# MICHAEL'S GEMSTONE DICTIONARY

## Metaphysical properties of gems and minerals

Written by

Judithann H. David Ph.D.
and
JP Van Hulle

# MICHAEL'S GEMSTONE DICTIONARY

## Metaphysical properties of gems and minerals

Published by the Michael Educational Foundation and
Affinity Press in Orinda, California

For information write:
Affinity Press
P. O. Box 877
Orinda, California 94563

*A Michael Speaks Book*

This book is dedicated to my beloved husband, Desai,
my precious daughter, Juliana, and to my mother
who worked to make this book possible even
though she doesn't "believe" in Michael.
Judie


I dedicate this work to my darlings: Aaron, Penny,
and Jessica and with love and gratitude to my
ever loyal parents: Joy and John Perasso.
Thank you.
JP

# TABLE OF CONTENTS

**We are deeply grateful to:**

Claire Hudson for the hours spent editing the manuscript.

Harvey Kushner for producing a truly spectacular cover photo.

Luba Yudovich for assistance with layout design.

Aaron Christeaan for the cover design and his technical assistance to create a beautiful finished product.

Christine Perasso for her creative illustrations.

J. Jones for the questions he submitted and material he transcribed from a channeling session with Shepherd Hoodwin of New York.

All Michael students who wrote us with questions and ideas for this revision.

Michael for providing us with all of this fascinating information.

# PREFACE

We wrote this book as a dictionary, to organize in a coherent fashion, the hundreds of gemstones and minerals whose metaphysical properties are defined here. All of the stones are listed alphabetically as well as by category. That way, if one is attracted to a piece of Orpiment found at a rock shop, it is possible to discover why one finds it attractive by looking up Orpiment in the alphabetical list and reading about it's properties. Conversely, if one wishes to feel, say, ambitious, one can turn to the section on "Personal Power" and look under "Ambition".

The first section entitled "Gemstones: Natures's Gift", discusses a variety of topics on the use of gemstones and minerals. Included is how to select gemstones for personal use, how to clean and re-energize them, how to program Crystals, how to design an environment, and much more.

The second section is a listing of gemstones and minerals by subject. There are three basic categories here. The first category, "Of General Interest", includes such topics as gemstones and minerals of use to children, those that aid one's gardening endeavors, those that promote prosperity or those that enhance one's spiritual awareness. The second category, "The Individual", describes stones, for example, that are healing to the emotions, those that stimulate the intellect and those that augment one's personal power.

The third category, "Well Being", discusses such topics as those stones that promote happiness, those that are healing to the physical body and those that affect the subtle body or personal energy field. The fourth category, "Relating to Others", describes gemstones and minerals, that foster good communication skills, support one's leadership abilities, promote love and intimacy and enhance one's personal relationships in general.

The next to the last section, "Michael's System of Personality" is a discussion of gemstones and minerals as they relate to the Roles, the overleaves, centering and body types;

concepts central to the Michael Teaching. Also included is a miscellaneous group that covers such topics as, channeling, parallel universes and walk-ins.

The last section of this book, is an alphabetical listing of gemstones and minerals by name. The name of each stone is followed by a brief description of its color and then its metaphysical or spiritual meaning is given. Where there is more than one effect a stone can have, they are listed more or less in order of importance, as a, b, c, etc. The final definition, where applicable, is a description of the effect that a gemstone or mineral has, using the terminology of the Michael Teaching. The alphabetical list has the fullest, and most extensive description of each stone.

Following the Alphabetical list, is the Subject Index. Here we have listed all the gemstones and minerals that are categorized by subject, and the page numbers on which they can be found. An index for the Alphabetical list is not included. Please note that alternate names of gemstones and minerals, such as Ruby Silver for Proustite, will be found only in the Alphabetical list.

In this edition, we've greatly expanded our information on how to use gemstones and minerals. We've also made an effort to describe the metaphysical values of the stones in terms that can be easily understood by all. Definitions using the terminology of the Michael Teaching, are presented only in the section on "Michael's System of Personality". Our hope is that with this book, others will have as much pleasure selecting and using their own gemstones and minerals as we have.

# INTRODUCTION

Ever since that evening in November of 1984, when we received channeling from Michael on the metaphysical properties of a few dozen popular gemstones, our fascination with this subject has grown. We and other Michael students, have collected and researched gemstones and minerals from all over the world. We have haunted gem shows and rock shops; questioned jewelers, geologists and gemologists; read dozens of metaphysical and scientific books; and channelled extensively on the topic.

The first stones on which we received channelling, were the most popular and readily available gems and minerals such as Diamonds, Sapphires, Gold Tiger Eye and Blue Lace Agate. They were easy to find and sold universally under the same familiar names.

Once we began gathering information on less common stones, however, we ran into some problems. Someone would bring us a stone, hearing of our research; we would channel on its usage; and then, innocently assume they had given us its correct name. Once we realized how often people were mistaken about mineral names, we began checking our data for inconsistencies and errors.

We found some stones had been mislabeled. For example, we found that Elinoclase was really Clinoclase and Tacchantite was really Tacharanite. We found other stones misidentified. Finally, we discovered Michael's ability to read a stone's metaphysical properties from it's chemical composition. That cleared things up considerably. We now did not necessarily have to have an example of the stone itself to determine its metaphysical value.

There are a few exceptions, however, the most notable of which relates to the fact that some stones have the exact same chemical composition, but different crystalline structures. In some cases, this changes their metaphysical properties as illustrated by Andalusite and Kyanite. In other cases, the metaphysical value remains the same as in the case of

Indialite and Iolite. So, we still need "hands on" samples and the assistance of a gemologist from time to time. In any case, we hope this revision has cleared up many of those inaccuracies.

We have also listed in this dictionary, every name we have run across for a particular gemstone or mineral. This includes nicknames such as "Cinnamon Stone" for Orange-Brown Grossular or "Hawk's Eye" for Blue Tiger Eye, because we have seen them sold often at various shows with those names. We would like our readers to be able to find the metaphysical meaning of any stone, regardless of what it may be called. Sometimes we only have a nickname for a stone and it is only later, we are able to find out the correct mineralogical term for that stone. Then we include it in our next revision.

Another problem is that a mineralogical term that was acceptable in the past, may have been replaced by a new term which those who decree such things, regard as more accurate. "Aegerine", for example, used to be the accepted mineralogical name for "Acmite": and yet, in California, it is still often found labled as Aegerine. In these cases, we have left both names in the dictionary referring readers from the older names to the new and presenting the definition under the newest name we've found. Obviously, this name changing practice provides us with continual revision opportunities!

Another challenge we've had in writing this book is the tendency that rock dealers have to name the same stone a different name if it's found in a different region. Hence "Sonoma Opal" in California, becomes "Mountain Opal" in Colorado and "California Opal" in Utah. How confusing. They are all the exact same Opal with the same metaphysical qualities.

Some of the gemstones and minerals you will see listed in the dictionary are rarer and more difficult to find than others However, this being a dictionary, we have included every stone that we have ever channeled on for the purpose of being as complete a reference as possible. There is always more than one stone that will accomplish the same purpose.

So, if you have difficulty finding something look for an alternative rather than be frustrated. With Michael's help we will continue to provide you with spiritual information on all the gemstones and minerals we can find.

## Who Is Michael?

"Michael" is the name taken by a group of 1050 individuals, once flesh and blood humans like ourselves. After completing their physical lives on Earth, they bonded in spirit form into an "entity" so cohesive that they now consider themselves a unit. Hence, the singular name "Michael".

Michael now teaches us, from a higher plane of existence speaking through human "channels". The goal of the Michael entity in teaching us, is to promote a planetary shift from a self-centered human society, to one of tolerance and mutual respect.

## What is the Michael Teaching?

Michael's teaching views life as a cosmic game in which one sets up lessons which continue over many lifetimes. These lessons are learned through the personality, that one's soul, or "essence", designs each lifetime. Michael's system describes the various different personality traits which can be chosen, and with the many options available, it is rare to find two individuals who are exactly alike in all aspects.

Michael teaches this system of personality so we can better understand the behavior and motivations of ourselves and those around us, and become more unconditionally tolerant and compassionate. The section of this book entitled "Michael's System of Personality", describes the metaphysical properties of relevant gemstones using the terminology of the Michael teaching.. Read it and see if you resonate with the system. You may become a "Michael student" yourself.

One of the most important principles of the Michael Teaching is that it is not a religion or dogma. Being a Michael student involves no uniformity of belief. We self-validate all channelled information and take nothing on faith, because channelling is not an exact science. All you need, to be a Michael student, is a desire to grow, a desire to see life in a new perspective, and a willingness to use those parts of Michael's information you accept for the highest purpose.

# A MESSAGE FROM MICHAEL. . .

We have presented all of the information we teach, so people can have their lives work in a more integrated and balanced fashion as they go through the lessons they are learning on the Physical Plane. Being physical means you are to use the physical body, and find out how to be competent around physical things. It means you are to be in complete acceptance of all things physical.

Many religious and philosophical organizations encourage you to "rise above" the physical, as you get to be an older soul. We say you cannot rise above the place where you are. As long as you have a physical body, it is important to use the physical body appropriately, and gently, or you will not be able to have higher-centered experiences or evolve eventually to a higher than physical state.

Because of this fact, we find it extremely important that people use the various tools available to them on the Physical Plane to be in balance, and to be healed: that they use their body appropriately and in a sacred fashion: that they take care of themselves physically while they pay attention in other ways to their emotional, psychological and spiritual natures.

Gemstones and minerals are one of the tools available on the Physical Plane, and are something that everyone uses whether they realize it or not. Almost no one is unaffected by stones. You see a pretty rock--you pick it up. You put it in your pocket. You don't even know why you like it. When you have the conscious knowledge of what is behind the usefulness of a particular stone, what happens is that its effect will be much more powerful. With conscious knowledge, you increase one-hundredfold the power of the rock that you were using anyway by having it close to you.

The benefit of using an appropriate stone is that it makes life easier. It makes you more capable of being balanced, of having good communication with others, and of getting along well with others. Even when you are all alone, you can use the appropriate gemstone for any of your intellectual, physical, emotional or spiritual types of work.  So, since you have the benefit of these gifts while you are on the Physical Plane, we would like you to use them to their fullest extent. Our work gets done here on the Physical Plane when people get to experience agape;  people get to experience truth;  and people get to experience their physicality at its highest level.

# GEMSTONES: NATURE'S GIFTS

Since early times, mankind has been fascinated with the beauty and power of gemstone and minerals. Druids used them for healing as well as for their religious rituals. Medieval Europeans ground them into powders for medicinal purposes. Gem encrusted seals were used to seal the letters of Rulers. The Tibetans regarded Quartz Crystals as one of the seven most precious substances of Buddha.

For thousands of years, South American Indians have used a variety of gemstones and minerals to insure the excellent growth of their crops. They bury them in the ground at strategic points throughout the fields and refuse to reveal the secret of exactly which stones they use, and where and how they are placed. It is well known, however, that the Amaranth crops of the Andes grown by these methods produce an incredible harvest.

In modern times, the interest in gemstones and minerals has continued unabated. Technological uses for gemstones are common: Rubies are used for lasers, Diamonds for cutting tools, and Quartz Crystals for electronic equipment. More people than ever, can afford to buy gemstones and minerals for beauty and adornment. Interest has revived in the metaphysical properties of gemstones and minerals and many people are exploring, yet anew, the power of gemstones and minerals to heal, to improve communication, to stay balanced and to achieve spiritual growth.

## THE EFFECT OF GEMSTONES

Gemstones and minerals represent energy in its most solid form. Each gemstone or mineral has its own energetic characteristics that allow us to distinguish one from the other. They vary in chemical composition, in type of crystalline structure (or lack of it), in degree of hardness and color. Michael tells us that as each gemstone or mineral varies in its physical characteristics, so they also vary in the effect they have on those around them in specific and predictable ways. This is so because people have their own electro-magnetic fields that are impacted by the energetic quality of each gemstone or mineral. This, in turn, creates an electrochemical response in the body which impacts our psychological and physiological functioning.

Gemstones and minerals exert a positive and beneficial effect on all who come in contact with them, whether they be humans, animals or plants, and on the environments in which they are placed. As we attune ourselves to the various energies of different stones, and learn to discriminate one from the other on finer and finer levels, our self awareness and environmental consciousness becomes more highly developed and refined. Understanding how the energy of gemstones and minerals affect our body and psyche, fosters an increased sense of awareness and sensitivity to all that is around us and in us. This not only promotes growth in the ability to handle our lives on a day to day basis, but also stimulates the evolution of our spiritual nature.

## SELECTION OF GEMSTONES

When selecting gemstones for one's own use, the most important guideline is that the stone is appealing. The body has a way of being attracted to a gemstone that is appropriate for use at the time, whether one realizes it consciously or not. Thus, one may be attracted to a piece of Howlite because one is entering a creative phase, or a piece of Youngite to help one quit procrastinating and get down to business. As one develops a sense of which gemstones or minerals "feel right" and which do not, the ability to use gemstones or minerals in an effective, powerful and appropriate way becomes simple.

In response to our queries about how we should go about building a collection of stones for our personal use, Michael gave us some rather entertaining material that we later turned into an article for the "Michael Connection". This is an excerpt from that article.

*Have you been paying attention to the rocks you wear or have scattered around your home? Possibly not. It is very easy to let such little things drop out of your consciousness in the press of daily duties. Go around your home now and collect all the gemstones, crystals and minerals you have. Yes, even those dusty ones you haven't looked at or worn for months. Lay them out in front of you and sit quietly, just gazing at them one by one.*

*You will notice that some will start to stand out to you and say, "Pick me up." Some will start to look very pretty and you will feel an urge to put on a ring or pendant you haven't touched for a long time. Others will look dull or downright ugly to you and you may wonder, "Why did I buy that?" All of these reactions are your Essence's way of letting you know what energies are appropriate for you to have on or around your person at present. None of the rocks are really more "pretty" or "ugly" than they were when you bought them. Later on, you will probably experience a complete reversal and you will wonder why that little chunk of Carnelian looked so ugly to you. You can now see it is really very darling.*

*Next, we would like you to become more conscious about how you use your gemstones and minerals. First, pay attention to where you have your mineral specimens placed and make sure the room or location is really appropriate. For example, it would be nice to have Mesolite or pink Tourmaline (go with the flow) rocks in your bedroom or bathroom: someplace you like to relax and just hang out. Garnets (productivity) would be good placed next to your desk or in any area you like to be well organized and efficient. Garnets in the bedroom, however, might not produce exactly the romantic atmosphere you were looking for with the love (or potential love) of your life.*

*Second, be conscious of the jewelry you wear every day. Now that you have examined all your jewelry, old and new, make a commitment that you will have all your gemstones identified as to what they are and how the energy of each affects the body. Then you can make a conscious decision every day about which gemstones you would like to wear that day or which energies or effects you wish to emphasize that day.*

*For example, you are going to be involved in a difficult business meeting. You know you tend to be wishy-washy and lose your capacity to remember where you really stand on an issue. Try taking some Smoky Quartz to enhance your discriminative powers and some Blue Topaz to bring out your latent leadership qualities. If you are afraid you will come on too strong, particularly when you are not accustomed to the energy of these rocks, throw in a little Malachite for balance and the ability to communicate well, and stick a lump of Manganocalcite in your pocket to create an aura of personal adorableness.*

*On the other hand, perhaps you have planned a luncheon with a new flame and you really want to make a hit with him or her, even though you will be dressed in a business-like manner to deal with the rest of your day. Put a Sodalite pendant or ring in a plastic bag, which muffles the energy of the rock. Just before lunch, whip it on and, Voila! You never knew how sexy you could look buttoned up to the throat.*

*With a little imagination and thought, learning about the gemstones you own and the conscious use of them, will provide you some hours of entertainment as well as some interesting lessons about yourself and others.*

### Basic Stones to consider

There are a few stones that are simply good "basics" to have in one's repertoire. First and foremost, are the multipurpose clear Quartz Crystals. Clear Quartz is not only useful for clearly seeing the truth, a highly important attribute, but is the most programmable stone of all the mineral kingdom. Everyone should also have a stone to reduce fear and anxiety. Leopard-Skin Agate is one of the best. It's easy to find, inexpensive and strong in effect. Bone and Shell fragments, though not stones, are also useful for calming anxiety.

Amethyst has a universal appeal. It increases serenity and spiritual awareness, while reducing impatience and frustration. Selenite is important as a cleanser and charger of other minerals (see more on Selenite below) and Smoky Quartz helps one be more discriminating about who or what one allows to be of impact.

Particularly beloved are Diamonds for excellence, Pearls for wisdom and Amber for intellectual clarity. Amazonite and Pyromorphite are money producers, and Variegated Jasper is one of the strongest all-purpose physically healing stones. Of equal importance is keeping the chakras open, aligned and balanced. Clear Quartz Crystal, Malachite, and the Aventurines are very powerful choices in this regard. Three other stones are a must: Rose Quartz to stay aligned with Essence, Fluorite to clear the aura, and Grey Jade for reducing tension.

Play with this group and with the 45 or 50 other most available gemstones and minerals. We find that the stones which are most readily available and popular, also have metaphysical properties that are the most useful and desirable. While it is great fun to collect the rarer varieties of gemstones and minerals, we generally find their metaphysical properties to be of a more limited or esoteric nature.

## Size

In general, the size of a stone does not matter as much as one might think. A very small stone can produce enough energy to stimulate one in a very powerful way. Examples that come to mind immediately are Diamonds, Rubies, Emeralds, Aquamarines and less well known stones such as Benitoite, Labradorite and Apatite. It seems equally apparent that a huge boulder of Rose Quartz is not going to pull a person any more into their body than a smaller rock that would fit in the pocket. One is either "all present and accounted for" or one is not and more or larger pieces will not affect that.

There is one way in which size does matter. Larger stones will generally have the same effect as smaller stones, but will cover a larger area. A pocket-sized piece of Amazonite, for example, will increase the fervor of the individual's efforts to progress, whereas a larger piece, say as large as an egg, can affect an entire office of co-workers simultaneously.

The factor which determines the <u>minimum</u> size of a stone needed to fully manifest its metaphysical nature, we call the "completeness" principle. What we mean by "completeness" is that the sample is completely itself; not bits and pieces in a neutral matrix. There must be enough of the particular specimen that it can be easily read by the body's electro-magnetic field. It can be readily seen, then, that only a small Diamond or Emerald is necessary to satisfy the "completeness" principle. On the other hand, a much larger piece of a banded Agate or Brecchiated Jasper would be needed for "completeness": i.e., before enough of it was present that it fully represented itself.

## Flaws and Inclusions

On an essence level, we do differentiate between flawed or perfect gemstones, because our essence responds energetically to the beauty of a stone and has an aesthetic appreciation of the quality of beauty. The body, however, does not differentiate on the basis of beauty and flaws in a gemstone such as fractures, do not alter the energetic impact of the stone or its metaphysical properties.

Inclusions of other minerals alters the metaphysical properties of a stone and can, also, affect its intensity. The Aventurines, for example, are Quartz Crystals with inclusions of Mica. Citrines are Quartz Crystals that get their unique color from the inclusion of Iron. The metaphysical properties of clear Quartz Crystals, the Aventurines and the Citrines vary widely. Rutilated Quartz is Quartz Crystal permeated with Rutiles of Iron Pyrite. The addition of the Rutiles, not only changes the metaphysical value of the stone, but intensifies it's energetic impact as well.

Inclusions of neutral substances such as clay, gases and liquids are fairly benign and affect the metaphysical properties of gemstones in very minor ways or not at all. Such inclusions do affect the clarity of a gemstone, however, and for a few stones this is a very important factor. Two major examples, are Chrysacolla and colorless Quartz Crystal. Much of their impact centers around "seeing clearly". The more perfectly clear the crystal, the more clarity it produces.

## Faceting and Shaping

Whether a gemstone or mineral is cut or uncut, polished or unpolished, faceted or unfaceted, does not alter its energetic impact or affect its metaphysical properties. Shaping and faceting, however, does affect the intensity and/or focus of a gemstone's energetic impact. The faceting of gemstones for jewelry intensifies the energetic impact in a general way, but does not give it greater focus. The faceting of wands, obelisks and pyramids, intensifies their energetic impact. Their pointedness makes it possible to focus and direct the energy of the stone in a very precise way. For this reason, these shapes are often used for healing.

The rounder, unfaceted shapes of eggs and spheres project the energy of the stone in a universal and widely dispersed way. This make it easier for the individual to access the energy of the stone and such shapes are often preferred for scrying or meditation. With rounder shapes, the energetic impact is not intensified.

## Synthetic Stones

With man-made stones, it is important to find out the chemical compositon, as this affects its nature. For example, a Cubic Zirconia is a man-made Garnet even though it is presented as a substitute for Diamonds, and corresponds to productivity rather than mastery. A stone that is sold as "synthetic" is exactly the same in crystalline structure, chemical composition, etc. as the same stone grown in nature. The body will experience a natural Sapphire and a synthetic Sapphire as the same substance. An "imitation" stone, however, could have no resemblance in its physical properties or structural nature to the natural stone it emulates.

## Questions

Michael, I am still somewhat confused about how to tell how big a piece of any particular gemstone I would need.

*Gemstones and minerals vary in terms of size and the degree of impact associated with the size. We feel it is important for you to start developing the inner sensing mechanism that will tell you how much is needed in any given situation. Pick up a stone you have never touched before and feel how intensely it affects you. If a thumbnail sized piece has a great impact, you will need less of it than a piece of the same size that feels mild in effect. You may need a large sample of a mineral that barely impacts you to get the maximum effect.*

Michael, this is a question about the quantity of the stones used at one time. Would it be more effective to use, say, a string of beads instead of a chip or one piece?

*Quantity is not the most important factor to consider. What is more important is whether one has enough of the mineral in question that its nature can be easily read by the body's electro-magnetic field. Thus, if one has beads in which the desired mineral is small pieces contained in matrix rock, one may need an entire string of such beads to feel an effect. On the other hand, a small piece of a mineral that is purely itself, unblended with any other substances, will be equally as effective.*

Let me ask you the opposite. Can too large a quantity, or mass, of a stone prove excessive, or harmful, or damaging, or dangerous in any way?

*Usually not. If a person is severely imbalanced, and a powerful stone which is maybe not very appropriate for that person is used, it could set in motion movement which is too fast for that person to handle. It isn't that the energy, in and of itself is harmful, but people can only change so fast. If the stone initiates change too quickly, then it can be experienced as being negative. That is a rare instance, and a neutral stone, like a clear Quartz Crystal, cannot be too large or too powerful for normal usage.*

This leads to another question. How does a person's sensitivity to the energy of stones affect their use?

*A good point to keep in mind is that individuals vary in the degree of sensitivity they have to the energy of gemstones. This is largely a matter of personal preference. Some individuals will allow themselves to experience various stones in their full intensity. Others set up personal barriers that inhibit or entirely neutralize a stone's impact. For example, an individual may not wish to be very influenced by the accepting qualitiy of Apatite; perhaps it makes them feel too vulnerable or unable to be discriminating. Subconsciously they will inhibit the effect of the gemstone or mineral and damp it down to a comfortable level. The point here is that individuals have a great degree of control over what comes into their personal space. One is not just automatically affected in a predictable way.*

Is there any other way that a person can affect the power of a gemstone or mineral?

*One's awareness and intention are also very important factors in affecting the power of a gemstone. If one is aware of the effect a particular gemstone has, that awareness synergistically interacts with the gemstone or mineral to boost its power. When one "holds the intention " that the gemstone act in a certain way, that intentionality gives it more clarity of direction and intensity of focus. For example, if one is wearing Sodalite; the awareness that this stone enhances one's sexual attractiveness intensifies the effect. If one also fully "intends" to be more sexually attractive, say, to one's mate, the effect of the stone is now focused with more impact in their direction. Awareness is the passive "intensity booster" and intention is the active power booster.*

## USE OF GEMSTONES AND MINERALS

### Cleaning Gemstones and Minerals

After being worn for a while, a gemstone or mineral can be drained of its energy, or soak up undesirable energies occurring in its proximity. There are a number of ways to restore a gemstone or mineral to its original freshness; i.e. recharge it, and empty it of unwanted negative influences; i.e. clean it up. One way is to place it in rock salt for 3 to 30 days. Exercise discretion in using this method as some minerals or gemstones are harmed by the salt such as Pearls or Halite.

One can also place a gemstone in the freezer for three hours to three days. Michael recommends using the freezer. As they put it, "is easiest on the stones because you're not putting them into a medium they can't handle. Any stone can handle freezing temperatures and it does cleanse them very, very effectively."

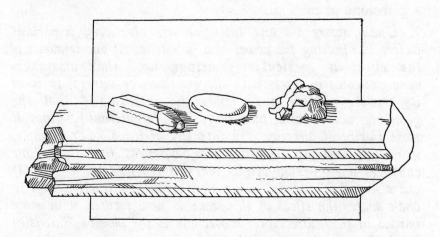

Selenite can be used to clean and recharge minerals and gemstones. One can place gemstones or minerals on top of the round, mushroomy type of Selenite. With Selenite that occurs in long crystals or spears, the stones can be place on top in a row. Selenite spears can also be used in another way.

Place the Selenite to point at a Rock Crystal and set the Rock Crystal to point at the gemstone or mineral you want to affect. The Selenite spear and the Quartz Crystal, that is placed in the middle, function as focusers and will super-clean any stone incredibly quickly: usually within 15 seconds.

Another method is to put the stone in some distilled water and place the container in the sunlight. Intention that the stones be cleansed is important here and one needs to tell the stones that it is time for them to "empty out". The water gives them a medium to release energy into and is a method of choice when a gemstone may have picked up energies one does not want discharged into the environment. A good example of this is when one is using gemstones for healing.

### Charging Gemstones and Minerals

Selenites can also be used in various ways to "charge" a stone. Such charging makes a stone more powerful in its energetic impact. A very simple way to increase a stone's potency, is to point a spear-shaped Selenite at a mineral for a few minutes. Also, stones left sitting on a Selenite spear or cluster for longer than it takes to clean them, get highly charged and project their qualities out to easily fill not just an entire room, but a large hall or warehouse, as well.

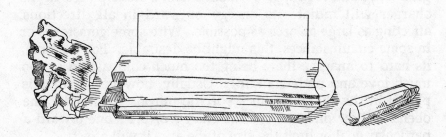

Selenite spears can also be used to imprint the metaphysical properties of one gemstone on to another. This is done by placing one mineral behind a Selenite spear (the imprintor) and another in front. In a few moments, the mineral in front of the Selenite spear will be imprinted with the property of the mineral behind. The imprinted mineral will now carry the metaphysical properties of both stones for at least 3 days. This method is particularly useful when a mineral you own is too large, too delicate or too inconvenient to carry around with you. Charge an easy-to-carry stone and have both energies available as pocket companions.

## Building a "Charger"

Another way to charge crystals, or amplify their power, is to build a crystal "charger". Michael has informed us that these chargers were used by ancient civilizations whose people were much more adept at crystal technology than ourselves. Chargers can be built of any natural substance; stone, wood, metal, bone, etc. Metals are best, of course, and of these, the most highly charging "conductor" is Copper.

The shape is simple: a cube with a four-sided pyramid resting above and on it. The height of the pyramid should be the height of the cube itself for maximum charging effect. At the tip of the pyramid, a crystal point can be placed if desired. We have also used a Fluorite octahedron quite successfully.

Surrounding the charger, a few inches out from the center of each of the four sides, should be four obelisks for grounding and focusing. Without these, a stone placed in the charger will radiate its energy outward in all directions affecting as large an area as possible. With some gemstones or in some circumstances, this might be desirable. For example, its hard to imagine there being too much compassion or too much love and understanding. Usually, however, a stone is placed in the charger with a specific purpose in mind. The obelisks allow one to focus the energy of the stone toward a particular goal or limit the size of the area it will affect.

The obelisks should be made of stone or metal, preferably; though again, anything natural will work. Width and depth of each obelisk is irrelevant, but each obelisk must be taller than the cube part of the charger. Each obelisk should also be about the same size and height as the other three obelisks for uniform grounding.

Lastly, a stone placed in the charger, should rest in the <u>center</u> of the charger. Rest it on a natural-material pedestal to do so. Copper is the best material for pedestals. Plastic neutralizes a stone's energy, and should not be used.

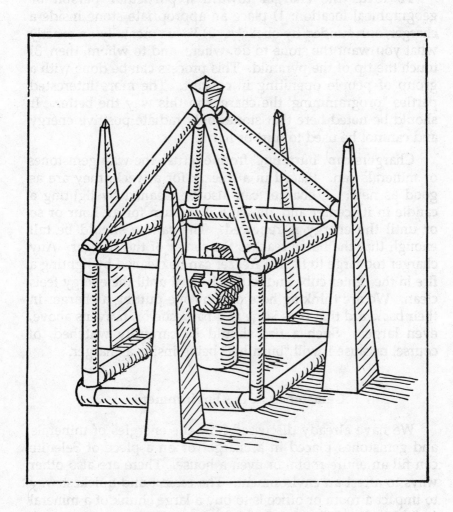

A charger is very effective in its ability to amplify the power of a gemstone or mineral. A stone placed in a charger will not only fill a room with its energy, but can impact an entire acre. Walls are irrelevant to chargers. A charger focused with obelisks and made of copper can send a beam of energy many miles away. A ball of Variegated Jasper placed in such a charger in California was deemed responsible for healing a deathly-ill woman in Ireland, for example.

To focus the charger toward a particular person or geographical location: 1) place an appropriate stone inside a charger, surrounded by obelisks. 2) Focus mentally on exactly what you want the stone to do, where, and to whom, then, 3) touch the tip of the pyramid. This process can be done with a group of people operating in concert. The more interested parties "programming' the charger in this way the better. It should be noted here that stones only radiate positive energy and can not be used to hurt or harm.

Chargers can "burn out" from overuse the way gemstones or minerals can. Placed in a freezer for a week, they are as good as new. A charger can also be cleaned by lighting a candle in its center and allowing it to burn for an hour or so or until the energy is renewed. The candle should be tall enough that the flame reaches the center of the charger. Any charger too large to fit in a freezer can be cleaned by lighting a fire in the center cube and letting it burn until the energy feels clean. We are thinking here of someone putting a charger in their backyard that is as large as a barbecue or, heavens above, even larger. Such a fire should be carefully watched, of course, because it will "burn hot" being inside a charger.

### Gemstones in the Environment

We have already discussed how the energies of minerals and gemstones placed in a charger or on a piece of Selenite can fill an entire room, or even a house. There are also other ways to affect an environment. The easiest and quickest way to impact a room or office is to buy a large chunk of a mineral (over 3 lbs) and simply place it in the room of your choice. A big piece of Iron Pyrite, for instance, can be helpful in an office setting, because it enables one to match and blend with others' paces. Ryalite is a wonderful stone to keep on the nightstand if you have fertility problems.

If smaller stones are placed in a room, the energy of the stones will completely permeate the room in no more than three weeks. When stones are removed, the energy can take up to a week to completely dissipate.

Another way to impact large spaces with stones is to place a small crystal in each corner of the room in question. Citrines are good when you have a lot of work to get done. Smoky Quartz pieces protect one's privacy and safety. Fluorite will inhibit cording and define what you want to happen in the space.

Finally; patterns, or grids, of stones can be placed on the floor, or a centrally-located table, for specific effects. Laying stones out in a triangle aids in healing conflicts, squares and diamond shapes build prosperity, and spirals are healing. You can lay out grids made of only small clear quartz crystal points; but, of course, using appropriate stones will give you a stronger effect: Jaspers for healing, Amazonites for prosperity, etc.

## Gemstones and the Body

The proper placement on the body enhances the effectiveness of many stones. For example, if one is using a stone that stimulates healing in the kidneys, it should be placed on or near the kidneys for maximum benefit. If one is using a gemstone that governs communication, the effect will be most intense when worn near the throat. Some stones have an ability to bring up certain issues when worn nearest the chakra associated with the issue. For example, Ivory, when worn near the heart chakra, brings up emotional issues related to one's survival and calms them as well.

Other gemstones are very non-specific with regard to placement on the body and will operate more or less powerfully as a function of its distance from one's body. A stone which is placed within a foot or less of one's body will affect it within minutes. One should also be aware that synthetic fabrics insulate the energy of gemstones. Such fabrics when worn on the body, do provide a barrier to impact. When gemstones are placed in a pouch, the pouch should always be made of natural fabrics, such as leather or cotton. If, on the other hand, one wishes to contain the energy of a gemstone and prevent it from impacting one's person or the environment, wrapping it in plastic or nylon will be very effective.

## QUARTZ CRYSTALS

Clear Quartz Crystals are the most versatile gemstones available for our use that we know of. They are powerful healers, promote clear sightedness, stimulate the energy field of the body, balance the chakras and are the most programmable stones of all the mineral kingdom.

Rock Crystals have the quality of individuality, a "pet-rock" feel, and resonate better to one individual than to another. Michael explains the phenomena this way.

*The basic thing about a Crystal in it's raw and natural state and a body in its raw, natural state is that they have to be attuned to one another. What makes people feel attuned to a particular Crystal, is that your body has its own particular dynamic energy and the Crystal has its own individual dynamic energy as well. So, the one that most closely matches your own energy will be the one that you will claim, "That's my Rose Quartz over there." or "That's my Amethyst over there." as opposed to someone else's. So you will reach out for the ones that most closely approximate your own energy pattern because they are most healing to you and to your environment even though they are, at the same time, general purpose Crystals and everyone will get some feeling from them.*

Quartz Crystals are also very powerful in their capacity to aid the healing process. Basic to the nature of clear Crystals is the ability to produce clarity. This makes it easier for the healer to see what needs to be healed and to proceed in an appropriate fashion. Crystals also produce clarity on the energetic level, at the level of body awareness, in addition to the level of conscious intellectual thought. The body then proceeds to clear itself in both energetic and physical realms. Chakras are cleared and balanced and unwanted negative energies cleared away. The process of clearing away toxins, unhealthy chemicals, disease producing agents, etc., is stimulated at the physical level. In a recent discussion on Crystals, Michael explained it this way:

*The best thing we can tell you is that Quartz Crystals are like a universal blood type. So that someone needed a blood transfusion, there would be a universal blood that could be absorbed by anyone regardless of blood type. Crystals are very, very similar to that.. They make one able to see whatever it is that one needs to see, and, therefore be able to heal whatever needs to be healed, or balance that which needs to be balanced. As soon as something can be noticed on an energetic level or on a more intellectual level, it can be altered. Then what you have is health and wellness.*

## Programming Quartz Crystals

To program a quartz point or wand, hold it in your left hand and concentrate on something you want to manifest in your life while looking at a particular facet of that crystal. When you have the idea well-focused on that facet, tap it with the forefinger of your right hand.

You can program every facet of a crystal this way and have a very useful stone indeed. It is always best to leave one facet free, however, for the crystal to retain its balance and observational quality. Whenever the crystal has manifested for you and you want to change the request you've put into a particular facet; blow quickly and deliberately on that facet while thanking the crystal and thinking of its release.

Crystals that carry lots of information can become exhausted more easily and can need to be cleaned or refocused regularly; whereas a mineral that has one specific purpose will retain its strength much longer. Still, many people find it easier to afford and carry one crystal rather than 30 other stones. It's always nice to have both options.

## Questions

We asked Michael a number of questions about programming Quartz Crystal and how to use them. Here are some of our questions. The first question had to do with the uses of Quartz Crystals.

*Something one can do with a Quartz Crystal, is literally drain it of any kind of character of its own and put into it any character that one would want it to have. So, that if one has a good Quartz Crystal that one feels attuned to on an individual basis, one can imbue into that crystal the properties of any of the other gemstones one would wish to bring into one's space. Let's say you just aren't able to run out to the gem store and buy some Wavellite or Pyromorphite ,at the moment, but you can encode a crystal with any desire or wish of your own. So, they are industrial-strength, multi-usage, totally multi-purpose stones.*

I find that when I encode a stone, I have to keep a little bit of intention there to keep it from slipping. It's like a radio frequency that likes to drift a little bit.

*Yes, you do. Actually, we even suggest keeping it stored in a tuning mechanism which we will discuss later.*

*What you don't want to do too often to a crystal, if you want a crystal to have strength of character, is switch its purpose all the time. If you're very impoverished and all you can afford is one crystal, you can do that. But, you are eventually going to drain it of any character because it's going to be tired, stretching out towards finding you a mate one day, healing a wart on your foot the next day, and endeavoring to bring in world peace on the next day! What will happen is you're going to wear that crystal out and it is going to take a nice long time to recharge. Until it's recharged, all it is going to do is sit there and make you clear. It isn't going to want to keep stretching in all those directions.*

*If you charge a Crystal for a particular purpose and you are going to have your attention on that purpose for a long period of time, it is better to get another Crystal if you have another purpose in mind. Very few people need to continually indulge in various whims momentarily and then zip to another whim. Most people are working on something for quite some time. You can always give a crystal rest, especially if after five or six months, you get what it is that you wanted and don't need the Crystal for that purpose any longer. You can cleanse it and then encode it for something else. What we are suggesting is not to rapidly and frequently switch its energy.*

In what direction should one place the point of a crystal? What different effect does this produce?

*Basically what you're doing with the point of a Crystal is directing energy. If there is an energy within the Crystal, that you wish to go toward someone you are healing,for example, the point ought to point toward them and, in particular, toward the area you want to heal.*

*If you are attempting to drain some energy out of the person, then what you want to do is put the butt end of the Crystal pointing out toward the Universe and not toward you or another person. For the purpose of draining energy out, you would not use a double-terminated Crystal as a point cannot absorb from a general area the way the flat, butt end of a crystal can. A Crystal with a flat end just generally absorbs from an area and puts it out through the point towards the Universe or wherever you want that energy to go.*

*There is a tendency when people wear a Crystal to have it pointing downward. This takes the energy and draws it down and essentially pulls their Essence down further towards their feet into their body. It functions similarly to a Rose Quartz. All Quartz Crystals will draw energy. Now, if you are a person that has an incredible amount of sixth and fifth chakra energy and you continue to hold it your head, you might want to wear a the point of a Crystal pendant or earring pointing downward as it will draw energy away from a total emphasis on the intellect.*

*If you have a Crystal point upwards, it brings up love, and survival and lower chakra issues such as money, power, health, and sex and stimulates these issues to rise up toward the intellect. If you are a person who has a tendency to be very emotional or very action oriented and you want to draw your consciousness into your head, then you will want to wear a Crystal with the point upward.*

*It is best to be aware of how comfortable or uncomfortable your body is with the Crystal you are wearing and the direction you have it pointing. So, if you have a Crystal and it is draining your energy, up or down, to some degree that is not particularly comfortable, your body will learn how to seal the effect of that crystal off, given a period of months. Then whenever you wear it, it won't have any effect on you at all, because it was beginning to feel uncomfortable, and bodies are very good at being able to wall off whatever feels uncomfortable.*

Michael, what is that tuning mechanism for Crystals you mentioned earlier, that keeps my programmed Crystal from losing its imprinting?

*The tuning mechanism is simple enough. Wrapping a Crystal in at least two loops of metal wire helps it say encoded. Though any conductive metal will work, Silver and Copper work exceptionally well in this capacity. It is no accident that "wire-wrapped" jewelry and Crystal wands are becoming so popular. Wire-wrapping is not only beautiful, but functional as well.*

# Part I

## SUBJECT LIST:

**Gemstones and Minerals Categorized
According to Their Metaphysical Properties**

# OF GENERAL INTEREST

## ANIMALS

These stones make it easier to relate to animals or to understand them better.

**Andrewsite:** Creates a greater bond between sentient and semi-sentient creatures. Can improve the relationship with one's pets, help one train animals, ask gophers to stay out of the yard and ask plants to grow larger.

**Atelestite:** Promotes communication between animals (mammals and birds) and humans. Makes one more empathically aware of the needs of animals and better able to relate to them.

**Azoproite:** Reduces fear of carnivorous animals.

**Ilmenite:** Increases understanding of the way other mammals think. Good for animal trainers, pet-owners, farmers, etc.

**Bonaccordite:** Same in effect as Ludwigite.

**Copralite:** Reduces fear of any kind of insect or animal life.

**Julienite:** Enables one to make mental contact with any life form that has thoughts no matter how rudimentary. This includes cats, dogs, birds, horses, cows, etc.

**Ludwigite:** Reduces fear of carnivorous animals.

**Jasper, Poppy:** Helps one relate well to animals.

**Thinolite:** Aids in training animals and communicating with them.

**Topaz, Clear:** For better relationships with non-human species on this planet: includes plants and animals.

**Veatchite:** Reduces fear of animals.

These stones all have some positive benefit for the animal such as balancing or producing healthy growth.

**Andersonite:** Encourages young animal reptile, bird or insect bodies to grow strong, large and healthy. Stimulates healthy plant growth as well.

**Beryllonite:** Balancing and calming to all mammals. Especially useful for calming nervous pets.

**Braunite:** Balancing for egg-laying animals: fish, reptiles and birds.

**Chlorargyrite:** Increases the speed of growth in plants and animals.

**Ilvaite:** Increases the appetite of animals that are off their feed.

**Quietite:** Very balancing and calming to domesticated animals. Makes wild animals nervous.

**Mimetite:** Keeps reptiles balanced.

**Phosgenite:** Helps birds, etc., lay stronger eggs.

**Stibiconite:** Balances fish and crustaceans.

## ARTISTIC and MUSIC ABILITY

**Aphthitalite:** Encourages one's musical ability and talent to be used to its fullest. True no matter how little ability one has. Cures songwriter's block.

**Charoite:** Enhances one's ability to appreciate beauty.

**Fuchsite:** Increases appreciation of artistic endeavors. Enhances one's talent around anything that requires artistic ability, flair or an eye for design.

**Valentinite:** Encourages one to sing and enjoy music.

**Yuksporite:** Promotes inventiveness in the use of language and creation of poetry.

## ASTROLOGY

**Agate, Enhydritic:** Accentuates the astrological influences of the water signs Cancer, Pisces, and Scorpio: i.e., those qualities become more pronounced.

**Agate, Pseudo:** Puts one in touch with the energetic qualities of other planets. By being more sensitive to planetary energies, one's awareness of astrological influences is enhanced.

**Marmatite:** Helps neutralize astrological influences. For example, great to wear when Mercury is retrograde or Saturn is transiting your Venus.

## CHILDREN

**Abelsonite:** Has a relaxing effect on children. Enables them to feel calmer and more able to handle stressful situations.

**Agrinierite:** Assists the pubescent adolescent in becoming aware of, and more comfortable with, their sexuality.

**Andersonite:** Encourages young human bodies to grow strong, large and healthy.

**Anhydrite:** Promotes a sense of peace and serenity even during difficult times. The violet tends to be more attractive to children and the light blue tends to be more attractive to adults.

**Bermanite:** Eases the transition from childhood, through puberty, and into adulthood by balancing the hormonal and chemical changes that take place in the body.

**Bowenite:** Balances the hormonal system. Healing and balancing to the female reproductive system and organs. Useful for girls going through puberty as it helps them stay on even keel. Helps alleviate cramps.

**Eosphorite:** Helps children to feel more secure and able to handle the absences of their parents for short periods of time.

**Goudeyite:** Decreases shyness and that agonizing flipping back and forth between low self esteem and arrogance.

Makes it easy to maintain a stable, positive sense of self. Good for children, because they usually go through episodes of this.

**Jokokuite:** Opens children to spiritually based, emotional experiences. Enables them to feel a sense of lovingness toward all beings.

**Molybdenite:** Makes one less afraid of the dark. Works equally well for adults and children.

**Palygorskite:** Makes children feel more experienced, more capable and more adult.

**Plancheite:** Aids children in going through the grieving process when they have lost someone they love.

**Quartz, Snow:** Good balancing stone for children. Helps them be clear about the world they're in and be comfortable in a child's body.

**Smithsonite, Pink:** Helps make children more psychic. Can also be used by adults, but more useful for children.

**Zapatalite:** Increases a younger person's understanding of the point of view of someone older than themselves.

**Zektzerite:** Protects any child under the age of five against threats to their survival.

## CRAFTSMANSHIP

**Agate, Dry-Head:** Increases precision and craftsmanship. Makes it easier to focus in on a project and be clear about each necessary detail. Produces a finer and finer mastery of one's craft or skill.

**Duftite:** Makes it easier to learn any mechanical skill. This includes, for example, basketweaving, car repair, woodcarving, and football.

**Plattnerite:** Produces greater craftsmanship and skill in using one's hands.

## CREATIVITY and IMAGINATION

**Acanthite:** Stimulates the imagination and pulls one into an artistic, creative mode.

**Actinolite:** For those who are doing artistic, creative projects: Enables one to stay focused and to handle several projects at once without getting scattered or sidetracked.

**Agate, Mustard Yellow:** Puts one into a creative, imaginative and unusually inventive mood. Keeps one original and fresh in one's approach.

**Agate, Plume:** Opens up one's creativity and encourages one to be more creatively expressive. Helps one to get past the tendency to be shy and hide one's creative talents.

**Amakinite:** A stone that enables one to turn the immediate environment into a vast, creative playground of energy that stimulates project initiation, the imagination, organic growth, and new inventions. Can have the side effect of making a very focused person feel temporarily dizzy and fuzzy. Use the stone for two or three hours of vast inventiveness, then return it to the freezer for at least 24 hours for recharging.

**Augelite:** For those who are doing artistic, creative projects: Makes it easier to manifest creative projects and to follow through with them to completion.

**Barbosalite:** Stimulates one's creativity and releases any blocks one has to being creative.

**Basaluminite:** Stimulates one to create technologically and to come up with ideas one could pursue of a technological nature. Promotes technological advances.

**Bismuth:** Stimulates the creative use of one's imagination.

**Bismuthinite:** Same in effect as Bismuth.

**Bismutite:** Same in effect as Bismuth.

**Clinoclase:** Increases one's ability to use one's imagination.

**Feldspar, Andesine:** Balances and grounds those involved in artistic or creative projects.

**Grunerite:** Same in effect as Bismuth.

**Gyrolite:** Enhances one's creativity.

**Hackmannite:** Same in effect as Sodalite.

**Hendricksite:** Enables one to get in touch with one's playful, creative side.

**Hexagonite:** Same in effect as Actinolite.

**Howlite:** Promotes the process of artistic creation and inspiration. Also stimulates creative ideas about new things to bring into one's life.

**Koettigite:** Enables one to feel less stressed when in the process of creation. As a result, one's projects run more smoothly.

**Llanoite:** For creativity of the "genius" sort. Promotes unusual thought patterns for the creation of highly inventive solutions to problems or the development of fresh perspectives.

**Mariposite:** Stimulates one toward self-expressiveness in the area of creativity.

**Microlite:** Same in effect as Actinolite.

**Opal, Boulder:** Inspires creativity of an unusual and, sometimes, bizarre sort. Stimulates one to come up with wild and crazy ideas, to make leaps to higher levels of knowledge, or to think of something that pulls a lot of ideas together in a way that suddenly works, when it didn't before.

**Opal, Sonoma:** Good for anyone who is pursuing a hobby, career or artistic endeavor that requires they be creative, and emotionally stable at the same time. Stabilizes mood swings and keeps one from getting easily upset.

**Prase or Prasolite:** Same in effect as Actinolite.

**Sapphire, Dark Blue:** Taps into creative potential and inspires people to express themselves creatively. Is grounding during the creative process, assists follow through and keeps one from getting too scattered.

**Sapphire, Lilac:** Encourages one's creativity to flow freely and intensely. Especially useful for those who are creatively talented, or involved in a creative project, and feel blocked.

**Scolecite:** Balancing for those who are involved in artistic or creative endeavors.

**Sodalite:** Stimulates one to use one's creativity.

**Todorokite:** Calms and soothes highly excitable, creative or artistic types of people.

**Tremolite:** Same in effect as Actinolite.

**Uvarovite:** Aids imagination and story-telling abilities.

**Villiaumite:** Enables one to appreciate the unusual, the eccentric and the bizarre.

**Zinkeinite:** Same in effect as Bismuth.


## DREAMS

**Diamond, Herkimer:** For vivid dreaming and astral clarity. Use with Rhodochrosite to remember dreams better.

**Enargite:** Promotes vivid dreaming. Makes it easier to remember one's dreams.

**Luzonite:** Same in effect as Enargite.

**Quartz, Strawberry:** Has an intense, dreamy quality. Helps one to remember dreams.


## FINDING THINGS

**Eucryptite:** Encourages anything hidden in its vicinity to reveal itself. Makes it easier to find lost things like keys or buried treasure.

**Manganaxinite:** Enables one to find things one has lost on, or under the ground. One's impulses prompt one to move in the right direction. Also, helps one find new things, located underground, one might like to have like crystals, gold or oil .

**Riebeckite:** Helps one recognize what's missing. One might identify what thieves took in a robbery or look at larger issues such as what is missing in one's life.

## GARDENING

**Andersonite:** Encourages healthy plant growth.

**Andrewsite:** Creates a bond of empathy and communication with the plants and animals in one's garden. Use it to ask gophers to leave your lawn area, plants to grow larger, etc.

**Babingtonite:** Makes one feel attached to the land and green growing things. Good for farmers, landscapers and weekend gardeners. Increases one's "green thumb" ability.

**Buergerite:** Same in effect as Black Tourmaline.

**Cornwallite:** Enables one to feel more attuned to natural organic substances, plants and natural settings.

**Margaritasite:** Gives one a green thumb. Expands one's ability to instinctively know how to take care of one's plants and help them grow.

**Nullaginite:** Makes one feel more in touch with the earth, and in fact, with all physical objects.

**Strashimirite:** Gives one a green thumb. Enhances one's natural empathy with plants.

**Topaz, Clear:** Enables one to relate better to one's plants. Enhances one's green thumb ability.

**Tourmaline, Black:** Healing for house plants. Has no effect on humans other than producing a mild empathy with the plant kingdom.

**Volkonskoite:** Makes one feel more in touch with the earth.

## KARMA

Eastern philosophy teaches that karma is our "fate" or destiny. It is the consequences of our actions during the successive phases of our existence. In the Michael teaching, karma is defined, in its largest sense, as "intensity", and operates according to the cosmic law of balance. If one person provides another with an intense experience, of either a positive or negative nature, something has been learned. At the same time, an imbalance has been created. The person on the receiving end has incurred a "karmic debt" and owes it to the other to teach a similar lesson in return. Once "pay back" has occurred, balance is restored and the two persons are no longer "in karma" with each other.

It is apparent, from the foregoing, that we can experience karma daily. That is, our interactions with others can provide experiences that vary in intensity from positive, to neutral, to negative every day. Under ideal circumstances, interactions are reciprocal, balance is restored, and karma is completed almost as soon as it is formed. If a karmic debt is not completed in one lifetime, it remains a debt, and an imbalance, until completion in a future lifetime.

People also have self-karma. Self karmas are lessons one gives one's self that are associated only indirectly with other people. In this case, one feels intense, or incomplete, about an issue or situation in one's life. Until one learns the lesson, one will not feel complete. Examples of self karmas include issues with one's health, one's self worth, or the use of one's power.

As stated previously, karmic exhanges can be either positive or negative, and are not necessarily to be avoided. While too much time in karma can be exhausting, too little time in karma can be boring. The following stones help one to balance the amount of time one spends doing karmic lessons.

**Calcite, Gray:** Neutralizes the impact of karmic influences. Allows one to see what's going on and remain neutral about it emotionally.

**Hubnerite:** Brings one's karmas in to one's life.. Good to use when life gets boring, or one is ready for a new cycle to begin.

**Jade, Blue:** Neutralizes the impact of karmic influences. Allows one to see what's going on and remain neutral about it emotionally.

**Jade, Brown or Gray:** Same in effect as Blue Jade and Gray Calcite.

**Legrandite:** For karmic intensification. Produces a sense of imbalance, which propels one either into self karma, or karma with another to feel balanced again. These karmas can be either pleasurable or not.

**Liebigite:** Attract's one's karmas and brings them into one's life when worn. These will be the karmas one had planned on having in one's life before birth. Do remember these could be positive karmas and highly desirable.

**Marmatite:** Makes it easier to avoid karmas and other predestined happenings, dictated by one's astrology.

**Paua Shell:** Reduces the stress associated with difficult karmas or soul-level transitions.

**Pickeringite:** Allows one to temporarily suspend karma, and create an island of calm.

**Wolframite:** Same in effect as Hubnerite.

## MISCELLANEOUS

**Boltwoodite:** Increases one's ability to hunt and forage for food. Sharpens the senses and one is better able to spot tracks, tell when one is upwind of the quarry, or find the elusive edible mushrooms.

**Bournonite:** Improves one's sense of direction. Makes it easier to find one's way home, or to find one's way about more easily.when in a strange town

**Carnotite:** Vastly increases one's puzzle-solving capabilities.

**Cornwallite:** Encourages one to feel more attuned to natural organic substances. One feels more comfortable absorbing the energy of natural settings. Makes it easy to make the transition from city to country.

**Corvusite:** When holding the rock, one will notice which objects in one's surroundings could be used as lethal weapons or as protective devices.

**Descloizite:** Promotes a tendency to reject anything foreign, including man-made objects, from one's environment.

**Glauberite:** Enables one to feel more comfortable around modern technological inventions. Helps ease the discomfort one feels with new advances in science and technology.

**Holmquistite:** Increases one's ability to understand and work with mathematical concepts and solve puzzles.

**Mottramite:** Increases one's ease with man-made objects. Makes it more comfortable to be surrounded by synthetics such as plastic, nylon, computers and the plethora of man-made items in our modern world.

**Scorzalite:** Deepens and underscores the effect of any other mineral it is bonded to or in matrix with. Doesn't work if another rock is merely set near it: must be a bonding or melding of materials. Often found with Andalusite, Citrine and Scorodite.

**Tinzenite:** Encourages one to lose the things one no longer has use for, but has been hanging onto.

## ORGANIZATION

**Dumortierite:** Encourages a business-like attitude. Use when one wants to prioritize, to get things organized and in order.

**Graphite:** Encourages a sense of orderliness, a desire for things to be in place, and makes it easier to get things done in an organized fashion.

**Huntite:** Allows one to prioritize so one can productively accomplish everything.

## PROBLEM SOLVING

**Aerugite:** Gives one a sense that things will go well and encourages one to look for positive solutions to whatever problems may exist.

**Bayleyite:** Helps one go straight to the core nature of a problem as well as its solution. Eliminates mental confusion.

**Crossite:**  Enables one to come up with creative solutions to problems in one's life about which one feels most miserable or desperate.  Since these solutions are accessed from one's deepest subconscious, they can be quite extreme and must be considered carefully for appropriateness.

**Jasper, Owyhee:**  Enables one to come up with unusual solutions to problems that are not easily solvable.

**Llanoite:**  Promotes unusual thought patterns and fresh perspectives for the creation of highly unusual solutions to problems.

**Metahewettite:**  Promotes one's ability to tackle one's problems forcefully and move into action dynamically and appropriately.

**Sapphire, Dark Blue:**  Helps one to find creative solutions to problems.

**Variscite:**  Enables one to come up with solutions for problems that create a win-win situation for everyone.

**Youngite:**  Inspires solutions to problems requiring action.  Energizes one to solve difficult problems.

## PROSPERITY

Everyone wants to feel prosperous.  Even a person with the mildest material desires, likes to have a full stomach, a cozy bed, and warm winter clothing.  And many people, of course, want much more.  Michael defines prosperity as having enough of what you want in your life.  This includes not only money, but enough time for relaxation or a satisfactory mated relationship.

There are three ways that gemstones and minerals can aid one in achieving prosperity:  1) they make a person lucky, 2), they instill a feeling of confidence and imbue one with the dynamism to manifest more abundance, and 3) they simply attract energy in the form or money or the material goods that one desires.

## Good Luck

**Aerugite:** Makes one feel lucky, which can lead to being lucky, because "you are what you think you are."

**Boleite:** A good-luck charm. Makes one feel lucky and receptive to the positive forces of fate.

**Sapphire, Green:** Good luck stone. Creates the atmosphere for serendipitous events to occur in one's life.

## High Havingness

**Amazonite:** Gives one the feeling that one can get out there and get the things or experiences one wants.

**Astrophyllite:** Promotes a sense of abundance and prosperity. Makes one feel wealthy and content with whatever one has.

**Bloodstone:** Inspires high prosperity consciousness and a willingness for abundance to show up in one's life. Engenders a strong feeling that it is all right to have what one wants and that it is only a matter of time until one gets it. One feels confident that life will be good.

**Connemara:** Promotes prosperity, the acquisition of wealth, and a sense of satisfaction.

**Cubic Zirconia:** Aids in maintaining a high productivity level and increases one's prosperity. When the color is other than clear, a slightly different twist is added to the basic energetic effect of productivity and prosperity.
>
  **Blue:** Adds an element of calm.
  **Brown:** Prompts the body to relax and let go of physical tension.
  **Green:** Puts a stronger emphasis on prosperity: focuses one on making one's life just like one wants it to be.
  **Pink, Lilac & Purple:** Creates a mood of relaxation and a desire for spiritual pursuits. Would not promote productivity in the arena of "getting things done."
  **Red:** Adds a little extra punch and a dynamic quality.
  **Yellow to Orange:** Adds an element of contentment or happiness: promotes a mildly pleasurable state.

**Diamond:** Promotes a feeling of richness and abundance.

**Garnet**: Promotes prosperity and helps one focus on having one's life exactly as one would like it to be. As the color changes, the characteristic of the Garnet shifts also. Garnet types are listed below by name.

**Garnet, Almandine**: Promotes prosperity with strong element of productivity, purposefulness and focus.

**Garnet, Pyrope**: Promotes prosperity with the qualities of abundance and happiness.

**Garnet, Rhodolite**: Promotes prosperity in the arena of one's career.

**Goosecreekite**: Helps one break through one's emotional and intellectual blocks to increase of prosperity.

**Merwinite**: Same in effect as Bloodstone.

**Jasper, Nunkirchner**: Same in effect as Bloodstone.

**Mullite**: Encourages thriftiness. Aids one in making a budget and sticking with it. Helps one acknowledge that one has personal, monetary limitations.

**Osarizawaite**: Promotes a fine, pin-point accuracy in whatever one attempts to manifest or bring into one's life. Whatever one is trying to produce, emerges in its purest, finest and most exact form.

**Zircon, Violet**: For monetary resourcefulness. Makes one feel like there will always be money, especially if it is really needed.

## Money

**Campiglaite**: Same in effect as Pyromorphite.

**Ettringite**: Tends to attract money or energy in the form of goods (things that are worth money) into your life.

**Pyromorphite**: Attracts money or energy in the form of goods.

**Saponite**: Same in effect as Pyromorphite.

**Sturmanite**: Attracts money and energy in the form of goods.

# PSYCHIC ABILITIES

Psychic ability is different from the ability required in channeling. The psychic is basically using his or her own awareness to discern what is not usually seen about another person or things. This awareness can be telepathic, empathic, telemetric, intuitive or prophetic.

**Aragonite:** Enables one to operate out of a high degree of empathic perceptivity and psychic awareness.

**Australite:** Same in effect as Moldavite.

**Barytocalcite:** Enhances one's empathic awareness.

**Desautekite:** Enables one to predict future trends and assess more accurately the probabilities of various events occurring in the future.

**Herrerite:** Enables one to open up one's psychic abilities particularly where blocked.

**Mirabilite:** Increases empathic perceptivity. Makes hunches stronger.

**Moldavite:** Enables one to communicate telepathically.

**Smithsonite, Pink:** Helps make one more psychic. Milder in effect than the purple variety of Smithsonite.

**Smithsonite, Purple:** Pulls one to the sixth chakra and makes it easier to use psychic abilities.

# SHAMANISM

**Enargite:** A shaman stone. Discovered centuries ago and used by shamans for vision quests and in combination with drugs for heavy hallucinatory experiences. Tends to put one more in alignment with one's astral self than one's physical self.

**Hauynite:** Amplifies shamanic abilities. Operates by pulling one into the emotions, and reconnecting one with the memories of those early lifetimes when one was still in touch with the Tao.

**Jasper, Morrison Ranch:** Same in effect as Morrisonite. Puts one in touch with the Universal Consciousness, or Tao, in a shamanistic way. Opens and connects all the chakras. Makes it easier to get in touch with inner parts of the self, using rituals and ritualistic symbology.

**Luzonite:** Same in effect as Enargite.

**Morrisonite:** Related to Shamanistic type rituals: Makes it possible to get more out of the ritual; to feel more connected to the Universal Consciousness, or Tao. Opens, and connects all the chakras. Choose stones with the greatest amount of the avocado green color, because that part of the stone carries the strongest impact.

## SPIRITUALITY

The stones in this section facilitate the development of one's spirituality and foster the conscious awareness of one's spiritual nature. They are of four types. 1) Those that create a state of readiness to move into spiritual awareness. 2) Those that put one in touch with one's capacity for unconditional love and acceptance toward one's self and others. This energy is often likened to "Christ Consciousness". 3) Those that expands one's ability to recognize ultimate truth and wisdom. 4) Those that transform consciousness and allow one to perceive one's unity and harmony with the Tao, God, or Universe as a whole.

In using the term "spirituality", we are not referring to one's individual religious or philosophical belief systems. We are referring to one's general, non-denominational connectedness to God, or, what could be termed, the Supreme Reality. We are also referring to the recognition of one's self or others as "spirit", soul or essence; that which one is when one is without a body. In general, the stones in this section enhance the conscious experience of one's spirituality and foster the conscious awareness and appreciation of one's spiritual nature.

## Spiritual Readiness

**Agate, Blue with White Stripes:** (Also called Neptunian Agate). Puts one in a dreamy, visionary, almost psychic frame of mind in which it becomes easier to appreciate questions of a spiritual nature.

**Agate, Holly Blue:** For being spiritually discriminating. Encourages one to be discriminating about what one will accept in the way of new beliefs, new spiritual paths, or new religions.

**Bentorite:** Increases spiritual awareness. Makes it easier to perceive the answers to questions of a cosmic nature.

**Celestite:** Inspires one to visionary and beautiful flights of fancy. Enables one to keep a level head and promotes the ability to stay grounded while in a state of spiritual inspiration.

**Halite, Pink:** Makes one feel visionary, larger than life, and inspired.

**Halotrichite:** Creates a sense of ascending into spiritual heights. Puts one in touch with one's spiritual nature.

**Opal, Cacholong:** Clears energy blockages in the body so one can open up to new experiences. This includes those of a spiritual nature.

## Unconditional Love

**Apatite:** An acceptance stone that with continued use, makes one unconditionally accepting of the people that come into one's life.

**Belovite:** Same in effect as Apatite.

**Beryllium:** Puts one in touch with the highest, most spiritual form of love possible. Also referred to as "Christ Consciousness".

**Bisbeeite:** Same in effect as Chrysocolla.

**Calcite, White:** Enables one to experience a feeling of love and connectedness with the entire universe. One feels worthy of being loved by the Supreme Being; and worthy of being connected to and experiencing higher planes of existence.

**Chalcanthite:** Opens one up to the feeling one can love all mankind. Helpful to those who are super intellectual or action oriented and have difficulty experiencing their finer emotions.

**Chrysocolla:** Crystallizes feelings of unconditional love, acceptance, and tolerance toward others.

**Chrysoprase:** Very similar in both chemical composition and function to Chrysocolla.

**Clinoptilolite:** Puts one in touch with unconditonal love, acceptance, and tolerance toward others..

**Eilat:** Blend of Chrysocolla, Turquoise and Malachite. The Malachite keeps one balanced and better able to use the energies of Chrysocolla and Turquoise.

**Gem Silica:** Same in effect as Chrysocolla, but stronger.

**Jasper, Parrot Wing:** A combination of Chrysocolla, Turquoise and Malachite. See Eilat.

**Spangolite:** Same in effect as Chalcanthite.

**Turquoise:** Centers one's being on love and connectedness with others. Pulls one into the experience of unconditional love for all beings.

**Turquoise, Navajo:** A combination of Sard and Turquoise. Green Turquoise in a yellow-brown matrix.. Centers one's being on love and connectedness with others. Also makes one feel secure and "at home" no matter where one is.

## Truth and wisdom

**Amethyst:** Helps one remember there is time enough for everything. Enables one to stay in the present moment and truly connected to what is going on with self and others. Keeps one in touch with one's highest ideals and able to discern the actions that would best serve all.

**Aragonite:** Enables one to simultaneously operate from a high degree of emotional perceptivity, intellectual clarity and the ability to see truth from a higher perspective. This stone will not be very attractive to those who like a lot of drama in their life or who are uncomfortable feeling very truthful.

**Betpakdalite:** Encourages one to think in a highly inspirational manner and see the higher truth in things.

**Calcite, Brown or Gold:** Enhances one's capacity to know what is true. Better able to appreciate such philosophers as Lao Tsu.

**Galena:** A truth stone. Aids in telling the truth and in looking for what's true.

**Kyanite, Green:** Opens one to inspirational bursts of truth, love, and wisdom from higher planes of existence.

**Pearls:** For wisdom. Each Pearl absorbs and holds a different inspirational thought and the energy of one doesn't blend with that of another. The more misshapen the pearl, the more eccentric the thought. Such Pearls are called baroque.

**Pearls, Biwa:** Same as Pearls but more for eccentric thought.

**Septarian Nodule:** Enhances the ability to perceive higher truth and love.

## Oneness with the Universe

**Calcite, Violet:** Enables one to feel harmoniously connected to, and at peace with, everything that is. Makes one feel that everything is perfect just as it is.

**Creedite:** Connects one with the Tao. One feels directly connected with God.

**Gaudefroyite:** Enables one to transcend ego and one's sense of individual identity. Enables one to go beyond one's self and feel a part of the greater whole.

**Granite:** Connects one with the Tao. One feels directly connected to God--the Supreme Reality.

**Hauynite:** Puts one in touch with the Tao and one's spiritual nature. Enables one to experience the connectedness of the whole and oneness with all that is. Promotes the ability to use symbolism to reach higher states.

**Heulandite:** For spiritual awareness. Enables one to experience the connectedness of the whole; oneness with all that is, and awareness of the Supreme Reality.

**Hiddenite:** Enables one to experience a feeling of love and connectedness with the entire universe. One feels harmoniously connected to the whole and that everything is perfect just as it is.

**Kammererite:** Gives one a sense of being at peace; a sense of harmony and connectedness with the whole.

**Lepidolite:** Same in effect as Kammererite.

**Opal, Black:** Makes one feel energetically connected to the whole, and one with all that is. Enables one to have a highly spiritual and divinely intense sexual experience, in which one loses the boundaries of one's ego, and merges with the cosmos.

**Opal, Jelly:** Functions the same as the Black Opal although it is not quite as powerful.

**Vanadinite:** For inspiration of a spiritual nature. Promotes the experience of an exalted, inspirational space wherein one is in touch with God, the Universal Consciousness.

### Oneness with Nature

**Agate, Enhydritic:** Puts one in touch with the spiritual nature of water.

**Coronadite:** Same in effect as Wulfenite.

**Murataite:** Same in effect as Wulfenite.

**Wulfenite:** Enables one to commune with the spirits of nature. Connects one to the spiritual energy of trees, clouds, water, plants, etc.

## TRANSFORMATION

The stones in this section relate to one's transformation in the deepest or most profound sense: transformation in relationship to one's essence or soul rather than one's surface personality and day to day existence. They fall into two categories: 1) enhancing or awakening inner awareness 2) stimulating or aiding, in some way, the evolution of the soul through growth experiences. As completing one's karmic debts also evolves the soul, please refer to the discussion on Karma included earlier in this section.

## Inner Awareness

**Apache Tears:** Makes it easier to be aware of, and communicate with, one's self on the essence level. Enhances awareness of one's true self.

**Esperite:** Enables one to get in touch with the overview of one's life, and to see the overlying patterns of one's existence. Helps one to identify one's purpose in life, and the tasks that will accomplish that purpose. Reveals to one, that which will advance the soul.

**Jinshajiangite:** Leads one directly and with surety to one's personal truths and inner principles. Eliminates self-deception and clarifies one's beliefs. Useful during meditation

**Quartz, Lavender:** An aid to meditation and self remembering. Self-remembering is being aware of what one is actually doing and saying on all levels. Stimulates an intense, supra-self awareness.

**Rose Quartz:** Puts one in touch with one's self on the essence level. Enhances awareness of one's true self.

**Shattuckite:** Puts one in touch with different degrees of essence: i.e., from the least to the most developed parts of one's essence. Allows one to experience the different facets of one's higher self. These facets include the ability to be in accord with nature and animals, to appreciate the finer aspects of power, prosperity, and relationships with one's fellow man, as well as the experience of higher truth and transcendent love and wisdom.

**Sphalerite:** For transcending ego; for spirituality and empathy. It takes one beyond petty problems and into a higher space of calm and true self-knowledge.

**Stellarite:** Puts one in touch with the highest degree of one's essence, or highest self.

## Evolution of Essence

**Agate, Brown with Gray, Black or Clear Stripes:** Enables one to invoke transformation in one's self and others. One becomes a catalyst for transformation.

**Amethyst:** Keeps one in touch with one's more noble, spiritual side: the part of one that urges one to do the best thing, even though that might not be the most serving of one's own interests. Enables one to act out of one's highest ideals rather than one's self-motivated interests. Action motivated out of higher ideals most effectively advances the evolution of the soul.

**Boltonite:** Same in effect as Peridot.

**Bukovskyite:** Same in effect as Peridot.

**Chenevixite:** Encourages powerfully intense growth experiences to occur in one's life.

**Cyanotrichite:** Transforming due to its ability to pull one into emotional intensity and depth.

**Epidote:** Promotes the regular and steady evolution of the soul and, at the same time, allows one to remain powerful as one evolves.

**Malachite:** Enables one to stay in a mood of loving tolerance toward others, balanced internally and able to respond flexibly to events, regardless of what is happening and no matter how bizarre and unsettling the events. One is able to be truly appropriate in one's reactions.

**Peridot:** Escalates growth: opens the box of adventure and brings in new challenges. The effect can be too intense for some. Yellower color produces the most intense effect; greener a milder effect. Wear with Amethyst and Citrine to slow the growth aspect down and keep one balanced.

**Pistacite:** Same in effect as Epidote.

**Sinhalite:** Similar in effect to Peridot.

**Stichtite:** Aids in completing old cycles and cleaning up one's incompletions. Cycles have a beginning, middle, and an end. Stichtite encourages one to continue through to completion.

**Zircon, Pink:** For growth on the Astral Plane. Pushes one to leave the body, at night while sleeping, and do astral lessons. Astral lessons are emotional in nature and can result in a rather restless night.

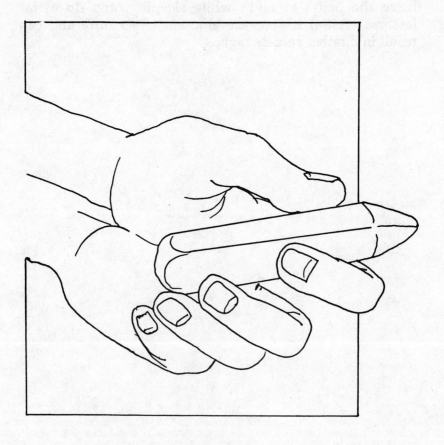

# THE INDIVIDUAL

## The Emotions

**Barytocalcite:** Enables one to be in touch with, and clear about, one's emotions. Heightens one's empathic awareness and ability to be emotionally perceptive about others.

**Calcite, Blue:** Balances one's emotional state and removes blocks so emotions can flow more easily.

**Calcite, Orange:** Balancing to the emotions. Increases feelings of happiness.

**Horn:** Balancing to one's emotional state. Makes one feel connected to others and loved.

**Lapis Lazuli:** Enhances neutrality of the emotions and enhances neutral emotional perceptivity. Allows one to perceive emotional issues more clearly.

**Mirabilite:** Increases one's emotional perceptivity and empathic understanding of others.

**Phenakite, Blue:** Keeps one from forming bad emotional habits. This includes throwing a tantrum when one doesn't get one's way, or any way of acting out of one's emotions inappropriately.

### EMOTIONAL OPENNESS

**Aplowite:** Brings emotions to the surface. Encourages honesty about one's feelings.

**Balyakinite:** Allows one to experience strong emotions with a feeling of safety and a sense that one's emotions will stay appropriately in check.

**Calcite, Red:** Allows one to feel safe to open up emotionally. Negative emotions are drained out of body rather than held or absorbed.

**Desautelsite:** Puts one in touch with one's primal emotions. Encourages one to process one's issues emotionally rather than intellectually.

**Glaucocerinite:** For emotional mastery. Makes one feel in control of one's emotions and gives one a comforting sense that one will make it through emotionally trying times.

**Heterosite:** For emotional openness. Most useful for people who are emotionally blocked.

**Quartz, Elestial:** Opens the emotions, releases emotional blocks and heals. Allows one to see one's emotional truths clearly.

**Smithsonite, Green or Blue:** Releases the emotions. Good for those who are emotionally blocked.

**Trippkeite:** Opens up one's ability to experience all one's emotions. Aids in experiencing one's love and joy to the fullest. If one has painful emotions to process, use this stone sparingly.

## EMOTIONAL STRESS

There are a number of stones that are useful when one is under emotional pressure. This first group reduces the intensity of various emotional states, help one stay in balance and are healing to the emotional center

**Aurichalcite:** Very useful when one has taken some very hard knocks and one is in need of emotional healing.

**Brucite:** Reduces the sense of being pressured, keeps one emotionally balanced, and helps one avoid a tendency to have hysterics.

**Calcite, Blue:** Reduces intensity, heals the emotions, and removes blocks so emotions can flow more easily.

**Calcite, Gray:** Gives one a break from emotional intensity, so one can take a look at the issues in one's life from a detached point of view.

**Calcite, Red:** Drains negative emotions out of the body.

**Carnotite:** Allows one to stay intellectually and emotionally clear when under stress, particularly if one's survival issues have been activated. Enhances one's ability to use logic and, simultaneously, heightens one's intuitiveness and emotional sensitivity

**Clinotryolite:** Same in effect as Aurichalcite.

**Franklinite:** Helps release emotional tensions. Keeps the emotions flowing in a steady fashion so they don't become blocked.

**Jasper, Spider Web:** Has a valium-like effect and is very soothing to frayed nerves.

**Paua Shell:** Helpful in times of difficult challenge or heavy transitions. Heals stress by keeping the body clear of stressful chemicals and hormones.

**Qingheiite:** Same in effect as Rosasite.

**Rosasite:** Helps one shift out of a negative emotional state into a more positive one. Works by enabling one to produce an appropriate action or thought, that then shifts the emotional state.

## Grief and Trauma

This next group of stones are particularly healing when one is experiencing a great deal of upset, grief or trauma.

**Benjaninite:** Acts as an anesthetic to the emotions when one has gone through great difficulties and is traumatized: like putting a bandage over emotional wounds.

**Edingtonite:** Eases grief and allows one to get through it without collapsing.

**Kinoite:** Softens grief and makes it easier to feel at peace.

**Plancheite:** Very strong healer when one is going through an intense tragedy or grieving period. Temporarily numbs the emotions until healing can begin: then, eases a person through the various stages of the grief process.

**Yecoraite:** Same in effect as Benjaninite.

## Anxiety

Anxiety is a difficult emotional state that is becoming more and more common in today's society. Very often, one is precipitated into the state of anxiety, with its attendant symptoms of fear, without knowing why. Other times one has an awareness of the source of one's anxiety, such as the possible loss of one's job, or not enough money to pay the bills, or a fear that a loved one will come to harm.

In all cases, anxiety is related to something that is not actually happening in the present. If that were so, we would call it fear and, most likely, some immediate action would be indicated. With anxiety, the precipitant is either unknown or the feared event takes place some time in the future. There is usually a belief or a feeling that one's survival is threatened; that whatever happens will be terrible. The following group of stones calm such fears and help one feel that survival is not an issue

**Abalone:** Makes one feel calmer and less afraid. Particularly useful for people who live very dramatic, intense lives.

**Agate, Leopard Skin:** Calms anxiety and is very healing when dealing with heavy emotional issues. Reduces free-floating anxiety: i.e., when one is worried or nervous but doesn't know why.

**Aventurine, Blue:** Calms anxiety and makes one feel more stable, balanced and well supported.

**Bone:** Helps calm anxiety and basic fears about survival whether one's issue is real or not. Makes one feel that everything will be fine in the long run.

**Chinese Writing Stone:** Helps calm anxiety and basic fears about survival. Makes one feel that everything will be all right.

**Coral, Apple:** Calms anxiety.

**Coral, Black:** Major healer of anxiety and primal fears. There are two basic emotions in the universe--fear and love--when one is healed of fear, what is left is love.

**Flint:** Heals one of fears surrounding survival.

**Grossular, Gray to Black:** Heals one of anxiety and fears about survival. Particularly good when facing survival issues such as the loss of a job. Functions similarly to Bone.

**Ivory:** Helps to calm anxiety and basic fears about survival whether one's issue is real or not. Makes one feel that survival is not an issue.

**Lawsonite:** Similar in effect to Leopard Skin Agate.

**Ludlamite:** Very calming, particularly when one has gone through difficult or anxious times. Keeps one from acting out one's stress with inappropriate behavior.

**Obsidian, Black:** Same in effect as Leopard-Skin Agate.

**Obsidian, Rainbow:** Calms, relaxes, and heals one of survival fears.

**Petrified Wood:** Same in effect as Bone.

**Shell:** Same in effect as Bone. Particularly useful for those whose lives are full of intensity.

**Volborthite:** Decreases one's tendency to worry, particularly if the worry is needless.

# The Intellect

## INTELLECTUAL PURSUITS

**Abernathyite:** Encourages one to operate from a very scholarly and intellectual point of view: to seek out the facts and to gather data rather than accept information on faith. Encourages good study habits.

**Agate, Gray or Brown-Gray with White Stripes:** Makes one appreciative of intellectual pursuits and promotes abstract, creative thought.

**Anthonyite:** Enables one to keep an emotional balance during prolonged intellectual pursuits. Speeds basic data manipulations such as categorizing. Relieves the stress of continual hard thinking and makes it easier to work longer on intellectual tasks without mental exhaustion.

**Brazilianite:** Stimulates one to investigate and do research in incredible detail, or into investigating the unusual, esoteric or bizarre.

**Chloroxiphite:** Promotes strong spurts of intellectual growth. Enables one to learn new information in large chunks.

**Coral, Blue:** Encourages the passionate pursuit of knowledge.

**Coral, Elephant Ear:** Stimulates one's passion for new philosophical concepts and encourages intellectual pursuits.

**Emerald:** Balancing to those who deal with processing a great deal of information. Helps one feel out the truth when there is a lot of information to sort through.

**Feldspar, Anorthite:** Promotes the pursuit of knowledge and keeps one from becoming close minded or overly theoretical.

**Goshenite:** An anti-pigheadedness stone. Useful for anyone who gets overly opinionated or into emotional pontificating. Centers a person in the positive use of one's intellect and in knowledge rather than theory.

**Phenakite, Colorless to White:** Keeps one from forming bad mental habits. For example, assuming that one is right, when one hasn't collected enough evidence, or had enough experience, to know.

**Sapphire, Light Blue:** Produces inspired conceptual thoughts. Will promote an inspired approach to one's intellectual projects.

**Sapphire, Yellow:** Puts one directly in touch with what one knows. Also helps one realize what one doesn't know. Enables one to use one's intellect and knowledge very appropriately. Also enhances one's ability to learn and retain information.

**Topaz, Imperial:** Makes one feel able to exercise all of one's scholarly abilities and talents. Makes one feel that one is intelligent enough, that one has enough information and, in general, that one has enough scholarly ability to handle any situation.

**Wermlandite:** Increases curiousity.

**Winstanleyite:** Increases one's curiousity.

**Zoisite, Brown:** Balances those engaged in intellectual pursuits. Prevents one from falling into an opinionated, "know-it-all" attitude.

## MEMORY

**Allophane:** Helps the brain work more efficiently and access those "tip of the tongue" thoughts, concepts or memories.

**Blixite:** Enhances short-term memory retention. Helps one on tests, to remember where one parked one's car or remember where one left one's keys.

**Brushite:** Helps one to forget. Use this method: Pull up an unpleasant memory. Concentrate on that memory while holding the rock for a few minutes. Do this every day for a period of time and the memory will be erased. Usually one or two weeks will suffice. Drains the emotion out of the memory.

**Carminite:** Increases short-term memory retention. Enhances one's ability to remember what happened within the last 24 hours.

**Eckermannite:** To stimulate one's memory of the key elements of any event. Useful for recalling key aspects of minor, as well as more major events.

**Enstatite:** Good for short-term memory retention. Useful in taking tests.

**Orthoferrosilite:** Enhances short-term memory.

**Rhodochrosite:** Increases long-term memory. One is better able to access memories from the present life, as well as from past lives. Also enables one to remember what one is supposed to be doing in the present moment: to stay aware, be present and be relevant.

**Sapphire, Yellow:** Enhances one's ability to memorize and retain information.

**Thenardite:** Improves memory by promoting a more efficient accessing of existing memory banks. Also promotes the more efficient storage of new information and aids in the creation of new memory banks.

**Tugtupite:** Sharpens the memory. Increases one's ability to remember.

## MENTAL CLARITY

**Amber:** Good for mental clarity. Enables one to maintain a sharp intellectual focus.

**Amber, Honey:** Same in effect as the clear Amber, but with a more inspirational quality.

**Bayleyite:** Good for eliminating mental confusion. Helps one go straight to the core nature of a problem, as well as its solution.

**Bellingerite:** Promotes mental clarity and discourages fuzzy thinking.

**Datolite:** Produces clearer thinking.

**Freibergite:** Puts one in a practical and reasonable frame of mind. Enables one to coolly and calmly perform tasks in the most logical manner.

**Gypsum:** For intellectual clarity and competency.

**Hyalophane:** Focuses the mind and increases mental activity. Enables one to think more quickly and of more things.

**Jarosite:** Helps one to gather scattered thoughts together or bring diverse and confusing ideas into focus.

**Jasper, Brecchiated**: Centers one intellectually and makes it easier to be logical, clear headed and clear thinking. Increases one's intellectual capacity.

**Jasper, Bright Green**: Draws one into a cool, calculating intellectual energy.

**Richterite**: Gives one mental stamina. Enables one to keep paying attention, for long periods of time, to even somewhat boring material. One can study tedious materials longer

**Smithsonite, Brown**: Produces clearer thinking.

**Topaz, White**: Opens the mind and allows one to maintain a clear, intellectual focus. Similar in effect to Amber.

**Tourmaline, Yellow, Brown or Clear**: Assists one in intellectual processing.

**Triplite**: Same in effect as Amber.

**Wermlandite**: Stimulates the intellect and allows one to think for long periods of time without mental fatigue.

**Winstanleyite**: Stimulates the intellect and allows one to think for long periods of time without mental fatigue.

**Xiangjiangite**: Enables one to use at least five more percentage points of one's mental capacity.


## MENTAL STRESS

The stones listed below, are particularly effective for enabling one to deal with a variety of stresses to the mind. Any of the stones listed above, that aid in producing mental clarity; that help one stay centered intellectually and to be logical and clear thinking, are also useful during times of stress. If one can maintain presence of mind in the midst of crises and emotional storms, it is much easier to deal with any difficulty.

**Amber, Red**: Enables the intellect to function smoothly by containing negative emotions.

**Ambroid:** Enables one to maintain an intellectual focus even when one's consciousness is dominated by primal fears or survival issues.

**Anthonyite:** Heals the mental stress of continual hard thinking. Makes it easier to work longer on intellectual tasks without mental exhaustion.

**Aragonite:** Reduces emotionality and drama. Enables one to simultaneously operate from a high degree of emotional perceptivity, intellectual clarity, and the ability to see truth from a higher perspective and psychically sense the flow of events.

**Burnite:** Enables one to effectively use one's intellect, and stay clearly observant, even when in crisis or strongly emotional.

**Carnotite:** Allows one to stay intellectually and emotionally clear when under stress, particularly if one's survival issues have been activated. Enhances one's ability to use logic and, simultaneously, heightens one's intuitiveness and emotional sensitivity

**Dioptase:** Physically healing to the brain. Reduces the stress of chemicals that are released into the brain from overworking or overstudying.

**Goldstone, Blue:** Very calming, particularly if one is intellectually stressed.

**Jasper, Brecchiated:** Makes it easier to be logical, clear headed and clear thinking, regardless of the circumstances.

**Opalite:** Keeps excess energy from building up, and can help release that "headachy" feeling one gets from overusing the mind.

**Polylithionite:** Corrects chemical imbalances in the brain.

## OBSERVATION

The stones in this section ensure that one's observations are very clear, sharp and insightful.

**Carminite:** Makes one extremely observant of all that is happening in the present moment.

**Crystal, Clear:** For clarity of observation. The clearer the stone, the clearer the observation.

**Diamond, Herkimer:** A more powerful version of clear Crystal.

**Geodes:** Geodes are unique and individual. Each one represents a different observation about something that's true. The most attractive Geodes remind one of a particular observation that one has made and that one wishes to remain aware of.

**Milarite:** Sharpens one's observations. Helps one see things with greater clarity.

**Quartz, Snow:** An observation stone. When snowy in color rather than clear, one moves into a childlike state from which one can observe from a place of innocence. One's insights are fresh and clear, free of preconceptions and free of cynical, "adult" viewpoints.

# Action

The gemstones and minerals described here, have the general effect of enabling one to move into action appropriately; enhancing one's decisiveness, alertness, productivity level, and ability to handle stressful situations effectively.

**Agate, Fire:** Same in effect as Fire Opal.

**Austinite:** Aids workaholics or nervous overachievers to slow down and work at an easier pace. Enables one to proceed in a more balanced fashion.

**Bellingerite:** Encourages one to be more decisive and to act on one's decisions. Discourages fuzzy thinking and delayed action.

**Bogdanovite:** Reduces harried hurriedness and encourages one to take things at a more appropriate pace. Increases one's effectiveness. One pays more attention to what one is doing.

**Metahewettite:** Promotes one's ability to tackle one's problems forcefully and to move into action dynamically and appropriately.

**Norbergite:** Stimulates one to act on one's thoughts. If one is thinking about something, the impulse will occur toward some action that takes care of what one was thinking about.

**Omphacite:** Enourages one to tackle one's tasks with fervor and boldness. When used with Garnet, adds the element of productivity.

**Opal, Fire:** Enables one to be powerful in circumstances that require action.

**Purpurite:** Enables one to stay balanced and moving into action appropriately.

**Sapphire, Yellow:** When wearing this stone, new opportunities start to arise, and new options open up for one to pursue..

**Topaz, Golden:** Useful for knowing what procedures will work in a particular situation. Enables one to delineate steps a, b, and c, without wasting time. Good with Garnets to pull in practical ways of being productive.

**Youngite:** Inspires solutions to problems requiring action on the physical plane. Energizes one to solve difficult problems.

## GET UP and GO

**Agate, Black with White Stripes:** Makes one very alert and ready for action.

**Cahnite:** Encourages the body to move at a quicker pace. Good for getting things accomplished and/or keeping the body exercised.

**Calomel:** Makes one feel more energetic and prompts one to move at a faster pace.

**Cumengite:** (Found as a growth on Boleite). Encourages a passionate fervor for taking advantage of the opportunities that come one's way, particularly those arising out of the good-luck energy stimulated by Boleite.

**Jasper, Red:** Produces a dynamic and lively energy.

**Opal, White:** Energizes the body and enhances productivity.

**Piemontite Epidote:** A very powerful stone. Makes one feel that one is pulsing with power and "get up and go" energy. A good cure for laziness.

**Smithsonite, Yellow:** Makes one more movement oriented and ready for action.

**Spectrolite:** Same in effect as White Opal, although more powerful in its action. May be too strong for some.

**Tiger Eye, Blue:** Same stone as Spectrolite.


## PRODUCTIVITY

**Adamite:** Adds the quality of specifity to one's productivity. Enables one to see the details of a situation and encourages one to proceed in a step-by-step, delineated fashion from a, to b, to c, etc.

**Agate, Dry-Head:** Enables one to be focused and precise. Promotes productivity by making it easier to focus in on a project and be clear about each necessary detail.

**Annabergite:** Enables those who approach life and its tasks from a widely focused-viewpoint, to narrow their focus and pay attention to details or prioritize cycles in order of importance. Curbs the tendency to do everything at one time.

**Austinite:** Same in effect as Labradorite.

**Cassiterite:** Enhances productivity. Keeps one focused, purposeful and able to get a lot accomplished.

**Chondrodite:** Enhances productivity. Enhances the qualities of bravery, protectiveness, acting from one's high ideals, feistiness, and the willingness to take orders. Promotes

Productivity in the office can be enhanced with the appropriate gemstones and minerals. Good choices are Atacamite for attention to detail, Huntite for prioritizing, Malachite for balancing and Clear Crystal for Clarity.

good strategic skills and the ability to work as a team with others.

**Cubic Zirconia:** Aids in maintaining a high productivity level and increases one's prosperity. When the color is other than clear, a slightly different twist is added to the basic energetic effect of productivity and prosperity.

>**Blue:** Adds an element of calm.

>**Brown:** Prompts the body to relax and let go of physical tension.

>**Green:** Puts a stronger emphasis on prosperity: focuses one on making one's life just like one wants it to be.

>**Pink, Lilac & Purple:** Creates a mood of relaxation and a desire for spiritual pursuits. Would not not promote productivity in the arena of "getting things done."

>**Red:** Adds a little extra punch and a dynamic quality.

>**Yellow to Orange:** Adds an element of contentment or happiness: promotes a mildly pleasurable state.

**Garnet:** Best all-round gemstone for productivity. As the color changes, the characteristic of the productivity shifts also.

**Garnet, Almandine:** Increases one's productivity. Enables one to stay focused and to get things done in a competent, purposeful fashion.

**Garnet, Pyrope:** For productivity, with the qualities of happiness and abundance. Keeps one not only producing, but producing abundantly with a sense of happiness at the same time.

**Garnet, Rhodolite:** Also for productivity, but related more specifically to one's career and feeling productive when on the job.

**Garnet, Spessartite:** A productivity rock for the homemaker. Focuses one on the home and enables one to get a lot accomplished.

**Garnet, Star:** For high-powered productivity. The productivity of the Garnet is powered by the Rutile that "stars" it, and keeps one moving "full steam ahead" for long periods of time.

**Hollandite:** Empowers one to be productive, purposeful, and focused in getting things accomplished.

**Huntite:** Clears any excess out of the space and allows one to concentrate on just what needs to be done. Allows one to prioritize so one can productively accomplish everything.

**Labradorite:** Enables one to work productively for long periods of time without tiring. Balances and re-energizes those who have been overworking.

**Opal, White:** Energizes the body and enhances productivity.

**Youngite:** Inspires solutions to problems requiring physical action. Very productivity oriented.

**Zoisite, Gray:** Keeps one organized, productive and able to get a lot accomplished without being insensitive to others, bossy or too demanding.

## SITUATIONAL STRESS

Very frequently stress is generated by external events that are difficult to handle. This can be a one-time event such as the break up of a relationship or getting fired. Stress can also be the result of a number of smaller difficulties, each of which could be handled easily, but when occurring together become overwhelming. Sometimes stress is generated by too many positive things happening at once, such as getting married, getting pregnant and being promoted on the job all in the same month.

The stones listed below are particularly good for handling a variety of situational stresses. Many helpful stones are also discussed in the section "Inner Strength".

### Coping

**Alforsite:** Allows one to accept whatever is happening, no matter how difficult, and deal with it rather than turn away. One must be cautious in using this stone as a person who tends to be naturally soft and passive might become overly pliant and lose the capacity to set limits.

**Andremeyerite**: Gives one a more humorous perspective during difficult times, and makes one feel more comfortable about one's problems. Others may feel offended if the holder of the stone makes "light" of their difficulties because of his ability to feel lighter himself.

**Arrojadite**: Allows one to close one's emotions down very tightly to handle extremely difficult situations.

**Bowenite**: Eases one's sense of being victimized by circumstances. Reduces feelings of helplessness.

**Calcite, Black**: Aids one in seeing anything that could possibly go wrong, and taking precautions so one will not fall into further problems or difficulties.

**Crossite**: Enables one to come up with creative solutions to miserable or desparate problems in one's life. Since these solutions are accessed from one's deepest subconscious, they can be quite extreme and must be considered carefully for social appropriateness.

**Jasper, Bruneau**: Enables one to handle crises or difficulties in a very balanced fashion.

**Jet**: Good to have around when one must deal with difficult situations. Keeps one's eyes open and alert for what might go wrong, so one can correct the situation with some kind of positive action.

**Soapstone, Pale Green**: (Translucent). Same in effect as Bowenite.

**Stringhamite**: Encourages one to take a strong leadership position, and enables one to stay on top of a difficult or confusing situation.

## Staying Calm

This group of stones are particularly good for staying calm under trying circumstances. In one way or another, they all enable one to remain serene and keep one's perspective.

**Analcime**: Enables one to handle anything that comes up with a sense of purpose and an ability to remain neutral.

**Anhydrite:** Promotes a sense of peace and serenity even during difficult times, and helps one stay objective and realistic about any problem.

**Callaghanite:** Enables one to hear, and calmly deal with, unpleasant news.

**Emerada:** For fearlessness. Wear in situations where one would normally feel afraid or anxious, and one will feel much calmer.

**Jade, Green:** Enables one to handle the unpleasant aspects of life that one cannot avoid, in a calm and capable manner. Promotes a tranquility that mitigates against depression.

**Jerrygibbsite:** Promotes a sense of calm and an ability to remain serene and keep one's perspective in the face of any mishap or difficulty.

**Pickeringite:** Allows one to create an island of calm in an otherwise frantic period.

**Rhodonite, Pink with Brown, Yellow or Grey markings:** Enables one to be cool and dignified even while facing stressful circumstances.

**Todorokite:** Calms and soothes highly excitable or creative types of people when they are under stress.

## We Will Survive

The stones included here are all useful when one's survival is threatened. They give one a sense that things will turn out all right.

**Acmite:** Encourages the belief that one can handle what may look to be an insurmountable difficulty. Very similar in effect to Gratonite, but it is not necessary for the circumstances to be so desparate before one finds Acmite valuable.

**Agate, Turitella:** Puts one in touch with any instinctive fears, or survival-based issues and helps one neutralize them.

**Flint:** Gives one a sense of confidence when going through experiences that threaten survival and encourages one to feel that one can survive, no matter what.

**Gratonite:** Encourages one to believe, even in the face of the most difficult circumstances, that one can not only survive, but one can thrive against all odds.

**Grossular, Gray to Black:** Enables one to face survival threatening events, such as the loss of a job, with equanimity. Promotes the feeling that things will ultimately turn out fine.

**Ramsdellite:** Gives one the courage to continue on in very difficult, or potentially dangerous situations. Helps one operate from "fight" rather than "flight."

**Sogdianite:** Enables one to push beyond one's ordinary limitations to survive.

**Tigillite:** Heals and calms one's strongest fears about survival.

# Personal Power

One's personal power, or the ability to act effectively in the world, is essential in creating a lifestyle that is personally satisfying. The gemstones and minerals included in this section enhance one's personal power in a variety of ways; from the ability to realize one's ambitions or build empires, to the ability to develop one's inner strength and withstand the self scrutiny necessary to eliminate self-defeating behavior patterns.

**Agate, Orange with Yellow or Brown Stripes:** Makes one feel, as well as project the image, that one is grounded, self-sufficient, capable and trustworthy. One has an aura of strength and competence.

**Agate, Fire:** Same in effect as Fire Opal.

**Aquamarine:** Helps one project an aura of real strength. Makes others pay attention, even when one may not fully believe in one's self.

**Aventurine, Red:** A powerful, all-purpose stone that stimulates one's creativity, enhances one's personal power and level of prosperity, promotes emotional availability, intellectual acuity and good communication. Enables one to use these various aspects of one's being in a harmoniously blended fashion.

**Charoite**: Enables those who are involved in teaching, the media, or any profession that involves the dissemination of information and/or wisdom, to feel powerful and project an aura of confidence and authority.

**Jasper, Red**: Puts one in touch with feeling powerful and reduces feelings of victimization.

**Magnetite**: Promotes a straight forward, reality oriented, truth-telling approach to life and its problems.

**Opal, Fire**: Allows one to project with incredible charisma. Increases one's personal power and the ability to operate effectively in the world.

**Quartz, Rutillated**: Enables one to project an aura of authority. Pulls one into being powerful and produces clarity with regard to what one is being powerful about. One not only looks very clear, and capable of handling everything, but one feels that way as well.

**Rutile**: Adds power to whatever rock it flows through. The rock then becomes a magnifier of the power of one's own personal aura. One stands out as a more powerful or noticeable person in one's way of being. It is important to note that it is the power of one's presence that is augmented, rather than one's actions becoming more powerful or having more power over another person.

## AMBITION

**Augite**: Promotes ambitions. Enables one to pull in what is needed to get ahead and to use one's personal power effectively to realize one's ambitions. Usually found in a matrix of Green Jade or Serpentine which adds the ability to stay tranquil and calm.

**Cacoxenite**: Makes one feel ambitious and, at the same time, very practical about achieving one's ambitions.

**Chalcosiderite:** Very powerfully assists one to get in touch with and manifest one's ambitions in a positive way.

**Olivenite:** Promotes success by putting one in the mood to do career work. Makes it easy to focus on work or career issues.

**Pyrolusite:** A stone that enhances qualities of determination, willfulness, and ambition. Makes it easier to keep going, when the going gets tough. Good for stiffening the spine of a passive, indecisive type of person. Often combined with White Calcite which adds an element of love and acceptance toward others, that tempers the willfulness of this stone.

## EMPIRE BUILDING

**Actinolite:** Helps one to build an empire in the area of art and creativity, or to master one's creative abilities.

**Andalusite:** Enables one to take on vast projects that require a great deal of foresight, planning, and staying power. A power stone of "empire-building" strength.

**Cassiterite:** Helps one to build an empire in the area of business or politics, or any arena that needs mastery of organizational and strategic skills.

**Diamond:** Helps one to build an empire of any sort and master any project that is of grand scale.

**Hexagonite:** Same in effect as Actinolite.

**Jasper, Stromatolitic:** Similar in effect to Andalusite with more emphasis on the element of risk taking.

**Jasper, Xmas-Tree:** Empowers one to achieve whatever one has set out to do. Keeps one anchored in mastery and excellence; completely focused and looking ahead to what one is going to accomplish next, without being distracted. One can produce a similar effect, by combining Garnet, Blue Topaz, and Rutillated Quartz. Michael suggests throwing in a little Blue Sapphire for compassion.

**Mariposite:** Helps one to build an empire that is based on communication or media skills.

**Microlite:** Same in effect as Actinolite.

**Sapphire, Orange:** For the individual who is comfortable with being very powerful, and is basically ready to build an empire based on scholarly pursuits. This could include the writing of books, doing research on a large scale, or being in charge of ten libraries at once.

**Tremolite:** Same in effect as Actinolite.

**Veszelyite:** Helps one to build an empire that is spiritually based; usually in the area of the ministry.

**Viridine:** Same in effect as Andalusite.

**Sillimanite, Dark Brown:** Same in effect as Andalusite.

**Zoisite, Green:** Inspires one to build an empire in the area of service to others.

## ENVISIONING POSSIBILITIES

**Celestite:** Inspires one to visionary and beautiful flights of fancy, while at the same time, enables one to keep a level head.

**Dypingite:** Enables one to stop all physical, emotional and mental activity. One can then sit back and, with this clean slate, envision new directions.

**Hambergite:** Pulls one into a visionary frame of mind in which one is inspired by utopian concepts and the wonderful possibilities in the universe. Works on fomenting ideas rather than manifesting them.

**Jade, Pakistan:** Enables one to come up with some great, wild, visionary ideas. Similar in effect to Hambergite.

**Jade, Southern:** Encourages one to come up with new possibilities in a situation instead of just accepting things as they are.

**Moonstone:** Helps one achieve one's heart's desire, by clearly seeing the variety of possibilities inherent in a situation, or in one's life.

**Sonolite:** Puts one into a spiritualistic, visionary frame of mind, able to envision all possibilities and open new horizons.

## GETTING RESULTS

**Chondrodite:** Promotes and enhances the qualities of bravery, protectiveness, acting from one's high ideals, feistiness, and the willingness to take orders. Promotes good strategic skills and the abililty to work as a team with others.

**Diamond:** Promotes the development of competence and feelings of mastery over situations external to one's self. Enables one to see ways to handle a situation one desires to master.

**Planerite:** For personal power and winning. Particularly good for winning arguments and resolving communication conflicts.

**Tiger Iron:** Promotes the mastery of skills necessary to deal effectively with situations external to one's self. Stimulates the pursuit and achievement of excellence.

**Variscite:** Empowers one to come up with solutions or actions that will produce win-win results for everyone. Allows one to see what it is that pulls everything together, and simultaneously, feel that one has the power to make it happen.

**Vesuvianite:** Helps one to compete, to come from a desire to win, and to be appropriate with one's competitiveness. Encourages a "win-win" attitude.

## INNER STRENGTH

**Anatase:** Makes one feel innately more powerful and capable of handling any difficulties that show up.

**Arsenoclasite:** Promotes a kingly sense of calm and power.

**Barkevikite:** Gives one a sense that one is in control of one's body, one's environment and one's destiny. Enables one to get in touch with, and use, one's will power.

**Brookite:** Increases one's sense of personal power. Enables one to feel more capable and confident about handling whatever difficulties might appear.

**Epidote:** Promotes the mastery of one's own power. Enables one to remain powerful in a situation where others would like to cause harm, or undermine one's power.

**Iolite, Gray:** Makes one feel confident about one's ability to take charge of one's life and be successful, particularly in the arena of one's career. Makes it difficult to feel that one is a victim of the circumstances.

**Jade, Black:** Enables one to deal with issues which involve survival, sex, and power, in a balanced fashion. Good to wear when one wants to open up, but feels attacked or that survival is an issue.

**Jasper, Gray:** Makes it easier to utilize one's own personal power and have confidence that one's power cannot be taken away.

**Jamesite:** Gives one a feeling of security. One feels that any endeavor undertaken will turn out well. One has a sense that support will be there if needed, which gives the confidence to take on projects that might otherwise seem too difficult or overwhelming.

**Jeanbandyite:** Enables one to remain firm in one's convictions. Keeps one from being wishy-washy, easily swayed, or convinced of something other than what one truly believes.

**Neptunite:** Same in effect as Gray Jasper.

**Pistacite:** Same in effect as Epidote.

**Spinel, Black:** Promotes a sense of beneficence. Makes one feel so in charge of situations and self that one can afford to be really giving and understanding of others, no matter what they're doing.

**Stanite:** Enables one to feel as stable as the rock of Gibralter and capable of standing up under any pressure.

**Topaz, Pink:** Promotes the qualities of integrity and honesty.

**Trevorite:** Encourages honesty.

**Tsavorite:** Promotes the ability to master one's personal issues and take control of one's own destiny. Gives one a feeling of happiness and confidence that one's life is in good shape whether it pleases someone else or not.

**Unikite:** Enables one to completely and totally take charge of one's own life. Helps protect personal power and fosters a sense that one is the guardian of one's own fate and cannot be taken over by anyone else.

### Bravery and Courage

The following group of stones are all about being brave and more courageous. They make it easier to do things that one fears. Examples might be trying to ski for the first time, or going off the high dive, or starting that new job that will call on skills one has never used before. Then, there are those people who find life itself very trying and who are always more or less afraid. They might like to have one or two around all the time just in case.

**Acmite:** Increases bravery and bolsters one's courage.

**Antigorite:** Enables one to be cautious when necessary without being overly fearful.

**Chalcocite:** Encourages a cautious, deliberate approach when appropriate, and keeps one from becoming overly fearful.

**Cervantite:** Same in effect as Stibnite.

**Clinochrysotile:** Same in effect as Antigorite.

**Clinosafflorite:** Enhances the qualities of bravery, fearlessness and courageousness.

**Emerada:** Enables one to feel less fear: an all around fear reducer.

**Ramsdellite:** A courage stimulator.

**Sarabauite:** Stimulates courageous action.

**Stibnite:** Enables one to feel more brave.

**Strengite:** Increases bravery and courage.

## Hanging In There

**Bracewellite:** Raises one's self esteem and makes one feel more capable of handling situations that one would normally avoid.

**Chalcocite:** Encourages one to perservere through any hardship. Increases one's emotional stamina and ability to stick with it.

**Benavidesite:** Same in effect as Jamesonite.

**Boulangerite:** Same in effect as Jamesonite.

**Citrine:** Builds up one's stamina and makes it easier to keep going through difficult processes.

**Jamesonite:** Helps one perservere through long, even life-long tasks.

**Jasper, Owyhee:** Useful when there is something one needs to deal with dynamically, but not too aggressively, over a long period of time. Enables one to perservere.

**Sanbornite:** Increases one's ability to perservere: to continue at a steady pace regardless of the circumstances.

**Strengite:** Enables one to perservere in the face of adversity.

**Tourmaline, Watermelon:** Increases one's quotient of "stick-to-itiveness" and strengthens the ability to perservere.

## Surrender

**Coffinite:** Encourages a feeling of surrender to the inevitable. One feels that all will turn out right in the end. Reduces one's fear that things will go wrong, which makes it easier to move ahead.

**Kunzite:** Enables one to accept something that's out of one's control and surrender to it. Very useful since people spend so much time resisting things that are truly out of their control. Michael regards this as one of the most useful of rocks and recommends it highly.

**Sapphire, Pink:** A delegation and surrender stone. Allows one to be more accepting of that which one cannot control.

Makes it easier to surrender to people who can handle things better than oneself. Will tone down dominance and aggression and let life flow more easily.

**Volcanic Ash:** For acceptance of, and surrender to, the inevitable. Helps one recognize, and then acknowledge, when nothing more can be done and surrender is appropriate.

**Woodhousite:** Makes it easier to surrender when necessary and not be so controlling.

## MAKING CHANGES

**Agate, Turitella:** Facilitates the process of taking something old, something new, and successfully putting them together in a new combination. Helps one adjust to changes in one's life that involve blending the old with the new.

**Ametrine:** Helps one adjust to changes in one's life that involve blending the old with the new. In this regard, similar in effect to Turitella Agate.

**Artinite:** Aids one in adapting to the changes in one's life, by encouraging one to have no preconceived ideas about what's supposed to happen.

**Cobaltite:** Helps one to integrate one's lessons, and pull the various aspects of one's life into a coherent whole. Useful for anyone with changes to be integrated into their lives.

**Cornwallite:** Encourages one to feel more attuned to natural organic substances. One feels more comfortable absorbing the energy of natural settings. Makes it easy to transit from city to country living.

**Ferberite:** Encourages acceptance of new things, people and places. One is more willing to let go of familiar structures, and be more flexible and fluid during times of change in one's life.

**Friedalite:** Enables one to feel more at home on the East Coast of the United States. This is also where it is found. Good for immigrants to the U.S, or citizens from other parts of the U.S. who are transplanted to the East Coast.

**Jasper, Morrison Ranch:** Enables one to feel more comfortable with important turning points in one's life and the "rituals" that often accompany them. Examples are: moving away from the home for the first time, graduating from college, getting married, having a baby, turning 40, etc. Makes one feel capable of handling these changes.

**Morrisonite:** Same in effect as Morrison Ranch Jasper.

**Stichtite:** Aids in completing old cycles and cleaning up one's incompletions. Cycles have a beginning, a middle, and an end. Stichtite encourages one to continue through to completion.

## MAKING DECISIONS

**Atacamite:** Enables one to discriminate appropriately about the new things one gets, new situations one enters into or new cycles one starts. Keeps one from accepting things that one might later regret.

**Chalcedony, Gray, Blue or Purple:** Helps one be aware of what one does not want in one's life. Gray helps one get rid of unwanted things. Purple makes one aware of the emotional experiences one doesn't want to have: usually related to the people in one's life. Blue relates to what one doesn't want intellectually in one's space. The gray is usually preferred, because most people would rather clear things out of their life, rather than people or ideas.

**Smoky Quartz:** Enables one to distinguish that which one wants, and that which one doesn't want, and be clear about which is which. Helps one be appropriately discriminating.

**Spinel, Blue to Gray:** Enables one to reject what one does not want in one's space. Great for cleaning the garage. Also good for getting out of sticky situations. Use with caution, as one can go overbaord.

**Tourmaline, Blue:** Enables one to be more discriminating about the people, situations or things, one wants in one's life. Helps one to reject things one doesn't want.

**Willemseite:** Helps one to make choices and be appropriately discriminating. Not good for people who are already very discriminating, as they may become too picky.

**Zorite:** Enhances one's ability to make accurate judgements. Good for discerning the appropriateness of one's choices. Also good for delicately balanced decision making, such as that which abitrators and judges engage in.

## OBJECTIVITY

**Anhydrite:** Gives one a sense of being above any problem, and able to be objective about it.

**Benjaminite with Aikinite:** Helps one to be realistic about the possibilities in the present, and in the near future.

**Burnite:** Promotes realism and objectivity. Enables one to remain neutral, and keep a realistic viewpoint, regardless of the situation.

**Jade, Orange:** Useful when one is unsure of one's sophistication about life. Reduces the tendency to be gullible and naive, about what's actually so.

**Jade, Pink:** Same in effect as Orange Jade.

**Jade, White:** Makes it easy to perceive objective reality.

**Magnetite:** Pulls one into objective reality. Promotes a straight forward, reality oriented, truth-telling approach.

**Perovskite:** Enables a person, who tends toward gullibility, to see what might be wrong with something that is being offered. Encourages one to develop some healthy cynicism.

**Rumanite:** Same in effect as Burnite.

## PERSONAL APPEAL

**Boothite**: For strong charismatic appeal. Inspires trust in others. Good for those in the public eye.

**Cymrite**: Makes one more appealing to others: one's best qualities show up to others. Even one's enemies will be drawn by, and be able to see, one's positive qualities.

**Feitknechtite**: Same in effect as Manganite.

**Groutite**: Same in effect as Manganite.

**Manganite**: Makes one more attractive or charismatic to others. Brings one's friendlier aspects to the fore and makes one appear more outgoing and approachable.

**Manganocalcite**: Makes one appear very charming and adorable to others.

**Stilbite**: Similar in effect to Manganocalcite. Need to have it very near one's body for the other person to regard one as adorable.

**Wogdinite**: Reminds everyone of the love they feel for the person wearing the stone.

**Yugawaralite**: Same in effect as Manganocalcite.

## PERSONAL APPEARANCE

**Bjarebyite**: Encourages one's feeling of attractiveness. Helps one to be more certain that one is making a good impression on others.

**Chalcedony, Pink**: Makes one more discriminating about one's appearance. Useful for people who don't pay much attention to how they look.

**Gmelinite**: Increases the delicacy of one's movements and aura of refinement in general.

**Rhodonite, Pink or Pink with Black markings**: For feeling, as well as projecting, an aura of elegance.

**Sauconite**: Same in effect as Rhodonite.

**Tephroite**: Gives one an air of dignity.

## RISK TAKING and ADVENTUROUSNESS

**Agate, Orange with White Stripes:** Makes one feel vigorous, energetic and ready to take on challenges. Increases one's willingness to take risks or be adventurous.

**Autinite:** Encourages one to feel more adventurous. Promotes one's willingness to try out some new places, people or things.

**Cinnabar:** Encourages one to be dynamic, adventurous, risk taking and assertive. Especially good for those who are too meek and mild.

**Hemimorphite:** Enables one to be assertive, enthusiastic and dynamic in one's undertakings.

**Sarabauite:** Increases one's willingness to take risks of an emotional, as well as of a physical nature.

**Ulexite:** For rising to the challenge, and willingness to be adventuresome. Makes one feel free to do whatever one wants to do, and not restricted or stuck. It seems possible to really make changes and transform one's self in a positive adventurous way.

## TACT and APPROPRIATE BEHAVIOR

**Alexandrite:** Produces a sense of sophistication and increases one's ability to behave in a refined and elegant manner.

**Axinite:** Enables one to maintain a clear perspective and stay balanced about important issues. Keeps one from going overboard into zealousness or fanaticism.

**Beryl, Pink to Pale Violet or Strawberry Red:** Makes one more mellow and flexible in one's attitude toward the differences one finds in others.

**Buttgenbachite:** Encourages one to pay attention to the appropriate and proper social behavior that is needed in any given situation. Enables one to act out a refined and exact role.

**Donathite:** Makes one notice when one is being arrogant or bossy. Encourages one to soften one's approach if indicated.

**Euclase:** Promotes a desire to be exactly correct on all levels. Good to wear when one wants to make a very good impression. And, if one needs to deal with difficult people or a challenging situation, it will encourage diplomacy and tact.

**Ferroaxinite:** Promotes care and forethought with regard to one's actions and communications. One proceeds deliberately, in an exact fashion and makes sure all bases are covered.

**Jasper, Pale Green to Yellow:** Calms aggressive energy.

**Pseudoboleite:** Contains impulsiveness. Encourages one to pay attention to appropriate and proper social behavior. Enables one to behave in a refined manner.

# Self Improvement

## SELF EXAMINATION

The gemstones and minerals described in this section, promote self awareness and assist one in the process of self examination. It can be helpful to use these stones along with others, to either enhance or soften the process. Rose Quartz to be "essence directed", Brown Calcite or Galena to stay in touch with one's inner wisdom, and Tsavorite or Unikite for self mastery, are all stones that have an enhancing effect. To soften the impact of looking at one's self, Blue Sapphire for compassion, White Sapphire for self nurturance, and Malachite or Amethyst to stay relaxed and balanced, would be good choices.

**Arsendescloizite:** Makes one clearer about one's own motivations. One can see the motive behind one's actions or words.

**Barnesite:** Enables one to understand one's own subconscious symbols more readily. Useful for guided meditations, dream work, art therapy, etc. Makes the symbolic meanings clearer.

**Cameo Shell:** Makes it easier to access unconscious motivations. Good for eliminating inappropriate behavior patterns. Allows one to evaluate the usefulness of any particular behavior pattern.

**Celadonite:** Makes one exquisitely aware of one's own flaws. One also feels less judgmental of the flaws of others. Since one can cringe under such ruthless self-scrutiny, it is recommended that one use this rock along with those that promote self esteem.

**Cobaltite:** Useful for those who wish to do some re-evaluation, and are taking a long, hard look at their lives. Helps integrate lessons about one's self, and one's life. Makes it easier to pull the various pieces together into a coherent whole.

**Diaspore:** For clarity of observation about one's personal life. Encourages one to look within and see what has been ignored.

**Dypingite:** Enables one to stop all physical, emotional and mental activity. One can then sit back and, with this clean slate, envision new directions or see old events in a new light.

**Hematite:** Promotes awareness of personal issues and patterns. Makes it easy to access anything subconscious.

**Jasper, Picture:** Aids in the evaluation of one's issues by prompting the recall of past experiences that are associated with the issue. One remembers the story that goes along with the memory, as well as what went wrong, or where one went off a correct path. Makes it clearer what needs to be done to resolve the issue, or what needs to be understood about it.

**Jinshajiangite:** Leads one directly and with surety to one's personal truths and inner principles. Eliminates self-deception and clarifies one's beliefs.

**Marcasite:** Similar in effect to Hematite, although somewhat more gentle. Kick back with slippers and pipe, and reflect for a while.

**Margerite:** Takes one back to a state of innocence and simplicity, with few preconceived notions about how things are. Enables one to take a look at what is going on in one's life, without a sense of struggle or resistance.

**Millerite:** Helps one to get in touch with, and eliminate, beliefs obtained from significant others during childhood: beliefs that are a part of one's imprinting, but have no actual basis in fact.

**Quartz, Lavender:** Promotes a very finely-tuned, self awareness. Increases awareness of what one is actually doing and saying on all levels.

## Emotional Issues

**Asbolan:** Enables one to bring up feelings of hate, anger, and revenge so that they can be dealt with. Particularly good for those who are in therapy. Lifts the repression of such feelings and the issues surrounding them. Use this rock sparingly and consciously.

**Desautelsite:** Puts one in touch with one's primal emotions. Encourages the emotional, rather than the intellectual, processing of one's problems.

**Quartz, Elestial:** Releases emotional blocks and heals. Allows one to see one's emotional truths clearly. Particularly good for those who have had a past history of abuse, or a very dysfunctional family, to heal up from.

**Trippkeite:** Opens up one's ability to experience all repressed emotions, but only while holding the stone. Lifts repression and enables one to get in touch with painful memories and issues. Use sparingly and consciously.

## Instinctive Issues

**Amianth:** Opens one's instinctive issues very quickly and effectively.

**Agate, Leopard Skin:** Puts one in touch with any instinctive terrors or fears so one can work on them and conquer them.

**Coral, Black:** A major healer of fear and anxiety. Heals fears by enabling one to get in touch with, and bring up intense, primal material to process.

**Jasper, Morrison Ranch:** Helps one bring instinctive issues to the surface, and makes one feel more comfortable handling them.

**Lawsonite:** Same in effect as Leopard-Skin Agate.

**Lizardite:** Enables one to access primitive, instinctive fears and issues: brings them to conscious awareness. Useful in therapy.

**Morrisonite:** Same in effect as Morrison Ranch Jasper.

**Obsidian, Black:** Same in effect as Leopard Skin Agate.

**Scheelite:** Opens up one's awareness of personal survival issues or deeply buried conflicts. Enables one to stay balanced while dealing with them.

## Past Lives

**Betafite:** Helps one remember past life lessons.

**Coral, Black:** Aids in remembering past lives.

**Hematite:** Useful for focusing on past lives for the purpose of working with issues related to them.

**Marcasite:** Similar in effect to Hematite.

**Jasper, Morrison Ranch:** An aid to remembering past lives.

**Jasper, Picture:** Enables one to recall past lives and the stories that went with them.

**Rhodochrosite:** Helps one bring up memories from previous lives.

**Skutterudite:** Puts one in touch with past life experiences.

**Staurolite:** Helps one to remember lessons from one's earliest lifetimes.

## Gaining Perspective

**Bostwickite:** Puts one in touch with the larger picture of one's life: where one is going, and what one is trying to accomplish. Helps one to develop long-range plans and strategies for achieving goals.

**Diadochite:** Puts one in touch with the larger picture of one's life. Enables one to step back and get perspective. Not good for planning; details tend to fall away.

**Emerald:** Useful when one is feeling a great deal of personal confusion and asking, "What should I do with my life?" Especially helpful when one is trying to answer this question from several different levels at once, sort through a lot of information, or a variety of options.

**Esperite:** Enables one to get in touch with the overview of one's life, and to see the overlying patterns of one's existence.

**Phillipsite:** Enables one to look at things from a broad perspective. One can step back and separate the "forest from the trees".

## DEVELOPING PATIENCE

Those who suffer from impatience feel there is not enough time, and operate from a fear "of missing out." Intolerance at its worst, and audacity at its best, characterizes impatience.

**Amethyst:** Gives one a feeling that there is time enough for everything. When feelings of impatience start to pop up, they are immediately followed by the awareness that there's no need to rush. Extremely popular, since most people feel victimized by their circumstances, at one time or another, in their lives.

**Danburite:** Enables one to be more patient. Particularly good for the very heavily impatient: for those who can be extremely intolerant: for the type of person who will hyperventilate if caught in a traffic jam because they can't stand the slow pace.

**Grossular, Pale Yellow:** Reduces any impatience one has about communication.

**Hedenbergite:** Promotes serenity, calms impatience and creates an ability to move at a slower pace.

**Hexagonite:** Keeps those involved in creative projects paying attention to detail, and being less impatient.

**Romerite:** Same in effect as Danburite.

## LEARNING FLEXIBILITY

Everyone is occasionally stubborn and inflexible. Stubbornness is based on fear: the fear of losing control or being overwhelmed by something one can't handle. The stones below make it easier to relax and be flexible, because they give one a feeling of security; that one's "moorings" cannot be easily swept away; that one doesn't have to fight to maintain one's own direction or purpose.

**Agate, Blue, White & Lavender Lace:** Softens stubbornness. Provides an especially strong feeling of security that if any new situations arise, they can be handled. One feels assured that one will not have to do something one doesn't want to do, or be plunged into something overwhelming. This makes it easier for even the most stubborn person to be more flexible.

**Agate, Sagenite:** Softens silent stubbornness, and makes one more willing to share one's communications

**Azurite:** Makes one less stubborn and more flexible in the area of one's communications. Allows one to be in better communication with others by fostering a willingness to listen. Gives a secure sense that one can listen in a flexible manner and not lose sight of one's own position.

**Beryl, Pink to Pale Violet or Strawberry Red:** Helps create a more mellow and flexible attitude toward the differences one finds in others.

**Dypingite:** Enables one to stop all physical, emotional and mental activity, sit back, and envision new directions or see old events in a new light. Helps one move out of stubbornness into a more flexible position.

**Ferberite:** Encourages one to be more willing to let go of familiar structures, and be more flexible and fluid during times of change in one's life.

**Tiger Eye, Gold:** Works in an unusual fashion. Pulls one into a more positive and flexible attitude and makes it possible to be determined rather than obstinate in one's approach. Especially effective for those who are very stubborn.

## BUILDING SELF ESTEEM

**Amazonite:** Raises self-confidence by giving one the feeling that one can have what one wants. Discourages one from behaving self-destructively when disappointed.

**Amblygonite:** Takes the attention off of the self, so one can become less self-conscious.

**Andorite:** Raises self confidence by reducing shyness.

**Aventurine, Green:** Enhances self esteem by making one feel good about oneself. Particularly useful for those who have been viewed as abnormal by the culture and have a lowered self esteem as a result. Feeling abnormal fosters a tendency to shut down and operate from survival fears.

**Billietite:** Reduces self centeredness. Enables one to stop focusing on one's self so exclusively, and begin to turn one's attention outward to noticing others. Decreases the feeling that one is "alone in the world."

**Bixbyite:** Enables one to feel comfortable with one's "differentness" whether real or imagined.

**Bloodstone:** Raises one's self esteem. One feels confident that one can be effective in one's life, and that life will be good.

**Carnelian:** Has the greatest potential of any stone to increase one's sense of self worth. Eliminates the fear of being inadequate.

**Chalcopyrite:** Raises self esteem by changing how one feels about one's self. Makes one feel very worthwhile and useful.

**Chromite:** Self esteem stimulator. Makes one notice when one is being self deprecatory, and makes it so clear that this is unnecessary, that it becomes embarrassing to continue.

**Columbite:** Promotes self confidence by making one less timid, less self-deprecatory and less embarrassed about one's self.

**Coquimbite:** Raises self esteem and makes one feel capable of handling whatever challenges might come one's way. Increases one's ability to feel pride in one's concrete accomplishments.

**Emerald:** Enhances one's self esteem and builds self confidence. Encourages one to notice the areas in which one excels, without, at the same time, feeling arrogant about these talents.

**Gorceixite:** Increases one's self confidence.

**Goudeyite:** Decreases shyness and that agonizing flipping back and forth between low self esteem and arrogance. Makes it easy to maintain a stable, positive sense of self.

**Palygorskite:** Makes the inexperienced person feel more experienced and capable.

**Powellite:** Promotes self confidence and imbues one with a sense of dignity. Particularly good for those who were brought up not to believe in themselves.

**Garnet, Spessartite:** Boosts one's self confidence and decreases self-deprecation and arrogance. Brings up such feelings as, "I'm a good person". . ."I have my niche and know where I belong. So, it's unecessary for me to compare myself with others in any way."

**Serandite:** Makes it easier to believe that one is valuable to others. Encourages the feeling that others would like to spend time with, work with, or love one.

**Spinel, Peach:** Aids in building self-esteem. Hits one very hard with the realization that one has just said or done something indicative of low self esteem, and this prompts self correction.

**Spinel, Yellow:** Encourages legitimate feelings of pride and confidence in one's accomplishments. Especially good for people with very low self esteem as it enables them to start believing in themselves.

**Uranophane:** Encourages a feeling of accomplishment. Allows one to savor completions.

**Zippeite:** Same in effect as Carnelian.

## ELIMINATING FEARS and PHOBIAS

Each of the following stones deals with a specific fear or phobia.

### Miscellaneous

**Celestite:** Helps one to adjust to heights or high altitudes. Good for air travel phobias or fear of heights in general.

**Copralite:** Reduces fear of any kind of animal life.

**Halotrichite:** Calms fear of heights. Most effective in calming fear of heights stemming from traumatic incidents in past lives.

**Molybdenite:** Helps one to feel more comfortable in the dark.

**Romanechite:** Heals the abnormal fear of open spaces.

**Triphylite:** Reduces the fear of accidents, and actually contributes to one having fewer accidents by keeping one's consciousness on what one is doing, rather than on one's fear of something going wrong.

### Related to People

**Andorite:** Reduces one's fear of being in crowds or speaking in public. Raises self confidence by reducing shyness.

**Bixbyite:** Reduces fear of not measuring up to another's standards. Enables one to feel more comfortable with one's "differentness" whether real or imagined. Particularly good for characteristics that either can't be changed, such as a harelip; or are difficult to change, such as biting one's fingernails.

**Hypersthene:** Helps reduce fear about being in public view. Good for public speaking, board meetings, or even crowded grocery stores.

## Related to Water

**Arsenocrandallite:** Gives one a sense of control when near, or on the water. One feels confident that one could be a master fisherman, sailor, olympic swimmer or master of the high dive. Also reduces an irrational fear of water.

**Borcarite:** Reduces fear of water and water-related activities. For example, one is less afraid of water on the face; or swimming, sailing, or drowning.

**Stilpnomelane:** Encourages within one the ability to work on, be comfortable with, swim in and make one's living from. . .water. Reduces fears of drowning.

## ADDICTIONS and BAD HABITS

These stones are useful for eliminating bad habits and addictive behaviors. Bad habits can run the gamut from leaving one's clothes on the floor, to eating junk food, to having a tantrum when one is crossed. Addictive behaviors are a little more difficult to break and include drinking, smoking and over-eating.

**Bindheimite:** Same in effect as Black and Brown Obsidian.

**Cameo Shell:** Useful for eliminating bad habits. Makes it easier to access unconscious motivations, and allows one to look at whether they need to keep the habit or not. Enables one to evaluate the usefulness of any particular habit.

**Laumontite:** Effectively reduces obsessive and/or compulsive tendencies. Obsessions refer to repetitive thoughts, and compulsions are repetitive behaviors one feels impelled to perform.

**Obsidian, Black and Brown:** Helps one eliminate one's addictive behaviors by reducing craving.

**Phenakite:** Helps prevent the formation of bad habits. Each color relates to a different arena in which a habit can be formed.

    **Blue:** Prevents formation of bad emotional habits.

    **Colorless:** Prevents formation of bad mental habits.

    **Yellow-Pink:** Prevents formation of bad physical habits.

**Trevorite:** Increases one's awareness of one's tendency to be sneaky. Makes it harder to cheat because it makes it embarrassing for one to sneakily continue the bad habit or addictive behavior. Encourages honesty.

**Witherite:** Helps control compulsive behavior by encouraging one to think before acting.

## CONQUERING SELF-DESTRUCTIVE TENDENCIES

Self-destructiveness is the act, or motivation, to harm oneself either physically or emotionally. This includes accidentally harming one's self, or using substances in a harmful way, such as; alcohol, drugs, and food. It also includes over doing things: like staying up all night, every night, the week after one has had a heart attack, then going to work the next day.

A person who is self destructive, has a fear that life will never be worth living; that whatever one wants, one cannot really have; that one is worthless and deserves nothing but misery. Life seems painful, and one is convinced there is really no way out of the pain. The stones described below, effectively counteract any self-destructive tendencies.

**Amazonite:** Gives one the feeling that it is possible to have whatever one wants. It makes one notice how self-destructive it is to take one drink too many, or engage in some other excessive behavior that is not in one's best interests.

**Bloodstone:** Engenders a strong feeling that it is all right to have what one wants, and that it is only a matter of time until it manifests. Produces high prosperity consciousness and willingness for abundance to show up in one's life. Makes one feel confident that life will be good.

**Merwinite:** Same in effect as Bloodstone.

**Jasper, Nunkirchner:** Same in effect as Bloodstone.

**Manjiroite:** Softens cruelty toward self or others. Operates by reducing the internal stress state that causes one to engage in compulsively destructive acts. Examples of such behaviors might be: pulling the wings off butterflies, burning one's self or a child with cigarettes, or slashing one's arm with razor blades. The intention behind these behaviors is to reduce the pain one feels inside. Manjiroite opens one up to other ways of reducing the pain, and makes one see how inappropriate such behaviors are.

**Microcline:** Same in effect as Amazonite. Stronger in its ability to make one see how unnecessary self-destructive behaviors are. Generic Microcline is white or pink. Amazonite is, technically, the blue-green variety of Microcline.

# WELL BEING

## The Psyche

The stones listed below promote feelings of serenity, tranquility and peacefulness. All enhance one's general sense of well being.

**Anhydrite:** Promotes a sense of peace and serenity.

**Calcite, Violet:** Gives a feeling of peacefulness and enables one to feel harmoniously connected to, and one with, everything that is.

**Cape Chrysolite:** Same in effect as Prehnite.

**Dundasite:** Makes one calm, serene and reflective.

**Hedenbergite:** Promotes serenity and an ability to move at a slower pace.

**Jade, Green:** Creates a mood of tranquility in which one emanates calm, peacefulness and harmony.

**Johannsenite:** Same in effect as Hedenbergite.

**Prehnite:** Calming.

**Quartz, Lavender:** Promotes peacefulness and intense self awareness. Good for meditation.

**Sapphire, White:** Encourages one to be good to oneself and self-nurturing. Makes sure one does nice things for oneself.

**Schrockingerite:** Promotes a deep sense of well being, happiness, and a sense of humor about life.

## HAPPINESS

Feelings of happiness, contentment and satisfaction are promoted by the stones listed below. We have included stones here that encourage an optimistic and idealistic outlook and make it difficult to be skeptical or cynical.

**Acanthite:** Promotes feelings of optimism and encourages one to be more idealistic.

**Agate, Green or Green with White Stripes:** Promotes happiness, expansiveness and sociability.

**Agate, Pale to Bright Yellow:** Puts one in a fun-loving, lighthearted and cheerful mood.

**Ajoite:** Puts one into a good mood. Enables one to see the lighter side of things.

**Alacranite:** For happiness. Makes it easy to shift into a more optimistic, upbeat or giggly mood, when one is feeling neutral. Has little effect when one is unhappy.

**Andorite:** Promotes feelings of optimism and encourages one to be more idealistic.

**Calcite, Orange:** A happiness stone. Creates the state of mind that everything is just fine.

**Chalcotrichite:** Promotes feelings of joy, happiness and contentment.

**Connemara:** Engenders a feeling of satisfaction and contentment.

**Fernandinite:** Stimulates feelings of pleasure. Makes one feel generally happy and optimistic.

**Jade, Lavender:** Promotes the qualities of optimism and idealism. Particularly useful for helping skeptics stay in a positive, optimistic mood.

**Jasper, Rain Forest:** Makes one feel expansive and happy.

**Kyanite, Green:** Creates delighted shivers and rushes of well being.

**Linarite:** Makes one feel very good humored and optimistic about life.

**Tyrolite:** Encourages one to feel happy and cheerful.

## ENTHUSIASM

**Coral, Apple:** Creates a feeling of enthusiasm for life and warm-hearted openness towards others.

**Coral, Blue:** Promotes a sense of adventurousness, and a general atmosphere of "Peter Pan"-like fun.

**Coral, Red, Pink & White:** Creates emotional openness, and a zesty enthusiasm about life, and one's relationships with others. White emphasizes the qualities of love and affection, while the pinker or redder the Coral is, the more passionate and sexual it becomes. Red is more intense in its effect than pink.

**Cumengite:** (Found as a growth on Boleite). Encourages a passionate fervor for taking advantage of the opportunities that come one's way, particularly those arising out of the good-luck energy stimulated by Boleite.

**Sapphire, Light Blue:** Inspirational. Makes one feel excited about life; that it will really work.

**Tantalite:** Helps those who tend to be repressed or restrained in manner, let go and move into open-hearted enthusiasm.

## HUMOR and FUN

We all need to laugh and have fun from time to time. These stones stand out for their ability to stimulate one's funny bone, or encourage one's sense of frivolity and playfulness.

**Andremeyerite:** Enables one to hang on to a more humorous, simple and innocent view of whatever is happening in one's immediate vicinity.

**Autinite:** Makes one feel more adventurous: encourages one to try out some new places, people or things and have a little fun.

**Bassetite:** Same in effect as Autunite.

**Bayldonite:** Increases cheerfulness and puts one in a happy, possibly even silly or giddy mood.

**Chiolite:** Same in effect as Ralstonite.

**Cryolite:** Same in effect as Ralstonite.

**Cuprosklodowskite:** Increases one's sense of fun.

**Hendricksite:** Makes one feel creative, expansive and playful.

**Jasper, Fancy:** A "let's party" stone. Particularly good for helping serious, highly focused types, to lighten up and have a little fun.

**Miserite:** Promotes a "holiday-like" atmosphere. Encourages one to let go, and get into the festivities.

**Philipsburgite:** Makes anything seem funny or amusing.

**Ralstonite:** Encourages one to see things with a sense of humor.

**Wolsendorfite:** Encourages one to laugh and giggle. Does not necessarily promote an internal sense of humor. Healing in its ability to promote laughter.

## HARMONY WITH ONESELF

The stones described below, are particularly good for reducing internal conflict, and creating a sense of balance and of harmony with oneself. Many also help one stay in a positive frame of mind, and avoid behaviors that are internally disrupting, such as being too impatient, too inflexible, or too arrogant.

**Agate, Brecchiated:** Creates a very positive approach toward life, in which one maintains a tranquil, optimistic, open-minded and realistic attitude. Allows one to avoid negative behavior patterns that create disharmony within, such as being too impatient, stubborn, or self-effacing. Enables one to feel harmoniously centered, and comfortably in touch with oneself.

**Aventurine, Red:** Enables one to use the various aspects of one's being in a harmoniously blended fashion. This includes one's creativity, power, emotional perceptiveness, and intellectual acumen.

**Barbertonite:** Creates a consciousness of being one with one's self, in all one's various aspects.

**Chalcopyrite:** Encourages eccentricity. Enables one to be eccentric, and comfortable with one's eccentricity as well. Keeps one feeling good about oneself and seeing oneself in a positive light.

**Jasper, Bruneau:** Same in effect as Brecchiated Agate. This stone is especially effective, for enabling one to handle crises or difficult challenges in a balanced fashion.

**Jasper, Rim:** Same in effect as Brecchiated Agate

**Jasper, Wood:** Same in effect as Brecchiated Agate.

**Realgar:** For feeling a sense of balance and harmony about one's life, one's relationships, and one's possessions.

## SECURITY and STABILITY

**Analcime:** Has a very stable, cleansing, and anchoring energy. Makes one feel very grounded and secure.

**Benavidesite:** Same in effect as Jamesonite.

**Boulangerite:** Same in effect as Jamesonite.

**Carrollite:** Promotes stability in the home and appreciation for it.

**Citrine:** Provides a sense of stability when things are moving along too fast.

**Coalingite:** Increases one's desire to own physical property. Works against the nomadic impulse.

**Corkite:** Makes one feel comforted, safe and secure. Soothes minor emotional aches and pains. Allows a sense of lightheartedness to creep in.

**Francevillite:** Makes one feel secure on one's own land, or home turf. Healing when one has been robbed.

**Garnet, Spessartite:** Makes one feel contented and happy with one's home life. One feels grounded, rooted and in one's niche.

**Jamesonite:** Helps one perservere through long, even life-long, tasks while providing a feeling of groundedness and security.

**Montroseite:** Same in effect as Sard.

**Sanbornite:** Promotes a feeling of security and great stability.

**Sard:** Encourages those who are without family or home, to feel more rooted and comforted. Keeps a person mindful of their emotional attachments and family commitments.

**Stanite:** Makes one feel as grounded, and as stable as the Rock of Gibralter.

**Tourmaline, Watermelon:** Enables one to draw on all of one's inner stability and reliability. Also enables one to impress others with these qualities.

**Yafsoanite:** Brings up thoughts of home, and keeps a person mindful of their emotional attachments and family commitments. Those who are without family or home, feel more rooted and comforted.

## RELAXING

**Bloedite:** Powerful in its ability to reduce tension. Operates by absorbing energy in its vicinity. Particularly good when one feels too jazzed or wired, and can't calm down.

**Bogdanovite:** Reduces freneticism and harried hurriedness. Slows one down and encourages one to take things at a more appropriate pace.

**Idocrase:** Releases tension. Drains out excess energy. The different varieties of Idocrase affect different types of tension.
> **Blue:** Releases emotional tension.
> **Green:** Releases physical tension.
> **Yellow:** Releases Intellectual tension.
> **Yellow-Green:** Releases primal, instinctive tension.

**Mesolite:** A "let's go on vacation" rock. Enables one to totally relax and detoxify. Can move immediately into a restful state, instead of taking several days to wind down.

**Miserite:** Releases tension, and encourages one to let go of stress.

**Pascoite:** Releases tension, and drains excess energy from the body, so one can relax.

**Tourmaline, Pink to Red:** Encourages one to go in the direction of least resistance. Makes it very easy to relax and unwind. Good to wear when one wants to take a week off. Not for use when one wants to be dynamic, and out in the world accomplishing things.

**Cassiterite, Wood-Tin:** Lowers one's internal energy and drive, so one can slow down, come to a standstill and get ready for a little reflection and re-evaluation.

## ENERGIZING

**Chapmanite:** Highly energizing. Stimulates the adrenal glands and can be tiring if used for too long. Best when used for a specific purpose or project.

**Goldstone, Blue:** Makes one feel a little peppier if tired: like taking a shower after hard work. Relaxes and gives one a feeling of being refreshed.

**Jasper, Green:** Enables those who like to take life at a slow pace, to feel peppier.

**Metatorbernite:** An energizer: it raises adrenalin levels.

**Opal, Black:** Makes one feel physically energetic and very alert.

**Opal, Jelly:** Same in effect as Black Opal, but milder.

**Septarian Nodule:** Very energizing. Keeps the energy moving throughout the body. The gray concretions are full of devas, which provide a source of energy that one can draw on.

## SEXUAL IDENTITY

**Anapaite:** Makes one more comfortable with one's sexuality and biological urges. Loosens one up to accept one's sexual impulses. As a result, there is sometimes an aphrodisiac effect. Also reduces feelings of shame or conflict around sexuality and makes one feel confident that one's sexual behavior is appropriate.

**Baricite:** Enables one to be more comfortable with one's sexual idiosyncrasies, or individual peculiarities in the sexual arena. Helps heal any lack of acceptance one has about one's sexuality.

**Cheralite:** Enables one to feel well balanced and satisfied with one's sexual functioning. One feels neither too repressed nor too preoccupied sexually.

**Chloromelanite:** Very balancing for women in the area of sexual identity. Gives a woman a clear sense of who she is as a woman; enables her to be comfortable and grounded in her femininity.

**Dyscrasite:** Encourages anyone in a male body to fully appreciate and operate from their innate maleness.

**Empressite:** Encourages anyone in a female body to fully appreciate, use, and feel fulfilled in their femaleness.

**Goethite:** Good for men having a hard time with masculinity issues, such as feeling they're not masculine enough, or not in touch with their innate maleness. Makes men feel more relaxed, and more secure about their masculinity.

**Jasper, Brick-Red:** Helps one get along better with one's own sex. If one is homosexual, makes one very comfortable with one's sexuality, and able to maintain compatible relationships.

**Joaquinite:** Heals fears or traumas in the area of one's sexuality. Healing for anyone who has ever been sexually abused or molested.

**Natrojarosite:** Reduces sexual repression and increases sexual passion.

# Well Being: The Physical Body

## HEALING THE BODY

All gemstones and minerals are "healing" in the sense that they have a positive effect on one's physical, emotional and intellectual functioning. The use of the term "healing" in this book, specifically indicates that a malfunction of some kind exists in the body and needs correction. Healing with stones will generally be successful, unless for subconscious reasons, the individual is not ready to be healed.

A word about clear Quartz Crystals is in order since they have a very strong reputation as healers. As we said in the discussion of clear Quartz Crystals earlier in this book, Quartz Crystals heal by <u>clearing</u> the area of the body they are placed near. Thus, if a chakra is blocked, a Crystal will clear it; if it is congested, a Crystal will clear up the congestion. In addition, each Crystal has a slightly different character and heals in a slightly different way. People will resonate to one Crystal and not to another. Clear Quartz Crystals are multi-purpose stones, and as discussed previously, they are easily programmed to be good conductors of healing energy. Other stones in the Quartz family are even better healers than Clear Crystal, though,since they were designed for that specific purpose. Variegated Jasper and Dendritic Agate are good examples of this.

Healing physical ailments with a gemstone or mineral, designed by nature to heal, is a very simple process. Simply place the stone as close to the area of the body that needs healing as possible. Of course, one should never put a mineral on a mucous membrane, or eat it. Just attach it nearby with a bandaid. Or, if that is inconvenient, rest quietly a few times a day, for 10 or 15 minutes, with the mineral near the area of the body that needs healing.

Another good way to heal the body, is with the use of stones or Crystal wands. Lying quietly on a flat surface, have a friend or healer concentrate on the spot to be healed. Focus the wand's healing energy to its point, and then touch the point to the area to be healed.

Placing healing stones or Crystals on a piece of Selenite, or in a charger, can create a healing environment throughout an entire room, or even send healing energy long distances to specific people or places. Healing stones placed in spiral patterns in a room can also radiate healing energy. With these methods, the afflicted person does not need to be touched with a stone, which can be desirable when working in a conservative setting.

Finally, for the most "new-age" of healings, one can heal by laying a crystal grid right on a person's prone body for a period of time. A stone to balance each chakra should be placed on each chakra. Good grounding stones should be placed above the head, below the feet, and at each side of the body; and a small spiral of healing stones near the area to be healed. Many people use Quartz Crystals for grounding stones and they work well. We have also noticed that Jaspers, Malachite, and Limestone work very nicely.

The chakra-clearing stones that are selected, should be specific to each chakra, and the spiral of healing stones should be made of stones specifically for healing the particular ailment if possible. Usually 15 minutes under a crystal grid is enough per session, though this can be repeated 2 or 3 times daily if desired.

The length of time the stone needs to be used will vary with the severity of the problem. It is important to realize that stones are not meant to replace appropriate medical or medicinal treatments. The stones mobilize the body's healing resources and capacity for regeneration, and when used in conjunction with more conventional modes of treatment, very satisfactory and, sometimes, spectacular results occur.

This first group of stones have a strong healing and balancing effect on the physical body in general. They are "non-specific" in their healing capabilities. For maximum effect, they should be placed near the part of the body to be healed.

**Agate, Dendritic:**  One of the most powerful healing stones available.  Can be used anywhere on one's body.

**Agate, Eye:**  One of the strongest healing stones for the body.

**Agate, Fern:**  Same in effect as Dendritic Agate, but milder.

**Agate, Moss:**  Same in effect as Dendritic Agate, but milder.

**Andersonite:**  Aids in healing, by promoting healthy cell growth.

**Bloedite:**  Place on sprains, bruises or a feverish head.  Works by absorbing the energy in its vicinity.

**Boevnite:**  Same in effect as Pharmacolite.

**Chrysoberyl:**  Healing to the physical body.  While any of the Chrysoberyls are healing for almost everyone, they are slightly more effective for one type of person or another as the color varies.  Michael says this effect is related to one's race or the geographical area in which one's race originated.
>   **Brown:**  General healing for Africans, Egyptians, and Caribbean Islanders..
>   **Cat's Eye:**  Generally healing for those of Asian, Mediterranean, and South American descent.
>   **Golden:**  Generally healing for Australians, Native Americans, Filipinos, and Polynesian Islanders.
>   **Yellow-Green:**  Generally healing for Northern Europeans, Russians, and North Americans of European descent.

**Copper:**  Releases energy blocks in the body.  When energy is stopped or blocked at any point in the body, difficulties can develop.  This stone can be used to remove the energy blocks, and thus promote the healing of various conditions.

**Dolomite:**  Promotes general internal bodily health.

**Hedenbergite:**  Healing to the physical body.

**Jasper, Variegated:**  One of the strongest healing stones for the physical body.  Especially for those who have been extremely ill and are recuperating.

**Johannsenite:**  Same in effect as Hedenbergite.

**Pharmacolite:**  Aids in healing by pulling impurities from the body.  Place on or near affected area.

**Spinel, Blue to Gray:** Enables one to clear that which is unwanted from one's body. This includes rejecting microbes. growths, chemicals, etc. Use consciously and with caution. Hold in one's hand or near the affected area for a short period of time, while concentrating on that which needs to be rejected from one's body. Note that nothing should be rejected from one's body without knowing the impact that will have on one's total well being. Place this stone in plastic when not in use.

**Thompsonite:** Same stone as Eye Agate.

This next group of stones are effective aids to healing specific areas of the body. Since the stones are grouped by category, some of the stones listed in this section also promote the healthy functioning of that area of the body

## Allergies

**Alunite:** Promotes resistance to allergy producing substances.

**Bakerite:** Reduces allergic reactions and promotes resistance to stress.

**Beryl, Gold:** Heals allergies to plants and pollens.

**Beryl, White:** Heals dust allergies.

**Calcite, Green:** Heals allergies to toxic fumes and chemicals.

**Hewettite:** Decreases allergic reactions to organic matter (plant or animal).

**Jasper, Poppy:** Reduces allergic reactions to animals or animal products.

**Kolwezite:** Reduces allergic reactions.

**Meneghinite:** Same in effect as Sulfur.

**Serpentine, Chartreuse:** Reduces allergic reactions to animals, birds, fish, reptiles, pets and meats to eat.

**Sulfur:** Heals plant allergies.

## Blood and Blood Vessels

**Andradite, Demantoid:** Heals veins.

**Anglesite:** Healing for hardening of the arteries.

**Arhbarite:** Promotes clotting and thickening of the blood

**Pyrophyllite:** Heals and detoxifies the blood.

## Fever

**Diopside:** Balances body temperature and reduces fever.

**Opalite:** Reduces fever.

**Violane:** Balances body temperature and reduces fever.

## Immune System

**Alunite:** Stimulates the production of antibodies to fight diseases that enter the body, and increases the production of white blood cells.

**Bakerite:** Strengthens the immune system.

**Brochantite:** Aids the healing of cancer occuring in the lungs, esophagus or throat.

**Chalcophanite:** Helps the body fight off invasive bacteria.

**Grossular, White:** Healing to the immune system.

**Kolwezite:** Builds the immune system and increases physical stamina.

**Limestone:** Heals and strengthens the immune system.

**Marialite:** Strengthens the immune system.

**Mizzonite:** Same in effect as Marialite.

**Monticellite:** Strengthens the immune system.

**Nontronite:** Helps the body fight off bacterial infections.

**Orthoclase:** Aids in the healing of cancer.

**Sanidine:** Aids in the healing of cancer.

## Miscellaneous

**Agate, Brazilian:** Healing to the kidneys.

**Andradite, Topazolite:** Heals synapses.

**Brochantite:** Heals the lungs, esophagus, and throat. Also heals cancer in those areas.

**Cerussite:** Fungus removal.

**Dioptase:** Healing to the brain. This includes anything that physically stresses the brain: e.g., edema, a mild concussion, or chemical substances.

**Euxinite:** Healing to the eyes. Helps heal injuries, eye strain and, in a very gradual fashion, can improve nearsightedness or farsightedness.

**Gordonite:** Healing to the myelin sheath; the outer covering of muscle cells.

**Leucite:** Helps clear mucus membranes. Good for colds.

**Minium:** Same in effect as Cerussite.

**Zircon, Red:** Helps ear infections heal more quickly.

## Pain

**Agate, Lattice:** Eliminates headaches.

**Biotite:** Helps relieve headaches by releasing excess energy from the head.

**Bowenite:** Helps alleviate cramps.

**Copper:** Useful for relieving arthritic pain, cramps, or tension headaches.

**Crocoite:** Heals back and headache pain.

**Opalite:** Helps relieve headaches by releasing excess energy from the head..

**Soapstone, Pale Green:** Translucent. Same in effect as Bowenite.

**Zircon, Brown to Brownish-Red:** Heals headaches. Drains excess energy from head, and keeps the energy balanced in that area.

## Skin

**Andersonite:** Promotes healthy cell growth in new skin.

**Andradite, Melanite:** Heals skin.

**Corderoite:** Maintains the skin in a healthy state. Good for the growth of new skin

**Descloizite:** Removes external aberrant growths such as warts, moles, skin growths, blisters and hives.

**Periclase:** Aids in healing sun-damaged skin.

## Wounds

**Andersonite:** Heals wounds by promoting healthy cell growth.

**Arhbarite:** Helps decrease blood loss from wounds by promoting clotting of blood.

**Copiapite:** Helps heals wounds or bites by poisonous insects or reptiles

**Corderoite:** Aids in the healing of wounds, burns and diseases of the skin.

**Euxinite:** Heals wounds to the eyes.

**Marialite:** Encourages wounds of a physical nature to heal more quickly.

**Mizzonite:** Same in effect as Marialite.

## HEALTHY FUNCTIONING

This group of stones all promote the healthy body's ability to function smoothly and well. Since the stones are grouped by category, there will be some listed here that are also effective aids to healing where damage or disease exists. Predominately, however, the categories will relate to healthy body processes.

## Bones, Joints & Teeth

**Andersonite:** Promotes healthy bone growth.

**Barite:** Encourages calcium retention in the bones. Especially good for women.

**Bolivarite:** Healing for the joints of the body.

**Desert Rose:** The rosette form of Barite. Same in effect as Barite.

**Dolomite:** Kills off aberrant cells and promotes correct bone growth. Mild in its action.

**Hopeite:** For healing bone marrow.

**Natrolunite:** Promotes healthy bone growth, and prevents cavities in teeth.

**Pectolite, White or Clear:** Augments the body's ability to use nutrients to strengthen bones, teeth and nails.

**Wavellite:** Healing for bones:
    **Blue:** Small bones
    **Brown:** Teeth.
    **Colorless:** Large bones.
    **Green:** Medium-size bones.
    **White & Yellow:** Bone marrow.

**Whiteite:** Decalcifies and demineralizes the joints.

## Cleansing and Purifying

**Calcite, Green:** Clears toxins from the body, and from the atmosphere.

**Copiapite:** Helps one recuperate from having had poisons or toxins in one's system.

**Kupletskite:** When toxic materials are present in the body, one will continue to crave and drink water until the body is flushed, while carrying this stone. Not useful for toxic processes in the body which cannot be altered by flushing such as fungal infections.

**Limestone:** Totally cleansing and purifying to the system.

**Litharge:** Encourages one's body to purge itself of ingested poisons or toxins through vomiting or diarrhea.

**Massicot:** Same in effect as Litharge.

**Moolooite:** Increases the retention of water in the digestive tract, and functions as a mild laxative.

**Pascoite:** Draws impurities to the surface of the skin to be dissipated into the air, or cleansed from the body with a bath. This includes physical matter such as chemicals and minerals, as well as nonphysical matter, in the form of energy, that needs to be released in order to balance the system.

**Tacharanite:** Aids the body's cleansing, flushing and elimination of any excesses: e.g., excess bacteria and viruses, excess toxins, excess water, excess fat

## Coordination

**Alabandite:** Helps the body maintain physical equilibrium and move in a coordinated and balanced fashion. Keeps one from being clumsy.

**Boltwoodite:** Increases eye-hand coordination in hunting activities. One is more accurate with a bow and arrow, knife, gun, etc.

**Nullaginite:** Makes one feel more in touch with the earth and physically balanced. Great for any endeavor where keeping one's balance is essential.

**Plattnerite:** Reduces clumsiness and increases one's ability to move with grace and ease.

**Purpurite:** Makes one more capable doing anything that requires agility and good motor coordination. Improves one's fine motor coordination as well.

**Rockbridgeite:** Improves one's coordination and physical balance. Decreases clumsiness.

**Siegenite:** Increases eye-hand coordination.

**Volkonskoite:** Improves one's ability to keep one's balance. One feels more in touch with the earth and physical objects.

**Xitieshanite:**  Increases one's overall physical agility and motor coordination.  Particularly enhances one's eye-hand motor coordination as required in finer applications, such as fencing, microcircuitry, surgery and art.

## Enjoying the Body

**Agate, Arizona:**  Brings out one's sensual qualities.

**Agate, Flame:**  For adjusting to, and being comfortable in one's body.  For enjoying one's body and the activities one does in it.

**Agate, Snake Skin:**  Puts one in a sensual loving mood appreciative of the body and its sensations.

**Agate, White or White with White Stripes:**  Puts one in a sensual, loving mood appreciative of the body and its sensations.

**Agate, Zebra:**  Same in effect as Flame Agate.

**Boracite:**  Enables men to feel more comfortable in their male bodies.  Enables both sexes to be more comfortable around male bodies.

**Breithauptite:**  Enables women to feel more comfortable with their female bodies.  Enables both sexes to be more comfortable around people with female bodies.

**Chloanthite:**  Encourages one to take on the qualities of the Venusian body type: i.e. to be sensuous, soft, warm and emotional.

**Moukaite:**  Same in effect as Flame Agate.

**Phenakite, Yellow or Pink:**  Keeps one from forming bad physical habits.  Examples are not eating right, or not exercising enough.

## Exercise

**Bronzite:**  Stimulates one to exercise.

**Cahnite:**  Encourages the body to move at a quicker pace.  Good for getting things accomplished and/or keeping the body exercised.

**Campbellite:** Stimulates the body to move. A good exercise motivator. Also gives the body a greater degree of endurance and stamina.

**Miargyrite:** Encourages athletic activity and stimulates one to hone one's athletic abilities.

**Obsidian, Silver or Gold Sheen:** Stimulates one to engage in activities that promote bodily health.

**Spectrolite:** Stimulates one to exercise. Makes one feel like hopping and skipping about.

**Strontianite:** Increases physical strength by energetically encouraging the body to build muscle.

**Tiger Eye, Blue:** Same stone as Spectrolite

## Food and Digestion

**Asbecasite:** Aids digestion for those who tend to have digestive problems.

**Afwillite:** Buffers the digestive system from the effects of psychological stressors, and allows one to digest one's food more thoroughly and with fewer problems.

**Ankerite:** Aids digestion, and promotes the smooth functioning of the alimentary canal.

**Antigorite:** Calming to the digestive tract. Reduces acidity and gas, particularly when one is under under stress.

**Dolomite:** A general aid to digestion.

**Eudialyte:** Aids vitamin absorption, particularly those that are fatty based or occur in complex or "yang" foods, e.g., nuts, fish, or meats.

**Long-Hair Asbestos:** When worn on the body, promotes a reduction in the amount of stomach acid production, which allows the body to digest food better.

**Merlinoite:** Strengthens the digestive system by promoting proper functioning of all aspects of digestion.

**Montroseite:** Same in effect as Sard.

**Jasper, Poppy:** Reduces allergic reactions to eating meats.

**Pioche:** Heals the digestive tract.

**Proustite:** Heals the colon.

**Sard, Light Brown:** Aids in digesting vegetable proteins.

**Sard, Red-Brown:** Aids in digesting animal proteins.

**Selenite:** Aids in the digestion and absorption of minerals.

## Hair

**Arsenuranospathite:** Strengthens hair follicles to produce healthier growth. Aids hair in recovering from chemical treatments such as bleaching, or from diseases, or treatments such as chemotherapy that have caused hair loss.

**Cyanotrichite:** Stimulates hair growth.

**Pectolite, White or Clear:** Augments the body's ability to use nutrients to strengthen the hair.

## Hormone balancing

**Bowenite:** Balances the hormonal system.

**Cyanotrichite:** Balances and stimulates the hormones

**Jasper, Pink:** Hormone balancing.

**Jasper, Yellow:** Hormone balancing.

**Soapstone, Pale Green:** Same in effect as Bowenite.

## Miscellaneous

**Aenigmatite:** Enables physical body to maintain a better fluid balance. Helps prevent dehydration or edema.

**Asbecasite:** Improves the physical stamina of thin people with delicate constitutions.

**Bournonite:** Improves one's sense of direction. Makes it easier to find one's way home, or to find one's way about more easily when in a strange town

**Laubmannite:** Encourages the muscles in one's feet to relax and stay in alignment.

**Northupite:** Increases muscle strength.

**Pectolite, Pink:** Enables one to increase the amount of oxygen one draws out of the air, as well as to increase the amount one utilizes as one breathes. Good for cigarette smokers, those with emphysema, or anemia (low red blood cell count). Do not eat.

**Purpurite:** Increases physical strength and stamina.

**Raspite:** Helps eliminate, or tone down, muscular tics and twitches.

**Vauxite:** Cures insominia by making a person very sleepy.

## Motion Sickness

**Baddeleyite:** Decreases motion sickness by stabilizing the inner ear.

**Kurnakovite:** Decreases motion sickness and reduces dizziness.

## Physical Growth

**Andersonite:** Speeds up the rate at which one grows physically.

**Chlorargyrite:** Speeds up the rate at which one grows physically.

## Sexuality

**Agate, Wonder:** For male sexuality: Increases sexual arousal, and the ability to get and maintain erections.

**Bowenite:** Healing and balancing to the female reproductive system and organs.

**Diabase:** For male sexuality: Increases one's ability to maintain erections. Has a beneficial influence on health of sex organs.

**Jasper, Serape:** For female sexuality. Stimulates sexual arousal, and facilitates getting pregnant.

**Jasper, Willow Creek:** Same in effect as Serape Jasper.

**Osumilite:** For male sexuality: Keeps sexual organs healthy and heals genital damage.

**Petalite:** Acts on the sexual organs of both males and females to stimulate healthy functioning.

**Ryalite:** A generic name for Serape Jasper and Wonder Agate. The more pink/orange the tones are, the more the stone relates to female sexuality. The more brown/gray/purple the tones are, the more the stone relates to male sexuality.

**Soapstone, Pale Green:** Same in effect as Bowenite.

**Xanthiosite:** Heals the sexual organs of illness, imbalance or disease. Works for all mammals, of both sexes.

## Reproduction

**Bowenite:** Good for women when pregnant: keeps mother and fetus in alignment. Keeps everything related to the pregnancy functioning normally and in good health. Reduces risk of birth defects, and protects the growth of the fetus, particularly if it is female.

**Braunite:** Generally healing and balancing to the reproductive system. Keeps eggs healthy, especially after fertilization.

**Bauranoite:** Increases hereditary red-headedness in children of the parents who wear it.

**Chabazite:** Increases fertility, and balances pregnant women.

**Conichalcite:** To put mother and fetus in balance with each other.

**Cornetite:** Increases fertility. Promotes sperm production; stimulates healthy functioning of reproductive organs.

**Cuprite:** Birth control rock. Aids in avoiding conception. Do not use this stone as the only form of birth control. This stone works only as long as intention is with it. If one, even subconsciously wants to get pregnant, this stone will not stop that from happening. (Poisonous. Don't eat it!).

**Diabase:** For fertility and potency. Makes it easier to "get" pregnant or "make" someone pregnant. Steps up sperm production, and has a beneficial influence on health of sex organs.

**Fayalite:** Increases female sexuality and fertility.

**Libethenite:** This stone is good to keep around when one is trying to get pregnant. It kills off aberrant sex cells, especially aberrant sperm cells. Thus, it lowers the risk of a baby that's mentally retarded or deformed.

**Mixite:** Similar in effect to Conichalcite.

**Osumilite:** For male sexuality. A powerful fertility stone. Steps up the production of strong, healthy sperm.

**Petalite:** Aids in fertility. Promotes sperm production.

**Soapstone, Pale Green:** Same in effect as Bowenite.

**Tilasite:** Encourages hereditary blondness and blue eyes.

**Zinnwaldite:** Encourages the manifestation of the dominant genes in one's children. Useful for those who have a recessive, gene-linked hereditary problem in the family.

### Temperature Tolerance

**Hidalgoite:** Increases tolerance of extreme temperatures: either hot or cold.

**Metatorbernite:** Helps one adjust to the cold by raising one's body heat.

**Murdochite:** Increases tolerance of high temperatures.

**Pokrovskite:** Enables one to tolerate low temperatures more easily, particularly when living in snowy areas for long periods of time.

### Weight Control

This group of stones aid one in gaining or losing weight, and primarily affect the body on the physical level. Also useful for weight control, are the stones included in the previous section on "Addictions and Bad Habits" as well as the following section on "Exercise." Please note that none of these stones are meant to be ingested. So--DO NOT EAT.

**Aenigmatite:** Balances water gain and loss in the body.

**Cahnite:** Speeds the metabolism. One side effect of speeding the metabolism is that it would be easier to lose weight, and another side effect is that it would be easier to keep warm when it's cold.

**Carnallite:** Helps body gain weight, by promoting maximum usage of caloric intake.

**Inesite:** Balances water gain and loss in the body.

**Lanarkite:** Helps one lose weight. Boosts the metabolic rate.

**Metatorbernite:** Aids in weight loss by raising the metabolic rate.

**Tacharanite:** Aids the body in cleansing, flushing and eliminating any excesses: e.g., excess water and fat. Good for losing weight.

**Tennantite:** Helps one gain weight. Slows down the metabolic rate.

# Well Being: The Subtle Body

The subtle body is the electro-magnetic field that encompasses and surrounds, the physical body. This includes the aura, which is that part of the subtle body that surrounds the physical body, and the chakras which are energy centers within the physical body.

## AURA CLEARING and DECORDING

Clearing one's aura involves restoring the integrity of the electro-magetic field surrounding one's body, and releasing any negative influences. As one goes through the day, interactions with the environment or other people can pull the electro-magnetic field out of balance leaving "holes" in some parts, and compressing it in other parts. Negative influences come from the absorption of other people's negative emotional states, such as pain, grief, anger, exhaustion, etc. Gemstones and minerals that are effective for clearing the aura, pull the electro-magnetic field back into shape, fluff it up, and rid it of unwanted energies.

"Cording", in Michael's teaching, refers to the energy that another person focuses on one, or in one's direction. "Cords" of energy tend to attach themselves to one's energy centers or chakras, and are experienced as energy drains from the point of attachment. People cord others unconsciously in order to get support and energy boosting. Decording stones exist to enable one to remove unwanted cording. They will not remove cords of attachment one wants to keep: for example, the energy attachments between parents and children, or between intimates or close friends. Freud referred to cording as cathexis.

**Alexandrite:** Limits and inhibits the energies one does not want around, particularly when worn on the left hand. This can include people, their emotions, or communications, as well as energies from non-animate sources such as microwaves or power lines. Prevents cording. Inhibits others from attaching energetically, and drawing on one's energy without permission.

**Bastnaesite:** Almost always found in Fluorite as Rutiles going through the crystal. Its effect is to augment the Fluorite's capacity to protect one's aura and prevent unwanted cording.

**Fluorite:** Excellent aura cleanser: fluffs the aura and rids it of any unwanted energies. Keeps others from making energetic attachments that are not desired. Hold to forehead for 15 seconds for rapid clearing of the aura. Colors are blue, clear, purple, yellow and green. All are equally effective. Use the color that one finds most attractive, for greatest compatibility.

**Jasper, Brown:** Prevents cording.

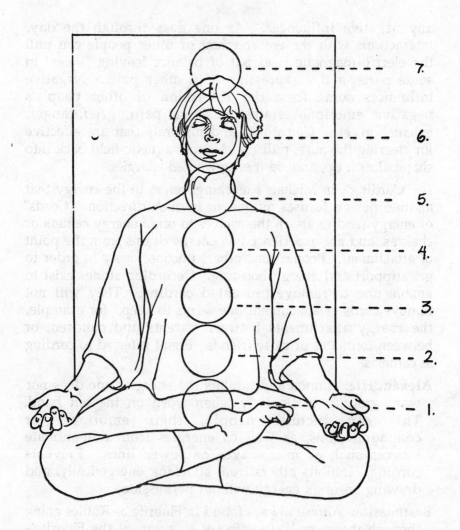

## CHAKRAS

| | | |
|---|---|---|
| 1 | First Chakra | Base of Spine |
| 2 | Second Chakra | Pelvis |
| 3 | Third Chakra | Solar Plexus |
| 4 | Fourth Chakra | Heart |
| 5 | Fifth Chakra | Throat |
| 6 | Sixth Chakra | Forehead |
| 7 | Seventh Chakra | Top of Head |

**Opal, Black:** Creates a field of resonance between oneself and others. Because of this, others are drawn to form energetic attachments, and one is easily corded when wearing this stone. Use with Fluorite, or another aura cleanser, to prevent unwanted cording.

**Opal, Jelly:** Same in effect as Black Opal, but milder.

**Yttrocerite:** Same in effect as Fluorite.

**Zircon, Colorless:** Aura cleansing: Fluffs the aura, rids it of any unwanted energies, or impurities from the environment. Prevents cording.

**Zircon, Yellow:** Clears the aura in the same way as colorless Zircon. Also pushes one to clear one's environment of clutter both materially and energetically.

## BALANCE and the CHAKRAS

Michael regards the stones for balancing, to be among the most important. To say that the chakras are "balanced", means that one's chakras are open and in alignment, so that energy can flow through the body freely. When the chakras are out of balance, and the flow of energy through the body is blocked, one becomes less conscious, and more liable to get stuck when dealing with life's problems or challenges.

A key to dealing with stressful situations is to approach them from a balanced state. Then, whatever happens is not nearly as stressful as those same things occurring when one is not in balance or in harmony with oneself. Most people get all "stressed out" and then look for some way to lower or handle the stress. Michael suggests we concentrate first on getting balanced, and then go out to deal with the stresses in our lives.

A chakra is an energy center which has a physical location in the physical body, but is not of the physical body. There are six chakras residing within the physical body and each has a physical referent. The seventh chakra is centered above the top of one's head, in one's aura. (See illustration for chakra names and locations).

Optimally, when the chakras are in balance, they are in alignment (synchronized with each other), neither too open nor too closed, and functioning normally (none shut down or ignored). Following is a list of gemstones that are particularly effective for keeping the chakras opened and aligned. Stones noted as "healing" are useful when something a little stronger is needed to get back in balance, such as a chakra that has been severely overused, or "blasted open", and cannot very easily return to normal.

In addition to gemstones discussed previously under the headings of "Relaxing" and "Energizing", there are a number of gemstones in this section that produce the same effect, but for different reasons. The word "energy", loosely defined, refers to the amount of "juice one has in one's batteries". A gemstone that is described as "stimulating" a chakra, adds energy to that chakra, and thus has an energizing effect. Gemstones that are described as "draining excess energy" from a chakra, help one to relax.

### First Chakra

This group of stones open and balance the first chakra. The first chakra relates to instinctive, survival-oriented issues. Contains memories of all past lives and unresolved conflicts.

**Abalone:** Balances and heals the first chakra. Reduces fear.

**Agate, Leopard Skin:** Heals and balances the first chakra. Powerful in its ability to calm anxiety.

**Amianth:** Opens the first chakra very quickly and very widely. Useful for those who are very shut down.

**Aventurine, Blue:** Keeps the first chakra, and the feet, open and unblocked so energy can flow through unimpeded.

**Benitoite, White:** Balances and heals the first chakra. Tiny amounts are very potent.

**Bone:** Balances and heals the first chakra. Calms anxiety.

**Idocrase, Yellow-Green or Brown:** Balances the first chakra and drains out excess energy.

**Ivory:** Balances and heals the first chakra. Strong in effect.

**Lawsonite:** Similar in effect to Leopard Skin Agate.

**Mother of Pearl:** Same in effect as Abalone.

**Obsidian, Black:** Same in effect as Leopard-Skin Agate.

**Scheelite:** Balances and opens the first chakra. Helpful because the first chakra is often closed down.

**Siderite:** Same in effect as Blue Aventurine.

## Second Chakra

This group of stones open and balance the second chakra. The second chakra is the center for sexuality and creativity.

**Agate, Plume:** Opens and balances the second chakra. Opens one up sexually, and reduces repression.

**Joaquinite:** Balances and heals the second chakra. Opens it if too closed, and closes it down and repairs it if ragged and bruised.

**Hackmannite:** Same in effect as Sodalite.

**Natrojarosite:** Balances and heals the second chakra. Reduces sexual repression and increases sexual passion.

**Sodalite:** Balances, heals and stimulates the second chakra. Very healing when the second chakra has been overused, or is too shut down.

## Third Chakra

This group of stones open and balance the third chakra. The third chakra relates to the movement of the body, and is the center for power, health and career issues.

**Bronzite:** Opens, aligns and stimulates the third chakra.

**Epidote:** Protects the third chakra.

**Jasper, Gray:** Balances, heals and protects the third chakra. Makes it easier to feel that one's power cannot be taken away.

**Jasper, Red:** Balances the third chakra. Reduces feelings of victimization.

**Neptunite:** Same in effect as Gray Jasper.

**Pistacite:** Same in effect as Epidote.

**Purpurite:** Keeps the third chakra balanced. Keeps movement steadily flowing.

**Smithsonite, Yellow:** Balance the third chakra. Pulls one into action.

**Spectrolite:** Same in effect as Bronzite. Keeps one active.

**Tiger Eye, Red:** Gives the third chakra a break. Slows the third chakra down, and flushes excess energy out.

### Fourth Chakra

This group of stones open and balance the fourth chakra. The fourth chakra governs feeling states such as happiness, love, sadness or anger.

**Aurichalcite:** Balances and heals the fourth chakra. Particularly healing to a fourth chakra that has been "blasted open".

**Benitoite, Pink:** Balances and heals the fourth chakra. Tiny amounts powerful.

**Calcite, Blue:** Balances and heals the fourth chakra. Clears energy blockages, so emotions can flow more easily.

**Calcite, Red:** Balances the fourth chakra, keeps it open and lets it feel protected.

**Clinotryolite:** Same in effect as Aurichalcite.

**Heterosite:** Balances and opens the fourth chakra.

**Horn:** Balancing to the fourth chakra. Promotes a warm-hearted feeling state.

**Idocrase, Blue:** Balances the fourth chakra and drains out excess energy.

**Lapis Lazuli:** Balances the fourth chakra. Increases the conscious awareness of one's emotional experiences.

**Smithsonite, Green or Blue:** Balances and clears the fourth chakra.

**Trippkeite:** Balances and heals a blocked fourth chakra. Removes one's defenses around feelings.

### Fifth Chakra

This group of stones open and balance the fifth chakra. The fifth chakra is about one's thoughts, one's insights, and communications.

**Amber:** Balances the fifth chakra. Clears one mentally.

**Amber, Honey:** Balance and heals the fifth chakra. Calms the mind.

**Anthonyite:** Balances and heals the fifth chakra. Particularly good for healing, and closing down a "blasted open" fifth chakra.

**Bayleyite:** Balances the fifth chakra and removes any superfluous negative energies.

**Benitoite, Clear:** Balances and heals the fifth chakra. Tiny amounts very powerful.

**Burnite:** Balances the fifth chakra.

**Datolite:** Balances the fifth chakra. Heals exhaustion around communication.

**Smithsonite, Brown:** Balances the fifth chakra and pulls one into using it.

**Topaz, White:** Balances the fifth chakra. Particularly good for opening a closed fifth chakra.

**Tourmaline, Yellow, Brown or Clear:** Balances the fifth chakra. Assists one in endeavors that require intellectual processing.

**Triplite:** Same in effect as Amber.

**Winstanleyite:** Balances the fifth chakra and strengthens it, to prepare for periods of heavy usage.

## Sixth Chakra

This group of stones open and balance the sixth chakra. The sixth chakra governs wisdom, knowledge, and the ability to know what's true. It is also the center for telepathic psychic ability.

**Benitoite, Blue:** Balances and heals the sixth chakra. Tiny amounts very powerful.

**Betpakdalite:** Opens the sixth chakra when it is too closed down.

**Calcite, Brown or Gold:** Balances and heals the sixth chakra. Puts one in touch with one's inner wisdom.

**Herrerite:** Balances and heals the sixth chakra. Particularly good for opening the sixth chakra when blocked.

**Howlite:** Balances and heals the sixth chakra. Especially good for one that has been overworked.

**Opalite:** Balances and heals the sixth chakra. Drains excess energy.

**Smithsonite, Pink:** Balances the sixth chakra. Most effective for children. Milder in effect for adults.

**Smithsonite, Purple:** Heals and balances the sixth chakra and pulls one into using it.

## Seventh Chakra

This group of stones open and balance the seventh chakra. The seventh chakra puts one in touch with the experience of unconditional love, and connectedness with the universe. Center for intuitive, empathic psychic ability.

**Benitoite, Purple:** Balances and heals the seventh chakra. Tiny amounts very powerful.

**Calcite, White:** Keeps the seventh chakra open, in balance, and gives a feeling of protectedness: that it is safe to be spiritually open and vulnerable.

**Chalcanthite:** Opens and balances the seventh chakra. Opens one's spiritual side.

**Cobalt:** Opens and balances the seventh chakra. Great for feeling connected with the Universe.

**Cobalt Glass:** Opens and balances the seventh chakra. Milder in effect than Cobalt, but pleasant.

**Eilat:** Balances and opens the seventh chakra. Infuses one with feelings of love.

**Jokokuite:** Opens and balances the seventh chakra. Opens one to spiritually-based, emotional experiences. Similar in effect to Chalcanthite.

**Spangolite:** Same in effect as Chalcanthite.

## All Chakras

This group of stones open and balance all chakras.

**Amethyst:** Balances and heals all chakras. Has a particularly strong impact on the third and seventh chakras. Calms the third chakra and the impatience that arises when one can't manifest as quickly as one would like. The seventh chakra quality, is that Amethyst keeps one in touch with one's more noble, spiritual side: the part of one that urges one to do the best thing, even though that might not be the most serving of one's own interests.

**Bazirite:** Balances all chakras. Similar in effect to Benitoite.

**Bone:** Balances all chakras. Very grounding and calming.

**Calcite, Blue:** Opens, heals and unblocks all chakras. Very intense and rapid in its effect. Similar to the Aventurines, although the latter operate more slowly and are gentler in effect.

**Cleavelandite:** Balances and heals all chakras.

**Crystal, Clear:** Crystals produce clarity in whatever way they are used, and this clarity does not have to be visual. When placed on a chakra, that chakra will be cleared of negative influences, opened, and balanced.

**Fluorite:** Balances all chakras. Wonderful for removing negative influences.

**Granite:** Balances all chakras. Makes one feel grounded and connected to the earth.

**Ivory:** Balances and heals all chakras. Has a capacity to calm survival fears associated with the chakra it is worn closest to. When worn near the second chakra, calms survival-related fears about one's sexuality or creativity. When worn near the third chakra, calms survival issues about money, or the use of power. When worn near the fourth chakra, one's emotions will not be survival based. When worn near the fifth chakra, calms survival-based thought patterns. When worn at the sixth chakra, produces inspiration about ways to solve survival issues.

**Jade, Brown or Gray:** Drains excess energy from all chakras, and allows chakras to realign themselves.

**Jasper, Brick-Red:** Balances all chakras. Mild in effect.

**Jasper, Green:** Balances and clears all chakras. Removes energy blocks in the body.

**Jasper, Morrison Ranch:** Opens, balances, and connects all the chakras. Makes it possible to feel more in touch with the "Universal Consciousness".

**Malachite:** Balances and heals all chakras. Very strong in effect.

**Morrisonite:** Same in effect as Morrison Ranch Jasper.

**Opal, Cacholong:** Balances and clears all chakras.

**Pascoite:** Balances all chakras. Drains any excess energy from the body.

**Pearls:** Balance and heal all chakras. Have the additional effect of enhancing one's wisdom. Pearls can be placed near a chakra, when one desires the highest truth and wisdom about an issue that pertains to that chakra.

**Pearls, Biwa:** Same in effect as Pearls, except that all wisdom is of an eccentric or innovative nature.

**Sugilite:** Balances and heals all chakras. Creates a state of receptiveness to higher influences.

**Yttrocerite:** Same in effect as Fluorite.

**Zircon, Light Blue:** Opens and balances all chakras. Uplifting.

## Two or More Chakras

Each of these stones balance and heal two or more chakras, though not all seven.

**Apachite:** Opens and balances the sixth and seventh chakras.

**Aragonite:** Keeps chakras four, five and six in balance and operating in a blended fashion. One simultaneously operates from a high degree of emotional perceptivity, intellectual clarity, and one has the ability to see truth from a higher perspective and psychically sense the flow of things. A favorite of those who like a high degree of truth in their lives.

**Aventurine, Green:** Keeps the sixth and seventh chakras open and unblocked so energy can flow unimpeded.

**Aventurine, Red:** Keeps the second, third, fourth and fifth chakras open and unblocked so energy can flow unimpeded.

**Barytocalcite:** Balances, opens and stimulates the fourth and seventh chakras. Fosters emotional strength and clarity with regard to the emotions.

**Benitoite:** Balancing and healing to five of the chakras. It is often found in very small pieces, but is so powerful in effect a large piece is not necessary. Benitoite comes in a variety of colors. Each color is related to a different chakra.
  **White:** First chakra.
  **Pink:** Fourth chakra.
  **Clear:** Fifth Chakra
  **Blue:** Sixth Chakra
  **Purple:** Seventh Chakra.

**Carnotite:** Heals and balances the first, fourth and fifth chakras. Allows them to work together in a blended fashion.

**Dypingite:** Balances and heals the third, fourth and fifth chakras. Particularly good for healing, and closing down these chakras when abused.

**Idocrase, Green:** Balances the second and third chakras, and drains out excess energy.

**Idocrase, Yellow:** Balances the fifth and sixth chakras, and drains out excess energy.

**Jade, Black:** Balances, opens and integrates the first three chakras, which involve survival, sex and power, so one can be appropriate with all three.

**Opal, Sonoma:** Creates a link between the second and fourth chakras. Keeps them aligned and operating in a blended fashion. This stabilizes the emotions of one who is involved in a sexual relationship or a creative project.

**Septarian Nodule:** Balances fourth, fifth and sixth chakras. Enables them to operate in a blended fashion.

## Special Effects

There are a number of gemstones, that while they do not balance or heal the chakras, do have an impact on selected chakras in special and specific ways.

**Alexandrite:** Alexandrite suspends intense emotional states to allow a person to operate in a more neutral way, when worn on the chest. When worn in the ears, it inhibits excessive intellectual processing, to allow one to maintain and outwardly-directed intellectual focus.

**Amber:** Has the capacity to put an intellectual focus on some chakras when worn near that chakra. When worn at the sixth chakra, eliminates confusion about what's really true and increases mental clarity. When worn at the fifth chakra, one is more intellectual and thoughtful in one's communications. When worn at the fourth chakra, intellect guides the emotions. When worn at the third chakra, one has more intellectual clarity about one's career, health or power issues.

**Amber, Honey:** Same in effect as Amber, but stronger in its ability to have a healing effect on the chakras.

**Diamond:** Promotes mastery of activities associated with the chakra it is worn closest to. For example, Diamonds worn near the second chakra, promote excellence as a lover and high quality in one's creative projects. Diamonds also come in a variety of colors and each color tends to resonate best to a different chakra.

| | |
|---|---|
| **Black:** | First chakra. |
| **Pink-red:** | Second chakra |
| **Clear:** | All chakras, but especially the third. |
| **Yellow:** | Fourth chakra. |
| **Green:** | Fifth chakra. |
| **Brown:** | Sixth chakra. |
| **Blue:** | Seventh chakra. |

**Triplite:** Same in effect as Amber.

## FREQUENCY and ENERGY BALANCE

"Frequency" is the rate at which one's essence vibrates. Frequency, as defined here, is <u>not</u> a measure of one's spiritual development. It is the rate at which one's internal clock runs, and it determines the pace one finds most comfortable as one moves through life.

The majority, of course, fall in the mid-range of the frequency spectrum. Most people move through life at a pace that seems to be, more or less, like everyone else's. For a high-frequency person, the internal clock runs faster. Such people are energetic, fast moving and want to zip through life. A person of low frequency, in contrast, tends to have a denser aura, and takes life at a more leisurely pace.

Each person has a natural set point with regard to frequency. When a very high or low-frequency person is energetically unbalanced, the internal clock begins to either speed one up, or slow one down to a rate that is uncomfortably outside one's normal pace. Those whose vibratory rate is in the mid-range, can get unbalanced in either direction: they can get too hyped, get too slowed down, or find their energy level bouncing around in an uncomfortably erratic fashion.

The gemstones or minerals listed below, are all-purpose, energetic balancers that allow one to stabilize, and maintain, one's frequency rate at a comfortable level. They are effective regardless of frequency type, and keep one moving through one's day, at a pace that feels just right. For mid-range frequency types, the stones listed below are the best choice for keeping one energetically balanced.

**Beryl, Pale Green:** An all-purpose energetic balancer, most effective for persons of mid-range frequency. Those who live life in the fast lane, or those who, like the turtle, live life by the side of the road may not feel much effect.

**Bone:** Balances one energetically and fosters a sense of practicality and grounded awareness. Similar in effect to Ivory, except that Ivory has a more refined quality to it.

**Ivory:** Stabilizes one's energy level and keeps one moving through life at a comfortable pace: one that is neither too hurried nor too plodding.

**Jasper, Brick-red:** A good, all-purpose energetic balancer, although milder in effect than others.

**Malachite:** One of the most powerful balancing stones. It is almost impossible to be around Malachite, and remain unbalanced for long.

**Obsidian, Rainbow:** An energetic balancer Stabilizes one's internal clock and allows one to move through one's life at a comfortable pace.

**Petrified Wood:** A good, all-purpose energetic balancer.

## High Frequency

When a high-frequency person is out of balance, they get overly hyped, too buzzy and are often unable to slow down. Gemstones and minerals that are balancing for a high-frequency person, slow the speed at which they're zipping about, to a level normal for that person and keep it stabilized there. Stones that balance a low-frequency person, have the effect of lowering the vibratory rate of a high-frequency person, giving them a chance to really slow down and mellow out.

**Abalone:** Balances high-frequency types of people. Particularly calming to those who tend to live in a very intense state.

**Agate, Copco:** Balances a high-frequency person, or helps a lower-frequency person raise their frequency. A very balancing and healing energy, surrounded with the loving emotionality of the Venusian body-type Agate.

**Agate, Dendritic:** Balances and calms overly-energized, high-frequency persons.

**Agate, Fern:** Same in effect as Dendritic Agate.

**Agate, Moss:** Same in effect as Dendritic Agate.

**Agate, Tree:** Same in effect as Dendritic Agate.

**Amethyst:** Balances those of high frequency. Calming and stabilizing when one feels frenetic or too highly energized.

**Carnelian:** Balancing for "buzzy", high-frequency people. Is energizing for the low-frequency types of people who take life at a slower pace.

**Emerald:** Balances persons of high frequency.

**Citrine:** Balances high-freqency types. Useful for the hyperkinetic person who can't seem to calm down, or for those super high-energy folks who can't seem to move at a slower pace.

**Clam Shell:** Especially healing for high frequency, "buzzy", types of people who often live in a very intense state. Helps them slow down and mellow out.

**Hedenbergite:** Balances high-frequency types of people. Calming to "buzzy" types of people who, when they become over stimulated, are often unable to slow down.

**Johannsenite:** Same in effect as Hedenbergite.

**Limestone:** Balances a high-frequency type of person.

**Mother of Pearl:** Same in effect as Abalone.

**Obsidian, Snow-Flake:** Balances and calms "high frequency", "buzzy" types of persons who move through life at a very fast pace.

**Tanzanite:** Calming to "high frequency", "buzzy" types of people who tend to live in a very intense state. Slows them down and mellows them out.

## Low Frequency

When a low-frequency person is out of balance, they start thinking and moving at a slower and slower pace, plodding along, unable to keep up with everyone else: often feeling confused and stupid. An effective frequency balancer, enables them to gain control of the rate at which they're moving and speed it up to appropriate and comfortable levels. Stones that balance a high-frequency person, have the effect of raising the vibratory rate of a low-frequency person above their normal set point, giving them an opportunity to really step up the pace from time to time.

**Azurite:** Balancing for low-frequency types. Creates a sense of harmony and balance for people who tend to take life at a slower pace.

**Apache Tears:** Balances and creates a sense of harmony for low-frequency types of people.

**Aventurine, Green:** Balances a low-frequency person.

**Bloodstone:** Creates a sense of harmony and balance for those who take life at a slower pace. Slows down a high-frequency person who tends to "buzz" through life.

**Coral, Black:** Balances a low-frequency person. High energy types, those who buzz through life at a very fast pace, might feel it slows them down too much. Or they might love it, because it can help them to relax and slow down.

**Jasper, Green:** Balances a low-frequency person and makes them feel peppier.

**Jasper, Imperial:** Balances a low-frequency person and makes them feel healed. Slower moving people often have difficulty feeling adequate, because they're always striving to move faster, than is really comfortable for them.

**Jasper, Nunkirchner:** Same in effect as Bloodstone.

**Limestone:** Balances a low-frequency type of person.

**Merwinite:** Same in effect as Bloodstone.

**Tiger Eye, Gold:** Balancing for low-frequency types: those who like to move slowly and take their time about things. Can help high-frequency types mellow out.

## Matching Frequency

It is possible to raise or lower one's frequency. Without realizing it, most people do this constantly as they interact with others throughout the day. That is, we slow down or speed up, to match ourselves to the pace of another person. With one person, we will find ourselves talking or moving more slowly and with another person, chattering like a magpie and bouncing around like a ball.

When another person's pace is markedly different from one's own, the effort to match the other's pace can be wearing. Gemstones are an aid in this regard, as they energetically assist this process. That is, they enhance one's ability to harmonize one's energy with another's and make it easier to move at the same pace, especially if that pace differs from one's own.

**Apache Gold:** Same in effect as Iron Pyrite.

**Bravoite:** Same in effect as Iron Pyrite.

**Limonite:** Same in effect as Iron Pyrite.

**Iron Pyrite:** Helps one match frequency with someone of a higher or lower frequency than oneself.

**Obsidian, Rainbow:** Stabilizes one internally and allows one to harmonize one's pace with another's: i.e., match frequency with someone of a higher or lower frequency than oneself.

**Pyrrotite:** Same in effect as Iron Pyrite.

**Tenorite:** Same in effect as Iron Pyrite.

## Metals and Frequency

It is the primary function of the metals to raise or lower frequency. Remember that when one's frequency is raised, one feels energetic. When one's frequency is lowered, one feels more mellow.

**Brass:** Lowers frequency, but not quite as much as gold.

**Bronze:** Lowers frequency, but not quite as much as gold.

**Copper:** Raises frequency most powerfully, and is thus, quite energizing.

**Gold:** Lowers frequency the most of any metal.

**Goldstone:** Glass with Copper flecks. Copper raises one's frequency or "buzziness", but is somewhat softened by the glass which surrounds it.

**Silver:** Raises frequency a moderate amount.

## MALE/FEMALE ENERGY

Energy can be divided into two types: "male" energy which is focused, organized, and very grounded, and "female" energy which is unfocused, creative, and expansive. Each person has a certain proportion of male energy to female energy that is not dependent on gender. Thus, a woman can be very high male energied or high female energied or just about 50/50, as can men.

"Balancing" one's female or male-energied side, means using the amount of male and female energy one has in a balanced fashion: that is, when one is operating primarily out of one energy, one stays enough in touch with the other energy to be appropriate, and not go overboard in one direction or another. For example, a person who is too male energied, can get overly focused and concentrated on one detail, fail to notice any other relevant details, and be unable to access their female-energied side which is needed to step back and see the larger picture.

A person using their female energy in an unbalanced fashion can be so lost in the vastness of their creativity, or going in so many different directions at once, they are unable to prioritize, or focus in on an appropriate direction, or are unable to "stick with it" long enough to guide their projects, ideas or desires to fruition.

The gemstones listed below help one access, balance, relate to, or, in some way get more comfortable with, one's creative, female-energied side, or one's focused, male- energied side.

**Agate, Dendritic:** Balances those who are either high-male energied or who are high-female energied. Promotes moderation in one's approach to life rather than a tendency to be either overly expansive or overly structured.

**Agate, Fern:** Same in effect as Dendritic Agate.

**Agate, Moss:** Same in effect as Dendritic Agate.

**Agate, Tree:** Same in effect as Dendritic Agate.

**Amethyst:** Balances high male-energied or high female-energied persons: those who are either highly focused and driven in their approach to life; or those who are highly creative, but chaotic in their way of dealing with life. Brings both out of the extremes into a more balanced state near the middle.

**Annabergite:** Enables those who have a wide focus-viewpoint; i.e., high-female energied, to narrow their focus and pay attention to details, or prioritize cycles in order of importance. Curbs the tendency to do everything at one time.

**Apache Tears:** Balancing and grounding for those who are either very high-male energied or who are very high-female energied. Promotes moderation in the use of one's male or female energy.

**Arsenopyrite:** Helps one match energies with one who is more female energied, or more male energied than oneself.

**Aventurine, Green:** Balancing and grounding for those who are either very high-male energied or who are very high-female energied. Promotes moderation in the use of one's male or female energy.

**Binghamite:** Goethite plus Quartz. Same in effect as Goethite.

**Bloodstone:** Balancing and grounding for those who are either very high-male energied or who are very high-female energied. Promotes moderation in the use of one's male or female energy.

**Carnelian:** Balances those whose proportion of male to female energy is more or less equal. Enables them to use their focused, organizational abilities (male-energied side), and their creative, innovative abilities (female-energied side) in a balanced fashion.

**Chlorite, Green:** Attractive to those with female bodies, or to those who are high-female energied. Creates comfort and compatibility for a high-female energied person with a male body or a high-male energied person with a female body.

**Colemanite:** Balances high male-energied types of people and enables them to use their female-energied side more effectively. Enhances creativity and widens one's focus to view things from the perspective of the "larger picture".

**Covellite:** Promotes focus, clarity and the ability to concentrate. Enables one to use one's male-energied side more easily, even if one is high-female energied.

**Emerald:** Balances those whose proportion of male to female energy is more or less equal. Enables them to use their focused, organizational abilities (male-energied side), and their creative, innovative abilities (female-energied side) in a balanced fashion.

**Goethite:** Similar to Chlorite, but attractive to those with male bodies or high-male energied types paired with a disparate energy or body. Makes high-female energied types more comfortable with a male body, and high-male energied types more comfortable with a female body. Because this stone reduces the amount of confict going on internally, one feels much more relaxed. Also good for men having a hard time with masculinity issues, such as feeling they're not masculine enough, or not in touch with their male side.

**Gyrolite:** Accentuates the qualities of female energy: e.g., expansiveness, versatility, and creativity. Puts one more in touch with one's female-energied side and one's ability to use it.

**Hendricksite:** Increases one's ability to work with one's female energy: get in touch with it, play with it, express it, and operate through it. One totally relaxes one's concentration, to be creative, expansive and playful.

**Jasper, Green:** Healing to highly focused, male-energied people, especially those who have worn themselves out with concentrating.

**Jasper, Imperial:** Balancing for those who have a high percentage of female energy. For someone who's very unfocused and wants to be more focused; for the high female-energied person who wants to be more grounded.

**Jasper, Nunkirchner:** Same in effect as Bloodstone.

**Limestone:** Balancing and grounding for those who are either very high-male energied or who are very high-female energied. Encourages a moderate approach to life, and softens the tendency such people have, to be either overly expansive and unfocused, or overly structured and highly focused. Brings both out of the extremes into a more balanced state near the middle.

**Marble:** Balances the male-energied side of everyone. Makes it easier to accomplish projects that require a high degree of focus and concentration. Darker colors are preferred by those with a high percentage of male energy or by the more solid roles such as Warriors, Kings and Scholars. Lighter colors of marble are preferred by high-female energied types, by the lighter roles, Artisans, Servers and Priests, and by those who feel very unhealed and sensitive. Comes in many colors and each color gives a slightly different flavor to the main definition.

> **Black:** Focuses one's energy in a very refined manner.
> **Brown:** Focuses one's attention a little more on issues relating to the home.
> **Gray:** No added qualities.
> **Green:** Focuses one's attention a little more on prosperity issues.
> **Pink:** Calms and heals.
> **Salmon:** Makes one more aware of what one might be angry about.
> **Tan:** Enables one to remain physically balanced.
> **White:** No added qualities

**Merwinite:** Same in effect as Bloodstone.

**Obsidian, Rainbow:** Enables one to use one's focused, organizational abilities (male-energied side), and one's creative, innovative abilities (female-energied side) in a balanced fashion.

**Okenite:** Balances high-female energied types and promotes creativity. Very useful, as it is easy for those with high-female energy to get out of balance.

**Onyx:** Balances the female-energied side of everyone. Useful when one wants to pursue creative projects and see things from a more expansive, "larger picture" perspective. Darker colors are more intense, and preferred by high male-energied types, or by the more solid roles. Correspondingly, lighter colors are gentler and usually preferred by high female-energied types. Comes in many colors and each color adds a slightly different flavor to the basic definition.

> **Black:** Calms primal or basic fears and enables one to feel stable and secure.
>
> **Milky White or Cream:** No added qualities.
>
> **Orange to Brown:** Enhances and intensifies the basic effects.
>
> **Pale Green or Olive Green:** Soothes and calms the emotions.
>
> **Red:** Adds a dynamic element.

**Tanzanite:** Balances high male-energied or high female-energied persons: those who are either highly focused and driven in their approach to life; or those who are highly creative, but chaotic in their way of dealing with life. Brings both out of the extremes into a more balanced state near the middle.

**Todorokite:** Balances, calms and soothes high-female energied, creative types of people when they are under stress. Helps a high-female energied person, when out of control and bouncing around energetically, to stabilize their energy and calm down.

**Tourmaline, Watermelon:** Has a stabilizing effect on everyone, but is especially good for those fluid, expansive, high female-energied types of people who can appear "fluff-headed". Helps them use their male-energied side more effectively, and enables them to be more focused and solidly grounded.

**Wyartite:** Enables very focused, high male-energied people to understand, and get along with, people who are very high female energied, and vice-versa.

### Male/Female Energy Type and Frequency Range

There are a number of gemstones and minerals that are not only balancing based on frequency type, but are also balancing depending on one's proportion of male to female energy. In the tables below, one can find those stones that have this dual capacity.

While gemstones and minerals do tend to be more effective when used by persons who fall in the frequency, or male to female energy ranges described, they should not necessarily be shunned on that basis. Any stone that one finds attractive, will also be the most appropriate. Also, there is no need for concern if one does not know one's frequency or male/female energy ratio. Again, always select stones for personal use based on the degree of affinity one feels for the stone.

The first table lists gemstones that are most effective for those who are either extremely male energied, or extremely female energied, or whose proportion of male to female energy is more or less equal. For example, Green Jasper balances a low-frequency person or a high male-energied person.

### Proportion of Male to Female Energy

| Frequency | Hi Male | Hi Female | Equal |
|---|---|---|---|
| High | | | Carnelian Emerald |
| Low | Jasper, Green | Jasper, Imperial | |

The second table, is a list of stones that balance either high male or high female-energied persons, or balance a person of either high or low frequency. Stones that balance those on the extreme ends of the male-to-female energy range, bring both extremes more to the middle. They soften the tendency of a high male-energied person to be overly structured and highly focused, and soften the tendency of a high female-energied person to be overly expansive and unfocused. Limestone, for example, promotes moderation for either high male-energied, <u>or</u> high female-energied persons, <u>or</u> balance someone whose frequency is either high <u>or</u> low.

## Proportion of Male to Female Energy

| Frequency | Hi-Male or Hi-Female Energied | |
|---|---|---|
| High | Agate, Dendritic<br>Agate, Fern<br>Agate, Moss<br>Agate, Tree | Amethyst<br>Limestone<br>Tanzanite |
| Low | Apache Tears<br>Aventurine, Green<br>Bloodstone | Jasper, Nunkirchner<br>Limestone<br>Merwinite |

# RELATING TO OTHERS

## Communication

Communication is extremely important in all phases of life. It is the grease that oils the wheels of civilization. Further, it is not possible for sentient beings to evolve without communication, because all evolution occurs through the process of relating to other sentient beings. The primary distinction between sentient beings and non-sentient beings, besides the awareness that "I am I", is the fact that sentient beings talk about things. If we stop talking about things, we really take a step backwards down the evolutionary scale. Communication need not be verbal, but it is necessary that, by some means, what is going on with one's self is communicated to others and similar communications received.

These stones are general, all-purpose aids to clear, clean communication. Each makes it easy to get one's point across.

**Agate, Sagenite:** Enables one to be more direct, clear and powerful in one's communications as well as more willing to share those communications.

**Antlerite:** Pulls one strongly into good, clear communication, and thus, eliminates arguing. Makes it difficult, if not impossible, to miscommunicate.

**Azurite:** Makes one clearer in one's communications, and able to put one's points across more effectively. Allows one to be in better communication with others by fostering a willingness to listen. Gilves a secure sense that one can listen and not lose sight of one's own position.

**Beryl, Pale Green:** An aid to communication. Encourages one to communicate relevant information, and promotes good listening habits.

**Chessylite:** Same in effect as Azurite.

**Emerald:** Keeps one balanced, in communication, and away from being arrogant or self-deprecating in one's communications.

**Grossular, Green:** Makes one comfortable with communicating. One feels more comfortable with what one wants to say, and with one's ability to communicate it.

**Kornerupine:** Enables one to communicate more clearly. The greener the color, the stronger the effect.

**Malachite:** Makes one feel grounded, balanced and very willing to communicate who one is, and where one is coming from. Promotes willingness to relate to others and to let them know what one's position is.

**Myrichite:** For accuracy and speed of communication. One feels a strong push to get one's communications out there quickly. Good for those in the media and for others who just need to have an "important" talk with someone.

**Tourmaline, Green to Dark Green:** Produces a charismatic ability to communicate.

The next set of stones all aid communication, but in a variety of specialized ways.

**Aplowite:** Brings emotions to the surface and encourages one to communicate more honestly about the emotional impact one has felt.

**Arthurite:** Opens up communication, and the desire to communicate where one has been silent before.

**Datolite:** Heals exhaustion around communication.

**Eucryptite:** Promotes honesty in communcations by making it difficult for either party to lie.

**Franklinite:** Allows one to communicate about intense issues in a calmer fashion. Releases emotional tension.

**Kidwellite:** Enables one to understand the hidden meanings in the communications of another person.

**Matildite:** Encourages inter-racial and inter-cultural communication. Makes one open to hearing about other perspectives.

**Planerite:** Enhances one's own personal power when communicating, as well as one's ability to debate effectively.

**Spinel, Yellow:** Encourages communication from the standpoint of a feeling of pride in oneself. "I am proud of myself and I want to tell you about it."

**Strunzite:** Increases one's ability to learn other languages easily.

## DISSEMINATION of KNOWLEDGE and TRUTH

**Charoite:** Enables those who are involved in teaching, the media, or any profession that involves the dissemination of information, truth and/or wisdom, to feel powerful and to project an aura of confidence and authority.

**Feldspar, Oligoclase:** Ensures that important information will be imparted clearly, and in a balanced fashion.

**Grossular, Pale Yellow:** Calms those who get frantic about whether they'll be able to get all the information they have, out to the appropriate listeners in a timely fashion. Slows one down kinesthetically, and creates the feeling that there is time enough to do and say it all. Very good for those in the acting professions or media.

**Hessonite:** Puts one in touch with basic truths, and the ability to communicate them.

**Mariposite:** Enhances one's self-expressiveness, and ability to communicate with others.

**Spinel, Dark Green:** Emphasizes the communication of information, wisdom and truth. Particularly assists in the communication of wisdom.

**Tourmaline, Green to Dark Green:** Produces a greater ability to communicate. Emphasizes the communication of information, wisdom and truth.

## OTHER SENTIENTS

These three stones enable one to communicate with other sentient beings.

**Australite:** Same in effect as Moldavite.

**Lodestone:** Helps one communicate with dolphins and whales.

**Melanotekite:** Same in effect as Tektite.

**Moldavite:** Enables one to communicate telepathically with other sentient beings both human and non-human.

**Tektite:** Assists in contacting and communicating with sentient beings from other planets.

## THE GENERATION GAP

These stones enable members of different generations to communicate with one another better.

**Agate, Crazy Lace:** A stone that effectively enhances the communication between different generations. Makes children understand parents and grandparents. Makes parents and grandparents understand children and grandchildren.

**Agate, Mexican Red Lace:** Makes it easier for family members and close friends to share emotional truths.

**Spinel, Violet:** Good for communicating with people who are very different in age from oneself (at least 20 years) either older or younger. A stone that helps bridge the generation gap.

**Zapatalite:** Helps a younger person understand an older person's point of view, but does not work in the other direction.

## STORYTELLING

**Bismuth:** A stone for "storytellers". Enhances one's storytelling abilities.

**Bismuthinite:** Same in effect as Bismuth.

**Bismutite:** Same in effect as Bismuth.

**Grunerite:** Same in effect as Bismuth.

**Uvarovite:** Aids imagination, and increases one's charisma and verbal abilities.

**Yuksporite:** Promotes inventiveness in the use of language, and creation of poetry.

**Zinkeinite:** Same in effect as Bismuth.

# For Those in Service to Others

**Bornite:** Promotes wider social consciousness. Enables one to be innovative in one's approach to social issues or the application of justice. Encourages one to be concerned with what will work for society. Promotes a love of justice and keeps one aware of one's higher principles. One wants to be sure things are fair and is willing to protest if they're not.

## CARETAKING

This group of stones are very popular, as most of us are in service to others at one time or another in our lives. Not only are there many professions that fall in this category, but the role of parent is a prime example of being in "service to others". These stones all make one feel comfortable with taking care of others.

**Clinochlore:** An other-directed stone that enhances one's ability to be nurturing, warm, aware of the needs of others and to enjoy seeing that those needs are met.

**Clinozoisite:** Helps those in positions of service to others remember that they need to take care of themselves, as well as others, in order to remain balanced.

**Cuprolite:** Enables one to be practical and grounded while working in a capacity of service to others. Makes it easier to pay attention to the details of what needs to be done, to create excellence in service.

**Endlichite:** Enables one to feel good about taking care of people on an individual basis, and to feel calm and serene about day-to-day mundane tasks that other people might consider drudgery.

**Erythrite:** Fosters one's capacity for selflessness. Good for those who have a tendency to be self centered and thinking only of their own needs.

**Feldspar, Red to Brown:** Enables those in a position of service to stay balanced and not fall into negative patterns, such as being overly emotional, overly involved, martyred or self deprecating.

**Heliodor:** Ensures that one feels comfortable about being of service to others: that one is able to approach giving to others in a relaxed fashion without feeling victimized or trapped. One of the most comforting types of stones to wear. More powerful than Rubies, but harder to find.

**Herderite:** Enables those in a position of service, to stay appropriately nurturing and care-taking. Particularly fosters the ability to know what would enhance the well being or growth of another person.

**Metatorbernite:** Makes one feel very enthusiastic about taking care of others and being of service.

**Ruby:** Makes one feel giving and happy about being able to be of service to others. Enhances one's ability to be warm, caring and tuned into the needs of others. Inspiring in its devotional quality.

**Spinel, Violet:** Most useful when one is feeling victimized about serving or taking care of others: enables one to pull out of being a victim and gain control.

**Sylvite:** Enables those in a position of service to stay appropriately nurturing, care-taking, and tuned into the needs of others.

**Torbernite:** Encourages compassionate and nurturing behavior toward others. Enables one to be effectively powerful in the ability to heal or aid others and in the ability guide others, toward the fruition and completion of projects that are beneficial to all.

**Zeunerite:** Same in effect as Torbernite.

**Zoisite, Green:** Balances those in a position of power in the area of service to others, and facilitates, for example, the relationship between doctor and patient, therapist and client, healer and healed. Enables one to use one's power to act effectively in the best interests of those one is responsible for.

**Zoisite, Pink:** Balancing to those in a position of service and keeps them from over-extending themselves, or falling into negative habit patterns, such as being overly bossy, too self-effacing or martyred.

## COMPASSION

**Sphene:** Promotes compassion of an extremely durable type. Helpful in situations that really put a strain on one's compassion, such as working in a hospital or with very disturbed people for extended periods of time.

**Veszelyite:** Allows one to be more compassionate.

## THE HEALING PROFESSIONAL

Many of the gemstones and minerals described in other sections of this book, are helpful to the healing professional. For the psychotherapist, the stones that aid the process of self examination, those that help one overcome addictions, bad habits and self-destructive tendencies, are particularly useful. Healers of the physical body, will find most useful, the section that discusses the stones associated with healing or maintaining the health of the physical body. All healing professionals will be able to find uses for the stones that heal and balance the chakras, as well as those that calm anxiety and heal survival-based fears. Presented below, is a miscellaneous collection of stones we wanted to be sure were not missed.

**Eucryptite:** Encourages anything hidden or secretive to reveal itself. In its presence, people share their secrets and say what's true for them.

**Fluorite:** Enables one to remain clear of unwanted energetic attachments from one's clients or patients, and prevents them from drawing on one's energy without permission.

**Jade, Nevada:** To become a master healer; really in charge of and in control of one's healing powers. Aids in helping and healing others rather than the self.

**Kidwellite:** Enables one to understand the hidden meanings in the communications of another person. Makes it easier to grasp the metamessage: i.e., the message within a message.

**Laumontite:** Reduces obsessive or compulsive tendencies. Useful for those who are trying to give up addictions, as one will notice that one is thinking about "reaching for that cigarette" and in noticing, one will feel uncomfortable and it will be easier to stop. If the obsession or compulsion is not related to an addiction, and is not apparently related to anything else, one should use this stone in conjunction with therapy. Therapists should note this stone brings to the surface, the anxiety an obssessive or compulsive behavior might be masking.

**Sapphire, Light Blue:** Has the capacity to produce inspired conceptualizations. Good for therapists, as it will inspire them to see through people's blocks and discover ways to work them out.

## THE TEACHER

**Charoite:** Enables those who are involved in teaching, the media, or any profession that involves the dissemination of information, truth and/or wisdom, to feel powerful and project an aura of confidence and authority.

**Cornubite:** Useful for anyone involved in teaching. Creates confidence in one's ability to teach. Makes it easy for one's knowledge to flow forth.

**Feldspar, Oligoclase:** Ensures that important information will be imparted clearly and in a balanced fashion.

**Hessonite:** Puts one in touch with basic truths and enhances the ability to communicate them.

**Petersite:** Enables one to become a better teacher. Increases one's clarity of presentation and improves one's public-speaking skills. Makes it possible to teach for longer periods of time without tiring, and heals teacher "burn-out".

**Spinel, Dark Green:** Emphasizes the communication of information, wisdom and truth. Particularly assists in the communication of wisdom.

**Tourmaline, Green to Dark Green:** Produces a greater ability to communicate. Emphasizes the communication of information, wisdom and truth.

## PUBLIC SERVANTS

**Aquamarine:** Helps one take command, especially in situations when one has to act powerfully. Helps one adjust to being authoritative and in control without feeling wishy-washy about it.

**Feldspar, Bytownite:** Balancing to those in a position of power.

**Tiger Iron:** Enables one to be powerful and influential in relationships, politics, or one's career. Particularly empowering in any area requiring mastery.

**Torbernite:** Balances those in positions of power that involve serving others. Enables one to be effective and powerful, in the ability to guide others toward the fruition and completion of projects that are beneficial to all.

**Zoisite, Green:** Balances those in a position of power in the area of service to others. This could be the administrator of a hospital, the director of a research project to find a cure for cancer, or the relationship between doctor and patient, therapist and client, healer and healed. Enables one to use one's power to act effectively in the best interests of the agency, the project or the individual.

**Zoisite, White:** Balancing to those in a position of power. Keeps one aware of the power of one's position, Enhances one's ability to use one's power appropriately. .

## SPIRITUAL LEADERS

**Feldspar, Albite:** Balances those who are involved in directing, or impacting in some way, the spiritual welfare of others. Keeps them from becoming martyred, self-deprecating, overly emotional or overly involved.

**Herderite:** Fosters the ability to know what would enhance the spiritual well being or growth of another person.

**Veszelyite:** Helps one to build an empire that is spiritually based; usually in the area of the ministry.

**Zeunerite:** Creates a sense of enthusiasm and inspired excitement about ways to be of spiritual aid to others.

# Leadership

The stones in this section foster the ability to take charge in a definitive manner, and to create "win-win" solutions for everyone. These stones pull one away from a tendency to be tyrannical or to misuse one's power.

**Agate, Fire:** Same in effect as Fire Opal.

**Aquamarine:** Helps one take command, especially in situations when one has to act powerfully. Helps one adjust to being authoritative and in control without feeling wishy-washy about it.

**Cacoxenite:** A powerful stone. Enables one to act from a position of authority and power, in a stable and grounded way that is not easily disrupted.

**Iolite, Gray:** Makes one feel comfortable taking a leadership role in one's job or profession and creating win-win situations for everyone. Promotes a sense of self-confidence that makes it easy for others to accept one's leadership. Particularly good for the overly mushy person.

**Opal, Fire:** Enables one to take command assertively and with good strategic vision.

**Stringhamite:** Allows one to take a leadership position, and guide a situation to an outcome that benefits all regardless of the difficulty encountered. Makes it very easy to be an authority figure and to convince others to follow one's lead.

**Topaz, Blue:** Brings forth one's leadership qualities, and enables one grasp control of the situations one encounters in one's life. Gives one an aura of competence that leads others to accept one's leadership.

**Xocomocatlite:** Reduces one's resistance to following another's lead. Enables one who is accustomed to leading, or who has a tendency to be pushy or domineering, to follow someone else's lead when necessary.

# Relationships

A variety of special effects are discussed in the group of stones listed below. Each stone stands on its own as a unique energy in its effect on the way we relate to others.

**Amblygonite:** Reduces arrogance by taking the attention off the self. Directs one's attention outward to noticing other people, or one's surroundings. Enables one to more in tune with any situation in which one finds oneself. Different colors are better for certain types:

> **Colorless:** Good for all.
> **Golden Yellow to Yellow:** For solid types: a person who is very grounded and organized.
> **Violet:** For fluid types: a person who's more flowing,

**Ardennite:** Makes it easier to talk to people one doesn't know well. Good in social situations where one would ordinarily be a wallflower. Helps one start to make friends.

**Arsendescloizite:** Makes one clearer about other people's motivations as well as one's own. One can see the motives that are behind actions or words.

**Beraunite:** Increases one's ability to trust others.

**Billietite:** Reduces self centeredness. Enables one to stop focusing on one's self so exclusively, and begin to turn one's attention outward to noticing others. Decreases the feeling that one is "alone in the world."

**Hanksite:** Encourages people to understand action-oriented and production-oriented people, if they aren't that themselves. Helps them deal with those people better. For instance, makes it easier to understand why one's mate is a workaholic.

**Hydrotalcite:** For feeling connected with anyone that has parallel experiences to one's own. Examples are: being involved in the same project, or going off to the same college. One feels in communion with, and empathetic with, that other person.

**Rauvite:** Enables a group of people to work together on an action-oriented project, with a great deal of synchronicity and telepathic awareness of the group dynamics.

**Opal, Black:** Creates an energetic field of resonance between oneself and others. Enables one to have the experience of being on the "same wavelength" as one's friends and intimates.

**Opal, Jelly:** Same in effect as Black Opal, although not quite as powerful.

**Spinel, Blue to Gray:** Helps those who've had many lifetimes, who have constant dealings with those souls with comparatively few lifetimes, to be appropriate in the way they relate.

**Topaz, Green:** Encourages one to be reserved and benevolent. Useful in situations where another person does something really stupid, and one would rather be benevolent and understanding than rub their nose in it and further the karma.

**Tourmaline, Yellow-Green:** Helps those souls with a lot of lifetimes of experience "under their belts" to relate to each other well

**Vivianite:** Helps one get along with those souls that are experiencing their first few lifetimes.

**Zircon, Green:** Similar in effect to Ardennite. Eases shyness.

## SOCIABILITY

These stones emphasize friendliness and encourage people to be sociable and have fun.

**Agate, Green or Green with White Stripes:** Promotes happiness, expansiveness and sociability.

**Alacranite:** Increases gregariousness. Encourages people to socialize and be involved in larger groups than they usually want to be involved with.

**Ardennite:** Encourages one to be more outgoing. Increases the ability to adapt to social situations, especially if one has a tendency to be a wallflower.

**Arsenbrackebuschite:** Encourages friendliness.

**Caledonite:** To feel more friendly and neighborly. Good for those who are "wooden" in social situations, and not very charismatic.

**Cuprosklodowskite:** Increases one's sense of fun, and encourages friendliness and greater affability. A great stone to take to parties, particularly if one is shy.

**Neoticite:** Increases the wearer's ability to seem friendly and outgoing, even though inside they may be feeling a little inhibited and closed down.

**Zircon, Green:** Increases gregariousness. Similar in effect to Ardennite.

## PRIVACY

**Bassanite:** Same in effect as black Jasper.

**Jasper, Black:** This stone has a repulsing quality. When carrying it, others will assume that privacy is desired and will not approach without a very good reason. Can also be used in one's environment to keep it protected. One should create the energy desired, then put the stone in place and it will repulse all unwanted energies.

**Sapphire, Star:** An isolation stone that says: "Don't interfere with me. I want some privacy right now." Colors are black, blue, white and red. Select the color that is the most appealing for best effect.

## FRIENDS AND LOVED ONES

**Agate, Covey Lace:** Helps one to get along with one's friends, and to be relaxed around them.

**Aheylite:** Draws in love relationships, and enables one to sense accurately if another person is truly appropriate for a strong relationship. This includes all types of relationships: people to whom one can relate as good friends, as family, as lovers, or as loyal business partners.

**Chalcophyllite:** Stimulates others to have emotional responses to the person carrying the stone. Useful to promote intimacy in a relationship, especially where there is good communication. Helpful to use in combination with a communication stone.

**Iolite, Blue:** Enables one to take a leadership role in one's friendships, and make things work out in a way that is satisfactory to all.

**Kettnerite, Green:** Helps one maintain friendly relationships with those one already knows, and to keep the lines of communication open.

**Kettnerite, Yellow:** Helps one attract new friends.

**Quenstedtite:** Attracts people to one another who have strong agreements to be together in the present lifetime. This includes all types of agreements such as mates, friends, and work partners.

**Serandite:** Makes it easier to believe that one is valuable to others. Encourages the feeling that others would like to spend time with, work with, or love one.

**Sunstone, Orange or Pink:** For finding sexual relationships. Gives the wearer an aura of sexual attractiveness.

### Support Circle

**Beyerite:** Enables one to find the friends one works with each lifetime, or the people one has "support" karmas with. A "support karma" is where one is owed support of a positive nature.

**Billietite:** Makes it easier to recognize the support that one is being given by others. Also makes it easier to see where possible sources of support exist and to ask for it. Decreases the feeling that one is "alone in the world."

**Iron Pyrite, Dodecahedron:** Iron Pyrite with a twelve-sided shape. Assists one in bringing the members of one's support circle into one's life, and makes it easier to feel comfortable with them. Enables one to match frequencies with members of one's support circle, which automatically eases the process of relating. Most effective with the friends one works with each lifetime.

**Sarcopside:** Encourages one to focus in on why one is lonely and/or not allowinn any support in from others. Stimulates a desire to shift, by sharpening the poignancy of aloneness.

**Weeksite:** Attracts in members of one's basic support group. That is, people who have support relationships of various types with one, even though one has not yet met them in this lifetime.

## Love and Understanding

**Apatite:** For unconditional love and acceptance of other people. Especially useful when one must work with difficult people in one's life.

**Arsenbrackebuschite:** Makes one feel more willing to see other people's good points, and to appreciate them. In turn, makes it easier to relate to them without one's usual judgments.

**Aubertite:** Encourages emotional closeness. Promotes a sense of camaraderie. Increases one's ability to feel friendly and loving.

**Belovite:** Same in effect as Apatite.

**Bieberite:** Same in effect as Laramar.

**Bisbeeite:** Same in effect as Chrysocolla.

**Cancrinite:** Same in effect as Orpiment.

**Chrysocolla:** Makes one very perceptive and understanding of other people. Promotes a loving acceptance of others, and an ability to forgive wrongdoings. One is able to see clearly what goes on with the other person.

**Chrysoprase:** Fosters one's ability to be loving, understanding and accepting of others. Focus is on one's own ability to be loving. One asks, "What can I do to be more understanding and forgiving of this other person?"

**Devilline:** Enables one to see when one is being loved and cared for. Enables one to see what one does, or is, that is appreciated by others.

**Gem Silica:** Same in effect as Chrysocolla, but stronger.

**Laramar:** For eternal love. Allows one to keep on loving wherever one has been loving. Very useful when a relationship is undergoing stress, and one feels that love may be jeopardized. Laramar ensures that the love that's underneath all the problems, will still be there.

**Natrolite:** Calms issues relating to love or support. Clears the energy blockages people put in their feet, relating to love issues (right foot), or support issues (left foot). Clear or yellow Natrolite is for the left foot, and red or white Natrolite is for the right foot.

**Orpiment:** For feeling nurtured and emotionally connected with others. Makes one feel that one is getting what one wants and needs, from loved ones.

**Reevsite:** Helps one empathize with, and have a clear intellectual understanding of, the point of view of someone who has a very different point of view from one's self. A harmonizer for those who are in great conflict. Does not change one's point of view, but it will enable one to really understand what's going on with the other person.

**Ruizite:** Helps one to feel a heart connection beyond death, or even though separated by great distances, continents, or oceans.

**Spinel, Black:** Promotes a sense of beneficence. Makes one feel so in charge of situations and oneself, that one can afford to be really giving and understanding of others, no matter what they're doing.

**Tourmaline, Blue-Green:** Makes one open-hearted, giving and accepting of other people.

**Willemite:** Makes one more appreciative of the people one cares about. Insures one will continue to appreciate those one cares about, instead of taking them for granted.

**Wogdinite:** When worn on or near the person, reinforces the love and affection one's friends and intimates have for one. Everyone is reminded of the love they feel for the person wearing the stone.

**Wyartite:** Enables very focused, straight-forward people to understand, and get along with, people who are very unfocused and scattered in purpose, and vice-versa.

**Veszelyite:** Makes one more accepting of people, particularly those with whom one is having difficulties.

## Relating to Same or Opposite Sex

**Boracite:** Encourages one to feel more comfortable around male bodies, and thus, reduces the fear that one can't relate to men very well.

**Breithauptite:** Enables both sexes to be more comfortable relating to, and being around, women.

**Jade, Yellow:** Takes the mystery out of the opposite sex, and gives one a sense that one really can understand what goes on with them.

**Jasper, Brick-Red:** Helps one get along with the same sex. If homosexual, makes one very comfortable with one's sexuality, and able to maintain compatible relationships.

## Ending Relationships

**Kettnerite, Blue:** Encourages one to do everything possible to save a failing friendship, and gives one the courage to end the relationship, if it is not successful.

**Scorodite:** Encourages one to leave hopelessly dysfunctional emotional relationships. Especially useful where one clings addictively to a relationship that will never work. Makes it easier to let go and move on.

**Sunstone, Blue or Green:** Enables one to end inappropriate or dysfunctional sexual relationships.

**Tinzenite:** Encourages one to lose the things one no longer has use for, but hse been hanging onto. This includes not only inanimate objects like an old sweater, but also includes outmoded relationships.

## INTIMATE RELATIONSHIPS

**Akatoreite:** Deepens the closeness in already established, mated relationships.

**Bafertisite:** Encourages one to remain satisfied with one's sexual partner. Enhances one's preference for monogamy.

**Iolite, Purple:** Enables one to take a leadership position in one's sexual relationships, and make things work out in a way that is satisfactory to all.

**Sapphire, Dark Blue:** For loyalty and bondedness.

**Sapphire, Pink:** Brings out one's ability to surrender to another person for the greater good. Allows one to be really devotional and appreciative of the person that one has surrendered to. A very people-oriented stone.

**Spinel, Pink or Red:** An other-oriented stone. Encourages devotion to those one loves. Enables one to surrender, and be devoted to another person. Can set one's ego aside when with a significant other, and be loving even when its tough. A good wedding ring stone.

**Sunstone, Clear or Yellow:** For maintaining sexual relationships, and keeping them balanced. All couples could use this. Helps avoid the tendency to blame the partner for difficulties.

## Mate Finding

Finding a good person to settle down with is one of life's major tasks. These stone help one draw in, and select, an appropriate mate.

**Agardite:** Helps one to attract appropriate potential mates. This stone increases one's pheromonic acuity; i.e., one is able to sense more clearly who would be an appropriate intimate partner. Good for people who continually make bad choices in this area.

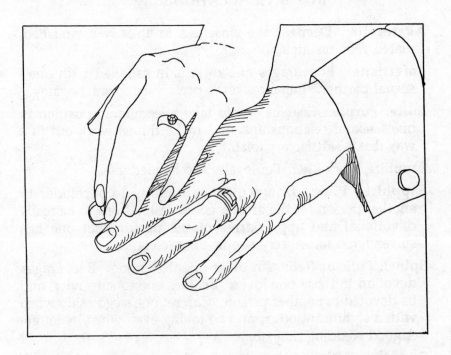

**Aheylite:** Draws in love relationships, i.e., people whom one can relate to as good friends, family, lovers, and loyal business partners. Increases one's pheromonic acuity like Agardite does. Thus, one is more able to sense accurately if another person is truly appropriate for a strong relationship.

**Boggildite:** Attracts one's sexual karmas and relationships to one, by augmenting one's pheromonic range. One broadcasts one's availability and readiness over a wider geographical area.

**Connelite:** Same in effect as Agardite.

**Quenstedtite:** Attracts people that one has strong agreements to be with, in the present lifetime. This includes mate agreements.

**Quetzalcoatlite:** Enables one to zero quickly in on whether someone else is appropriate mate material or not. A mate screening rock.

## Soul Mates

An essence twin is what is popularly referred to as one's "soul mate."

**Amethyst Quartz:** Purple and white stripe. Helps essence twins get along with each other.

**Halite, Blue:** Helps to attract an essence twin into one's life. If already acquainted with one's essence twin, this stone helps one to get along with them.

**Serpentine, Red:** Helps one have good sex with one's essence twin.

## Sexual Attractiveness and Desire

**Agate, Plume:** Encourages the expression of one's sexuality. Enables one to be more open sexually and less repressed. Increases one's sensuality and sexual attractiveness. Makes one feel sexually desirable.

**Agate, Wonder:** Stimulates sexual desire and arousal in males.

**Agrinierite:** Encourages one to seek out and engage in more sexual activity. If mated, one seeks out one's partner. If unmated, one seriously looks at finding one.

**Anapaite:** Stimulates sexual desire by making one more comfortable with one's sexual urges, and more accepting of one's sexual nature.

**Botryogen:** Renews one's ability to be sexually excited, when one's sexuality has been repressed or shut down for a period of time.

**Burckhardtite:** Enables one to feel sexually excited with no loss of intensity as one grows older.

**Coral, Purple:** Encourages an interest in offbeat or "kinky" sexual experiences. Also encourages homosexual attractions.

**Coral, Sponge:** Encourages recreational and non-karmic sex of the "let's have fun" variety. Associated with a more childlike and innocent view of sex. Also increases enjoyment of flirtations.

**Hackmannite:** Same in effect as Sodalite.

**Jasper, Serape:** Stimulates sexual interest and arousal in women.

**Jasper, Willow Creek:** Same in effect as Serape Jasper.

**Natrojarosite:** Reduces sexual repression, and increases passion by lifting the lid off the repression.

**Obsidian, Mahogany:** Increases one's sexuality and sensuality. One feels sexier and more "in touch with touch."

**Opal, Black:** Makes it easy to resonate to, and connect with, others on an energetic level. Increases mutual sexual interest and sexual attractiveness. Can inspire a highly spiritual, sexual experience.

**Opal, Jelly:** Same in effect as Black Opal, except milder.

**Sodalite:** Increases sensuality, sexual attractiveness and sexual interest.

**Szaibelyite:** Increases sensuality, sexual attractiveness and sexual interest.

## FAMILY

**Agate, Crazy Lace:** An "intergenerational" stone. Makes children understand parents and grandparents. Makes parents and grandparents understand children and grandchildren. It encourages the different generations to feel they can enjoy one another.

**Agate, Mexican Red Lace:** Similar in effect to Crazy-Lace Agate. Enables the generations to understand one another better and get along. The red color adds an additional emotional element, which encourages family members and close friends to tell each other their emotional truths. They confess they love one another, or that they are angry with one another, or perhaps just need some attention.

**Agate, Turitella:** Same in effect as Ametrine.

**Akatoreite:** Makes one feel close to, and appreciative of, one's family and closest friends.

**Ametrine:** Good for blending the old with the new, so assists "blended" families with the process of creating a stable, smoothly-functioning unit. A blended family comes into being when one marries, and there are children that are "his, hers, and ours".

**Arseniosiderite:** Encourages maternal inclinations. Thoughts of getting pregnant begin to enter one's mind if they have not been there before. Those who have children already, feel more like putting their attention on them and are more interested in all activities related to mothering.

**Arsenuranylite:** Encourages one to be home oriented. Brings up a desire for activities like baking cookies with the children, and snuggling in front of a warm fire. One feels the home is a cozy place, that is nice to curl up in.

**Carrollite:** Promotes stability in the home, because one feels a desire for rootedness. Encourages appreciation for one's home, and enjoyment in focusing one's attention on it. Don't wear a rock like this, put it somewhere around the house.

**Garnet, Spessartite:** Makes one feel grounded and rooted in the home. Brings forth a strong feeling of belonging with the family. Makes one feel happy and contented with one's home life.

**Gehlenite:** Encourages one to strengthen family ties, and to recognize the family as important. Also makes one willing to go out of the way to ensure the biological success of one's genes, and thus, protect the family lineage.

**Getchellite:** Encourages one to take risks to protect one's loved ones. Whatever risk is necessary will be undertaken, including the possible loss of one's life.

**Iolite, Purple:** Enables one to take a leadership role in familial relationships. Makes others more accepting of one in that role. Good for wishy-washy parents.

**Montroseite:** Same in effect as Sard.

**Sard:** "Homestone". Brings up memories of home, and reminds a person of their emotional attachments and family commitments. Those who are without family or home, feel more rooted and comforted.

**Taikanite:** Promotes loving alignment, understanding and great depth of empathy between parents and children of the same sex.

**Turquoise, Navajo:** A combination of Sard and Turquoise. Green Turquoise in a yellow-brown matrix. Centers one's being on love and connectedness with others. Also makes one feel secure and "at home" no matter where one is.

**Yafsoanite:** Brings up thoughts of home, and keeps a person mindful of their emotional attachments and family commitments. Those who are without family or home, feel more rooted and comforted.

**Yedlinite:** Encourages strong feelings of loyalty and faithfulness toward one's mate. Or, of one has no mate, towards one's intimate family members, primarily focusing on one's parents. Increases the bondedness of the immediate family.

**Yoshimuraite:** Promotes loving alignment, understanding and great depth of empathy between parents and children of the opposite sex.

## TRIBAL UNITY

**Akatoreite:** Encourages a sense of tribal unity. Has a "homey" feeling of togetherness.

**Zunyite:** Encourages one to have a deep sense of patriotism toward one's tribe, nationality, race, religion--anything that distinguishes one as a group member.

## OTHER CULTURES, OTHER BEINGS

**Agate, Pseudo:** Puts one in touch with the energetic qualities of other planets: i.e., ways of being, or perceiving, of the inhabitants of other planets; or the general, energetic qualities of another planet if it is not inhabited.

**Australite:** Same in effect as Moldavite.

**Beryl, Pink to Pale Violet or Strawberry Red:** Heals prejudice and intolerance toward others. Makes one more mellow, and helps create a more flexible attitude toward the differences one finds in others.

**Julienite:** Helps one get in touch with, and maintain, mental contact with other sentient beings and species on this planet and others. Must be discriminating about who one has contacted, as this stone helps one make contact with any life form that has thoughts no matter how rudimentary.

**Matildite:** Encourages inter-racial and inter-cultural communication. Makes one open to hearing about other perspectives.

**Moldavite:** Enables one to communicate telepathically with other sentient beings, both human and non-human. The other sentient beings on this planet are whales and dolphins. Would also aid one to connect telepathically with sentient beings on other planets.

**Polyhedroids:** Enables one to relate to alien thoughts and cultures.

**Takovite:** Promotes understanding of other people's tribal, racial, nationalistic, patriotic, philosophical, or religious orientation. Puts one in touch with why that person likes being identified with that particular group.

**Zebra Gneiss:** Anti-prejudice or anti-xenophobia rock. Puts one in alignment with those one regards as different from one's self. Enables one to feel that one can understand other races and other sentient beings. Makes it easier to understand how they're thinking and what they're doing.

# MICHAEL'S SYSTEM OF PERSONALITY

The gemstones and minerals in this section, are presented in terms of their relationship to Michael's view of the universe. The conscious use of these stones, is a concrete, and effective way, to experience various aspects of the Michael teaching. For those who are unfamiliar with the Michael system, an effort has been made to define relevant terms and concepts clearly. If one would like a more in-depth treatment of these concepts, we recommend "Michael, The Basic Teachings" listed in the reference section. All the stones listed in this section have also been included elsewhere, under another subject heading, and discussed in a general, non "Michaelese" fashion.

Michael's system of personality is composed of three parts: Roles, overleaves, and body types. The <u>Role</u> describes one's essence, or the way of "being" one has throughout one's lives. The <u>overleaves</u>, taken together, describe basic personality characteristics, that change with each lifetime to provide a variety of different lessons. The <u>body type</u>, describes the physical characteristics one has chosen in a given lifetime, and also adds another dimension to one's personality characteristics.

The individual's Role, overleaves, and body type, taken together, comprise the personality traits that describe a particular individual. For each Role, overleaf, or body type, there is a positive and a negative way of manifesting the associated energy. This is referred to as the positive or negative pole of the personality trait. Gemstones produce only positive energy, and will always pull one into the most positive way of manifesting the qualities of each trait. i.e, into the positive pole.

Selecting stones associated with one's own personality traits, or overleaves, gives one a chance to experience functioning in the most positive way on a consistent basis. It is also interesting, as well as useful, to select stones associated with other Roles, overleaves or body types, in order to pull different experiences into one's life. For example, if there is a need to go into a difficult situation with one's eyes open, one might wish to choose Jet, a stone for cynicism even though one is not a Cynic. Or if one is a Cynic, and a little weary of it, one might select some Lavendar Jade to pull a little optimism into one's life.

For those who have no idea what their Role, overleaves, or body type might be, remember the general rule of thumb: if one is attracted to any particular gemstone, it has something to offer that one needs. One can also think of the gemstones and minerals described here, as reflecting various qualities, and make choices in terms of a quality one wants to have or experience. For example, some "Warrior" stones reflect the quality of productivity and organized efficiency, while many of the stones listed under the category of "Priest", are inspirational and foster compassion toward others.

# Roles

An essence's "Role" is it's primary way of being, or the "underlying perception" through which it experiences its lessons through a variety of lifetimes. One's Role shapes the way one relates to others, and interprets one's experiences.

Gemstones and minerals associated with a specific Role, enables persons of that Role to feel more in harmony with who they are, be in balance, and be able to manifest the most positive aspects of their Role. Thus, Sages can stay in communication with others, rather than falling into nonstop talking at someone. Or, Servers can be warm, nurturing and devoted to the well being of others, without slipping into manipulativeness or martyrdom.

Gemstones and minerals associated with a specific Role, are also useful to the other Roles. They allow one to experience the qualities of that Role, or to be more effective when engaged in tasks typical of a Role other than one's own. For example, a person who is not a Server, but who is serving others (e.g., parenting, teaching, healing), might select a "Server" stone to enhance their own nurturing, care-taking qualities, as well as to make the process easier and more enjoyable.

Another example is Tiger Iron, which is a power stone for Kings. It enables Kings to manifest powerfully in any area of their lives they choose. Other Roles would find it useful only when engaged in King-like behavior: i.e, attempting to master, or perfect something in themselves or the environment, or when being a leader of people. A Scholar using Tiger Iron, for example, would not experience a more powerful thirst for knowledge, (a Scholar trait), but would be more powerful in the mastery of skills necessary to acquire knowledge, or would be more masterful in their ability to teach or lead others.

In what follows, we have defined a few terms used constantly throughout this section, in describing the way a stone affects the Role.

**Soul Ages:** According to Michael's Teaching, people progress in Soul Age from Infant to Baby, then Young, Mature and Old, through many lifetimes of growth. This does not refer to chronological age.

**Power stones:** A stone referred to as a "power" stone, empowers the person, of the Role it is associated with, to operate powerfully in all areas of their life. Other Roles will be enabled to operate powerfully in activities typical of that Role.

**Balances:** "Balances" Servers, or "balances" Artisans, etc., means that a stone keeps a person of that Role aligned with their essence, making them feel more at home with themselves. It also pulls persons of that Role into manifesting the positive pole regardless of what they're doing, and persons of other Roles into manifesting the positive pole of the Role when engaged in activities typical of the Role: e.g., more nurturing when serving, or more creative when involved in a creative project.

## SERVER

Servers are inspiring, and care for others by finding ways to serve them. They are nurturant, loving, other-directed, trustworthy, and friendly. In the negative pole, Servers can be covertly controlling of others, on the one hand, and easily feel victimized and trapped by those they are serving on the other hand.

**Clinochlore:** Helps all roles to get in touch with their Server qualities.

**Clinozoisite:** Reminds those in positions of service to take care of themselves. Servers particularly tend to forget they need to take care of themselves, as well as others, to remain balanced.

**Cuprolite:** For service, practicality, and attention to detail. Enables Servers, and those in a service capacity, to work in a very practical, grounded way with the ability to pay attention to the details of what needs to be done.

**Endlichite:** Enables one to feel good about taking care of people on an individual, day-to-day basis.

**Feldspar, Red to Brown:** Balances, grounds, and integrates Mature and Old Servers. Keeps one from falling into the negative aspects of Mature and Old soul while serving: martyred, self-deprecating, overly emotional or overly involved.

**Heliodor:** Balances Mature and Old Servers. Similar in effect to Red to Brown Feldspar.

**Herderite:** A power stone for Servers and Priests.

**Metatorbernite:** Stimulates one's enthusiasm about being of service to others.

**Ruby:** Makes one feel giving, and happy about being able to be of service to others. Inspiring in its devotional quality.

**Sapphire, White:** Keeps one serving oneself appropriately, by making sure one does nice things for oneself. Servers especially need to stay appropriate in taking care of themselves.

**Spinel, Purple:** Most useful when one is feeling victimized about serving: enables one to pull out of being a victim and gain control. A Server stone since this most often happens to them.

**Sylvite:** A power stone for Servers. Particularly empowers Servers in manifesting the positive pole of their Role.

**Torbernite:** A power stone for Servers and Priests. Promotes leadership, and balances Servers and Priests in positions of power.

**Zeunerite:** A power stone for Servers and Priests. Enables them to be powerfully inspired in every area of their life.

**Zoisite, Pink:** Balances Infant, Baby and Young Servers. Keep anyone from manifesting the negative pole of Server.

**Zoisite, Green:** A power stone for Servers. Also enables Servers in positions of power to stay balanced.

## PRIEST

Priests are concerned with the spiritual welfare of others. They are very inspirational, compassionate, emotionally connected, healing and warm. In general the Priest stones are useful, when one is actively involved in facilitating the spiritual growth, psychological development, or physical healing of individuals or groups: for ministers, healers and parents. In the negative pole, Priests can be overly enthusiastic to the point of zealousness, impractical, unthinking, and vague.

**Axinite:** For Infant, Baby and Young Priests. Keeps them from going into total zealousness, unable to maintain balance, and being totally fanatical about things. Older soul ages rarely allow themselves to go overboard this much.

**Feldspar, Albite:** Balances, grounds and integrates Mature and Old Priests. Keeps one from falling into the negative aspects of Mature and Old soul, while doing Priest-like duties: martyred, self-deprecating, overly emotional or overly involved.

**Herderite:** A power stone for Priests and Servers.

**Sapphire, Light Blue:** Produces inspired, conceptual thoughts. The darker the blue, the more creative a Sapphire is, and the lighter the blue, the more intellectually centered and philosophical it is.

**Sphene:** Balances Priests. Enables them to stay compassionate even in situations that make this difficult. Priests of different soul ages will find certain colors more effective than others.

| | |
|---|---|
| Black or Brown: | Infant Priests. |
| Clear: | Baby Priests. |
| Green: | Young Priests. |
| Yellow: | Mature Priests. |
| Orange-brown: | Old Priests. |
| Red-brown: | Old Priests. |

**Torbernite:** A power stone for Priests and Servers. Promotes leadership, and balances Priests and Servers in positions of power.

**Vanadinite:** Produces an exalted, inspirational space.

**Veszelyite:** A power stone for Priests of "empire building" strength. Particularly enhances the capacity for compassion. For Young Priests, this stone has the same effect as Sphene.

**Zeunerite:** A power stone for Priests and Servers. Enables them to be powerfully inspired in every area of their life.

**Zircon, Light Blue:** Balances Priests and those with Priest essence twins: makes them feel stable.

## ARTISAN

Artisans are the creators, the innovators, and are often eccentric. They are constantly involved in the creation of moods, of ideas, of emotions or of physical objects. They are the lightest and most fluid of roles. In the negative pole, Artisans can be flaky, moody, and self deceiving. They can be easily influenced and often feel victimized.

**Acanthite:** Balances Artisans. Stimulates the imagination, and pulls one into an artistic, creative mode.

**Actinolite:** A power stone for Artisans of "empire building" strength. Particularly enables Artisans to focus their power in the area of creativity and handle several projects at once, without getting scattered or sidetracked.

**Agate, Sagenite:** Balancing for highly expressive people such as Sages or Artisans

**Amakinite:** A power stone for Artisans. Vastly increases creativity.

**Augelite:** A productivity rock for Artisans. Makes it easier to manifest and follow through with projects to completion. Particularly useful for Mature and Old Artisans as they tend to go too much to "seed": i.e., get lazy and fail to complete projects.

**Feldspar, Andesine:** Balances, grounds and integrates Mature and Old Artisans.

**Hexagonite:** Same in effect as Actinolite.

**Howlite:** A sixth chakra rock that Artisans adore. Pulls one into artistic creation, and inspiration of a higher-intellectual sort.

**Koettigite:** Releases stress for Artisans, and those involved in creative projects.

**Mariposite:** A power stone for Artisans.

**Microlite:** Same in effect as Actinolite.

**Opal, Boulder:** An enjoyable stone for Artisans. Enables one to come up with highly inspirational, but unusual or bizarre ideas.

**Opal, Sonoma:** Balances and stabilizes Mature Artisans. Creates a link between the 2nd and 4th chakras and keeps them aligned. This stabilizes the emotions of anyone who is involved in a creative project.

**Prase or Prasolite:** Similar in effect to Actinolite, but milder.

**Quartz, Strawberry:** Balances Artisans. Has an intense, dreamy quality. Keep's one attached to one's body.

**Sapphire, Dark Blue:** Opens the second chakra. Pulls one into manifesting creatively.

**Sapphire, Lilac:** Very balancing for Mature and Old Artisans and those who have already learned to use their creativity, but who are feeling lazy or blocked because they're in the negative pole of their Chief Feature.

**Scolecite:** Balances Infant, Baby and Young Artisans. Enables them to stay out of self-deception, moodiness and wishy-washiness.

**Todorokite:** Calms and soothes Artisans and any highly creative, excitable type of person.

**Tremolite:** Same in effect as Actinolite.

## SAGE

Sages are the informers, disseminators and truth-tellers. They make sure the rest of us know what is going on. They are entertaining, perceptive, and quick witted. They make good critics, wise teachers, and fun friends. In the negative pole, they talk too much, crave attention, can be overly dramatic and irresponsible.

**Agate, Sagenite:** Balancing for highly-expressive people such as Sages or Artisans

**Andremeyerite:** Promotes the Sage-like ability to hang on to a humorous, more simple and innocent perspective of whatever is happening in one's immediate vicinity.

**Charoite:** A power stone for Sages of "empire-building" strength. Enables Sages to focus their power in the media, or any arena that requires the mastery of good communication skills.

**Emerald:** Balances Sages. Makes anyone feel more like communicating. Balances those who deal with communication or with processing a great deal of information.

**Feldspar, Oligoclase:** Balances, grounds and integrates Mature and Old Sages.

**Grossular, Pale Yellow:** Balances Infant, Baby and Young Sages. Calms Sages and those who get overbuzzed and frantic about whether they'll be able to get all the information out. Slows one down kinesthetically, and creates the feeling that there is time enough to do and say it all. Very good for those in the acting professions or media.

**Hessonite:** Balances Mature and Old Sages.

**Mariposite:** Power stone for Sages of "empire building" strength.

**Spinel, Dark Green:** Balances Sages. Emphasizes the communication of information, wisdom and truth.

**Tourmaline, Green to Dark Green:** Balances Sages. Produces a greater ability to communicate in everyone. Emphasizes the communication of information, wisdom and truth.

## WARRIOR

Warriors are the "doers", and make life work in a practical manner. They are persuasive, productive, energetic and are very loyal friends. They have high ideals, are great at strategic planning, and make fine generals or mothers. In the negative pole, they can be bullying, narrow minded, or violent.

**Adamite:** A "specificity" rock. Makes one more able to see details and to proceed in a step-by-step, delineated fashion. It enables one to focus on the details or specifics of one's situation: a Warrior quality useful to other Roles as well. As this stone helps bring one out of confusion, it is helpful for those in the negative pole of Growth. It is also useful for Sages, Priests, and Kings because they tend to look at whole pictures, and have trouble getting down to particulars.

**Agate, Dry-Head:** A stone Warriors like. It enhances one's ability to be focused and precise: to really zero in on a project and be clear about each necessary detail. This keeps one from wasting time and speeds up productivity.

**Austinite:** Same in effect as Labradorite. Helpful to overly-focused Warriors, or others, who won't slow down.

**Cassiterite:** A power stone for Warriors.

**Chondrodite**: Balances Warriors. Encourages Warrior-like behavior in everyone, even if not of the Role of Warrior. This includes bravery, feistiness, protectiveness, acting from one's high ideals, willingness to take orders, good team work, strategizing, and productivity.

**Garnet**: (Comes in a variety of colors. Rose-red, red, and red-brown are colors specific to Warriors). A power stone for Warriors. Enables one to be focused, productive, and able to get things done in a competent, purposeful fashion.

**Garnet, Star**: The Garnet produces Warrior-like productivity, and the star pulls in the power to back the productivity and keep it going.

**Hollandite**: A power stone for Warriors. One feels productive, organized and efficient.

**Huntite**: A productivity rock. It clears any excess out of the space, and allows one to concentrate on just what needs to be done. Allows one to prioritize, so one can productively accomplish everything.

**Labradorite**: Balancing for Mature and Old Warriors. Makes a Warrior feel like a Warrior, more than any other stone. Makes non-Warriors more Warrior-like: i.e., more organized, capable of being focused, productive, and maintaining concentration for long periods of time without tiring. Makes people feel energized; and, even if they have been over-producing or over-scheduling themselves, that they have their energy back and are healed. Useful for anyone who tends to overwork themselves: will feel re-energized.

**Zoisite, Gray**: Balances Infant, Baby and Young Warriors. Keeps one productive and organized and keeps one from acting out one's more aggressive impulses or being a narrow-minded bully.

**Youngite**: A power stone for Warriors and Kings. Inspires solutions to problems requiring physical action. Very productivity oriented.

## KING

Kings strive to master themselves and their environment. They are expert at whatever they do; self-assured, natural leaders and good advisors. They are gentle in nature and, at the same time, charismatic and powerful. In the negative pole, Kings can be tyrannical, haughty, intolerant and inflexible.

**Arsenoclasite:** A power stone for Kings. Promotes excellence and perfection in all that one attempts to do.

**Diamond:** A power stone for Kings of "empire-building" strength. Promotes the pursuit of excellence, of perfection, and the mastery of one's self or one's environment. Enables one to take on projects that are vast in scope, and succeed with them. Promotes a feeling of richness and abundance. Most exact and male-energied crystalline structure of all the stones. Certain Roles resonate best with certain colors.

| | |
|---|---|
| Black: | Kings |
| Blue: | Priests |
| Brown: | Scholars |
| Clear: | Warriors |
| Pink-Red: | Artisans |
| Yellow: | Servers |

**Feldspar, Bytownite:** Balances, grounds and integrates Mature and Old Kings, or those in a position of power.

**Tiger Iron:** A power stone for Kings.

**Tsavorite:** For self mastery. Produces a feeling of self-mastery, happiness and confidence about one's life, even though these feelings may not be noticeable to others. Thus, it is not as revealing as a Diamond.

**Unikite:** To completely and totally take charge of one's own life. Helps protect personal power and not allow others to dominate.

**Zoisite, White:** Balances Infant, Baby and Young Kings and any of the younger soul ages when in a position of power.

**Youngite:** A power stone for Kings and Warriors.

## SCHOLAR

Scholars are the most curious of all the roles. They are driven "to know" and ato ssimilate knowledge. They are also honest, diligent and thoughtful. They lend an air of neutrality and stability, to what goes on around them. In the negative pole, Scholars can be overly theoretical and intellectualized, pompous, opinionated or reclusive.

**Anthonyite:** Balances Scholars. Enables one to stay emotionally and intellectually balanced during prolonged intellectual pursuits. Can work longer without mental exhaustion.

**Abernathyite:** Balances Scholars.

**Brazilianite:** Balances Mature and Old Scholars. Stimulates incredibly detailed investigations, or investigation of the unusual, esoteric or bizarre. Prevents "burn out".

**Cornubite:** Creates confidence in one's ability to teach and makes it easy for one's knowledge to flow forth.

**Feldspar, Anorthite:** Balances, grounds, and integrates Mature and Old Scholars. Promotes the pursuit of knowledge and keeps one from becoming close minded or overly theoretical.

**Goshenite:** Balances Infant, Baby and Young Scholars. An anti-pigheadedness stone. Centers a person in the positive pole of the Intellectual Center, and in the positive pole of Scholar. Promotes the acquisition of knowledge, and discourages rigid, opinionated theorizing and pontificating.

**Sapphire, Yellow:** A power stone for Scholars. Puts one directly in touch which what one knows, and the ability to use that knowledge appropriately. Maintains one in the positive pole of Intellectual Center, and makes it difficult to have opinions based on inappropriate use of the other Centers.

**Sapphire, Orange:** A power stone for Scholars of "empire building" strength. For the Scholar who is comfortable with being very powerful, and is basically ready to be in charge of the lives of many, or influence the world in a big way.

**Topaz, Imperial:** A Scholar power stone. Makes Scholars feel good about themselves, and reduces their tendency toward self-deprecation when involved in a project that involves use of intellect and knowledge. Makes anyone feel they will be able to exercise all their abilities and talents, that they are intelligent enough, that they have enough information and, in general, that they have enough scholarly ability to handle any situation.

**Zoisite, Brown:** Balances Young Scholars. Takes away pomposity and a "know-it-all" attitude.

## ROLE-RELATED GEMSTONES

Grouped below, are several gemstones and minerals that relate to the Roles on the basis of color, but are not themselves Role stones. Each color is most effective for a particular Role. If one's Role is not known, select on the basis of the color one finds most attractive.

**Brucite:** Makes one feel calmer, and more competent when under emotional pressure.

| | |
|---|---|
| Server: | Yellow. |
| Priest: | Clear to White. |
| Artisan: | Pale Blue. |
| Sage: | Pale Green. |
| Warrior: | Brownish-red. |
| King: | Gray. |
| Scholar: | Brown. |

**Gorceixite:** Increases one's self confidence. Makes it easier to believe in one's self. When found as a mixture of colors such as yellow-green or orange-red, Gorceixite works equally well for all roles.

| | |
|---|---|
| Priests and Servers: | Red. |
| Sages and Artisans: | Orange. |
| Kings and Warriors: | Yellow. |
| Scholars: | Green. |

**Gypsum:** Promotes intellectual clarity, and competency.

| | |
|---|---|
| Server: | Yellow. |
| Priest: | Yellow-Green. |

| Artisan: | White. |
| Sage: | Green. |
| Warrior: | Light Brown. |
| King: | Champagne and Pink. |
| Scholar: | Clear. |

**Sphalerite:** For transcending ego; for spirituality and empathy. Transcends ego by lifting one beyond petty problems and into a higher space of calm and in touch with one's real self.

| Server: | Yellow. |
| Priest: | Purple. |
| Artisan: | Red. |
| Sage: | Orange/Pink. |
| Warrior: | Black. |
| King: | Brown. |
| Scholar: | Clear. |

**Feldspar:** The Feldspars are in a class all by themselves, and relate to the different Roles in a very unique way. Each Role has a favorite chakra of specialization, and the Feldspar's keep one balanced in their use. Favorite chakras as they relate to Role are:

| King: | First chakra. |
| Artisan: | Second chakra. |
| Warrior: | Third chakra. |
| Server: | Fourth chakra. |
| Sage: | Fifth chakra. |
| Scholar: | Sixth chakra. |
| Priest: | Seventh chakra. |

In order to understand how the Feldspars work, it is necessary to say a few words about how a person working "in Role" operates. Each Role has a favorite chakra through which they work, and can be said to specialize in, when engaging in the functions most particular to the manifestation of their Role.

A lack of balance occurs, when this favorite chakra, as it is used, becomes more open, while the other chakras either have not changed, or have closed down. The function of Feldspar, is to keep the Role-preferred chakra synchronized with the other chakras, so that all are in alignment, and no one chakra is more open than another. This allows a person to stay balanced, to feel grounded, and to consistently manifest the most positive aspects of their Role.

# Overleaves

One's soul, or essence, develops over many lifetimes of experience. Each lifetime, this "higher self" expresses itself through different personality traits or "overleaves". While one's Role remains the same throughout an entire cycle of lifetimes, the soul selects a new Goal, Mode, Attitude, Centering, Chief Negative Feature, and Body Type. for each. This gives the individual an ever-new personality to work with, and provides a fresh range of opportunities and challenges.

This section describes all the overleaf choices in Michael's system of personality, and describes stones that enable one to use each of the overleaves effectively. If uncertain which overleaf applies, use the stone that seems most appealing.

## GOALS

The Goal one's essence chooses, in a particular lifetime, determines the bottom line issue in every experience during that life. The biggest challenges essence gives itself, are related to the achievement of the Goal, and mastering those challenges will do the most to advance one's evolution on the essence (or soul) level. The Goal, then, is the underlying accomplishment that the essence aims for in any given lifetime.

### Growth

A life with the Goal of Growth is set up as a series of challenges and obstacles that temper essence's character and spiritual nature. The purpose of a Goal of Growth, is to evolve on the essence level through dealing effectively with the challenges one encounters.

The stones in this section keep one moving, without becoming driven or confused. Anyone who feels stuck in a rut, or confused about the direction they should take in their life, will find these stones useful.

**Boltonite:** Same in effect as Peridot.

**Bukovskyite:** Same in effect as Peridot.

**Chenevixite:** Encourages powerfully intense experiences to occur in one's life.

**Epidote:** Pulls one into the positive pole of Growth and promotes regular and steady evolution. Protects the third chakra and enables one to remain powerful as one evolves.

**Liebigite:** Brings intense, growthful experiences into one's life and spiritual debts to complete.

**Peridot:** For growth, but can be intense. When worn, growth escalates, the adventure box is opened, and new challenges abound. If one is already in a strong growth cycle, then wearing this stone could be overkill. Combine with Amethyst and Citrine to temper the effect.

**Pistacite:** Same in effect as Epidote.

**Sinhalite:** Similar in effect to Peridot.

**Zircon, Pink:** For growth on the Astral Plane. Pushes one out of the body at night to take on lessons of an emotional nature on the Astral Plane. Can result in a restless night.

## Re-Evaluation

Re-evaluation is the opposite of the Goal of Growth, in the sense that it limits the scope of life in such a way, that one can examine one or more major issues fully. It is inner directed and past directed.

While the gemstones in this section are useful for anyone who wishes to examine themselves or their lives more fully, they are especially useful for those with the goal of Growth, who need to slide to Re-evaluation once in a while for a rest. Also good for Priests or those who keep their attention focused out into the future, and miss all the middle parts of life, and those in Passion mode who tend to enthusiastically skip past things they need to learn.

**Cobaltite:**  Helps one to integrate one's lessons, and pull the various aspects into a coherent whole.  Also useful for those at the third level (introspective level) of any soul age.

**Hematite:**  Useful when one wants to really look something over; pulls up everything that needs to be looked at, and makes it really clear what one's issues are.

**Marcasite:**  Similar in effect to Hematite, although a little more gentle.

**Margerite:**  Takes one back to a state of innocence and simplicity, with few preconceived notions about how things are.  Enables one to take a look at one's life without a sense of struggle.  Good for Cynics and Skeptics.

**Jasper, Picture:**  Enables one to effectively use past life, or earlier in this life, memories to recall the story that goes along with the issue one is re-evaluating.

### Acceptance

The issue for a person with this Goal is learning to accept themselves, their lives and the people in it.  They also focus on being accepted by others and are usually friendly, outgoing individuals.  The spiritual task for those with a Goal of Acceptance, is learning to accept themselves and others just as they are.

In the negative pole, people with a Goal of Acceptance can be ingratiating and people pleasing; glossing over their real feelings and thoughts so they won't "make waves" or get rejected.  The gemstones in this section make one generally more loving and accepting, and can be helpful to all in getting along better with others.

**Alforsite:**  Encourages one to accept whatever is happening, no matter how difficult or disgusting the situation is, and then deal with it rather than turn away.  One must be

cautious in using this stone, /          a person wh      *nds to
be naturally soft and passi                              'ant,
and lose all capacity to disc

**Apatite:** An Acceptance st(                           pulls
one into a spiritual sta                                 ward
others. It is almost Acce,                               :cause
of the willingness it fosters to a..._,         . could
possibly flow into one's life; or a Green ب.    one  it says
"give me more" rather than less. Due to its qualities of
unconditional love and acceptance, this stone is useful
when one must work with difficult people or situations.

**Belovite:** Same in effect as Apatite.

**Tourmaline, Blue-Green:** Wear to be more open-hearted,
giving, and accepting of what's going on in one's life, or of
other people. Invites people in, rather than closes them
out. Useful for those in Impatience, as it pulls one out of
intolerance into tolerance.

**Volcanic Ash:** For acceptance and surrender to the inevitable.
Helps one recognize, and then acknowledge, when nothing
can be done about a situation, and that surrender is
appropriate.

## Discrimination

The purpose of this Goal is to learn to be discriminating;
to pick and choose what one does, or does not want, in one's
life, rather than accepting everything in a meaningless
fashion. People with this Goal develop their critical faculties,
are very sophisticated, and have refined tastes and excellent
judgment.

In the negative pole of Discrimination, however, one can
be indiscriminately rejecting, prejudiced or opinionated. The
gemstones in this section help one to stay appropriately
discriminating: neither overly rejecting or accepting. These
stones are especially useful, when one has important or
difficult choices to make in one's life.

**Atacamite:** Enables one to be more discriminating about new
surroundings; i.e., a new job, a new house, or even a new

couch. More specific than Smoky Quartz. Great for starting a new cycle, and not accepting things one might later regret, as those in Acceptance are prone to do. Enables one to discriminate appropriately about structuring a new situation: saves one the trouble of having to change the status quo later on.

**Chalcedony, Gray, Blue or Purple:** Helps one be aware of what one does not want in one's life. Gray helps one get rid of unwanted things. Purple makes one aware of the emotional experiences one doesn't want to have, which are usually related to the people in one's life. Blue relates to what one doesn't want intellectually in one's space. The gray is usually preferred because most people prefer to clear things out of their life, rather than people or ideas.

**Chalcedony, Pink:** Makes one more discriminating about one's appearance. Useful for people who don't pay much attention to how they look. People who are intellectually or moving centered, tend to ignore their appearance a lot.

**Spinel, Blue to Gray:** Strongest Discrimination stone. Enables one to reject anything: germs out of the body; people out of one's life. Wonderful for illness and big dump jobs. Paradoxically, this stone helps Young, Mature or Old souls who have constant dealings with Infant or Baby souls, to relate to them better. One is able to discriminate very clearly about how to behave around a Baby soul, and thus, be more appropriate. Have to exercise some caution here, because one can also be rejecting with this stone.

**Smoky Quartz:** Enables one to discriminate what one does, or does not, want in one's life. Assists one in "cutting the dead wood", out of one's life appropriately. Wear Hematite and Smoky Quartz to evaluate personal matters. Helps those in Acceptance "clean out the garage".

**Tourmaline, Blue:** Makes one very clear, calm and centered about what one doesn't want in one's life. For some, this calm can verge on being cold and calculating. Use in conjunction with light blue Sapphire (compassion) or blue-green Tourmaline (acceptance) to soften this aspect.

**Willemseite:** Enables those who do not have a Goal of Discrimination, to be more appropriately discriminating. If one is already in Discrimination, the use of this stone could make them too picky.

**Zorite:** Increases one's ability to discern the most appropriate choice, in any given situation, more accurately.

## Dominance

People with a Goal of Dominance, approach life from the standpoint of winning and being in control. They are driven to win whatever challenge they have taken on, whether this be overcoming a personal challenge or guiding others. They make excellent leaders, and are very grounded and competent in whatever they do.

In the negative pole, Dominance can become dictatorial, pushy, insensitive and overwhelming to others. The gemstones listed here, help one stay in the positive pole of Dominance, exercising the best qualities of leadership, and creating win-win situations for everyone.

**Iolite:** A very strong Dominance stone. One feels confident that one is a good leader, should be listened to. Others will accept this, because of the aura of self-confidence one projects. Particularly good for the overly mushy, overly ingratiating, and overly submissive person. Different colors affect different areas of one's life.

> **Blue:** Leadership in friendships.
> **Gray:** Leadership in career.
> **Purple:** Leadership in one's sexual and familial relationships.

**Planerite:** Makes one feel personally competent and powerful. Encourages a winning attitude. Particularly good for winning arguments, or resolving conversational conflicts.

**Stringhamite:** Enables one to take the leadership position, and guide a situation to an outcome that benefits all. Makes it very easy to be an authority figure, and convince others to follow one's lead. Also makes it easier to operate powerfully, regardless of the amount of difficulty encountered.

**Topaz, Blue:** Facilitates one's leadership abilities. Makes one feel more in control of one's self, or of the situations one encounters; able to take the lead, and handle things in a competent fashion. Wear for meeting with the IRS.

**Variscite:** Empowers one to come up with solutions or actions, that will produce win-win results for everyone. Allows one to, simultaneously, see what it is that pulls everything together, and to feel that one has the power to make it happen.

**Vesuvianite:** Enables one to come from a desire to win, and be appropriate with one's competitiveness. Encourages a "win-win" attitude, rather than one of tromping on the competition.

**Xocomocatlite:** Reduces one's resistance to following another's lead. Enables one who is accustomed to leading, or who has a tendency to be pushy or domineering, to follow someone else's lead when necessary.

## Submission

This Goal involves learning to be devoted to a cause, or totally supportive of another person or group of people. People in Submission, are inspired to "win" through support of another or a cause. They can be very selfless, sensitive, and caring.

In the negative pole, a person in Submission can become submissive or subservient, forgetting to take their own needs and desires into account. They can fall into helplessness or martyrdom, forgetting that it is they who choose who and what to support. The stones in this section, bring out the best qualities of devotedness and surrender.

**Kunzite:** For surrender. Makes one feel that one can accept something that's out of one's control, and surrender to it. Does not foster the devotional form of Submission. Very useful, because people spend so much time resisting things that are truly out of their control. Michael regards this as one of the most useful of rocks and recommends it highly.

**Sapphire, Pink:** Brings out one's ability to surrender, or devote oneself to a cause, or another person for the greater good. A delegation and surrender stone, that allows one to surrender power or control, to people who can handle things better. Allows one to be really devotional and appreciative of those one has surrendered to. A very people-oriented stone. Also makes it easier to accept when one is not "in control". Good for those in Aggression Mode or with a Goal of Dominance: tones them down and enables them to let life flow a little more.

**Spinel, Pink or Red:** An other-oriented stone: fosters submission and devotion to those one loves. Enables one to surrender, and be devoted to another person. Can set one's ego aside when with them, and be loving even when its tough. A good wedding ring stone.

**Woodhousite:** Makes one feel one can submit to the greater good. Makes it easier to surrender, and not be so controlling.


## Stagnation

The purpose of having a Goal of Stagnation is to learn to "go with the flow", to relax, to let go of resistance, and take things as they come. People with this Goal are generally easy going and fun-loving. This Goal is also called Relaxation.

In the negative pole, a person in Stagnation can become lazy, inert, or "stuck in the mud": unable to take action or shift appropriately to deal with new circumstances.

**Agate, Covey Lace:** Same in effect as Pink Tourmaline.

**Mesolite:** A "go with the flow" rock. Pulls one into the positive pole of Stagnation and encourages one to be more free-flowing. Particularly good for those who are over-stressed or who work too hard. Enables them to relax somewhat, to be less stressed, and stop putting "boulders in the middle of their own stream".

**Tourmaline, Pink to Red:** Enables one to go with the normal flow of one's life rather than be in resistance to it. One does not surrender, but goes with the flow, in the direction of least resistance; but always toward what one wants to resolve in a situation.

## MODES

The Mode, is the way one goes about achieving one's goals in life. It is one's modus operandi: the way one operates in the world. All of the stones in this section, encourage one to use any of the Modes in the most positive way, and keep one balanced in the use of one's own Mode.

### Repression

The positive pole of Repression Mode involves a sense of restraint, discipline and refinement. Life is approached in a very polished, dignified and civilized fashion. Immediate reactions are held back, and raw emotions are expressed with constraint. People in Repression Mode have an air of reserve, are often elegant, and appreciate beauty and culture.

**Alexandrite:** A sophisticated stone that brings life to the more refined and elegant side. Represses unwanted energies from others.

**Buttgenbachite:** Contains impulsiveness, and puts one in touch with the internal monitor that keeps the expression of one's emotions appropriate. Encourages one to pay attention to the proper social behavior needed in any given situation. Encourages refined behavior.

**Euclase:** Motivates one to strive for excellence, and to achieve perfection. Makes one want to be exactly correct on all levels.

**Gmelinite:** Increases the delicacy of one's movements and creates an aura of refinement in general.

**Pseudoboleite:** Contains impulsiveness. Encourages one to pay attention to appropriate and proper social behavior. Encourages refined behavior.

**Tantalite:** Helps those in Repression use Passion Mode.

## Passion

People in Passion Mode live their lives in a very enthusiastic and passionate way. They are energetic and open, have a tendency toward strong emotional reactions, and are very involved with life. Passion Mode promotes the realization of one's ambitions and self-actualization.

**Coral, Apple:** Creates a feeling of enthusiasm for life, and a warm-hearted openness toward others. Eliminates fears of closeness.

**Coral, Blue:** Promotes a sense of adventurousness, and Peter Pan-like fun.

**Coral, Red, Pink & White:** Creates emotional openness in one's relationships with others, and a zesty enthusiasm for life. White emphasizes the qualities of love and affection, while the pinker or redder the Coral is, the more passionate and sexual it becomes. Red is more intense in its effect than pink.

## Caution

In the positive pole of Caution Mode, one proceeds in a deliberate, careful fashion, taking one's time and avoiding any unnecessary risks or dangers. The motto here is "look before you leap". People in Caution Mode are quite tactful and diplomatic, and their presence adds an element of stability.

**Antigorite:** Enables one to be cautious when necessary, without being overly fearful.

**Chalcocite:** Encourages one to be appropriately cautious.

**Citrine:** Use to slow things down, and to create a steady pace. Provides a sense of stability, especially when things are moving too quickly. Good combined with Power Mode stones or Peridot, as it makes the use of power or the process of growth steady and predictable, rather than impulsive. Also useful for the hyperkinetic, or those super high-energy folks who can't seem to calm down or slow down.

**Clinochrysotile:** Same in effect as Antigorite.

**Ferroaxinite:** Fosters a sense of caution about one's actions, thoughts, feelings, or one's communications. Encourages one to proceed carefully, deliberately, exactly, and to make sure that one has all bases covered.

## Power

A person in Power Mode projects an aura of strength and is very noticeable. Their presence is very commanding and people often look at them as figures of authority; as people who will know the answers. The aura of power is in their quality of being, rather than anything specific that they do.

**Agate, Fire:** Same in effect as Fire Opal.

**Agate, Orange with Yellow or Brown Stripes:** Makes one feel, as well as project to others, that one is grounded, self-sufficient, capable and trustworthy. Gives one an aura of strength and competence.

**Aquamarine:** Enhances one's personal powe,r and helps one project an aura of real strength. Commands others attention, even though one may privately feel unsure of one's strength. Helps one adjust to being authoritative and in control, without feeling wishy-washy about it.

**Piemontite Epidote:** A very powerful stone. Good for getting people motivated, and ready to go. Makes one feel infused with power, and "get up and go" energy. A good cure for laziness.

**Opal, Fire:** Allows one to project incredible charisma. Increases one's personal power and ability to operate effectively in the world.

**Quartz, Rutillated:** Enables one to project an aura of authority. Pulls one into powerfulness, and produces clarity with regard to what one is being powerful about. One not only looks very clear and capable of handling everything, but one feels that way as well.

**Rutile:** Adds power to whatever rock it flows through. The rock then becomes a magnifier of the power of one's own personal aura. One stands out as a more powerful or noticeable person, in one's way of being. It is important to note, that it is the power of one's presence that is augmented, rather than one's actions becoming more powerful, or having more power over another person.

### Perserverance

In the positive pole of Perserverance, one has a great deal of staying power, stick-to-itiveness and the ability to complete long-term tasks or karmas.

**Benavidesite:** Fosters feelings of security and stability.

**Boulangerite:** Same in effect as Jamesonite.

**Chalcocite:** Encourages one to perservere through any hardship. Increases one's emotional stamina, and ability to stick with it.

**Jamesonite:** For stability, security and steadfastness. Makes one feel grounded and secure, that one can perservere over very long periods of time regardless of what comes up.

**Jasper, Owyhee:** A combination of Uranian Agate (eccentric body type energy), bright red Jasper (aggressive energy and dynamism), and a pale yellow to green Jasper. The pale color is an aggresson calmer, so the entire combo would put one into Perserverance Mode with the Uranian Agate adding a higher intellectual or unique, eccentric way of looking at one's problems. Useful to have around when there is something one needs to deal with dynamically, but not too aggressively, over a long period of time. Enables one to come up with unusual solutions, for problems that are not easily solveable.

**Sanbornite:** Increases one's ability to perservere: to continue at a steady pace regardless of the circumstances.

**Strengite:** Enables one to perservere in the face of adversity.

**Tourmaline, Watermelon:** Increases one's "stick-to-itiveness" and the ability to perservere. Enables one to feel, as well as to project, that one is stable and reliable.

## Aggression

Those in the positive pole of Aggression Mode, are very dynamic, adventurous, risk-taking and assertive. They are willing to step in, and take action where others might hesitate.

**Cinnabar:** Enables one to be dynamic, and enhances everything that Aggression Mode entails. Especially good for those who are too meek and mild, or who have overleaves that are a little too submissive.

**Hemimorphite:** Enables one to be assertive, enthusiastic, and dynamic in one's undertakings.

**Jasper, Red:** Produces a dynamic and lively energy.

**Metahewettite:** Promotes one's ability to tackle one's problems forcefully, and move into action dynamically and appropriately.

**Omphacite:** Fills one with a sense of adventure. Increases boldness, and prepares one to tackle the next task with fervor.

## Observation

People in Observation Mode like to stand back, and take a look at what's happening before they move into action. They are very attentive to the environment, and aware of what's happening. They like clarity and neutrality in their perceptions

**Carminite:** Makes one extremely aware, and observant of what is happening in the present moment.

**Crystal, Clear:** For clarity of observation. The clearer the stone, the better for observation. Crystals produce clarity in whatever way they are used, and this clarity does not have to be visual. For example, if placed on a chakra, that chakra will become clear, and thus more healed or energized.

**Diaspore:** For clarity of observation about what is going on with one personally. Encourages one to look within, and see what one has been ignoring.

**Geodes:** Geodes are unique and individual. Each one represents a different observation about something that's true. One will be attracted to the Geode, that reminds one of a particular observation that one wishes to stay aware of.

**Diamond, Herkimer:** A more powerful version of clear Crystal.

**Milarite:** Sharpens one's observations. Helps one see things with greater clarity.

**Quartz, Snow:** An observation stone. When snowy in color rather than clear, one moves into "childlikeness" and can observe from a place of innocence. One's insights are fresh and clear, free of preconceptions, and free of "adult" cynical viewpoints. Sages are attracted to Snow Quartz because they grow up at a slow rate, and often feel like their bodies are maturing at a faster rate than they are.

## ATTITUDES

One's Attitude is one's basic point of view: the stance from which one looks at things, or how one goes about deciding what to do. All of the stones in this section, enable one to experience a point of view, or Attitude toward life other than one's own; and keep one balanced and positive, in the use of one's own Attitude.

### Stoic

In the positive pole, Stoics manifest an aura of tranquility, and emanate a sense of calm, peacefulness, and harmony. They reserve their emotions and are stable.

**Arrojadite:** Increases stoicism, and one's capability to be emotionally detached. Closes the Emotional Center down very tightly, so it is best not to use this stone unless one's circumstances warrant it.

**Dundasite:** Makes one calm, serene and reflective.

**Jade, Green:** Produces a tranquil attitude. Good to use when one is depressed. Resigns one to difficult or unpleasant aspects of life that cannot be avoided; those situations in life one simply has to handle. Allows one to feel more grounded and capable of dealing with difficulties.

**Jerrygibbsite:** Promotes a sense of calm. Enables one to remain serene, and to maintain one's perspective no matter what's happening.

## Spiritualist

The Spiritualist is a visionary, and is able to see the variety of possibilities inherent in a situation, and enjoys "pursuits of a philosophical nature".

**Celestite:** Inspires one to visionary and beautiful flights of fancy, while at the same time, enables one to keep a level head. Helps one feel comfortable with the "higher altitudes" of inspirational philosophy.

**Halite, Pink:** One feels visionary, larger than life, and inspired, when using this stone.

**Hambergite:** Pulls one into a spiritualistic, utopian viewpoint: i.e., inspired by utopian concepts and wonderful possibilities in the universe. Works on fomenting ideas rather than manifesting them.

**Moonstone:** A visionary stone. Reduces tunnel vision. Helps one achieve goals, by seeing the possibilities more clearly.

**Jade, Pakistan:** Enables one to come up with some great, wild, visionary ideas. Similar in effect to Hambergite.

**Jade, Southern:** Pulls one gently into Spiritualism, from Stoicism.

**Sonolite:** Puts one into a spiritualistic, visionary frame of mind, able to envision all possibilities and open new horizons.

## Skeptic

The Skeptic likes to investigate matters, and consider all aspects of a situation before acting. A Skeptic does not believe in anything without proof, and constantly strives for knowledge.

**Aerugite:** Reduces a tendency toward innappropriate cynicism or skepticism, and encourages one to look for positive solutions to problems. Gives one a sense that things will go well.

**Beraunite:** Increases one's ability to trust others. Pulls one out of the negative pole of Skeptic, and reduces suspiciousness, wariness, and innappropriate skepticism.

**Calcite, Orange:** A happiness stone. Reduces innappropriate skepticism, and puts one in the state of mind that everything is fine.

**Jade, Orange:** Useful when one is unsure of one's sophistication about life. Reduces any tendencies to be gullible and naive, about what's actually so.

**Jade, Pink:** Same in effect as Orange Jade.


## Idealist

The Idealist is an optimist, who can see how things should be if they were ideal. An Idealist strives continually to improve the status quo, and seeks ways to combine the best of all possibilities, into a unified whole.

**Acanthite:** Helps one be more idealistic, especially when ine is not an Idealist. Makes one feel more optimistic in general.

**Andorite:** Makes one feel generally more optimistic, and encourages one to be more idealistic.

**Jade, Lavender:** Useful when one feels too cynical or unimaginative. Skeptics like it, because it puts them in an optimistic mood.


## Cynic

The Cynic is able to see all the possible pitfalls, or contradictions inherent in a situation: is good at constructive criticism, and "questioning commonly held beliefs".

**Aerugite:** Reduces a tendency toward innappropriate cynicism or skepticism, and encourages one to look for positive solutions to problems. Gives one a sense that things will go well.

**Calcite, Black:** Allows one to look at things in the worst possible light, if that's what is needed. Reveals everything that could possibly go wrong. Thus, one can take precautions, or work through possible problems, instead of passing them over.

**Jet:** Wear when it is necessary to go into a situation with one's eyes open; e.g., being in a war where it's useful to stay survival oriented, or in business where much back biting occurs, or when being undermined,

**Perovskite:** Promotes healthy cynicism, especially in a person who is too gullible.

### Realist

The Realist is able to see a situation objectively and realistically.

**Anhydrite:** Gives a sense of being above, and objective about, any problem.

**Benjaminite with Aikinite:** Helps one to be realistic about the possibilities in the present, and in the near future.

**Burnite:** Encourages the realistic viewpoint, especially when worried about one's ability to see things objectively and remain neutral in a situation. Helps one see clearly what there is to see, without feeling either pessimistic or overly optimistic.

**Jade, White:** Makes it easy to perceive objective reality. Good for people who daydream or "float out of their bodies" a lot. Can have an extremely calming effect for those who usually can't tell what's going on. White Jade makes them feel grounded and that they know what's really so.

**Magnetite:** Pulls one into objective reality. Promotes a straight forward, reality oriented, truth-telling approach.

**Rumanite:** Same in effect as Burnite.

## Pragmatist

The Pragmatist is practical, efficient, and a sensible rule maker

**Freibergite:** Makes one more pragmatic. Puts one into a practical and reasonable frame of mind. Enables one to coolly and calmly perform tasks in the most logical manner.

**Topaz, Golden:** Useful for knowing what procedures will work in a particular situation. Enables one to delineate steps a, b, and c, without wasting time. Good with Garnets, as this combination will pull in practical ways of being productive.

## CENTERS

The Centers govern how we process data, how we process feelings, and how we respond to stimuli of any sort. Each Center corresponds to a chakra, but is the <u>psychological</u> or <u>experiential</u> component of that chakra. There are seven Centers: Instinctive, Higher-Moving, Moving, Emotional, Intellectual, Higher-Intellectual and Higher-Emotional.

Below is a chart which shows each chakra and the Center to which it corresponds. The Roles, and the chakra of specialization for each, are also included.

| Center | Chakra | Location | Role |
|---|---|---|---|
| Instinctive | First | Base of Spine | King |
| Higher Moving | Second | Pelvis | Artisan |
| Moving | Third | Solar Plexus | Warrior |
| Emotional | Fourth | Heart | Server |
| Intellectual | Fifth | Throat | Sage |
| Higher Intellectual | Sixth | Forehead | Scholar |
| Higher Emotional | Seventh | Top of Head | Priest |

The Instinctive Center stores survival information gathered in this life, or from past lives, and signals a warning when it senses similar possible dangers. This we experience by feeling that our survival is at stake. The three Higher Centers are transformational states of awareness, achieved during peak experiences or meditation states. They are always available for use, but are not lived in moment to moment.

The remaining three Centers, Moving, Emotional and Intellectual, are in constant use on an every-day basis. Even though all Centers are used, each person chooses a particular Center that he or she will specialize in during tha lifetime. This is referred to as one's "centering". In Michael terms, that person is then said to be "moving centered", "emotionally centered", or "intellectually centered."

Moving-centered people tend to be physically active, mechanically skilled, sport loving, and enjoy travel. Emotionally-centered people tend to be perceptive, psychic, have hunches, be more emotional or dramatic, and experience life through "likes and dislikes". Intellectually-centered people tend to be more verbal, well-read, educated, philosophical and logical.

Another set of terms you will encounter, refer to the various planes of existence. According to Michael, there are seven, basic planes of existence and certain types of lessons to be learned on each plane. A description of each plane of existence follows.

**Physical Plane:** Life on the planet Earth in the form of our physical bodies. This is where we experience being solid, being separate, and being forgetful.

**Astral Plane:** Life is begun here when we are no longer incarnating. It is also where we go in between lives. This is where we experience more advanced emotional lessons, and start to recombine with other souls most similar to ourselves. When 1000 or more souls have recombined, they are referred to as an "entity".

**Causal Plane:** Where the entity learns more advanced intellectual lessons, and the nature of cause and effect. This entity will recombine with another entity before advancing to the Mental Plane. The entity, Michael, teaches from the Causal Plane.

**Neutral Plane:** The Neutral Plane, or Akashic Record, is where all of the experiences in the Universe are recorded. It is an energetic "computer" which stores everything that happens, on all planes of existence. We, on the physical plane, do not have direct access to the Akashic Record.

**Mental Plane:** Here, the entity has direct intellectual contact with the Tao, and is most involved with higher truth and wisdom, as it is possible at this level, to have an intellectual perception of the whole. Many of the gemstones and minerals that stimulate the Higher-Intellectual Center, also connect one with the Mental Plane. Lao Tsu was an entity who taught from this plane.

**Messianic Plane:** Where one experiences total agape and unconditional love toward other beings. There is a direct emotional perception of the Tao and consciousness begins to grasp the infinity of the Universe. Many of the gemstones and minerals that stimulate the Higher-Emotional Center, also allow one to experience the energy of the Messianic Plane. Jesus Christ was an entity who taught from this plane.

**Buddhaic Plane:** Where one merges with the totality of the Universe, and ultimately, with the Tao. Many of the gemstones and minerals that stimulate the Higher-Moving Center, also provide an energetic experience of the Buddhaic Plane. Buddha was an entity who taught from the Buddhaic Plane.

**Tao:** The Tao is composed of all the physical, and all the non-physical elements, of all the planes of existence in the universe. It is the "Universal Consciousness", that contains the totality of all of the individual consciousnesses, of all sentient beings of all planets of origin. It is also referred to as the "Supreme Reality", the "All-Pervading Consciousness", and "All That Is". The entities of the other planes of existence, who make themselves available to us energetically, have evolved to their present state through the human form, and learned their Physical Plane lessons on the planet Earth.

When it is said that a certain gemstone or mineral connects with one with the energy of the Mental, Messianic, or Buddhaic Planes, that means the energy of that plane is made available for one to experience. They are an aid to experiencing the energy of planes beyond our current, physical existence.

Below is a chart which outlines these concepts. Notice the location of the three Higher Centers. Two are at the top of the head (6th and 7th chakras), and a third is located in the lower part of the body (2nd chakra). Michael says this is so higher-centered energy can flow throughout the body.

### Planes of Existence

| | |
|---|---|
| **Physical Plane** | **Mental Plane** |
| Physical lessons | Higher Intellectual |
| **Astral Plane** | **Messianic Plane** |
| Emotional lessons | Higher Emotional |
| **Causal Plane** | **Buddhaic Plane** |
| Intellectual lessons | Higher Moving |

The gemstones and minerals listed in this section, work specifically through one chakra, or sometimes, a combination of chakras to stimulate the Centers. This brings one into a balanced and clear experience of a Center, or combination of Centers. As indicated previously, many of these stones also enable one to connect with sources of "higher consciousness" on other planes of existence.

The ability to use all Centers appropriately, is considered important in Michael's system of personality, and one will find all of these stones useful at some time or another. We might suggest, though, that one always have a few Instinctive-Center stones around, since they keep us balanced and out of our survival issues.

### Emotional Center

The Emotional Center governs feeling states such as happiness, grief or anger, and the ability to be emotionally perceptive.

**Aurichalcite:** For stress-related emotional healing. Particularly useful when one has taken some real hard knocks emotionally, and the Emotional Center, (heart chakra), needs healing.

**Balyakinite:** Allows one to experience strong emotions with a feeling of safety, and a sense that one's emotions will stay appropriately in check.

**Calcite, Blue:** Removes blocks, so emotions can flow more easily.

**Calcite, Orange:** Increases feelings of happiness.

**Calcite, Red:** Keeps the heart open, and lets it feel protected and not so vulnerable. One feels that it's okay to open up, as any negativity one encounters will be flushed right out. Negative emotions are drained out of the body rather than held or absorbed.

**Clinotryolite:** Same in effect as Aurichalcite.

**Desautelsite:** Puts one in touch with one's deepest feelings. Encourages one to process one's issues emotionally, rather than intellectually.

**Franklinite:** Helps release emotional tensions. Keeps the emotions flowing in a steady fashion, so they don't become blocked.

**Heterosite:** For emotional openness. Puts one in touch with the Emotional Center, and opens up the emotions. Most useful for people who are emotionally blocked.

**Horn:** Makes one feel connected to other live, warm creatures, and feel that one is loved.

**Idocrase, Blue:** Balances the Emotional Cente,r and drains out excess energy.

**Lapis Lazuli:** Enhances neutral perceptivity. Not useful for calming down when one feels overly emotional: this stone does not affect the type of emotion felt, or its intensity. It allows one to perceive emotional issues more clearly.

**Mirabilite:** Increases one's emotional perceptivity, and empathic understanding of others.

**Plancheite:** Very strong healer, when one is going through tragedy or grief. Temporarily numbs the emotions until healing can begin, then, eases a person through the various stages of the grief process.

**Qingheiite:** Same in effect as Rosasite.

**Quartz, Elestial:** Opens the emotions, releases emotional blocks, and heals. Allows one to see one's emotional truths clearly.

**Rosasite:** Most useful when one is stuck in the negative pole of the Emotional Center, and experiencing only negative emotions. Stimulates the Moving or Intellectual Centers to produce an action or thought, that balances the Emotional Center. Good for those who are emotionally centered, as they most often get trapped in this manner.

**Smithsonite, Green or Blue:** Makes it easier to experience one's emotions, particularly if one has been emotionally blocked.

**Trippkeite:** Opens up one's ability to experience all emotions. Aids in experiencing love and joy to the fullest. If one has painful emotions to process, use this stone sparingly.

## Higher-Emotional Center

The Higher-Emotional Center governs one's connection to the Messianic Plane, and the experience of unconditional love and acceptance.

**Apatite:** An acceptance stone that with continued use, makes one unconditionally accepting of the people that come into one's life.

**Belovite:** Same in effect as Apatite.

**Beryllium:** Connects one strongly with the Messianic Plane and the experience of love for all.

**Bieberite:** Same in effect as Laramar.

**Bisbeeite:** Same in effect as Chrysocolla.

**Calcite, White:** Enables one to operate from a feeling of love and connectedness with the universe. Keeps the seventh chakra open, and gives a feeling of protection; i.e., that it is safe to operate from the higher centers. Also, one feels loving, and worthy of being loved by the Supreme Being, and worthy of being connected to, and experiencing higher planes of existence.

**Chalcanthite:** Opens one up to the feeling that one can love all mankind. Opens one up to spiritually-based, emotional experiences. Helpful to those who are intellectually or moving centered, and have difficulty experiencing their finer emotions. Connects one to the energy of the Messianic Plane.

**Chrysocolla:** Crystallizes feelings of higher-centered unconditional love, acceptance and tolerance toward specific others. Makes it possible to forgive others their wrongdoings towards oneself, and to be loving and understanding, using one's abililty to see such people clearly and objectively. Clarity of this Crystal is important: the clearer the Crystal, the clearer one's perceptions of others are. An outwardly directed stone. One becomes very perceptive and clear about others while using it, but not necessarily about oneself.

**Chrysoprase:** Very similar in both chemical composition, and function to Chrysocolla. A little more inwardly focused. One asks: "How can I be more loving and understanding and forgiving of this other person?" Perceptiveness about others, is not quite as sharp as with Chrysocolla. Clarity of stone is also very crucial with Chrysoprase. This stone is especially inspiring to Artisans.

**Clinoptilolite:** Puts one in touch with unconditonal love, acceptance, and tolerance toward others..

**Eilat:** A blend of Chrysocolla, Turquoise and Malachite. The Malachite keeps one balanced, and better able to use the higher-centered energies of the Chrysocolla and Turquoise.

**Gem Silica:** Same in effect as Chrysocolla, but stronger.

**Hiddenite:** Encourages Higher-Emotional or Higher-Moving Centered states. Connects one with the Messianic Plane or the Buddhaic Plane.

**Jasper, Parrot Wing:** A combination of Chrysocolla, Turquoise & Malachite. Same in effect as Eilat.

**Jokokuite:** Opens one to spiritually-based, emotional experiences. Enables one to feel a sense of lovingness toward all beings. A stone that is particularly appealing to children. The younger the child is, the stronger the attraction. The effect of this stone on a person, however, is the same regardless of age: it is only affinity to the stone that shifts. Similar in effect to Chalcanthite. Connects one with the energy of the Messianic Plane.

**Laramar:** For eternal love. Allows one to keep on loving where one has started loving. Also makes the wearer feel emotionally supported. Very useful when a relationship is undergoing stress and love may be jeopardized. Laramar ensures that the love that's underneath the obstacles and challenges, will still be there. Also good in a divorce or a split relationship, where both parties would like to remain friends.

**Spangolite:** Same in effect as Chalcanthite.

**Turquoise:** Centers one's being on love and connectedness with others. Pulls one into the experience of unconditional love for all beings. Creates a feeling of higher-centered emotional connectedness and love.

**Turquoise, Navajo:** A combination of Sard and Turquoise. Green Turquoise in a yellow-brown matrix. Centers one's being on love and connectedness with others. Also makes one feel secure, and "at home" no matter where one is.

## Intellectual Center

The Intellectual Center governs conceptualizing, thinking, gaining insight, and communication.

**Allophane:** Helps the brain work more efficiently to access those "tip of the tongue" thoughts, concepts or memories.

**Amber:** Clears one mentally. Pulls one away from emotional and moving-centered experiences, into an intellectual focus. Amber will also put an intellectual focus near the center it is worn closest to. When worn at the sixth chakra, eliminates confusion about what's really true, and increases mental clarity. When worn at the fifth chakra, one is more intellectual and thoughtful in one's communications. When worn at the fourth chakra, intellect guides the emotions. When worn at the third chakra, one has more intellectual clarity about one's career, health or power issues. A good, all-purpose balancer of the Intellectual Center.

**Amber, Honey:** Same in effect as the clear Amber, but with a more inspirational quality.

**Amber, Red:** Enhances the operation of the Intellectual Center, by containing or deleting negative emotion. Keeps one from being overly emotional, and is calming. Related to the Intellectual Center by default, as it keeps other influences out of the picture.

**Anthonyite** Enables one to keep an emotional balance while engaged in prolonged intellectual pursuits. Speeds basic data manipulations such as categorizing. Relieves the stress of continual hard thinking, and makes it easier to work longer on intellectual tasks without mental exhaustion.

**Bayleyite:** Promotes clarity of thinking, and eliminates mental confusion.

**Bellingerite:** Promotes mental clarity, and discourages fuzzy thinking.

**Burnite:** Enables one to continue to use the Intellectual Center, and stay clearly observant, even when in crisis or strongly emotional.

**Chloroxiphite:** Promotes strong spurts of intellectual growth. Enables one to learn new information in large chunks.

**Coral, Elephant Ear:** Stimulates one's passion for new philosophical concepts, and encourages intellectual pursuits.

**Datolite:** Produces clearer thinking.

**Goshenite:** Balances those who are intellectually centered, and have little or no emotional empathy. Corrects an inappropriate use of the Intellectual Center.

**Gypsum:** For intellectual clarity and competency. Certain colors work best for certain roles.

| | |
|---|---|
| Champagne: | King. |
| Clear: | Scholar. |
| Green: | Sage. |

| Lt. Brown: | Warrior. |
| White: | Artisans. |
| Yellow: | Server. |
| Yellow-Green: | Priest. |

**Hyalophane:** Focuses the mind, and increases mental activity. Enables one to think more quickly, and of more things.

**Jarosite:** Helps one gather scattered thoughts together, or bring diverse and confusing ideas into focus.

**Jasper, Brecchiated:** Heals mental stress. Makes it easier to be logical, clear headed and clear thinking. Wakes one up, and increases intellectual capacity.

**Richterite:** Gives one mental stamina. Enables one to keep paying attention, for long periods of time, to even somewhat boring material.

**Sapphire, Yellow:** Maintains one in the positive pole of the Intellectual Center. Makes it difficult to have opinions based on the inappropriate use of other Centers. Puts one directly in touch with one's knowledge, and enhances one's ability to learn and retain information.

**Smithsonite, Brown:** Encourages one to use the Intellectual Center more often.

**Triplite:** Same in effect as Amber.

**Topaz, White:** Opens up the Intellectual Center, and allows one to maintain a clear, intellectual focus. Similar in effect to Amber.

**Tourmaline, Yellow, Brown or Clear:** Assists one in endeavors that require intellectual processing.

**Wermlandite:** Increases one's curiousity, stimulates the Intellectual Center, and allows one to think for long periods of time without mental fatigue.

**Winstanleyite:** Stimulates the intellect, and allows one to think for long periods of time without mental fatigue.

## Higher-Intellectual Center

The Higher-Intellectual Center governs one's connection to the Mental Plane, and the experience of truth and wisdom.

**Betpakdalite:** Encourages one to think in a highly inspirational manner, and see the higher truth in things.

**Calcite, Brown or Gold:** Enhances one's capacity to know what is true. Makes one better able to appreciate such philosophers as Lao Tsu. Creates a state of joyous clarity.

**Esperite:** Enables one to get in touch with the overview of one's life, and to see the overlying patterns of one's existence. Helps one to identify one's purpose in life, and the tasks that will accomplish that purpose. Reveals to one, that which will advance the soul.

**Galena:** A truth stone. Aids in telling the truth, and in looking for what's true.

**Herrerite:** Enables one to open up one's psychic abilitie,s particularly where blocked.

**Howlite:** Brings new ideas into clear focus. Pulls one into artistic creation and inspiration. Helps one bring new things into one's life in a creative way. Artisans, in particular, enjoy using this stone.

**Jinshajiangite:** Leads one directly and with surety to one's personal truths and inner principles. Eliminates self-deception, and clarifies one's beliefs. Useful during meditation.

**Kyanite, Green:** Creates delighted shivers, and rushes of well being. Opens one to inspirational bursts of truth, love, or healing from higher planes of existence. Connects one with the energy of the Mental Plane.

**Pearls:** For wisdom. Each Pearl absorbs and holds, a different inspirational thought, and the energy of one doesn't blend with that of another. The more misshapen the Pearl, the more eccentric the thought.

**Pearls, Biwa:** Same in effect as Pearls, but for more eccentric thought.

**Sphalerite:** For transcending ego; for spirituality and empathy. It takes one beyond petty problems, and into a higher space of calm and true self-knowledge.

## Moving Center

The Moving Center governs movements of the body; i.e., walking, dancing, crocheting or just fidgeting. One also processes, through the Moving Center, issues that relate to power, health, career, travel, environment, mechanical skills, and prosperity.

**Bronzite:** Stimulates one to exercise.

**Duftite:** Makes it easier to learn any skill that involves the Moving Center. This includes, for example, basketweaving, car repair, woodcarving, and football.

**Epidote:** Promotes the mastery of one's own power. Enables one to remain powerful in a situation where another would like to cause harm, or undermine one's power.

**Jasper, Gray:** Makes it easier to own one's personal power, and feel that it cannot be taken away.

**Jasper, Red:** Produces a dynamic and lively energy, and puts one in touch with being powerful. Reduces feelings of victimization.

**Miargyrite:** Encourages athletic activity, and stimulates one to hone athletic abilities.

**Neptunite:** Increases self confidence. Same in effect as gray Jasper.

**Norbergite:** Stimulates one to act on one's thoughts or plans. If one is thinking about something, the impulse will occur to take some action, that handles whatever one was considering.

**Obsidian, Silver or Gold Sheen:** Energizes by getting one in touch with the movement of one's body. Stimulates one to engage in activities that promote bodily health.

**Opal, White:** Encourages usage of the Moving Center. Energizes the body, and makes one feel like getting a lot accomplished.

**Pistacite:** Same in effect as Epidote.

**Purpurite:** Keeps the Moving Center balanced, and action steadily occurring in every area of life governed by the Moving Center.

**Smithsonite, Yellow:** Makes one use the Moving Center more often, and feel ready for action when necessary.

**Spectrolite:** Similar in function to Bronzite. Stimulates one to exercise, dance, hop, and skip about.

**Strontianite:** Increases one's physical strength, by energetically encouraging the body to build muscle.

**Tiger Eye, Blue:** Same in effect as Spectrolite.

**Tiger Eye, Red:** Gives the Moving Center a rest. One can become too hyperactive in a moving-centered or physical way. Red Tiger Eye slows this Center down and flushes excess energy out of the body for sleep or rest.

**Witherite:** Helps control compulsive behavior by encouraging one to think before acting. Balances the use of the Moving Center. Compulsions are defined as being trapped in the Emotional Part of the Moving Center.

## Higher-Moving Center

The Higher-Moving Center governs beauty, sexuality, creativity and perfection of physical form. It also connects one to the Buddhaic Plane, where one feels a sense of connectedness and oneness with the Universe.

**Agate, Plume:** Opens up one's expression of sexuality and creativity. Enables one to be sexually open and less repressed. Plume Agate also enables one to express more creativity, and get past the tendency to be shy and hide one's talents.

**Calcite, Violet:** Enables one to feel harmoniously connected to, and at peace with, all that is. Makes one feel that everything is perfect just as it is. Connects one with the energy of the Buddhaic Plane.

**Creedite:** One feels directly connected to God: the Supreme Reality.

**Gaudefroyite:** Enables one to transcend ego, and one's sense of individual identity. Enables one to go beyond one's self, and feel a part of the greater whole.

**Granite:** One feels directly connected to God: the Supreme Reality.

**Hackmannite:** Same in effect as Sodalite.

**Hauynite:** Enables one to experience the connectedness of the whole, and oneness with the All. Promotes the ability to access subconscious symbols, to reach higher spiritual states of awareness. Connects one with the energy of the Buddhaic Plane.

**Heulandite:** Enables one to experience the connectedness of the whole, oneness with all that is, and awareness of the Supreme Reality. Connects one with the energy of the Buddhaic Plane.

**Joaquinite:** Balances the Higher-Moving Center. Healing particularly in the arena of one's sexual issues.

**Kammererite:** Gives one a sense of being at peace, a sense of harmony and connectedness with the whole, and at one. Connects one with the energy of the Buddhaic Plane.

**Lepidolite:** Same in effect as Kammererite.

**Natrojarosite:** Balances, and heals the Higher-Moving Center. Reduces sexual repression, and stimulates sexual passion.

**Opal, Black:** Connects one to the whole of humanity. Sexual connections are especially noticeable.

**Opal, Jelly:** Functions the same as the Black Opal, although it is not quite as powerful.

**Sodalite:** Increases the energy running through this Center. Increases ones sexuality, sexual attractiveness and creativity.

### Instinctive Center

The Instinctive Center governs automatic body functions, primal emotions, and drives. It contains memories of all past experiences and conflicts, and specializes in handling survival issues.

**Abalone:** Healing to the Instinctive Center. While wearing Abalone, one feels calmer and less afraid.

**Agate, Leopard Skin:** Balances and heals the Instinctive Center. Very grounding and healing when dealing with heavy emotional issues. Reduces free-floating anxiety; i.e., when one is worried and anxious, but doesn't know why. Good for anyone, but especially grounding for people who are paranoid or schizophrenic, or those who are totally unstable and cannot handle life.

**Agate, Turitella:** Calming to the Instinctive Center. Puts one in touch with any instinctive-centered fears, or survival issues, and helps one neutralize them.

**Ambroid:** Enables one to maintain an intellectual focus, even when one's consciousness is dominated by instinctive fears or survival issues.

**Amianth:** Opens the Instinctive Center very quickly and very widely. Useful for those who need to do instinctive-center work and are very shut down.

**Aventurine, Blue:** Keeps the Instinctive Center, and the feet, open and unblocked so energy can flow through unimpeded.

**Benjaninite:** Heavy-duty Instinctive Center healer and anesthetic: like pouring a gelatinous bandage over the Instinctive Center. Useful when one has seen, or participated in, very traumatic circumstances such as murder, rape, or war. Later on, when numbing is no longer appropriate, and when one is ready to process the experience, this stone can be put aside and another Instinctive Center healer chosen.

**Bone:** Healing and calming to the Instinctive Center. Same in effect as Ivory, except that Ivory has a more refined energy. Grounds the body, and while wearing Bone, all actions will be sensible and calm.

**Cameo Shell:** Good for eliminating bad habits. Opens the Instinctive Center, and allows evaluation of the usefulness of any particular habit.

**Chinese Writing Stone:** Calms the Instinctive Center.

**Coral, Apple:** Calms instinctive fears. Creates a feeling of enthusiasm for life.

**Coral, Black:** Major healer of instinctive-centered fear. There are two basic emotions in the universe--fear and love. When one is healed of fear, what is left is love. Black Coral heals fears, by helping one to examine what's going on; i.e., opens the Instinctive Center and brings up instinctive material to process. This includes past lives.

**Flint:** Heals one of survival fears. Good when one has had very difficult survival experiences. Makes one feel that one can survive no matter what.

**Gratonite:** A survival stone. Helps one to believe that even under the most difficult of living situations, such as poverty, starvation, and extreme illness, that one can not only survive, one can thrive against all odds. The promotion of this attitude enables one to keep going when others would lose heart.

**Grossular, Gray to Black:** Heals the Instinctive Center. Particularly good when facing survival issues such as the loss of a job. Functions similarly to Bone.

**Idocrase, Yellow-Green or Brown:** Balances the Instinctive Center and drains out excess energy.

**Ivory:** Strong instinctive healer. Helps to calm basic fears about survival. Makes one feel that survival is not an issue. When worn on the chest, one's emotions will not be coming from survival-related fear. When worn at the ears, it produces inspiration about ways to solve survival issues.

**Jade, Brown or Gray:** Very relaxing: it drains excess energy from all chakras out through the Instinctive Center. When worn during the day, keeps excess energy from building up, and helps one to operate from a more relaxed state.

**Jasper, Morrison Ranch:** Useful in doing Instinctive Center work such as past-life regressions. Helps bring instinctive issues to the surface, and makes one feel more comfortable handling them.

**Lawsonite:** Calms instinctive fears. Same in effect as Leopard Skin Agate.

**Lizardite:** Calms the Instinctive Center. Enables one to access primitive, instinctive fears: i.e, brings one's fears up to conscious awareness so they can be processed.

**Ludlamite:** Very calming to the Instinctive Center, particularly when it is "blasted." When the Instinctive Center has been severely taxed, one can behave in some rather bizarre ways that society might label "crazy". This rock is strong enough to calm even the most severely stressed Instinctive Center.

**Morrisonite:** Same in effect as Morrison Ranch Jasper.

**Mother of Pearl:** Same in effect as Abalone, except it is more useful for those with ordinal Modes, Goals, and Attitudes. Very strong Instinctive Center healer.

**Obsidian, Black:** Same in effect as Leopard-Skin Agate.

**Obsidian, Rainbow:** Calms, relaxes, and heals one of survival fears. Makes one feel safe. Also balances those who are mentally unstable due to extreme chemical imbalances, such as that found in Schizophrenia or Manic Depressive llnesses.

**Petrified Wood:** Calms instinctive fears. Extremely grounding. Makes one feel they are a part of agelessness; nothing could go wrong. One feels one will last forever.

**Scheelite:** Balances and opens the Instinctive Center. Good because this Center is so often closed down.

**Siderite:** Same in effect as Blue Aventurine.

**Yecoraite:** Same in effect as Benjaninite.

## Center Combinations

The following stones pull one into an experience of two or more Centers.

**Aragonite:** Enables one to have an emotional focus, as well as an intellectual focus, and combine that with the truth-accessing ability of the sixth chakra. Thus, one simultaneously operates from a high degree of emotional perceptivity, intellectual clarity, and the ability to see truth from a higher perspective and psychically sense the flow of things. Prevents one from being overly emotional, or too dry intellectually. This stone will not be very attractive to those who like a lot of drama in their lives, or who are uncomfortable feeling very truthful.

**Asbolan:** Enables one to bring up feelings of hate, anger, and revenge, so that they can be dealt with. Particularly good for those who are in therapy. Lifts the repression of such feelings, and the issues surrounding them. Use this rock sparingly and consciously. Balances and opens the Instinctive, Emotional, and Higher-Moving centers.

**Aventurine, Green:** Green Aventurine is particularly good for those who have been viewed as abnormal by the culture, such as those who are very high-female energied (i.e., flaky) or those who are very high-male energied (very focused and often scary particularly when combined with a low frequency). Feeling abnormal makes it more difficult to keep the Higher-Intellectual and Higher-Emotional Centers open, which allow one to operate from universal truth and love. This stone curtails the tendency to shut down, and operate from instinctive, survival fears.

**Aventurine, Red:** Aligns the Moving, Emotional, Intellectual, and Higher-Moving Centers, and enables them to work in a blended fashion. Very important and powerful stone.

**Barytocalcite:** Balances, opens, and stimulates the Emotional, and Higher-Emotional Centers. Fosters emotional strength, and clarity with regard to the emotions.

**Calcite, Blue:** Unblocks all the Centers. Very intense and rapid in its effect. Similar to the Aventurines, although the latter operate more slowly and are gentler in effect.

**Carnotite:** Heals and balances the Instinctive, Emotional, and Intellectual Centers. Allows them to work together in a blended fashion.

**Dypingite:** Balances and heals the Moving, Emotional, and Intellectual Centers. Particularly good for closing them down when abused.

**Fluorite:** Keeps others from making energetic attachments that are not desired. Balances all Centers. Wonderful for removing negative influences.

**Galena:** A truth stone. Aids in telling the truth, and in looking for what's true. Operates through the Intellectual and Higher-Intellectual Centers.

**Idocrase, Green:** Balances the Moving and Higher-Moving Centers, and drains out excess energy.

**Idocrase, Yellow:** Balances the Intellectual and Higher-Intellectual Centers, and drains out excess energy.

**Jade, Black:** Balances, opens, and integrates the Instinctive, Moving, and Higher-Moving Centers, which involve survival, sex and power, so one can be appropriate with all three. Good to wear when one wants to open up, but feels attacked or that survival is an issue.

**Malachite:** Balances and heals all Centers. Very strong in effect. One of the most powerful balancing stones. Impossible to be around Malachite for long, and remain unbalanced.

**Opal, Sonoma:** Balances the Emotional, and Higher-Moving Centers. Creates a link between these two Centers, and keeps them operating in a blended fashion. This stabilizes the emotions of one who is involved in a sexual relationship, or a creative project.

**Septarian Nodule:** Balances the Emotional, Intellectual, and Higher-Intellectual Centers. Enables them to operate in a blended fashion. This combination enhances the ability to perceive higher truth and love.

**Smithsonite:** Smithsonite comes in several colors. Each color works on a different Center. In general, the effect is to pull one into the use of a particular Center, and to clear that Center of any blockage.

> **Green or Blue:** Makes it easier to experience one's emotions, particularly if they've been blocked.
> **Purple:** Pulls one into the Higher-Intellectual Center, and makes it easier to use psychic abilities.
> **Brown:** Makes one more intellectually centered.

**Yellow:** Makes one more moving centered, and ready for action.

**Pink:** Helps make children more psychic. Can also be used by adults, but more useful for children.

**Yttrocerite:** Same in effect as Fluorite.

## CHIEF NEGATIVE FEATURES

The Chief Negative Feature, is the only overleaf that is not chosen prior to the lifetime. Instead, it is selected sometime prior to one's 20th birthday, and occasionally later. Chief Features are based on fear, and are pulled into use in an attempt to protect one's self, when one feels off balance or threatened. While all Chief Features are used at one time or another, each person has a favorite that they use most frequently, and this "favorite" is referred to as one's Chief Negative Feature. Chief Negative Features also stimulate growth, as they form a primary stumbling block that makes it possible to learn about the characteristics, and consequences, of the associated fear.

The gemstones in this section work in several ways. Some make one more aware that one is in one's Chief Negative Feature, and this awareness softens the Feature, by making it more difficult to continue. Others pull one into the positive pole, and as one begins to manifest the positive aspects of the Chief Negative Feature, one begins to move out of it. The third type of effect, is that the stone simply puts one into a different place altogether. A good example of this is Chalcopyrite, which changes one's self-deprecatory feelings to positive self regard, and an ability to see one's self in a positive light.

### Self-Deprecation

With Self-Deprecation, one's self worth is felt to be very low. The basic fear is that of being inadequate: of not being good enough. Those with a Feature of Self-Deprecation constantly compare themselves to others, and never feel they quite measure up. In the positive pole, Self-Deprecation becomes appropriately humble, and one is gentle and unassuming. In the negative pole, a person in Self-Deprecation is self abasing, dresses poorly, and allows themselves little in the way of satisfactory jobs, relationships, or material possessions.

**Agate, Copco:** Same in effect as Carnelian. A very balancing and healing energy, surrounded with the loving emotionality of the Venusian body-type Agate.

**Bixbyite:** Reduces the fear of not measuring up to the standards of others. Enables one to feel more comfortable with one's "differentness", whether real or imagined.

**Carnelian:** Softens Self-Deprecation and Arrogance, particularly Self-Deprecation. Allows one to temporarily put aside major self-esteem issues. Gives one a break from needing to be better than anyone else, or agonizing over how inferior one feels. This creates the space for some positive feedback to flow in.

**Chalcopyrite:** Boosts self-esteem and increases positive self regard. The energy of this stone keeps one feeling good about one's self, and seeing one's self in a positive light. While many stones affect a Chief Feature by helping one notice what one is doing, this stone works to change how one actually feels about oneself.

**Chromite:** Softens Self-Deprecation. Makes one notice how self-deprecating one is being, and then it becomes too embarrassing to continue. Usually found with Kammererite which connects one with the Buddhaic Plane. Hard to maintain belief that one is worse than everyone else, when one feels a part of everything that is.

**Columbite:** Aids one in feeling more self confident, by decreasing timidity, false humility, and self deprecation.

**Coquimbite:** Boosts self esteem, and fosters feelings of adequacy. Makes one feel proud of the things that one has accomplished. Pulls one out the negative pole of Self-Deprecation into the positive pole of Arrogance.

**Gorceixite:** Increases one's self confidence. Makes it easier to believe in one's self. Different colors work best for different types of Roles. Choose the color one resonates to the most, if one's Role is unknown. When found as a mixture of colors such as yellow-green or orange-red, it works equally well for all Roles.

| | |
|---|---|
| Red: | Priests and Servers. |
| Orange: | Sages and Artisans. |
| Yellow: | Kings and Warriors |
| Green: | Scholars. |

**Powellite:** Builds self esteem, and imbues one with a sense of dignity. Particularly good for those who were brought up not to believe in themselves.

**Serandite:** Makes it easy for one to believe in one's own valuableness to others. Encourages the feeling that others would like to spend time with one, work with one, or love one.

**Garnet, Spessartite:** Softens Self-Deprecation and Arrogance. Makes one feel contented and happy with one's niche in life. Fosters the awareness that it is unnecessary to be self-deprecating or arrogant.

**Spinel, Peach:** Softens Self-Deprecation and Arrogance. Makes it easy to notice when one has just said, or done, something self-deprecating or arrogant.

**Spinel, Yellow:** Softens Arrogance and Self-Deprecation. Pulls one into the positive pole of Arrogance. This enables one to push away from Self-Deprecation, into a feeling of pride. Particularly good for people who are extremely self-deprecating.

**Zippeite:** Same in effect as Carnelian.

## Arrogance

Arrogance is low self esteem covered by a facade of 'I'm O.K.", or with an air of superiority. While one may appear to be self confident, underneath there is a fear of being judged and found wanting. A person with the Chief Feature of Arrogance feels vulnerable and fears exposure. Interestingly enough, shyness is a form of arrogance. In the positive pole, a person in Arrogance takes pride in themselves, and works to make themselves appear worthy in their own eyes. In the negative pole, Arrogance can be haughty and judgmental of one's self and others.

**Amblygonite:** Reduces Arrogance by taking the attention off the self. Directs one's attention outward to noticing other people or one's surroundings, and enables one to tune into the situation in which one finds oneself. Different colors are better for certain types:
>    **Colorless:** Good for all.
>    **Violet:** For fluid types: a person who's more flowing,
>    **Golden Yellow to Yellow:** For solid types: a person who is very grounded and organized.

**Billietite:** Softens Arrogance, and reduces the tendency to be self centered. Enables one to stop focusing on one's self so exclusively, and begin to turn one's attention outward to noticing others. Decreases the feeling that one is "alone in the world."

**Celadonite:** Deflates Arrogance, by making one exquisitely aware of one's own flaws. Since one can cringe under such ruthless self scrutiny, it is recommended one use this rock along with those that promote self-esteem or self-love.

**Coquimbite:** Boosts self esteem, and makes one feel proud of the things that one has accomplished. Pulls one into the positive pole of Arrogance.

**Donathite:** Softens Arrogance. Makes one notice when one is being arrogant or bossy. Encourages one to soften one's approach if indicated.

**Emerald:** Softens Arrogance. Brings up the question, "Am I thinking I am better than anyone else? I know I'm privileged, rich, and good-looking, but am I using this to make me think I'm better than somebody else?" Sages, Kings, and Priests are particularly prone to this problem.

**Goudeyite:** Decreases Arrogance, and keeps one from having "shy episodes:" i.e., that agonizing flipping back and forth between Self-Deprecation and Arrogance. This stone short-circuits the process. Good for children because they usually go through episodes of this.

**Garnet, Spessartite:** See Self-Deprecation.

**Spinel, Peach**: See Self-Deprecation.

**Spinel, Yellow**: See Self-Deprecation.

## Self-Destruction

Self-Destruction is characterized by an act, or the motivation to harm oneself either physically or emotionally. A person in Self-Destruction feels too unworthy to exist, and thinks that they can never have what they want in life. The fear is that life will never be worth living.

In the positive pole, a person in Self-Destruction can be self-sacrificing, perhaps dying in order to save others. In the negative pole, they can be suicidal, have little self esteem, and have self-destructive habits and beliefs. To move out of Self-Destruction, Michael recommends aiming for the positive pole of Greed, in order to foster the feeling that one can have what one wants in life.

**Amazonite**: Softens Self-Destruction, and pulls one into the positive pole of Greed. Makes one notice how self-destructive it is to take one drink too many, or engage in some other excessive behavior that is not in one's best interests. Gives one the feeling that it is possible to have whatever one wants.

**Manjiroite**: Softens cruelty toward self or others. Operates by reducing the internal stress state that causes one to engage in compulsively destructive acts. Examples of such behaviors might be pulling the wings off butterflies, burning one's self or a child with cigarettes, or slashing one's arm with razor blades. The intention behind these behaviors is to reduce the pain one feels inside. Manjiroite opens one up to other ways of reducing the pain, and makes one see how inappropriate such behaviors are.

**Microcline**: Same in effect as Amazonite. Stronger in its ability to make one see how unnecessary self-destructive behaviors are. Generic Microcline is white or pink, and Amazonite is the blue-green variety of Microcline.

## Greed

The Chief Feature of Greed arises out of the experience of wanting or desiring, coupled with a fear there will not be enough to go around.  The positive pole of Greed manifests as a lust for life, and an ability to appreciate one's experiences and possessions.  It is marked by the quality of "high havingness".  In the negative pole of Greed, one can become voracious, find it difficult to be satisfied, and go on binges to overcome the fear that there will not be enough.

**Astrophyllite:**  Makes one feel wealthy and contented with whatever one has.  One notices and appreciates what one has:  promotes a sense of abundance and prosperity.

**Bloodstone:**  Pulls one into the positive pole of Greed.  Engenders a strong feeling that it is all right to have what one wants, and that it is only a matter of time until one gets it.  Produces high prosperity consciousness, and willingness for abundance to show up in one's life.  Makes one feel confident that life will be good.

**Jasper, Nunkirchner:**  Same in effect as Bloodstone.

**Merwinite:**  Same in effect as Bloodstone.

## Martyrdom

Martyrdom is characterized by the feeling that one is a victim of the circumstances, and that those circumstances are beyond one's control.  A person with the Chief Feature of Martyrdom, most fears being out of control, and at the same time, is often unable to see that one really is in control of one's own life.

In the negative pole of Martyrdom, one feels victimized, out of control, and tries to control others by making them feel guilty.  In the positive pole, a person in Martyrdom can be selfless, and give much time and energy to the care of others, or to support a spiritual cause.

**Barkevikite:**  Gives one a sense that one is in control of one's body, one's environment, and one's destiny.  Enables one to get in touch with, and use, one's will power.

**Bowenite:** Anti-martyrdom stone. Eases one's sense of being victimized by others, or by one's circumstances. Also useful for those in Impatience or Stubbornness who use Martyrdom occasionally.

**Epidote:** Promotes the mastery of one's own power. Enables one to remain powerful in a situation where another would like cause harm, or undermine one's power.

**Erythrite:** Softens Martyrdom, and pulls one into the positive pole. Fosters one's capacity for selflessness. Good for those who have a tendency to be self centered, and thinking only of their own needs.

**Iolite, Gray:** Makes one feel confident about one's ability to take charge of one's life and be successful, particularly in the arena of one's career. Makes it difficult to feel that one is a victim of the circumstances.

**Jasper, Gray:** Makes it easier to own one's own personal power, and to have confidence that one's power cannot be taken away.

**Neptunite:** Same in effect as Gray Jasper.

**Pistacite:** Same in effect as Epidote.

**Soapstone, Pale Green:** Same in effect as Bowenite.

**Unikite:** Enables one to completely and totally take charge of one's own life. Helps protect personal power, and fosters a sense that one is the guardian of one's own fate and cannot taken over by anyone else.

## Impatience

Impatience is the Chief Feature most ruled by time. A person in Impatience has difficulty being in the present moment, and often feels there will not be enough time. The fear is that one will miss out on something important. In the positive pole, a person in Impatience can be audacious and daring. In the negative pole, Impatience is characterized by intolerance, and a constant feeling of being pressured.

**Amethyst:** Softens Impatience. Gives one a feeling that there is time enough for everything. When feelings of impatience start to pop up, they are immediately followed by the awareness that there's no need to rush. Extremely popular, since most people at one time or another, feel victimized by the circumstances in their lives.

**Danburite:** Enables one to be more patient. Particularly good for the very heavily impatient, and those who can be extremely intolerant; for the type of person who will hyperventilate if caught in a traffic jam, because they can't stand the slow pace.

**Romerite:** Same in effect as Danburite.

## Stubbornness

Stubborness is used as a braking mechanism to slow down the growth process, and to enable one to resist situations that seem threatening. In the positive pole, a person in Subbbornness operates with a great deal of determination and purpose, and has the ability to overcome obstacles to get what they want. In the negative pole, a person in Stubbornness can become obstinate, even when this is not in their best interest, and be unable to listen to the advice or suggestions of others. The fear is of being pushed beyond one's limits and being overwhelmed, or of losing one's self.

**Agate, Blue, White & Lavender Lace:** Softens Stubbornness. Provides an especially strong feeling of security, that if any new situations arise they can be handled. One feels assured that one will not have to do something one doesn't want to do, or be plunged into something overwhelming. This makes it easier for even the most stubborn person to be more flexible.

**Agate, Sagenite:** Softens silent stubbornness, and makes one more willing to share one's communications

**Azurite:** Enables one to be in better communication with others, by fostering a willingness to listen. Gives a secure sense that one can listen in a flexible manner, and still maintain one's own position.

**Tiger Eye, Gold:** Works in an unusual fashion. Pulls one into the positive pole of one's Attitude, while it softens stubbornness, making it possible to be determined rather than obstinate. Especially effective for those who are very stubborn.

### All Chief Features

There are several stones that <u>erase</u> <u>all</u> <u>Chief</u> <u>Negative</u> <u>Features</u>, and pull one into the positive pole of one's Attitude. This enables one to handle stresses in a balanced fashion, without being too stubborn, too impatient, too martyred, too self-deprecatory or arrogant, or too self-destructive or heedless. One will also be able to maintain a positive point of view, in which one is tranquil, optimistic, open-minded and realistic.

**Agate, Brecchiated:** Reduces all Chief Features, and pulls one into the positive pole of one's Attitude.

**Agate, Canal:** Same stone as Brecchiated Agate.

**Agate, Tubular:** Same stone as Brecchiated Agate.

**Jasper, Bruneau:** Same in effect as Brecchiated Agate. It is especially effective, for enabling one to handle crises or difficult challenges, in a balanced fashion.

**Jasper, Rim:** Reduces all Chief Features, and pulls one into the positive pole of one's Attitude.

**Jasper, Wood:** Same in effect as Rim Jasper.

# Body Types

Choosing a body type is similar to choosing an overleaf. It is chosen prior to birth, and will in some way facilitate the lessons and karmas for that particular life. The effect of body type is less than that of the other overleaves, but still impactful. The body type determines one's physical characteristics, colors one's personality traits, and influences one's psychological strengths and weaknesses, including one's emotional and intellectual capacities.

There are seven basic body types which correspond to the Sun, the Moon, and the five closest planets: Mercury, Venus, Mars, Saturn, and Jupiter. Most individuals will choose a body type that comes under the influence of two or more planets: for example, 70% Venusian, 20% Mercurial and 10% Lunar. Pure body types are rare, and are found mainly in mythology, fairy tales or archetypes. There are three additional body types, associated with the more distant planets Uranus, Neptune, and Pluto. These influences are chosen more rarely, and used for more obscure karmas.

Below are listed the ten body types, along with a series of adjectives that best describe the psychological and physiological characteristics of each. Included are the stones most energetically representative of each body type. In developing descriptions for these stones, and effort was made to capture the essence of each body type fully. Brevity, however, is always somewhat limiting, and in studying the longer list of adjectives, one might develop a fuller, more comprehensive sense of each body type and what it involves.

The gemstones and minerals described here, give one an energetic experience of what it is like to have a partituclar body type. These stones will also help one to heal conflicts, that have characteristics typical of a particular body type. For example, if one has a hard time relaxing into one's sensuality, a Venusian body-type Agate or stone will help resolve the problem.

## SOLAR

**Sun:** Refined features. Slight figure. Radiant. Creative. Lighthearted. Cheerful. Elegant. Dignified. Fun-loving. Child-like. Innocent. Androgynous.

**Agate, Arizona:** Brings out warm, sensuous, sunny, light, and androgynous qualities. A body-type Agate mixing qualities that correspond to Solar and Venus body types.

**Agate, Pale to Bright Yellow:** Puts one in a fun-loving, lighthearted and cheerful mood. A Solar body-type Agate.

**Agate, Yellow with White Stripes:** A Solar body-type Agate.

**Asbecasite:** Balances, strengthens, and improves the physical stamina of the Solar body types.

## LUNAR

**Moon:** Luminous. Pale skin. Moon faced. Passive. Patient. Tenacious. Sensitive. Imaginative. Maternal. Sympathetic. Receptive. Calm. Methodical. Solitary. Detail oriented. Mathematical. Can have genius intelligence.

**Agate, Gray or Brown-Gray with White Stripes:** Makes one appreciative of intellectual pursuits and promotes abstract, creative thought. A Lunar body-type Agate.

**Agate, Pink with Gray and White Stripes:** A Lunar body-type Agate. .

## VENUSIAN

**Venus:** Full-bodied. Voluptuous. Soft. Warm. Loving. Approachable. Adept in the art of harmony. Gentle. Non-judgmental. Sensual. Extremely loyal. Appreciative of beauty.

**Agate, Arizona:** Brings out warm, sensuous, sunny, light, and androgynous qualities. A body-type Agate mixing qualities that correspond to Solar and Venus body types.

**Agate, Copco:** (Carnelian with a thin layer of white Agate on top). A very balancing and healing energy surrounded, with the loving emotionality of the Venusian body-type Agate.

**Agate, Snake Skin:** Puts one in a sensual loving mood, appreciative of the body and its sensations. A Venusian body-type Agate.

**Agate, White or White with White Stripes:** Puts one in a sensual, loving mood, appreciative of the body and its sensations. A Venusian body-type Agate.

**Chloanthite**: Encourages one to take on the qualities of the Venusian body type: to be sensuous, soft, warm, and emotional.

## MERCURIAL

**Mercury**: Slender and quick moving. Intellectually active and perceptive. Clever. Versatile. Able to communicate clearly through speech. Sunny disposition. Youthful appearance.

**Agate, Black with White Stripes**: Makes one very alert and ready for action. A Mercurial body-type Agate.

## MARTIAL

**Mars**: Red hair and skin commonly with freckles. Very active physically, emotionally and intellectually. Decisive. Freedom-loving. Pioneering. Direct. Brutally honest. Strong leader in crisis. Highly productive. Energetic. Passionate. Highly sexed.

**Agate, Orange with White Stripes**: Makes one feel vigorous, energetic and ready to take on challenges. Increases one's willingness to take risks, or to be adventurous. A Martial body-type Agate.

## JOVIAL

**Jupiter**: Santa Claus or Falstaff type. Short and stout. Magnanimous. Compassionate. Generous. Caring and maternal. Philosophical in outlook. Breadth of vision. Well-directed mental powers. Good fortune. Sense of justice.

**Agate, Green or Green with White Stripes**:. Promotes happiness, expansiveness and sociability. A Jovial body-type Agate.

## SATURNIAN

**Saturn:** Uncle Sam or Abe Lincoln type. Large boned. Prominant features. Serious but gentle appearance. Self-controlled. Good natural leader. Diplomatic. Moderate. Trustworthy. Paternal. Capacity for long-thought and good memory.

**Agate, Orange with Yellow or Brown Stripes:** Makes one feel, as well as project to others, grounded, self-sufficient, capable and trustworthy. Gives one an aura of strength and competence. A Saturnian body-type Agate.

## NEPTUNIAN

**Neptune:** Dreamy, creative and unworldly in appearance. Large, saucer-like eyes. Idealistic. Spiritual. Imaginative. Sensitive. Subtle. Artistically creative.

**Agate, Blue with White Stripes:** Puts one in a dreamy, visionary, almost psychic frame of mind in which it becomes easier to appreciate questions of a spiritual nature. A Neptunian body-type Agate.

## URANIAN

**Uranus:** Pale or unusual skin. Large bodied. Natural drive towards fame as Yul Brunner or Grace Jones. Independent. Original. Loathing restrictions. Strong-willed. Versatile. Inventive. Sensuous. Humanitarian. Good-willed. Often naturally or deliberately bald.

**Agate, Mustard Yellow:** Puts one in a creative, imaginative and unusually inventive mood: Original and fresh in approach. A Uranian body-type Agate.

# PLUTONIAN

**Pluto:** Intellectually brilliant. Able to see the big picture. Transforming, able to evoke transformation in others. Able to see through deceptions or conventions.

**Agate, Brown with Gray, Black or Clear Stripes:** Enables one to invoke transformation in one's self and others. One becomes a catalyst for transformation. A Plutonian body-type Agate.

## BODY-TYPE AGATES

| Agate | Body Type |
|---|---|
| White or White with White Stripes | Venusian |
| Black with White Stripes | Mercurial |
| Green or Green with White Stripes | Jovial |
| Pink with Gray and White Stripes<br>Brown-Gray with White Stripes<br>Gray with White Stripes | Lunar |
| Orange with White Stripes | Martial |
| Pale to bright Yellow<br>Yellow with White Stripes | Solar |
| Orange with Brown Stripes<br>Orange with Yellow Stripes | Saturnian |
| Blue with White Stripes | Neptunian |
| Mustard Yellow | Uranian |
| Brown with Gray, Black and Clear Stripes | Plutonian |
| Creamy with White Stripes | Solar/Venusian |

# Michael's Miscellaneous

## THE CHANNEL

The stones in this section accomplish two things: 1) They enable one to connect with those beings of higher consciousness in the universe, who are one's spirit guides and teachers. 2) They enable one to channel beings of higher consciousness for the purpose of communication to others.

Channeling is defined as bringing an energy from a higher plane of existence, an energy that is not one's own, into one's body to be shared with others. This energy then translates into intellectual information one can communicate, an emotional impact one can create, or healing energy one can use to enhance well being. The channel, is a vehicle through which beings of higher consciousness, can facilitate the spiritual growth of their students on the Physical Plane. "Channeling one's own essence", or "higher self", is not what we mean by channeling. We define "channeling one's higher self" as being in touch with that aspect of one's self that is wisest. "Channeling one's spirit guides" means channeling Astral entities who are personally interested in aiding one's spiritual development.

Gemstones and minerals aid the channel in three specific ways. 1) They keep the chakras open. 2) They keep the chakras balanced and aligned, and the channel gounded. 3) They aid the channel in focusing on the specific source of higher consciousness they wish to contact.

## Opening the Chakras

The stones discussed below, enhance one's ability to remain open to allowing the channeled energy into one's body. Most channels bring this energy in through the seventh chakra, though not all, and all the chakras need to be open, so energy can flow in and out freely. A more comprehensive list of stones that have this same effect, can be found in the section, "Balance and the Chakras".

**Apachite:** Opens the seventh chakra. This opens one to spiritual information from higher sources.

**Aventurine, Green:** Opens and unblocks the sixth and seventh chakras

**Cobalt Glass:** Opens the seventh chakra.

**Chalcanthite:** Opens the seventh chakra. The effect is very strong and it is important to be grounded and have all chakras aligned and balanced before using this stone to channel.

**Jokokuite:** Opens the seventh chakra. Similar in effect to Chalcanthite.

**Spangolite:** Same in effect as Chalcanthite.

**Sugilite:** Very powerful channeling stone. Opens up all chakras to higher influences, particularly the seventh chakra.

## Aligning and Balancing Chakras

These gemstones and minerals keep all the chakras aligned and balanced, so the intense channeled energy doesn't deplete or exhaust the physical body. This will also enable one to channel for a longer period of time.

**Amethyst:** Balances and heals all chakras, particularly the third and seventh chakras. Keeps one grounded while channeling.

**Aventurine, Red:** Unblocks and balances the second through fifth chakras.

**Aragonite:** Keeps chakras four, five, and six open, in balance and aligned.

**Benitoite:** Healing to the chakras.

**Calcite, Blue:** Opens, heals and unblocks all chakras.

**Cobalt:** This stone has the effect of a combination of Sugilite and Clevelandite. Very useful for opening up one's channeling abilities.

**Cleavelandite:** Channeling aid. Balances and grounds while channeling. Keeps chakras automatically balanced, aligned and healed. Enables a person to channel twice as long without getting tired.

**Fluorite:** Useful as a channeling aid. Allows the channel to remain uncorded while channeling. Also balances all chakras.

**Granite:** Balances all the chakras and grounds one while channeling.

**Jade, Black:** Balances the lower three chakras.

**Opal, Cacholong:** Balances all chakras and clears energy blockages in the body so one can open up to new experiences.

**Septarian Nodule:** Composed of Concretions, Aragonite and Brown Calcite. Most useful if one is already a channel. The concretions contain devac energy and can also provide a base for one's Astral guides to connect with one. This lends one a great deal of energy, support, and power during the channeling process. The Aragonite keeps chakras four, five and six open, in balance and aligned. The Brown Calcite allows one to connect with the Mental Plane, which is a source of informational energy and higher truth.

**Yttrocerite:** Same in effect as Fluorite.

### Selecting the Source

Some people have difficulty channeling a specific source or entity. Instead, they have energy flooding in from everywhere. Gemstones and minerals are the perfect tools to help a channel focus on the specific source of higher consciousness they wish to contact. These entities, or sources of "higher consciousness", are accessed from five, specific, non-corporeal, planes of existence: the Astral Plane, the Causal Plane, and the three higher planes; the Mental Plane, the Messianic Plane, and the Buddhaic Plane.

In the section that follows, those gemstones and minerals that connect one with these five, nonphysical, planes of existence are described, as well as those stones that connect one energetically to the Tao. Stones that connect one with the Tao, are not useful tools for channeling as it is not possible to source everything, or channel "All That Is". One must make contact with someone, an entity with a separate consciousness, to form a connection. The highest form of consciousness that still exists as a separate entity is on the Buddhaic Plane.

## PLANES OF EXISTENCE

According to Michael, there are seven, basic planes of existence: the Physical Plane, the Astral Plane, the Causal Plane, The Akashic Record, the Mental Plane, the Messianic Plane, and the Buddhiac Plane. The Tao encompasses all planes of existence and is existence itself. A more complete discussion of these planes of existence, can be found in the section on "Centers".

Gemstones and minerals are an aid to experiencing the energy of planes beyond one's current, physical existence. They are particularly valuable for fostering the conscious awareness of one's spiritual nature, as well as making one more receptive to spiritual influence, and enlightening inspiration from higher planes of existence.

### Astral Plane

**Apache Tears:** Particularly good for channeling in one's spirit guides. Enables one to receive messages from those who are on the Astral Plane.

**Apachite:** Puts one in touch with one's spirit guides and friends on the Astral Plane.

**Apophyllite:** Connects one with the cycled-off members of one's entity, who are on the Astral Plane.

**Heulandite:** Connects one with the cycled-off members of one's entity, who are on the Astral Plane. Same in effect as Apophyllite, except that it is more easily used by those who are skeptical and cautious of accepting the unusual without a lot of proof.

**Julienite:** Enables one to channel sentient as well as non-sentient beings: any life form that has thoughts. Not only helps one to be in touch with people from other planes of existence, but also helps one to be in touch with other sentient species, whether on this planet or others.

**Kyanite, Black:** Enables one to contact beings from the lower Astral Plane. This refers to people between lives, or devas who have not yet had a lifetime. Must use caution when using this stone, as it will open one up to anyone without a body, even not very developed beings.

**Muscovite:** Connects one with one's spirit guides who are on the Astral Plane. Assists solid roles, Kings, Warriors and Scholars in leaving their bodies.

**Rose Quartz:** Assists one in communicating with one's spirit guides. Since Rose Quartz keeps one in one's body, the communication takes place internally.

**Septarian Nodule:** The "concretions" contain devac energy one can draw on to increase one's stamina when channeling, and can also provide a base for one's Astral guides to connect with one.

**Zircon, Pink:** For growth on the Astral Plane. Pushes one out of the body at night to take on lessons of an emotional nature on the Astral Plane. Can result in a restless night.

### Causal Plane

**Kyanite:** Connects one with the energy of the Causal Plane. This connection is not usually of interest, unless one has a teacher on that plane. Michael is a Causal Plane teacher and those who wish to connect with him or another such teacher will find this stone useful.

**Sillimanite, Pale Blue:** Same in effect as blue Kyanite.

## Mental Plane

**Calcite, Brown or Gold:** Connects one with the Mental Plane. Makes one better able to appreciate such philosophers as Lao Tsu.

**Kyanite, Green:** Connects one with the energy of the Mental Plane. Opens one to inspirational bursts of truth, love, or healing from higher planes of existence.

**Septarian Nodule:** Contains Brown Calcite which connects one with the energy of the Mental Plane.

## Messianic Plane

**Beryllium:** Connects one strongly with the Messianic Plane and the experience of love for all.

**Calcite, White:** Connects one with the energy of the Messianic Plane and unconditional love. Keeps the seventh chakra open and gives a one feeling of protection. One feels safe to operate out of Higher Centers.

**Chalcanthite:** Opens one up to the energy of the Messianic Plane, and a spiritual feeling one can love all mankind.

**Hiddenite:** Connects one with the Messianic Plane, the energetic source of unconditonal love for all.

**Jokokuite:** Opens one to spiritually-based, emotional experiences. Enables one to feel a sense of lovingness toward all beings. Connects one with the energy of the Messianic Plane. Similar in effect to Chalcanthite.

**Spangolite:** Same in effect as Chalcanthite.

## Buddhaic Plane

**Calcite, Violet:** Connects one with the energy of the Buddhaic Plane. Enables one to feel harmoniously connected to, and at peace with, all that is.

**Hauynite:** Enables one to experience the connectedness of the whole and oneness with the all. Connects one with the energy of the Buddhaic Plane.

**Heulandite:** Enables one to experience the connectedness of the whole, oneness with all that is, and awareness of the Supreme Reality. Connects one with the energy of the Buddhaic Plane.

**Hiddenite:** Connects one with the Buddhaic Plane, source of the energetic experience of being connected with the all.

**Kammererite:** Connects one with the energy of the Buddhaic Plane. Gives one a sense of harmony and connectedness with the whole.

**Lepidolite:** Same in effect as Kammererite.

### The Tao

**Creedite:** One feels directly connected to God: the Supreme Reality.

**Gaudefroyite:** Enables one to transcend ego and one's sense of individual identity. Enables one to go beyond one's self and feel a part of the greater whole.

**Granite:** One feels directly connected to God: the Supreme Reality.

**Hauynite:** Puts one in touch with the Tao, and creates greater awareness of one's spiritual nature.

**Jasper, Morrison Ranch:** Puts one in touch with the Tao in a shamanistic way.

**Morrisonite:** Same in effect as Morrison Ranch Jasper.

**Vanadinite:** Promotes the experience of an exalted, inspirational space wherein one is in touch with the Tao, or God, the Universal Consciousness.

### DEVAS

Devas are elemental life forms. They are the bit of universal consciousness in every rock, tree, cloud and puddle of water. Michael tells us that all spirits coming to this planet to see if they would like to call it home, begin their spiritual path on this planet as devas. After experiencing the Physical

Plane for a period of time as a deva, a spirit may choose to remain one; or move on to a series of human lifetimes. The following stones connect one empathically to the devas.

**Agate, Enhydritic:** Puts one in touch with water devas, who represent the spiritual nature of water.

**Coronadite:** Same in effect as Wulfenite.

**Julienite:** Enables one to make mental contact with any life form that has thoughts no matter how rudimentary. This includes devas.

**Murataite:** Same in effect as Wulfenite.

**Wulfenite:** Connects one to the devas. One feels in touch with their energies and intentions.

## PARALLEL UNIVERSES

Michael tells us that each soul inhabits a multiplicity of parallel universes all existing simultaneously. These universes are inhabited by the same people, in the same bodies, with the same personality traits. As life progresses, each individual is presented with a series of lessons, which provides the opportunity to choose to experience each lesson or to decline it. At this point, a new parallel universe comes into existence. This enables the soul to experience one parallel universe in which it proceeds with the lesson presented, and one in which it does not.

**Barbertonite:** Makes one feel at ease with the fact that in different parallel universes, one is making decisions to go in different directions. One can feel in harmony with one's self, and that one is a unit, even though parallel aspects of one's self are proceeding in different directions. Creates a consciousness of being one with one's self, in all one's various aspects.

**Hydrotalcite:** Allows one to feel in alignment with, and attuned to, parallel selves that are taking different paths from the path one is taking in this universe.

## SOUL-AGE DIFFERENCES

**Sphene:** Encourages compassion of an extremely durable type. Each color is resonates best to a specific soul-age perspective.

| | |
|---|---|
| Infant Souls: | Black or Brown. |
| Baby Souls: | Clear to Gray. |
| Young Souls: | Green. |
| Mature Souls: | Yellow. |
| Old Souls: | Orange-Brown. |
| Old Souls: | Red-Brown |

**Spinel, Blue to Gray:** Helps Young, Mature, or Old souls who have constant dealings with Infant or Baby souls, to relate to them more comfortably.. Helps one to discriminate very clearly, about how to behave appropriately around an Infant or Baby soul.

**Tourmaline, Yellow-Green:** Helps those souls with a lot of lifetimes of experience "under their belts" to relate to each other well. Helps Old, Mature and Young souls relate to one another comfortably.

**Vivianite:** Helps one get along with those souls that are experiencing their first few lifetimes. Helps one get along with Infant and Baby souls.

## WALK-INS

This is a new category that has come into being as "New Age" spirituality or metaphysics has developed. Michael explains the phenomenon of "walk-ins" in this way. Most of us come into a body around the moment of birth and grow up with that body. A "walk-in" is an essence who comes into an adult body (with the permission of the departing essence) and does not go through childhood.

A new essence can only "walk into" the body of a person whose essence is complete with that lifetime, for whatever reason, and yet agrees not to have the body die, which is the usual course of events as an essence leaves. The arriving essence is usually one that knows the departing essence quite well, and has business with at least some of the people that the departing essence already knows. The body's memories stay intact from birth and become the memories of the new essence so there is continuity of the personality's experience.

However, new essences must meld with a body that belonged to someone with different tastes, talents, and lessons. This is a seven year process, since the new essence has no childhood in which to adjust to the body and develop it properly. The stones in this section aid "walk-ins" in their adjustment process.

**Agate, Turitella:** Assists walk-ins because this stone is about taking something old and something new and putting them together to make a successful blend.

**Ametrine:** Promotes a blend of the old and the new and, thus, assists walk-ins in adjusting to the physical plane. Amethyst has a high frequency like the Universe itself. As it heats to become Ametrine, it becomes more focused and more physical. As this is similar to the adjustment process walk-ins go through, it is probably one of the best stones for them to use.

**Rose Quartz, Tourmaline, Pink to Red, & Kunzite** combination: This is an excellent combination for walk-ins: Rose Quartz keeps one in the body; Pink Tourmaline encourages one to go with the flow and not resist; and Kunzite is for surrender.

# Part II

## AN ALPHABETICAL LIST:

Gemstones and Minerals Listed in
Alphabetical Order by Name

# AN ALPHABETICAL LIST
## Of Gemstones and Minerals

**Abalone:** (The inside lining of an Abalone shell that is pearlized silver and blue in color). **a)** Helps one feel calmer and less afraid especially in the arena of one's instinctive or survival-oriented issues. **b)** Particularly calming to "high frequency", "buzzy" types of people who tend to live in a very intense state. **c)** Balances and heals the first chakra. **d)** In the Michael system, healing to the Instinctive Center; balances high-fre2quency types; especially effective for those who are Kings, Priests, or Sages; <u>or</u> who have a Goal of Dominance, Acceptance, or Growth; <u>or</u> who have the Attitude of Spiritualist, Idealist, or Realist.

**Abelsonite:** (Pink to purple). Has a relaxing effect on children. Enables them to feel calmer and more able to handle stressful situations. For example, this stone would be good for a child whose parents are divorcing, or a child who's flying on an airplane for the first time. Has a similar, but much milder effect on adults.

**Abernathyite:** (Yellow). **a)** Encourages one to operate from an intellectually-based point of view, to seek out the facts and to gather data. Fosters a scholarly demeanor. **b)** Encourages good study habits. **c)** In the Michael system, balances Scholars, and is particularly adored by Scholars as it makes them feel at home with themselves.

**Acanthite:** (Silver colored). **a)** Promotes feelings of optimism, and encourages one to be more idealistic. **b)** Stimulates one's imagination, and pulls one into an artistic, creative mode. Helpful for those who are not usually in touch with their artistic talents or creativity. **c)** In the Michael system, balancing and calming to Artisans.

**Achroite:** A clear variety of Tourmaline.

**Acmite:** (Gray-black, dark brown or black crystals). Increases bravery and bolsters one's courage. Encourages the belief that one can handle what may look to be an insurmountable difficulty. Similar in effect to Gratonite, but in contrast to that stone, it is not necessary for the circumstances to be desparate before one finds Acmite valuable.

**Actinolite:** (A flinty metallic stone, green to black in color). **a)** Enables one to focus one's power in the area of creativity, and handle several creative projects at once, without getting scattered or sidetracked. **b)** In the Michael system, a power stone for Artisans. Enables Artisans to be very powerful in any area they choose, whether it's in relationships, in politics, making money, or just pursuing a creative project. Useful for all other Roles when involved in a creative project.

**Adamite:** (Yellow-green to green or brownish-yellow in color). **a)** A "specificity" rock. Produces a quality of particularness, that makes one more able to see details and to proceed in a step-by-step, delineated fashion from a, to b, to c, etc. **b)** Helps bring one out of confusion and enables one to focus on the details, or specifics of a situation. **c)** In the Michael system, a stone that Warriors like. Useful for Sages, Priests, and Kings, as they tend to look at whole pictures, and have trouble getting down to particulars.

**Adularia:** Same stone as Moonstone.

**Aegerine:** Same stone as Acmite.

**Aenigmatite:** (Black in color). Enables the physical body to maintain a better fluid balance. Balances water gain and loss in the body. Helps prevent dehydration or its opposite, edema.

**Aerugite:** (Green in color). **a)** Makes one <u>feel</u> lucky which can lead to <u>being</u> lucky, because "you are what you think you are". **b)** Reduces inappropriate cynicism and skepticism, and encourages one to look for positive solutions to problems. Gives one a sense that things will go well.  c) In the Michael system, pulls one into the positive pole of the Attitude of Skeptic and Cynic.

**Afwillite:** (Glassy white in color).  Aids digestion.  Buffers the digestive ststem from the effects of psychological stressors, and allows one to digest one's food more thoroughly and with fewer problems.  Especially useful for those who tend toward indigestion or ulcers.  Do not eat.

**Agalmatolite:** (A denser variety of Pyrophyllite).  Same in effect as Pyrophyllite.

**Agardite:** (Blue-green in color).  Helps one to attract appropriate potential mates.  This stone increases one's pheromonic acuity: i.e., one is able to sense more clearly who would be an appropriate intimate partner.  Good for people who continually make bad choices in this arena.

**Agate, Arizona:** (Pale creamy-yellow in color).  a) Brings out warm, sensuous, sunny, light, and androgynous qualities.  b) In the Michael system, a body-type Agate mixing qualities that correspond to Solar and Venus body types.

**Agate, Banded:** Another name for brown Agate with red, pink, gray, black or clear stripes.

**Agate, Black with White Stripes:** a) Makes one very alert and ready for action.  b) In the Michael system, a Mercurial body-type Agate.

**Agate, Blue Lace:** (Pale blue in color with white lacy patterns).  a) Softens stubbornness.  Provides an especially strong feeling of security that if any new situations arise, they can be handled.  One feels assured that one will not have to do something one doesn't want to do, or be plunged into something overwhelming.  This makes it easier for even the most stubborn person to be more flexible.  Stubborn types of people can operate with a great deal of determination and purpose, but they can become obstinate and refuse to budge, even when this is not in their best interest.  b) In the Michael system, pulls one into the positive pole of the Chief Negative Feature of Stubbornness.  Makes it difficult to continue on a path of self-defeating stubbornness by calling the wearer's attention to it.

**Agate, Blue with White Stripes: a)** Puts one in a dreamy, visionary, almost psychic frame of mind in which it becomes easier to appreciate questions of a spiritual nature. **b)** In the Michael system, a Neptunian body-type Agate.

**Agate, Botswana:** Same stone as gray or brown-gray Agate with white stripes, or pink Agate with gray and white stripes.

**Agate, Brazilian:** (Pale brownish yellow with green, gray, white or black splotches). Healing to the kidneys.

**Agate, Brecchiated:** (Also called Tubular or Canal Agate. Broken Agate pieces held together with Quartz. Usually brown in color). **a)** Creates a very positive approach toward life, in which one maintains a tranquil, optimistic, open-minded and realistic attitude. Allows one to avoid negative behavior patterns that create disharmony within, such as being too impatient, stubborn, or self-effacing. Enables one to feel harmoniously centered, and comfortably in touch with oneself. **b)** In the Michael system, softens all Chief Negative Features and pulls one into the positive pole of one's Attitude.

**Agate, Brown with Gray, Black or Clear Stripes: a)** Enables one to invoke transformation in one's self and others. One becomes a catalyst for transformation. **b)** In the Michael system, a Plutonian body-type Agate.

**Agate, Canal:** Same stone as Brecchiated Agate.

**Agate, Copco:** (Carnelian with a thin layer of white Agate on top). **a)** A very balancing and healing energy surrounded with the loving emotionality of the Venusian body-type Agate. **b)** Allows one to temporarily put aside major self esteem issues. Gives one a break from needing to be better than anyone else, or agonizing over how inferior to others one _feels_. This creates the space for some positive feedback to flow in. **c)** Balances a "high frequency" or "buzzy" person. Helps them bring their frequency rate down to a lower level, even though still higher than what is comfortable for other folks, and allows them to keep it stabilized there without expending much energy to do so. **d)** Enables one to use one's focused, organizational abilities, and one's creative, innovative abilities, in a balanced fashion. **e)** In the Michael system, softens the Chief Negative Features of Arrogance and Self-Deprecation. Balances high-frequency types of people, or those whose proportion of male to female energy is more or less equal.

**Agate, Covey Lace:** (Turquoise and white pattern. Found in Hawaii). **a)** Enables one to feel relaxed and willing to go with the flow. **b)** Helps one to get along with one's friends and feel relaxed around them. **c)** In the Michael system, pulls one into the positive pole of the Goal of Stagnation.

**Agate, Crazy Lace:** (Gray with bluish, white, or brown tints swirled in a lacy pattern). This is an "intergenerational" stone. Makes children understand parents and grandparents. Makes parents and grandparents understand children and grandchildren. It encourages the different generations to feel they can enjoy one another.

**Agate, Dendritic:** (Milky, translucent Agate with black or brown fernlike patterns). **a)** One of the most powerful healing stones available. Can be used anywhere on one's body. For swiftest action, place near the body part most in need of healing. **b)** Promotes moderation in one's approach to life rather than a tendency to be either overly expansive or overly structured. **c)** Balances and calms "buzzy," highly energetic persons. Helps them mellow out and move at a slower, more comfortable pace. **d)** In the Michael system, balances high-frequency types of people and/or those who are high-female energied or high-male energied.

**Agate, Dry-Head:** (Rust, red, orange with black thin stripes in Geodes). **a)** Increases precision, productivity, and craftsmanship. Enhances one's ability to be focused and precise: to really zero in on a project and be clear about each necessary detail. This keeps one from wasting time and speeds up productivity. Produces a finer and finer mastery of one's craft or skill. **b)** In the Michael system, a rock that Warriors like all the time, and other Roles will find attractive when they want to be productive and precise.

**Agate, Enhydritic:** (Agate nodules with water trapped inside) **a)** Puts one in touch with the spiritual qualities of water. **b)** Accentuates the astrological influences of the water signs, Cancer, Pisces, and Scorpio: the qualities of those signs become more pronounced. **c)** In the Michael system, puts one in touch with "water devas" who represent the spiritual nature of water.

**Agate, Eye:** (White with green "eyes"). One of the strongest healing stones for the body. Can be placed anywhere on the body to promote healing of that area.

**Agate, Fern:** Same in effect as Dendritic Agate.

**Agate, Fire:** (A brown, opalized stone). Same in effect as Fire Opal.

**Agate, Flame:** Same stone as Zebra Agate.

**Agate, Gray or Brown-Gray with White Stripes: a)** Makes one appreciative of intellectual pursuits and promotes abstract, creative thought. **b)** In the Michael system, a Lunar body-type Agate.

**Agate, Green or Green with White Stripes: a)** Promotes happiness, expansiveness and sociability. **b)** In the Michael system, a Jovial body-type Agate.

**Agate, Holly Blue:** Lilac with pale blue-gray stripes). For being spiritually discriminating. Encourages one to be discriminating about what one will accept in the way of new beliefs, new spiritual paths, or new religions.

**Agate, Lattice:** (Pieces of Agate that crisscross in lattice format. Usually light brown in color). Eliminates headaches.

**Agate, Lavender Lace:** (Pale lavendar in color with white, lacy patterns). Same in effect as Blue Lace Agate.

**Agate, Layer:** Same stone as Lattice Agate.

**Agate, Leopard Skin:** (Pale yellow, brown or pink with darker leopard-like spots). **a)** Very grounding and healing when dealing with heavy emotional issues. Reduces free-floating anxiety; i.e., when one is worried and anxious, but doesn't know why. Good for anyone, but especially grounding for people who are paranoid or schizophrenic, and those who are totally unstable and cannot handle life. **b)** Puts one in touch with any instinctive terrors or fears, so one can work on them and conquer them. **c)** Balances and heals the first chakra. **d)** In the Michael system, balances and heals the Instinctive Center. Called Wolfstone at one time because unconsciously it was recognized that the wolf is directly related to, and is the symbol for, the emotional part of the Instinctive Center.

**Agate, Mexican Red Lace:** (Looks like red, white and gray lace). **a)** Similar in effect to Crazy-Lace Agate. Enables the generations to understand one another better and get along. **b)** Family members and close friends are encouraged to tell each other their emotional truths. They confess they love one another, or that they are angry with one another, or perhaps just needed some attention.

**Agate, Moss:** (Clear or milky with green or red mosslike patterns). Same in effect as Dendritic Agate.

**Agate, Mustard Yellow: a)** Puts one into a creative, imaginative and unusually inventive mood: Keeps one original and fresh in one's approach. **b)** In the Michael system, a Uranian body-type Agate.

**Agate, Orange with White Stripes: a)** Makes one feel vigorous, energetic and ready to take on challenges. Increases one's willingness to take risks or be adventurous. **b)** In the Michael system, a Martial body-type Agate.

**Agate, Orange with Yellow or Brown Stripes: a)** Makes one feel, as well as project to others, grounded, self-sufficient, capable and trustworthy. One has an aura of strength and competence. **b)** In the Michael system, a Saturnian body-type Agate.

**Agate, Plume:** (Red or yellow feathery occlusions in a clear matrix). **a)** Enables one to be more open sexually and less repressed. Makes one feel sexually desirable. **b)** Opens up one's creativity and encourages one to be more creatively expressive. Helps one get past the tendency to be shy and hide one's creative talents.  c) Opens and balances the second chakra.  d) In the Michael system, balances and heals, the Higher-Moving Center.

**Agate, Pseudo:** (Unusual triangular shape. Colored in varieties of brown). a) Puts one in touch with the energetic qualities of other planets. If the planet is inhabited, puts one in touch with those who live there, and their ways of being or perceiving.  b) This sensitivity to planetary energies, also enhances one's awareness of astrological influences.

**Agate, Sagenite:** (Purple with threads of white). a) Enables one to be more direct, clear, and impactful in one's communications.  The white Crystals function to make one's communications more purposeful and powerful.  b) Softens silent stubbornness, and makes one more willing to share one's communications   c) In the Michael system, particularly balancing for highly expressive people such as Sages or Artisans.  Pulls one into the positive pole of the Chief Negative Feature of Stubbornness, and makes one more willing to communicate. Affects the communication process only.

**Agate, Snake Skin:** a) Puts one in a sensual loving mood, appreciative of the body and its sensations.  b) In the Michael system, a Venusian body-type Agate.

**Agate, Tree:** Same in effect as Dendritic Agate.

**Agate, Tubular:** Same stone as Brecchiated Agate.

**Agate, Turitella:** (Black Agate dotted with gray and white little fossils). a) Helps one combine the old with the new. Facilitates the process of taking something old, and taking something new, and successfully putting them together in a new combination.  b) Helps one adjust to changes in one's life that involve combining something old with something new.  c) Helps "blended" families with the process of creating a stable, smoothly-functioning unit. A blended family is the result of a marriage with children that are "his, hers, and ours". **d)** Assists "walk-ins" in the process of taking an "old" essence and putting it into a new body. **e)** Puts one in touch with any instinctive fears, or survival-based issues and helps one neutralize them. **f)** In the Michael system, calms the Instinctive Center.

**Agate, White Lace:** (Milky white with white lacy patterns). Same in effect as Blue Lace Agate.

**Agate, White or White with White Stripes: a)** Puts one in a sensual, loving mood appreciative of the body and its sensations. **b)** In the Michael system, a Venusian body-type Agate.

**Agate, Wonder:** (Swirled gray, maroon and tan in color). For male sexuality: increases sexual arousal and the ability to get and maintain erections.

**Agate, pale to bright Yellow: a)** Puts one in a fun-loving, lighthearted and cheerful mood. **b)** In the Michael system, a Solar body-type Agate.

**Agate, Yellow with White Stripes:** Same in effect as pale to bright yellow Agate.

**Agate, Zebra:** (Maroon, cream and brown stripe). For adjusting to, and being comfortable in, one's body. Helps one enjoy one's body and the activities one does in it.

**Agrinierite:** (Orange in color). **a)** Increases sexual activity. Encourages people who have sexual partners to engage in more sexual activity. Encourages those who have been celibate or downplaying their sexuality, to look at having more sex in their lives. **b)** Assists the pubescent adolescent in becoming aware of, and more comfortable with, their sexuality.

**Aheylite:** (Blue-green in color). **a)** Draws in love relationships: those persons one can relate to as good friends, family members, lovers, or loyal business partners. **b)** Increases one's pheromonic acuity in the same way Agardite does. One is more able to sense accurately if another person is truly appropriate for a strong relationship.

**Ainalite:** Same stone as Wood-Tin Cassiterite.

**Ajoite:** (Opaque green-blue with brown or white flecks). **a)** Puts one in a good mood. **b)** Enables one to be good humored and see the lighter side of things.

**Akatoreite:** (Orange to brown in color). **a)** Encourages a sense of tribal unity. Has a "homey" feeling of togetherness. **b)** Makes one feel close to, and appreciative of, one's family and closest friends. **c)** Deepens the closeness in already established mated relationships.

**Alabandite:** (Black crystals). **a)** Helps the body maintain physical equilibrium and move in a coordinated and balanced fashion regardless of the circumstances. Keeps one from being clumsy. For example, makes it easier to walk on a tight rope or on a boat. **b)** Helps counteract the effects of inner ear problems or other diseases that affect the body's ability to move in a coordinated and balanced fashion.

**Alabaster:** (White, pink, or brown in color). A denser variety of Gypsum. Same in effect as Gypsum.

**Alacranite:** (Orange-yellow in color). **a)** Increases gregariousness. Encourages people to socialize and be comfortable in larger groups than they usually want to be involved with. **b)** For happiness. Makes it easy to shift into a more optimistic, up-beat or giggly mood when one is feeling neutral. Has little effect when one is unhappy.

**Albite Feldspar:** See Feldspar, Albite.

**Alexandrite:** (Purple. Shifts to green with light changes). **a)** A sophisticated stone that brings life to the more refined and elegant side. **b)** Limits and inhibits the energies one doesn't want around, particularly when worn on the left hand. This can include people, their emotions, or communications, as well as energies from inanimate sources such as microwaves or power lines. **c)** Prevents cording. Inhibits others from attaching themselves energetically and drawing on one's energy without permission. **d)** Suspends intense emotional states to allow a person to operate in a more neutral way, when worn on the chest. When worn in the ears, it inhibits excessive, intellectual processing to allow one to maintain an outwardly-directed intellectual focus. **e)** In the Michael system, facilitates the positive expression of Repression Mode.

**Alforsite:** (A variety of colors). **a)** Encourages acceptance. Allows one to accept whatever is happening no matter how difficult or disgusting the situation is. It then encourages one to deal with it rather than turn away. One must be cautious in using this stone, as a person who tends to be naturally soft and passive could become overly pliant and lose all capacity to discriminate or set limits. **b)** In the Michael system, pulls one into the positive pole of the Goal of Acceptance.

**Allophane:** (Glassy blue). **a)** Helps one reach for thoughts that are just out of one's grasp: concepts or memories that are on the "tip of the tongue". Helps the brain work more efficiently to access these elusive items. **b)** In the Michael system, enhances the use of the Intellectual Center.

**Almandine Garnet:** See Garnet, Almandine.

**Almandite:** Another name for Almandine.

**Alunite:** (Granular pink). **a)** Stimulates the production of antibodies to fight diseases that enter the body. Increases the production of white blood cells. **b)** Promotes the body's resistance to allergy-producing substances.

**Alurgite:** (Red flakes). Same stone as Muscovite.

**Amakinite:** (Pale green in color). **a)** A stone that enables one to turn the immediate environment into a vast, creative playground of energy, that stimulates project initiation, the imagination, organic growth, and new inventions. Immediate environment means 30 feet in any direction from the stone. **b)** Can have a side effect of making a very focused person feel temporarily dizzy and fuzzy. Bring the stone out for two or three hours of vast inventiveness, then return it to the freezer for at least 24 hours for cleaning and recharging. c) In the Michael system, a power stone for Artisans. Other Roles are attracted to this stone when they desire the particular effects outlined above.

**Amatrix:** (Light green in color with clear crystals). A combination of Variscite and clear Quartz. Same in effect as Variscite and clear Quartz.

**Amazonite:** (Blue-green Microcline). a) Raises self confidence and gives one the feeling that it is possible to have whatever one wants. Discourages one from behaving self-destructively when disappointed. One feels confident that, in time, all one's desires can be fulfilled. b) Makes one notice any self-destructive behavior that is not in one's best interests, such as taking one drink too many, or refusing to take care of oneself after one has been very ill. c) In the Michael system, pulls one out of the Chief Negative Feature of Self-Destruction into the positive pole of Greed.

**Amber:** (A clear gold-brown color). a) Clears one mentally and promotes the smooth functioning of the intellect. Pulls one away from emotional or physical experiences into a sharp, intellectual focus. b) Balances the fifth chakra. c) Has a capacity to put an intellectual focus on some of the chakras. When worn near the sixth chakra, helps eliminate confusion about what's really true. When worn near the fifth chakra (throat), produces mental clarity and one is more thoughtful and intellectual in one's communications. If worn near the fourth chakra (heart), intellect guides the emotions. When worn at the third chakra (solar plexus), one has more intellectual clarity about one's career, health or power issues. d) In the Michael system, balances the Intellectual Center.

**Amber, Black:** Another name for Jet.

**Amber, Honey:** (Milky gold color). Same in effect as the clear Amber, but with a more inspirational quality.

**Amber, Red:** (Clear, dark red color. Can occur naturally but is often manufactured). a) Aids the operation of the intellect by containing or deleting negative emotions. Is calming and keeps one from being overly emotional. **b)** In the Michael system, enhances the functioning of the Intellectual Center.

**Amber, Sea:** Same stone as Burnite.

**Amblygonite:** (Golden yellow, yellow, colorless and pale violet). **a)** Takes the attention off the self, so one can be less self-conscious. Directs one's attention outward to noticing other people or one's surroundings and enables one to tune into the situation in which one finds oneself. **b)** In the Michael system, softens the Chief Negative Feature of Arrogance. **c)** Different colors are better for certain types:

  **Colorless:** Good for all.

  **Violet:** For fluid types: a person who's more flowing, expansive and fluffy.

  **Golden Yellow to Yellow:** For solid types: a person who is very grounded and organized.

**Ambroid:** (Amber pressed into forms. Opaque. Dark red-gold in color). **a)** Enables one to maintain an intellectual focus even when one's consciousness is dominated by instinctive fears or survival issues. **b)** In the Michael system, calms the Instinctive Center and allows the proper functioning of the Intellectual Center.

**Amethyst:** (Clear, deep purple) **a)** Keeps one in touch with one's spiritual side and truly connected to what is going on with oneself as well as with others. Enables one to act out of one's highest ideals, for the good of all, even though this may not immediately serve oneself. **b)** Calms impatience. Gives one a feeling that there is time enough for everything. When feelings of impatience start to pop up, they are immediately followed by the awareness that there's no need to rush. Extremely popular, since most people feel victimized by the circumstances, at one time or another, in their lives. **c)** Balances and heals all chakras. Has strongest impact on the third and seventh chakras. **d)** Balances and calms "buzzy," highly energetic persons. Helps them mellow out and move at a slower, more comfortable pace. **e)** Promotes moderation in one's approach to life, rather than a tendency to be over-expansive or overly structured.  **f)** Keeps one grounded while channeling.  **g)** The more transparent and dark purple the color, the more intense the effect.  **h)** In the Michael system, balances high-frequency types and those who are high-female or high-male energied.  Softens the Chief Negative Features of Impatience and Martyrdom. Balances all Centers.

**Amethyst, Cape:**  See Cape Amethyst.

**Amethyst Quartz:**  (Purple and white stripes).  Helps essence twins get along with each other.  An essence twin is what is popularly known as one's soul mate.

**Ametrine:**  (Clear purple and gold-yellow striations).  Can occur naturally or can be created by subjecting Amethyst to a heat treatment process).  **a)** Facilitates the process of taking something old, something new, and successfully putting them together in a new combination.  Helps one adjust to changes in one's life that involve blending the old with the new.  **b)** Helpful with the creation of blended families.  A blended family is a marriage with children that are "his, and/or hers and ours.  **c)** Ametrine formed by subjecting Amethyst to a heat treatment process, very effectively assists walk-ins in adjusting to the physical plane.  Amethyst has a high frequency like the Universe itself.  As it heats to become Ametrine, it becomes more focused and more physical.  As this is similar to the adjustment process walk-ins go through, it is probably one of the best stones for them to use.

**Amianth:**  (Green and white web).  **a)** Opens up one's awareness of one's survival issues.  Operates very quickly and thoroughly.  Useful for those who are unaware of more deeply buried, internal processes.  Enables them to work on these issues.  **b)** In the Michael system, opens the Instinctive Center.

**Ammonite:**  (Fossilized Shells).  Same in effect as Shell.

**Analcime:**  (Like Crystal, clear, white or pink but is formed in squares instead of points).  **a)** Has a very stable, cleansing, and anchoring energy. Makes one feel very grounded and secure. **b)** Enables one to handle anything that comes up with a sense of purpose and an ability to remain neutral.

**Analcite:** Another name for Analcime

**Anapaite:** (Green in color). **a)** Makes one more comfortable with one's sexuality and biological urges. Loosens one up to accept one's sexual impulses. For this reason, it can seem to operate like an aphrodisiac. **b)** Makes one feel morally correct, and confident that one's sexual behavior is appropriate. **c)** Reduces feelings of shame, or conflicts about one's sexuality.

**Anatase:** (Gray, pale brown, yellow or deep blue in color). A power stone. Makes one feel innately more powerful, and capable of handling difficulties that show up. A mineral that works its way into matrixes. Has a preserving quality.

**Andalusite:** (Clear green-brown, pale olive or gray-green). A power stone of "empire-building" strength. Combines qualities of discrimination, power, and perserverance. Enables one to take on vast projects that require a great deal of foresight and staying power. The Chiastolite variety is the strongest. Similar to Xmas Tree Jasper in effect.

**Andersonite:** (Yellow-green in color). Encourages physical growth and healing. Encourages young human, animal, reptile, bird or insect bodies to grow strong, large and healthy. Encourages healthy plant growth as well. Aids in healing by promoting healthy cell growth as is needed for mending broken bones, healing wounds, or, more simply, for new skin healing over a scrape .

**Andesine Feldspar** See Feldspar, Andesine.

**Andorite:** (Black, non-shiny and metallic). **a)** Makes one feel generally more optimistic. **b)** Encourages one to be more idealistic. **c)** Raises self confidence by reducing shyness. **d)** Reduces one's fear of being in crowds or speaking in public. **e)** In the Michael system, pulls one into the positive pole of the Attitude of Idealist.

**Andradite, Demantoid:** (Emerald Green). Aids in the healing of veins.

**Andradite, Melanite:** (Black). Aids in the healing of the skin.

**Andradite, Topazolite:** (Yellow). Aids in the healing of synapses.

**Andremeyerite:** (Pale emerald green in color). **a)** Promotes the ability to hang on to a humorous, more simple and innocent perspective of whatever is happening in one's immediate vicinity. Makes one feel more comfortable about one's problems. Others may feel offended if the holder of the stone makes "light" of their difficulties because of his ability to feel lighter himself. **b)** In the Michael system, a Sage stone.

**Andrewsite:** (Green in color). Creates a greater bond of communication and oneness between sentient and semi-sentient creatures. One feels more attuned to all semi-sentient species. This includes plants, as well as animals and insects. Can improve the relationship with one's pets, help one train animals, ask gophers to stay out of the yard, or ask plants to grow larger.

**Angel Stone:** Same stone as Apophyllite.

**Angelic Feathers:** Another name for Pickeringite.

**Angelite:** Same stone as Blue Anhydrite.

**Anglesite:** (Clear or translucent white crystals). Helps prevent hardening of the arteries.

**Anhydrite:** (Light purple, light blue and white). **a)** Gives a sense of being above any problem and able to be objective about it. Promotes a sense of peace and serenity even during difficult times. **b)** The violet tends to be more attractive to children and the light blue tends to be more attractive to adults. **c)** In the Michael system, pulls one into the positive pole of the Attitude of Realist.

**Anhydrite, Smoky:** Same stone as Elestial Quartz.

**Ankerite:** (Pale brown). Aids digestion and promotes the smooth functioning of the alimentary canal.

**Annabergite:** (Pale green to intense yellow-green in color). **a)** Enables those who approach life and its tasks from a widely focused-viewpoint, to narrow their focus and pay attention to details or prioritize cycles in order of importance. Curbs the tendency to do everything at one time. **b)** In the Michael system, balances high-female energied types of people and helps them use their male energied side more effectively.

**Anorthite Feldspar:** See Feldspar, Anorthite.

**Anthonyite:** (Lavendar in color). **a)** Enables one to keep an emotional balance during prolonged intellectual pursuits. Speeds basic data manipulations such as categorizing. Relieves the stress of continual hard thinking and makes it easier to work longer on intellectual tasks without mental exhaustion. **b)** Balances and heals the the fifth chakra. **c)** In the Michael system, balances Scholars.

**Antigorite:** **a)** Calming to the digestive tract. Reduces acidity and gas, particularly when one is under stress. **b)** Enables one to be cautious when necessary, without being overly fearful. **c)** In the Michael system, balances those in Caution Mode.

**Antimonite:** Same stone as Stibnite.

**Antlerite:** (Dark green or brown in color). Pulls one strongly into good, clear communication and eliminates arguing. Makes it difficult, if not impossible, to miscommunicate.

**Antozonite:** (Often found with Salmon Calcite). Same stone as purple Fluorite.

**Anyolite:** (Moss green in color). Same stone as Green Zoisite with Ruby crystals.

**Apache Gold:** (Black with metallic gold streaks). Helps one slow down or speed up to match another person's pace. Same in effect as Iron Pyrite.

**Apache Tears:** (Clear dark brownish-black in color). **a)** Makes it easier to be aware of, and communicate with, one's self on the essence level. Enhances awareness of one's true self. **b)** Particularly good for channeling in one's spirit guides. Enables one to get in touch with those higher beings who care about one and desire to communicate. **c)** Promotes moderation, rather than a tendency to be over-expansive or overly structured in one's approach to life. **d)** Creates a sense of harmony and balance for people who tend to take life at a slower pace. **e)** In the Michael system, balances low-frequency types or those with a high percentages of male or female energy. Connects one with the Astral Plane.

**Apachite:** (Blue in color). **a)** Enables one to communicate with entities from higher planes of existence. Puts one in touch with one's spirit guides or those higher beings who care about one and desire to communicate. **b)** Opens and balances the sixth and seventh chakras. This can be experienced as a tingling in the head, or as a feeling that one is rising up out of one's body, which is the result of the seventh chakra opening suddenly and widely. **c)** The clearing of an overstuffed, and blocked sixth chakra, helps to eliminate "writer's block". **d)** An aid to channeling. **e)** In the Michael system, connects one with beings of higher consciousness on the Astral Plane.

**Apatite:** (Usually yellow. Can also be colorless, pink, green, blue or violet. Green variety called Asparagus Stone). **a)** An acceptance stone that, with continued use, puts one into a spiritual state of unconditional love toward others. Promotes a willingness to accept everything that could possibly flow in, and one says "give me more" rather than less. **b)** Due to its qualities of unconditional love and acceptance, this stone is useful when one must work with, or in some way accept, difficult people or situations into one's life. **c)** All colors have the same effect, but it is best to select the color one resonates to best. Very potent, so only a small piece is needed. **d)** In the Michael system, pulls one into the positive pole of the Goal of Acceptance.

**Aphthitalite:** (Clear and colorless). Encourages one's musical ability and talent to be used to its fullest. This is true no matter how little one might have. Cures songwriter's block.

**Aplowite:** (Pink in color). Brings emotions to the surface. Encourages one to communicate more honestly about the emotional impact one has felt.

**Apophyllite:** (Clear Square crystals). **a)** Connects one with those spirits one is closest to, who are no longer incarnating on the physical plane. **b)** In the Michael system, connects one to the Astral Plane and the cycled-off members of one's entity.

**Apple Coral:** (Smooth, fibrous material that varies from brown to rose red. Sometimes with branch-like striping). **a)** Enables one to be very deeply caring and warm-hearted about people. One is open to loving and being involved with others and, at the same time, healed of fear about such closeness. **b)** Creates a feeling of enthusiasm for life. **c)** Calms instinctive, survival-based fears. **d)** In the Michael system, balances the Instinctive Center.

**Aqua-Aura Crystal:** See Crystal, Aqua Aura.

**Aquamarine:** (Clear, pale to medium blue in color). **a)** Augments one's personal power and helps one project an aura of real strength. Commands other's attention, even though one may privately feel unsure of one's strength. **b)** Enables one to take command especially in situations where one must act powerfully. Helps one adjust to being authoritative and in control without feeling wishy-washy about it. **c)** In the Michael system, pulls one into the positive pole of Power Mode.

**Aragonite:** (White, brown, yellow, or reddish in color). **a)** Enables one to operate from a high degree of emotional perceptivity and intellectual clarity. Enhances one's ability to see the truth from a higher perspective and psychically sense the flow of things. **b)** Prevents one from being over-emotional or too dry intellectually. This stone will not be very attractive to those who like a lot of drama in their lives or who are uncomfortable with truth. c) Keeps chakras four, five and six in balance, and operating in a blended fashion. d) In the Michael system, balances the Emotional, Intellectual and Higher-Intellectual Centers.

**Ardennite:** (Yellow and brown in color). Increases gregariousness and fosters the ability to adapt to unfamiliar social situations. Especially good if one has a tendency to be a wallflower. Makes one feel more sociable, outgoing and willing to make new friends.

**Argentite:** (Lead gray in color). Alters to Silver when heated. Same in effect as Silver.

**Arhbarite:** (Blue in color). Helps decrease blood loss from cuts, wounds, etc. by promoting the thickening and clotting of blood.

**Arrojadite:** (Dark green in color). a) Increases stoicism and one's capability to be emotionally detached. Allows one to close one's emotions down very tightly to handle extremely difficult situations. Use with caution and when the situation is extreme enough to warrant it. (We think Florence Nightingale probably had some). b) In the Michael system, pulls one into the positive pole of Stoic.

**Arsenbrackebuschite:** (Honey yellow in color). Encourages friendliness. Makes one feel more willing to see people's good points and appreciate them. In turn, makes it easier to relate to them without one's usual judgments.

**Arsendescloizite:** (Pale yellow in color). Makes one clearer about other people's motivations as well as one's own. Makes it easier to see the motive behind actions or words.

**Arseniosiderite:** (Rich yellow in color). Encourages maternal inclinations. Thoughts of getting pregnant begin to enter one's mind if they have not been there before. Those who have children already, feel more like putting their attention on them and are more interested in all activities related to mothering.

**Arsenoclasite:** (Red in color). a) Pulls up a kingly sense of calm and power. One feels masterful, and at home, in one's surroundings. Promotes the pursuit of excellence and perfection in all that one attempts to do. **b)** In the Michael system, a power stone for Kings.

**Arsenocrandallite:** (Blue or bluish-green in color). Gives one a sense of control over water. One feels confident that one could be a master fisherman, sailor, olympic swimmer or master of the high dive. Also reduces an irrational fear of water.

**Arsenopyrite:** (Metallic silver-white or silver-gray in color). **a)** Helps one harmonize with those who tend to be either more structured or more expansive than one's self in their way of being. **b)** In the Michael system, helps one match energies with one who is more female energied or more male energied than oneself.

**Arsenuranospathite:** (Pale yellow in color). Strengthens hair follicles to produce healthier growth. Good for recuperating from diseases or treatments such as chemotherapy that has caused hair loss. Aids hair in recovering from excessive bleaching or other chemical treatments.

**Arsenuranylite:** (Orange in color). Encourages one to be home oriented. Brings up desire for activities like baking cookies with the children and snuggling in front of a warm fire. One feels the home is a cozy place that is nice to curl up in.

**Arthurite:** (Apple green in color). Opens up the possibility of communication and the desire to communicate where one has been silent before.

**Artinite:** (Translucent, reddish brown in color). **a)** Helps one adapt to new surroundings or to changes in one's life. **b)** This stone does not allow one to have any preconceived ideas as to what's supposed to happen. It is 100% unfocused, expansive energy and such energy can take on anything; it just engulfs a situation in its energy pattern. This effect helps one avoid the disappointment that can occur, when one has pictures or expectations about the future.

**Asbecasite:** (Bright yellow in color). a) Most useful for a thin, androgynous person with a weak digestive system and a "delicate" constitution. Helps the body maintain a balanced state and increases physical stamina so the body has an easier time staying healthy. b) Aids digestion for those who tend to have digestive problems. c) In the Michael system, balances and improves the physical stamina of Solar body types.

**Asbestos, Long Hair:** (Golden yellow or dark blue in color). Aids in digestion when worn on the body close to the esophagus or stomach. It reduces stomach acid production and allows the body to digest food better. Also aids digestion when eating unfamiliar foods or eating unusual amounts of food. Do NOT eat the stone.

**Asbolan:** (Black in color). a) Enables one to bring up, and focus on, feelings of hate, anger and revenge so that they can be dealt with. Aids in lifting the repression of these feelings and issues surrounding such feelings. Particularly useful for those who are in therapy. Best to use this stone sparingly, consciously, and with caution. b) In the Michael system, balances and opens the Instinctive, Emotional and Higher-Moving Centers.

**Asparagus Stone:** Same stone as green Apatite.

**Astrakhanite:** Same stone as Bloedite.

**Astrophyllite:** (Golden in color). a) Makes one feel wealthy and contented with whatever one has. One notices and appreciates what one has. Promotes a sense of abundance and prosperity. b) In the Michael system, pulls one into the positive pole of Greed.

**Atacamite:** (Vivid dark green in color). a) Enables one to be more discriminating, about what one accepts, in new situations or surroundings, such as a taking another job, getting married or moving to another state. Makes it easier to structure a new situation appropriately, and not accept things one might later regret. Saves one the trouble of having to change the status quo later on. b) Also makes one more discriminating about the new things one brings into one's life, such as a new house or new furniture. **c)** Similar to, but more specific in usage than, Smoky Quartz. **d)** In the Michael system, a stone for the Goal of Discrimination.

**Atelestite:** (Yellow in color). Promotes communication between animals (birds and mammals) and humans. Makes one more empathically aware of the needs of animals and better able to relate to them. Good for animal trainers, raising livestock, pet owners, etc.

**Attapulgite:** Same stone as Palygorskite.

**Aubertite:** (Azure blue in color). Encourages emotional closeness. Promotes a sense of camaraderie. Increases one's ability to feel friendly and loving.

**Augelite:** (Clear, colorless stone). **a)** Enables those who are doing artistic, creative projects to stay productive. Makes it easier to manifest creative projects and follow through with them to completion. **b)** In the Michael system, balances Mature and Old Artisans.

**Augite:** (Tiny, bright, brown to black crystals). **a)** Promotes ambitiousness. Enables one to pull in what is needed to get ahead, and to use one's personal power effectively to realize one's ambitions. **b)** Usually found with Green Jade or Serpentine. This adds to the ability to stay in a tranquil, calm state and not be pulled apart by one's ambitiousness.

**Aurichalcite:** (Delicate, pale blue crystals). **a)** For emotional healing. Aids in restoring one's emotions to a sense of balance and well being. Particularly useful when one has taken some hard knocks emotionally and is finding it difficult to recover. **b)** Balances and heals the fourth chakra. **c)** In the Michael, balances and heals the Emotional Center.

**Austinite:** (Colorless, white, pale yellow or bright green sharp little crystals). **a)** Aids workaholics or nervous overachievers to slow down and work at an easier pace. Enables one to proceed in a more balanced fashion. **b)** In the Michael system, balances overly-focused Warriors who won't slow down.

**Australite:** Same in effect as Moldavite.

**Autinite:** (Brown/green or yellow in color). Makes one feel more adventurous and willing to try out some new places, people or things. Encourages one to let go and have a little fun.

**Aventurine, Blue:** (Varies in color from light to very dark blue. Also called Blue Quartz). a) Calms anxiety and makes one feel more stable, balanced and grounded. b) Opens and unblocks the first chakra and energy points in the soles of the feet, so energy can flow through unimpeded. c) In the Michael system, balances and clears the Instinctive Center.

**Aventurine, Green:** (Varies in color from a pale clear green to a dark, mossy green). a) Enhances self esteem by making one feel good about oneself. Enables one to operate from a sense of universal truth and love. Particularly useful for those who have been viewed as abnormal by the culture and have a lowered self esteem as a result. Feeling abnormal fosters a tendency to shut down and operate from survival fears. b) Keeps the sixth and seventh chakras open and unblocked so energy can flow unimpeded. c) Creates a sense of harmony and balance for people who tend to take life at a slower pace. d) Promotes moderation rather than a tendency to be over-expansive or overly structured in one's approach to life. e) Useful as an aid in channeling. f) In the Michael system, balances high male-energied or high female-energied persons, as well as low-frequency types. Pulls one into the balanced use of the Higher-Intellectual and Higher-Emotional Centers.

**Aventurine, Red:** (Varies in color from dark red through peach to brown). a) An all-purpose stone that stimulates one's creativity, enhances one's personal power and level of prosperity, promotes emotional availability, intellectual acuity and good communication. Enables one to use these various aspects of one's being in a harmoniously blended fashion. b) Keeps the second, third, fourth and fifth chakras open and unblocked so energy can flow unimpeded. **c)** In the Michael system, balances and aligns the Higher-Moving, Moving, Emotional and Intellectual Centers. Allows them to work in a blended fashion.

**Axinite:** (Blue or blue-gray. Technically, Axinite is the name of a group of stones. This particular form of Axinite is more accurately called Magnesio-axinite. Axinite in shades of brown is Ferro-axinite. Pink to purplish gray is Manganaxinite. The yellow to red variety is Tinzenite). **a)** Keeps one from going overboard into total zealousness, unable to maintain balance and being totally fanatical about things. Enables one to maintain perspective and stay balanced about important issues. **b)** In the Michael system, this stone is particularly useful for Infant, Baby and Young Priests.

**Azoproite:** (Black in color). Reduces fear of carnivorous animals. Similar in effect to Ludwigite.

**Aztec Stone:** Same stone as Smithsonite.

**Azulisite:** Same stone as Labradorite.

**Azurite:** (Dark blue in color). **a)** Makes one clearer in one's communications, and able to put one's points across more effectively. Allows one to be in better communication with others, by fostering a willingness to listen. Gives a secure sense that one can listen and not lose sight of one's own position. **b)** Softens stubbornness, but is mild in effect. **c)** Creates a sense of harmony and balance for people who tend to take life at a slower pace. **d)** In the Michael system, softens the Chief Negative Feature of Stubbornness and balances low-frequency types of people.

**Babingtonite:** (Small dark green to black platey crystals). Makes one feel attached to the land and green growing things. Good for farmers, landscapers and weekend gardeners. Increases one's "green thumb" ability.

**Baddeleyite:** (Black in color). Decreases motion sickness by stabilizing the inner ear.

**Bafertisite:** (Red to Orange in color). Encourages one to remain satisfied with one's sexual partner. Enhances one's preference for monogamy.

**Bahia-Topaz:** Same stone as Citrine.

**Bakerite:** (White and Porcelain like). **a)** Reduces allergies and increases the body's ability to withstand stress. **b)** Builds the immune system.

**Balas Ruby:** Same stone as Red Spinel.

**Balyakinite:** (Blue-green in color). **a)** Allows one to experience strong emotions with a feeling of safety, and a sense that one's emotions will stay appropriately in check. **b)** In the Michael system, balances one in the use of the Emotional Center.

**Barbertonite:** **a)** Creates a consciousness of being one with one's self in all one's various aspects. **b)** Makes one feel at ease with the fact that in different parallel universes one is making decisions to go in different directions. One can feel in harmony with one's self, and that one is a unit, even though parallel aspects of one's self are proceeding in different directions.

**Barbosalite:** (Dark blue-green in color). Increases creativity and releases any blocks one has to being creative.

**Baricite:** (Blue). Enables one to be more comfortable with one's sexual idiosyncrasies or individual peculiarities in the sexual arena. Helps heal any lack of acceptance one has about one's sexuality. Goes well with Zebra Agate.

**Barite:** (Brown, yellow, colorless, light pink or blue-gray in color). Encourages calcium retention in the bones. Especially good for women.

**Barkevikite:** (Black in color). **a)** Increases the feeling that one is in control of one's body, one's environment, and one's destiny. Enables one to get in touch with, and use, one's will power. **b)** In the Michael system, pulls one out of the negative pole of Martyrdom.

**Barnesite:** (Dark red in color). Enables one to understand one's own subconscious symbols better. For example, the symbolic meaning of one's dreams would become more clear. Also useful for guided meditations, art therapy, etc.

**Baryte:** Same stone as Barite.

**Barytocalcite:** (Transparent and yellow-white in color). **a)** Enables one to be in touch with, and clear about, one's emotions. Heightens one's empathic awareness and ability to be emotionally perceptive about others. **b)** Balances, opens and stimulates the fourth or seventh chakra. Does not open the seventh and fourth chakras simultaneously. One must be clear about which chakra one wishes to focus on. **c)** An aid to channeling. Opens one to spiritual information from higher sources. Encourages astral travel. **d)** In the Michael system, balances, opens and stimulates either the Emotional or the Higher-Emotional Center, but not both at the same time.

**Basaluminite:** (White and powdery). **a)** Aids energetically in technological pursuits and advances. Bask in its energy field and use it to stimulate ideas about projects one can pursue of a technological nature. **b)** People can also use this mineral as a component substance in making anything from pans to computers.

**Bassanite:** Same in effect as black Jasper.

**Bassetite:** (Yellow in color). Same in effect as Autunite.

**Bastnaesite:** (Yellow in color). Almost always found in Flourite as rutiles going through the crystal. Its effect is to augment the Fluorite's capacity to protect one's aura and prevent cording when it is not desired. Cording refers to the energy a person focuses in one's direction.

**Bauranoite:** Increases hereditary red-headedness in children of the parents who wear it.

**Bayldonite:** (Green in color). Increases cheerfulness. Puts one in a happy, possibly even silly or giddy mood.

**Bayleyite**: (Yellow in color. Under black light changes to bright green). **a)** Eliminates mental confusion. Helps one go straight to the core nature of a problem as well as its solution. **b)** Balances the fifth chakra and removes any superfluous, negative energies. **c)** In the Michael system, balances the Intellectual Center.

**Bazirite**: (White). Balances all chakras. Same in effect as Benitoite.

**Beccarite**: Same stone as Green Zircon.

**Bellingerite**: (Green in color). Encourages one to be more decisive. Discourages fuzzy thinking and delayed action.

**Belovite**: (Yellow). Same in effect as Apatite.

**Benavidesite**: Same in effect as Jamesonite.

**Benitoite**: (Most commonly dark blue in color). **a)** Benitoite is very healing to the chakras. It is often found in very small pieces, but it is very powerful in effect, so a large piece is not necessary. **b)** In the Michael system, balances the Centers listed below. **c)** Benitoite comes in a variety of colors. Each color is related to a different chakra or Center, and is most effective balancing and healing that chakra or Center:

| | | |
|---|---|---|
| White: | 1st chakra. | Instinctive Center. |
| Pink: | 4th chakra. | Emotional Center. |
| Clear: | 5th chakra. | Intellectual Center. |
| Blue: | 6th chakra. | Higher-Intellectual Center. |
| Violet: | 7th chakra. | Higher-Emotional Center. |

**Benjaminite with Aikinite**: (Thin Silver metal on Quartz). **a)** Helps one to be realistic about what is possible in the present and in the near future. **b)** In the Michael system, pulls one into the positive experience of the Attitude of Realist.

**Benjaninite**: (Orange to yellow crystals). **a)** Acts as an anesthetic to the emotions when one has gone through great difficulties and is traumatized around survival issues: like pouring a gelatinous bandage over emotional wounds.

Most useful when one has seen, or participated in, very traumatic circumstances such as murder, rape, or war. Later on, when numbing is no longer appropriate, and when one is ready to process the experience, this stone can be put aside and another healing stone chosen.  b) In the Michael system, powerful healer of the Instinctive Center.

**Bentorite:**  (Bright violet in color).  Increases spiritual awareness.  Makes it easier to perceive the answers to questions of a cosmic nature.

**Beraunite:** (Red to reddish-brown in color).  a) Increases one's ability to trust others.  Reduces suspiciousness, wariness and skepticism.  b) In the Michael system, pulls one into the positive pole of the Attitude of Skeptic.

**Bermanite:** (Reddish-brown in color).  Eases the transition from childhood, through puberty, and into adulthood by balancing the hormonal and chemical changes that take place in the body.

**Beryl, Colorless:**  Same stone as Goshenite.

**Beryl, Emerald Green:**  Same stone as Emerald.

**Beryl, Gold:**  Helps alleviate allergies to plants and pollens.

**Beryl, Pale Green:  a)** An aid to communication.  Encourages one to communicate relevant information and promotes good listening habits.  b) Is energetically balancing for most people.  Stabilizes one's energy level and keeps one moving through life at a comfortable pace: one that is neither too hurried nor too plodding.  Those who live life in the fast lane or, those who like the turtle, live life by the side of the road, may not feel much effect.  c) In the Michael system, an all-purpose, frequency balancer.

**Beryl, Pink to Pale Violet or Strawberry Red:** Heals prejudice and intolerance toward others.  Helps create a more mellow and flexible attitude toward the differences one finds in others.

**Beryl, White:**  Helps alleviate dust allergies.

**Beryl, Pale Yellow to Green-Yellow:** Same stone as Heliodor.

**Beryllium:** (Lilac colored). **a)** Puts one in touch with the highest, most spiritual form of love possible. Also referred to as "Christ Consciousness". **b)** In the Michael system, connects one with the energy of the Messianic Plane.

**Beryllonite:** (Colorless, white or weak yellow). Balancing and calming to all mammals. This includes human beings. Especially useful for calming nervous pets.

**Betafite:** (Looks like Sandstone. Dark brown in color). Helps one remember past-life lessons.

**Betpakdalite:** (Bright yellow in color). **a)** Encourages one to think in a highly inspirational manner and see the higher truth in things. Enables one to make intuitive leaps with great ease. **b)** Opens the sixth chakra and makes it available for use. **c)** In the Michael system, balances the Higher-Intellectual Center.

**Beyerite:** (Yellow, yellow-green, green in color). Enables one to find the friends one works with each lifetime, or the people one has "support" karmas with. A "support karma" is where one is owed support of a positive nature. Long-lasting friendships often grow from these associations.

**Bieberite:** (Rose red). Same in effect as Laramar.

**Biggs Jasper:** See Jasper, Biggs.

**Billietite:** (Yellow in color). **a)** Makes it easier to recognize the support that one is being given by others. Also makes it easier to see where possible sources of support exist and to ask for it. Decreases the feeling that one is "alone in the world." **b)** Reduces self centeredness. Enables one to stop focusing on one's self so exclusively, and begin to turn one's attention outward to noticing others. **c)** In the Michael system, softens the Chief Negative Feature of Arrogance.

**Bindheimite:** (Rich yellow). Same in effect as Black and Brown Obsidian.

**Binghamite:** (Goethite plus Quartz). Same in effect as Goethite.

**Binnite:** Same stone as Tennantite.

**Biotite:** (Dark brown to black or dark green. Occurs in thin, ribbon-like sheets). Helps relieve headaches by releasing excess energy from the head.

**Bisbeeite:** (Light blue-green). Same in effect as Chrysocolla.

**Bismuth:** (Rainbow-colored, metallic crystals arranged geometrically). a) A "storyteller" stone. Enhances one's storytelling ability. b) Stimulates the creative use of one's imagination.

**Bismuthinite:** (Rainbow-colored metallic prisms). Same in effect as Bismuth.

**Bismutite:** (Usually yellow, green, or gray metallic). Same in effect as Bismuth.

**Biwa Pearls:** (Fresh water Pearls). See Pearl, Biwa.

**Bixbite:** Same stone as Strawberry Red Beryl.

**Bixbyite:** (Small, black, lustrous cubes). a) Reduces the fear of not measuring up to other's standards. Enables one to feel more comfortable with one's "differentness" whether it is real or imagined. Particularly effective if one has an idiosyncrasy or personal peculiarity that one knows is not really socially acceptable but that can't be changed (like a harelip), is very difficult to change (like fingernail biting), or that one does not want to change. b) In the Michael system, pulls one out of the negative pole of the Chief Negative Feature of Self-Deprecation.

**Bjarebyite:** (Emerald green in color). Encourages one's feeling of attractiveness. Helps one to be more certain that one is making a good impression on others.

**Blende:** Same stone as Sphalerite.

**Blixite:** (Pale yellow in color). Encourages short-term memory retention. Helps one on tests, or to remember where one has parked one's car, to find where one left one's keys, etc.

**Bloedite:** (Clear or flat grey. Also spelled Blodite). **a)** Powerful in its ability to reduce tension. Operates by absorbing energy in its vicinity. Particularly good when one feels too jazzed or wired and can't calm down. Best to use this stone with conscious intention, as it can become exhausting to be around. **b)** Place on sprains, bruises or a feverish head to reduce the fever. Works by absorbing excess energy from the distressed spot.

**Bloodstone:** (Dark green, sometimes with red flecks). **a)** Promotes high prosperity consciousness and a willingness for abundance to show up in one's life. Engenders a strong feeling that it is all right to have what one wants, and that it is only a matter of time until one manifests it. Softens the fear that there will never be enough and the panic that goes with the fear of missing out. **b)** Raises one's self esteem. One feels confident that one can be effective in one's life, and that life will be good. **c)** Creates a sense of harmony and balance for those who take life at a slower pace and slows down those who tend to "buzz" through life. **d)** Promotes moderation in one's approach to life, and softens tendencies to be overly expansive or overly structured. **e)** In the Michael system, pulls one into the positive pole of Greed, a Chief Negative Feature. Balances low-frequency types of people or those who are either high-male or high-female energied.

**Blue Aventurine:** See Aventurine, Blue.

**Blue Halite:** See Halite, Blue.

**Blue Lace Agate:** See Agate, Blue Lace.

**Boevnite:** Same in effect as Pharmacolite

**Bogdanovite:** (Rosy brown to bronze in color). Reduces freneticism and harried hurriedness. Encourages one to mellow out and take things at a more comfortable pace. Increases effectiveness as one can pay more attention to what one is doing.

**Boggildite:** (Red in color). Attracts one's sexual karmas and relationships, to one, by augmenting one's pheromonic range. One broadcasts one's availability and readiness over a wider geographical area.

**Boleite:** (Dark blackish-blue cubes). A good-luck charm. Makes one feel lucky and receptive to the positive forces of fate. Brings positive energy flowing into one's life.

**Bolivarite:** (Green, white or gold-yellow in color). Aids in healing the joints of the body.

**Boltonite:** (Crystals of white Peridot). Same in effect as Peridot.

**Boltwoodite:** (Yellow in color). **a)** Increases one's ability to hunt and forage for food. Sharpens the senses and one is better able to spot tracks, tell when one is upwind of the quarry, or find the elusive edible mushrooms. **b)** It also increases eye-hand coordination in hunting activities. One is more accurate with a bow and arrow, knife, gun, etc.

**Bonaccordite:** (Reddish brown in color). Same in effect as Ludwigite.

**Bonamite:** Same stone as Smithsonite.

**Bone: a)** Helps one feel calmer and less afraid, especially in the arena of one's instinctive or survival-oriented issues. Makes one feel that everything will be fine in the long run. Fosters a sense of practicality and grounded awareness. Keeps one's actions sensible and calm. **b)** Good, all-purpose energetic balancer. Stabilizes one's energy level and keeps one moving through life at a comfortable pace: one that is neither too hurried nor too plodding. Makes one feel at home in one's body. **c)** Balances all chakras. Has a particularly strong healing and calming effect on the first chakra. **d)** Same in effect as Ivory, except that Ivory has a more refined quality to it. **e)** In the Michael system, balances all Centers and is particularly healing and balancing to the Instinctive Center. Balances one energetically and enables one to keep one's frequency rate stable.

**Boothite:** (Blue in color). Helps one project a strong, charismatic appeal. Inspires trust in others. Good for those in the public eye.

**Boracite:** (Transparent pale, green-blue crystals). Enables men to feel more comfortable in a male body. Enables both sexes to feel more comfortable around people in male bodies. Reduces the fear that one cannot relate to men very well.

**Borcarite:** (Blue-green). Reduces fear of water and water related activities. For example, one is less afraid of water on the face, or swimming, sailing or drowning.

**Bornite:** (Dark blue in color). Promotes wider social consciousness. Enables one to be innovative in one's approach to social issues or the application of justice. Encourages one to be concerned with what will work for society. Promotes a love of justice and keeps one aware of one's higher principles. One wants to be sure things are fair and is willing to protest if they're not.

**Bort:** Gray Diamonds.

**Bostwickite:** (Dark red in color). Increases one's ability to see the larger picture. Enables one to see where one is going with one's life and aids in the development of long-range plans. It also helps one to develop, and hone, strategic skills.

**Botrygen:** (Red to orange). Renews one's ability to be sexually excited when one's sexuality has been repressed or shut down for a period of time.

**Botswana Agate:** See Agate, Botswana.

**Boulangerite:** (Fibrous, gray masses). Same in effect as Jamesonite.

**Bournonite:** (Metallic, steel gray to black). Improves one's sense of direction. Makes it easier to find one's way home, or to find one's way about more easily when in a strange town

**Bowenite:** (Translucent pale green to yellow-green with waxy luster. A form of Serpentine). **a)** An anti-martyrdom stone. It eases one's sense of being victimized by others or by one's circumstances. Reduces feelings of helplessness. Good to give to anyone in the generation that went through the depression, since most have a sense of martyrdom they've never been able to shake.  **b)** Balances the hormonal system.  **c)** Healing and balancing to the female reproductive system and organs. Useful for girls going through puberty as it helps them stay on even keel. Helps alleviate cramps.  **d)** Good if pregnant. Keeps mother and fetus in alignment. Keeps everything related to the pregnancy functioning normally and in good shape. Reduces risk of birth defects and protects growth of the fetus, particularly if female.  **e)** In the Michael system, softens the Chief Negative Feature of Martyrdom.

**Bracewellite:** (Deep red to black in color). Encourages one to feel physically stronger, more capable, and more courageous. These are psychological effects. One is not actually stronger or more courageous. However, the effect of feeling this way, would raise one's self esteem and make one more capable of handling a situation one might previously have shunned.

**Brass:** Helps one to relax and move at a slower pace. Lowers one's frequency. Mild in effect.

**Braunite:** (Black or brownish-black crystals).  **a)** Generally healing and balancing to the reproductive system. In particular, keeps eggs healthy especially after fertilization.  **b)** Also balancing for egg laying animals such as chickens, fish, reptiles and birds of all kinds.

**Bravoite:** (Bright, steel-gray mineral). Same in effect as Iron Pyrite.

**Brazilian Agate:** See Agate, Brazilian.

**Brazilianite:** (Yellow or green-yellow crystals).  **a)** Stimulates one to investigate and research things in incredible detail or to investigate the unusual, esoteric or bizarre. Prevents "burn out".  **b)** In the Michael system, balances Mature and Old Scholars,

**Brecchiated Agate:** See Agate, Brecchiated.

**Brecchiated Jasper:** See Jasper, Brecchiated.

**Breithauptite:** (Copper-red in color). Enables women to be more comfortable with their female bodies. Makes it easier for both sexes to relate to women, those with female bodies, and to feel that they are less mysterious.

**Brochantite:** (Green and blue in color). Healing to the lungs, esophagus, and throat. Also aids the healing of cancer in those areas.

**Bronze:** Helps one to relax and move at a slower pace. Lowers one's frequency. Mild in effect.

**Bronzite:** (Metallic green-brown. Now called Enstatite). **a)** Stimulates one to exercise or simply move about vigorously. **b)** Opens, aligns and stimulates the third chakra. **c)** In the Michael system, balances and activates the Moving Center.

**Brookite:** (Dark brown to black crystals). Increases one's sense of personal power. Enables one to feel more capable and confident about handling whatever difficulties might appear.

**Brucite:** **a)** Makes one feel calmer and reduces one's tendency to have hysterics, when under emotional pressure. Makes one feel less pressured. **b)** In the Michael system, the effectiveness of each color is related to a particular Role. Different people will resonate to different colors. If one's Role is unknown, choose the color one finds most attractive.

| | |
|---|---|
| Priest: | Clear to White. |
| Server: | Yellow. |
| Sage: | Pale Green. |
| Artisan: | Pale Blue. |
| King: | Gray. |
| Warrior: | Brownish-red. |
| Scholar | Brown. |

**Bruneau Jasper:** See Jasper, Bruneau

**Brushite:** (White). Helps one to forget. Use this method: Pull up an unpleasant memory. Concentrate on that memory while holding the rock for a few minutes. Do this every day for a period of time and the memory will be erased. Usually one or two weeks will suffice. Drains the emotion out of the memory.

**Buergerite:** Same in effect as Black Tourmaline.

**Bukovskyite:** (Yellow-green in color). Same in effect as Peridot.

**Burckhardtite:** (Red to violet-red). Enables one to feel sexually excited, with no loss of intensity, as one grows older.

**Burmite:** Another name for Burnite.

**Burnite:** (Also called Sea Amber as it is found on Baltic beaches. Solid and dark golden brown in color). a) Enables one to remain neutral, and keep a realistic viewpoint in difficult situations. Helps one see clearly, without being either too pessimistic, or too optimistic. Especially helpful when one is worried about one's ability to see things objectively. b) Enables one to effectively use one's intellect, and stay clearly observant, even when in crisis or strongly emotional. c) Balances the fifth chakra. d) In the Michael system, pulls one into the positive pole of the Attitude of Realist. Balances the Intellectual Center.

**Bustamite:** Same stone as pink Rhodonite.

**Buttgenbachite:** (Dark blue in color). a) Contains impulsiveness and puts one in touch with the internal monitor that keeps the expression of one's emotions appropriate. Encourages one to pay attention to the proper social behavior needed in any given situation. Stimulates refined behavior. b) In the Michael system, teaches the appropriate use of Repression Mode.

**Butterfat Jade:** See Jade, Butterfat.

**Byssolite:** (Blue-green in color. A type of Actinolite that occurs in long crystals). Same in effect as Actinolite.

**Bytownite Feldspar:** See Feldspar, Bytownite.

**Cacholong Opal:** See Opal, Cacholong.

**Cacoxenite:** (Brick-red to black in color). **a)** Encourages an ambitiousness that is practical, as well as powerful. **b)** Enables one to handle a position of authority and power, in a stable and grounded way that is not easily disrupted.

**Cahnite:** (White to beige to orange in color). **a)** Speeds the metabolism. One side effect of speeding the metabolism is that it would be easier to lose weight; another side effect is that it would be easier to keep warm when it's cold. **b)** Encourages the body to move at a quicker pace. Good for getting things accomplished and/or keeping the body exercised.

**Cairngorm:** Scottish name for Smoky Quartz.

**Calamine:** Same stone as Hemimorphite.

**Calcite, Black: a)** Promotes a healthy cynicism. Allows one to look at things in the worst possible light if that's what one feels the need to do. Enables one to see everything that could possibly go wrong. Thus, one can take precautions, or work out all possible problems instead of passing them over. **b)** In the Michael system, promotes appropriate use of the Attitude of Cynic.

**Calcite, Blue: a)** Balances one's emotional state and removes blocks, so emotions can flow more easily. Reduces intensity. **b)** Balances, heals and unblocks all chakras. Particularly effective for balancing and healing the fourth chakra. Very rapid in its effect. **c)** In the Michael system, balances and heals all Centers with particular emphasis on balancing the Emotional Center.

**Calcite, Brown or Gold: a)** Enhances one's capacity to know what is true. Creates a sense of joyous clarity. Makes one better able to appreciate higher wisdom and philosophers such as Lao Tsu. **b)** Balances and heals the sixth chakra. **c)**

In the Michael system, balances the Higher-Intellectual Center and connects one with the energy of the Mental Plane.

**Calcite, Dog's Tooth:** (Gray in color. Crystals formed in sharp, tooth-like spikes). Same stone as Gray Calcite.

**Calcite, Gray: a)** Gives one a break from emotional intensity, so one can take a look at the issues in one's life from a detached point of view. **b)** Temporarily eliminates and neutralizes the impact of karmic influences. Allows one to see what's going on and remain neutral about it emotionally.

**Calcite, Green: a)** Aids in healing toxic fume damage. Clears toxins from the body and the atmosphere. Useful to keep in the car, in the hot tub (we live in California, folks!), in the swimming pool or anywhere one wishes to keep toxins to a minimum. **b)** Also aids in healing allergies to toxic fumes and chemicals.

**Calcite, Orange: a)** A happiness stone. Reduces skepticism and puts one in the state of mind that everything is just fine. **b)** In the Michael system, balances the Emotional Center and pulls one to the positive pole of the Attitude of Skeptic.

**Calcite, Red:** (Pink to Salmon in color). **a)** Encourages one to feel that it is safe to open up emotionally. Allows negative emotions to be drained out of the body rather than held or absorbed. Makes one feel protected emotionally, and not so vulnerable. **b)** Balances the fourth chakra. **c)** In the Michael system, balances the Emotional Center.

**Calcite, Violet: a)** Enables one to feel harmoniously connected to, and at peace with, everything that is. Enables one to feel comfortable with any circumstances one encounters. Encourages one to feel that everything is perfect just as it is. **b)** In the Michael system, balances the Higher-Moving Center and puts one in touch with the energy of the Buddhaic Plane.

**Calcite, White or Clear: a)** For spiritual awareness. Enables one to experience a feeling of love and connectedness with the entire universe. One feels certain that one is loveable; that one is worthy of being loved by the Supreme Being and that one is worthy of being connected to, and experiencing, higher planes of existence. b) Balances the seventh chakra, and gives one a protected feeling: that it is safe to be spiritually open and vulnerable. c) In the Michael system, balances the Higher-Emotional Center, and connects one with the energy of the Messianic Plane.

**Calcite, Window Pane:** Same stone as White Calcite in blocky crystals.

**Caledonite:** (Dark green crystals). Makes one feel friendly and more comfortable relating to others. Helpful for those who are wooden in social situations and not very charismatic. Encourages one to feel neighborly.

**California Opal:** See Opal, California.

**Californite:** Same stone as green Idocrase.

**Callaghanite:** (Royal blue). Enables one to hear, and calmly deal with, unpleasant news.

**Callais:** Same stone as Turquoise.

**Calomel:** (Pale metallic crystals). Makes one feel more energetic and prompts one to move at a faster pace.

**Cameo Shell:** (Peach and cream layers). a) Good for eliminating bad habits and inappropriate behavior patterns. Makes it easier to access unconscious motivations, and allows one to look at whether one needs to keep the behavior pattern or habit. Allows evaluation of the usefulness of any particular behavior pattern or habit. b) In the Michael system, opens the Instinctive Center and enables one to access unconscious motivations.

**Campbellite:** Stimulates the body to move. A good exercise motivator. Also gives the body a greater degree of endurance and stamina.

**Campigliaite:** (Vivid yellow or light blue color). Same in effect as Pyromorphite.

**Cancrinite:** (Bright yellow or orange in color). Same in effect as Orpiment. Often found with Sodalite.

**Cape Amethyst:** Same stone as Lavender Quartz.

**Cape Chrysolite:** Same stone as Prehnite.

**Cave Onyx:** Same stone as Calcite except occurring in Stalactite form.

**Carbonado:** Same as Black Diamonds.

**Carbuncle:** Another name for Garnet.

**Carminite:** (Red. Can be dull or bright). **a)** Increases short-term memory retention. Enhances one's ability to remember what happened within the last 24 hours. **b)** Makes one extremely observant of all that is happening in the present moment. **c)** In the Michael system, pulls one into the positive pole of Observation Mode.

**Carnallite:** (Transparent colorless crystals that absorb water). Helps the body gain weight. Encourages maximum usage of caloric intake.

**Carnelian:** (Orange to orange-brown and tan in color). **a)** Increases one's sense of self worth and helps eliminate the fear of being inadequate. Allows one to temporarily put aside major self esteem issues such as "What am I really worth?" Major questions like this, as well as others such as "I'm so embarrassed to be seen in public with my new hairdo", feel laid to rest--not that they're handled or will never come up again. Thus, one gets a break from needing to be better than anyone else or agonizing over how inferior to others one feels. This creates the space for some positive feedback to flow in. **b)** Balancing for "buzzy", fast-moving people and is energizing for those who take life at a slower pace. **c)** Enables one to use one's focused, organizational abilities, and one's creative, innovative abilities, in a balanced fashion. **d)** In the Michael system, softens the Chief Negative Features of Arrogance and Self-Deprecation. Balances high-frequency types of people, or those whose proportion of male to female energy is more or less equal.

**Carnotite:** (Yellow to orange in color). **a)** Enhances one's ability to use logic and reason is and heightens one's intuitive and emotional sensitivity. Allows one to stay intellectually and emotionally clear when under stress, particularly if one's survival issues have been activated. **b)** Vastly increases one's puzzle-solving capabilities. **c)** Balances and heals the first, fourth and fifth chakras. Allows them to work together in a blended fashion. **d)** Often found with Metahewettite and Rauvite. **e)** In the Michael system, balances and heals the Instinctive, Emotional and Intellectual Centers.

**Carrollite:** (Yellow, mustard, yellow-green, green or brown in color). Promotes stability in the home. Stimulates a desire to put down roots. Encourages the appreciation of one's home, and enjoyment in focusing one's attention on it. Don't wear a rock like this, put it somewhere around the house.

**Cassiterite:** (Brilliant black crystals. Also pale brown). **a)** A power stone that enables one to be more productive, organized, focused, and forceful. **b)** Enables one to build an empire in the area of business or politics, or any arena that needs mastery of organizational and strategic skills. **c)** In the Michael system, a power stone for Warriors.

**Cassiterite, Wood-Tin:** (Yellow-brown to red-brown lumps). For lowering one's internal energy and drive so that one can slow down, come to a standstill, and get ready for a little reflection and re-evaluation. Doesn't help one re-evaluate, it helps one get off the merry-go-round.

**Celadonite:** (Dull green in color). **a)** Deflates arrogance. Makes one aware of one's own flaws. One also feels less judgmental of the flaws of others. Since one can cringe under such ruthless self scrutiny, it is recommended that one use this rock along with those that promote self-esteem or self love. **b)** In the Michael system, softens the Chief Negative Feature of Arrogance.

**Celestine:** Same stone as Celestite.

**Celestite:** (Blue to blue-gray crystals). **a)** Inspires one to visionary and beautiful flights of fancy. Enables one to keep a level head and promotes the ability to stay grounded while in a state of spiritual inspiration. Makes one feel more comfortable with the "higher altitudes" of inspirational philosophy. **b)** Helps one adjust to heights or to high altitudes. Good for air-travel phobias or a general fear of heights. **c)** In the Michael system, creates a positive experience of the Attitude of Spiritualist.

**Celunite Rose:** Another name for Desert Rose.

**Cerargyrite:** Same stone as Chlorargyrite.

**Cerussite:** (Gray, black, brown, tan or colorless). Aids in fungus removal.

**Cervantite:** (Rich yellow). Same in effect as Stibnite.

**Ceylonite:** Same stone as dark green Spinel.

**Chabazite:** (Translucent pink, salmon or red-brown, yellow or white in color). Increases fertility and balances pregnant women.

**Chalcanthite:** (Poisonous Copper Sulfate in vivid blue crystals). **a)** Opens one up to spiritually-based, emotional experiences. Promotes a feeling that one can love all mankind. Helpful to those who are super intellectual or action oriented and have difficulty experiencing their finer emotions. **b)** Opens and balances the seventh chakra. **c)** A good channeling stone. The effect is very strong and it is important to be grounded and have all chakras aligned and balanced before using this stone to channel. See sections on Channeling and Chakras. **d)** In the Michael system, balances the Higher-Emotional Center, and opens one up to the energy of the Messianic Plane.

**Chalcedony, Gray, Blue or Purple: a)** Helps one be aware of what one does not want in one's life. Gray helps one get rid of unwanted things. Purple makes one aware of the emotional experiences one doesn't want to have, which are usually related to the people in one's life. Blue relates to what one doesn't want intellectually in one's space. The gray is usually preferred because most people prefer to clear things out of their life, rather than people or ideas. b) In the Michael system, pulls one into the positive pole of the Goal of Discrimination.

**Chalcedony, Green:** Same stone as Chrysoprase.

**Chalcedony, Pink:** a) Helps one be very discriminating about one's appearance. Useful for people who don't pay much attention to how they look. Creates a greater sense of self-esteem by making one feel that one is taking better care of one's self. This stone is useful for people who are intellectually oriented as they tend to ignore their appearance a lot. b) In the Michael system, promotes a positive experience of the Goal of Discrimination.

**Chalcocite:** (Dull, metallic grey-black to black in color). a) Encourages one to perservere through any hardship. Increases one's emotional stamina and ability to stick with it. b) Encourages a cautious, deliberate approach when appropriate, and keeps one from becoming overly fearful. c) In the Michael system, pulls one into the positive use of Caution or Perserverence Mode.

**Chalcolite:** Same stone as Torbernite.

**Chalcophanite:** (Brownish-black or black). Helps the body fight off invasive bacteria. An immune system booster when invading bacteria are present.

**Chalcophyllite:** (Green or blue green in color). Stimulates others to have emotional responses to the person carrying the stone. Useful to promote intimacy in a relationship with good communication. Helpful to use in combination with a communication stone.

**Chalcopyrite:** (Brassy yellow or many hued). a) Raises one's self-esteem and increases one's positive self regard. The energy of this stone keeps one feeling good about one's self and seeing one's self in a positive light. Makes one feel that one is a worthwhile and useful member of society. b) Also encourages eccentricity. Enables one to be eccentric and comfortable with one's eccentricity as well. c) In the Michael system, softens the Chief Negative Feature of Self-Deprecation. While many stones affect a Chief Feature by helping one notice what one is doing, this stone works to change how one actually feels about oneself.

**Chalcosiderite:** Very powerfully assists one to get in touch with, and manifest, one's ambitions in a positive way.

**Chalcotrichite:** (Bright orange to red in color). Promotes feelings of joy, happiness, contentment. Similar in effect to Orange Calcite.

**Chalybite:** (Gold-brown, red-brown crystals). Same stone as Siderite.

**Chapinite:** Same stone as Chapmanite.

**Chapmanite:** (Beige-pink, yellow or green in color). Highly energizing. Sends bursts of energy throughout the body. Stimulates the adrenal glands and can be tiring if used for too long. Best when used for a specific purpose or project. If one is already feeling energetic, one will either blend with the energy of this rock and not notice its effect, or one will become super-energized and hyperactive. Good short-term pick me up when tired. Clean after each use, by placing it in the freezer for at least 12 hours.

**Charoite:** (Purple with fine white lacing). a) Puts one in touch with a sense of beauty and refinement. Makes one more aware of what one likes and what is perceived as an object of beauty. Enhances the desire and willingness to have beautiful things in one's life. b) Enables those who are involved in teaching, the media, or any profession that involves the dissemination of information, truth and/or wisdom, to feel powerful and project an aura of confidence and authority. c) In the Michael system, a power stone for Sages

**Charolite:** Same stone as Charoite

**Chelset:** Same stone as Pink Chalcedony.

**Chenevixite:** (Yellow-green to rich olive green in color). **a)** Encourages powerfully intense growth experiences to occur in one's life. Best used when one has a lot of time on one's hands, and one is ready for a new experience. **b)** In the Michael system, pulls one into the positive pole of the Goal of Growth.

**Cheralite:** (Red to Green) Enables one to feel well balanced and satisfied with one's sexual functioning. One feels neither too repressed nor too preoccupied sexually. Useful only for adults. Has this effect only after the hormonal balance is well established.

**Chert:** Same stone as Flint.

**Chessylite:** Same stone as Azurite.

**Chiastolite:** (Brown and black with Maltese Cross-like markings). A type of Andalusite.

**China Jade:** Another name for Bowenite.

**Chinese Writing Stone:** (Greenish black with white-gray markings). **a)** Helps calm anxiety and basic fears about survival. Makes one feel that everything will be all right. **b)** In the Michael system, calms the Instinctive Center.

**Chiolite:** Same in effect as Ralstonite.

**Chloanthite:** (White. Often coated with green Annabergite). **a)** Encourages one to be sensuous, soft, warm, and emotional. **b)** In the Michael system, a Venusian body-type Agate.

**Chlorargyrite:** (White). Increases speed of physical growth in plants, animals and people.

**Chlorite, Green:** (Clear with green fuzzy inclusions). **a)** Creates comfort and compatibility for a person in a female body whose energy is highly focused and concentrated. Has the same effect on a person in a male body whose energy is very fluid, creative, and expansive. Because this stone reduces the amount of conflict going on between body type and energy, one feels much more relaxed. **b)** Often found with Quartz which adds an element of observation and clarity to the adjustment process. **c)** A counterpart to Goethite. **d)** In the Michael system, attractive to those with female bodies, or to those who are high-female energied and paired with a disparate energy or body type.

**Chloromelanite:** (Black Jade and bright green Jadeite mixed together). Very balancing for women in the area of sexual identity. Gives a woman a clear sense of who she is as a woman; enables her to be comfortable with, and grounded in, her femininity.

**Chlorophane:** Same stone as Fluorite.

**Chloroxiphite:** (Emerald Green). **a)** Encourages strong spurts of intellectual growth. Enables one to learn new information in large chunks. **b)** In the Michael system, balances the Intellectual Center.

**Chondrodite:** (Deep brown-red clear crystals). **a)** Enhances productivity. **b)** Brings forth the qualities of bravery, protectiveness, acting from one's high ideals, feistiness, and the willingness to take orders. Promotes good strategic skills and the abililty to work as a team with others. **c)** In the Michael system, balances Warriors.

**Chromite:** (Brown in color). **a)** Self-esteem stimulator. Makes one notice when one is being self deprecatory. It then becomes too embarrassing to continue feeling worthless. Often found with Kammererite, which brings one into a state of perceiving one's connectedness to the whole. It is hard to maintain a belief that one is worse than everyone else, when one can perceive one's connectedness to them. **b)** In the Michael system, softens the Chief Negative Feature of Self-Deprecation.

**Chrysoberyl:** Healing to the physical body. While any of the Chrysoberyls are healing for almost everyone, they are slightly more effective for one type of person or another as the color varies. Michael says this effect is related to one's race and the geographical area in which it originated.

> **Brown:** General healing for Africans, Egyptians, and Caribbean Islanders.

**Cat's Eye:** Generally healing for Asians, Mediterraneans and South Americans.

**Golden:** Generally healing for Australians, Native Americans, Filipinos, and Polynesian Islanders.

**Yellow-Green:** General healing for Northern Europeans, Russians, and North American of European descent.

**Chrysocolla:** (Light green). a) Crystallizes feelings of spiritually-centered unconditional love, acceptance and tolerance toward others. Makes it possible to forgive others their wrongdoings and be more loving. Gives one the ability to see clearly what goes on with the other person. An outwardly directed stone. One is very perceptive and clear about others, but not necessarily about the self. Clarity of crystal is important: the clearer the crystal, the clearer one's perceptions of others are. b) In the Michael system, balances the Higher-Emotional Center and connects one with the energy of the Messianic Plane.

**Chrysolite:** Same stone as Peridot.

**Chrysopal:** Same stone as Prase.

**Chrysoprase:** (Green in color). a) Similar in effect and chemical composition to Chrysocolla. Chrysoprase, however, focuses one a little more inwardly on one's own ability to be loving. One asks: "What can I do to be more understanding and forgiving of this other person?" While one is still very perceptive about others, observation is not quite as sharp as with Chrysocolla. The clearer the stone, the greater the perceptual clarity. b) in the Michael system, balances the Higher-Emotional Center and connects one with the energy of the Messianic Plane. This stone is especially inspiring to Artisans.

**Chrysotile:** Same stone as Long Hair Asbestos.

**Cinnabar:** (Red in color). a) Enables one to be a dynamic "go getter". Encourages one to be dynamic, adventurous, risk-taking and assertive. Particularly good for those who are too meek or mild. b) In the Michael system, enables one to use the positive qualities of Aggression Mode. A stone that Warriors find attractive.

**Cinnamon Stone:** See Hessonite.

**Citrine:** (Light yellow to orange). **a)** Useful when one wants to slow things down and create a steady pace. Provides a sense of stability especially when things are moving along too fast. **b)** Builds up one's stamina and makes it easier to perservere through difficult processes or karmas. **c)** Useful for the hyperkinetic or those super high-energy folks who can't seem to calm down and move at a slower pace. Citrine helps them slow down and mellow out. **d)** Color varies from light yellow to orange. The lighter the color, the milder the effect. **e)** Helpful to combine with Aquamarine, Blue Topaz or Peridot as it makes the use of one's power, or the process of growth, steady and predictable rather than impulsive. **f)** In the Michael system, pulls one into the positive pole of Caution Mode. Balances high-frequency types of people.

**Clam Shell:** Especially healing for "high frequency", "buzzy", types of people who often live in a very intense state. Allows them to slow down and set a more comfortable pace. .

**Cleavelandite:** (White or grayish-white in color. Bladed form of Albite Feldspar). **a)** Balances and heals all chakras. **b)** An aid for those who are channels. Keeps one balanced and grounded while channeling. Enables a person to channel twice as long without getting tired.

**Cleiophane:** Another name for clear green or yellow Sphalerite.

**Clinochlore:** (Translucent in thin flakes. Blackish green in color). **a)** An other-directed stone that enhances one's ability to be nurturing, warm and responsive to the needs of others. **b)** In the Michael system, balances Servers. Helps all roles get in touch with their Server qualities.

**Clinoclase:** (Dark green). Increases the ability to use one's imagination.

**Clinochrysotile:** Same in effect as Antigorite.

**Clinoptilolite:** (Red in color). **a)** For spiritual awareness. Inspires one with a feeling of love and connectedness with the entire universe. One feels worthy of being loved by the Supreme Being and worthy of being connected to and experiencing higher planes of existence. **b)** In the Michael system, balances the Emotional Center and connects one with the energy of the Messianic Plane.

**Clinosafflorite:** (White to yellow silvery tiny crystals). Enhances the qualities of bravery, fearlessness and courageousness.

**Clinotryolite:** (Emerald green to blue in color). Same in effect as Aurichalcite.

**Clinozoisite:** (Pale to medium brown, light green or grayish-green in color). **a)** Enables those who take care of others, to be able to better take care of themselves. Those in positions of service tend to forget that they need to take care of themselves, as well as others, in order to remain balanced. **b)** In the Michael system, balances Servers.

**Coalingite:** (Red-brown in color). Increases one's desire to own physical property. Operates against the nomadic impulse and promotes the desire for roots and settling down.

**Cobalt:** (An orchid color rock in a brown matrix). **a)** Makes one feel connected with the Universe and receptive to spiritual influences. **b)** Keeps all chakras aligned and balanced. **c)** A channeling aid. Has the effect of Sugilite and Cleavelandite combined. Very useful for opening up one's channeling abilities. **d)** When heat treated, Cobalt becomes Cobalt Glass and is much milder in effect.

**Cobalt Glass:** (Blue, orange or red in color). **a)** Makes one feel connected with the Universe and receptive to spiritual influences. **b)** Opens the seventh chakra.

**Cobaltite:** (Tin-white with a metallic luster). **a)** Helps one integrate lessons about oneself and one's life, and pull them together into a coherent whole. Useful for anyone with changes to integrate into their lives. Also useful for those who wish to do some re-evaluation, and are taking a long, hard look at their lives. **b)** In the Michael system, pulls one into the positive use of the Goal of Re-Evaluation.

**Coffinite:** (Rich black in color). Encourages a feeling of surrender to the inevitable. One feels that all will turn out right in the end. Reduces one's fear that thing's will go wrong and makes it easier to move ahead.

**Coesite:** Same stone as Quartz Crystal.

**Colemanite:** (Colorless, white, faintly straw-yellow or grayish). **a)** Encourages one to relax one's concentration and widen one's focus to view things from a "larger picture" perspective. Enables one to operate in a more expansive, fluid manner. Especially good for those who use their energy in a highly focused, concentrated manner most of the time, and need help shifting. **b)** In the Michael system, balances high male-energied types of people and helps them use their female-energied side more effectively.

**Collophane:** Same stone as Apatite.

**Colorado Ruby:** Same stone as Pyrope.

**Columbite:** (Black square crystal). **a)** Boosts one's self confidence by decreasing any tendencies one has toward timidity, false humility, embarrassment or self-deprecation. **b)** In the Michael system, softens the Chief Negative Feature of Self-Deprecation.

**Conchiolin:** Same material as Pearls.

**Conichalcite:** (Vivid green). Good when pregnant. Puts mother and fetus in balance with each other.

**Connelite:** Same in effect as Agardite.

**Connemara:** (Green and black. A type of Marble). Promotes prosperity, the acquisition of wealth, and strong feelings of satisfaction and contentment.

**Copco Agate:** See Agate, Copco.

**Copiapite:** (Bright yellow in color). Helps one recuperate from poisons in one's system. This not only includes literal poisons such as arsenic, snake venom, etc., but also substances one is allergic to, such as bee stings, or ant and spider bites. Use by holding in one's hand. DO NOT EAT. Not a substitute for appropriate medical care.

**Copper:** a) An energizer. Makes one feel more energetic or "buzzy." b) Releases energy blocks in the body. When energy is stopped or blocked at any point in the body, difficulties can develop. Copper can be used to remove the energy blocks, and thus promote the healing of various conditions. For example, useful for relieving arthritic pain, cramps, or tension headaches. c) In the Michael system, raises one's frequency.

**Copper, Peacock:** Same stone as Chalcopyrite and Copper Pyrite.

**Copper, Pyrite:** Same stone as Peacock Copper and Chalcopyrite.

**Copralite:** (Petrified dinosaur dung. Mottled red, green and brown). Promotes a feeling a kinship or fellowship, with other forms of animal life. Reduces fear of all kinds of animals. This includes all mammals, birds, insects and fish.

**Coquimbite:** (Purple sometimes surrounded by a bright yellow matrix). a) Increases one's self esteem. Enables one to feel adequate to, and capable of, handling whatever challenges one might face. b) Makes one feel proud of the things one has accomplished. Also increases one's pride in one's children, one's mate, cohorts and anyone else one feels a close connection with, or with whom one identifies. c) In the Michael system, softens the Chief Negative Feature of Self-Deprecation and pulls one into the positive pole of Arrogance.

**Coral, Apple:** (Smooth, fibrous material that varies from brown to rosy red with black, branch-like striping). a) Makes one open to loving and to being involved with others and, at the same time, healed of fear about such closeness. As a result, one is very warm-hearted and deeply caring. b) Creates a feeling of enthusiasm for life. c) In the Michael system, calms the Instinctive Center. Pulls one into the positive pole of Passion Mode.

**Coral, Black:** a) Major healer of fear and anxiety particularly in the area of one's instinctive or survival-oriented issues. It heals fear by helping one to examine what's going on. The importance of this is that there are two basic emotions in the universe--fear and love--when one is healed of fear, what is left is love. b) Good for past life and early life review, as it aids in the accessing and processing one's deepest issues. c) Creates a sense of harmony and balance for those who take life at a slower pace. High energy types, those who buzz through life at a very fast pace, might feel it slows them down too much. Or they might love it, because it can help them to relax and mellow out. d) In the Michael system, balances the Instinctive Center, and low-frequency types of people

**Coral, Blue:** a) Promotes a sense of adventurousness and Peter Pan-like fun. b) Encourages the passionate pursuit of knowledge. c) In the Michael system, pulls one into the positive pole of Passion Mode.

**Coral, Elephant Ear:** (Pale celery green, yellow and white in color). a) Stimulates one's passion for new philosophical concepts and encourages intellectual pursuits. b) In the Michael system, pulls one into the positive pole of Passion Mode and gives one an experience of intellectually-centered enthusiasms.

**Coral, Purple:** a) Encourages homosexual attraction. b) Encourages an interest in offbeat or "kinky" sexual experiences.

**Coral, Red, Pink or White:** a) Wear to create emotional openness and enthusiasm. White emphasizes the qualities of love and affection while the pinker or redder the Coral is, the more passionate and sexual it becomes. Goes well with dark green Tourmaline for communication. b) In the

Michael system, pulls one into the positive pole of Passion Mode.

**Coral, Sponge:** (White or coral pink, porous, sponge-like material). **a)** Encourages recreational and non-karmic sex of the "let's have fun" variety. Not very intense, but fun. Associated with a more "childlike" and innocent view of sex: one without too many expectations or preconceived ideas. **b)** Encourages one to enjoy flirtations.

**Corderoite:** (Light pink to brown in color). Useful to maintain the skin in a healthy state. Also, a general healer for the skin. Heals wounds, burns and diseases of the skin.

**Cordierite:** Same stone as Indialite and Iolite.

**Corkite:** (Rich, pure yellow in color). Makes one feel comforted, safe and secure. Soothes minor emotional aches and pains. Allows a sense of lightheartedness to creep in when one is feeling emotionally "under the weather".

**Cornetite:** (Dark green or blue in color). Increases fertility. Promotes sperm production and stimulates the healthy functioning of male and female reproductive organs.

**Cornubite:** (Green in color). **a)** Useful for anyone involved in teaching. Creates confidence in one's ability to teach. Makes it easy for one's knowledge to flow forth. **b)** In the Michael system, balances Scholars.

**Cornwallite:** (Dark green in color). Encourages one to feel more attuned to the earth and all of its natural substances. One feels more comfortable absorbing the energy of natural settings. Neutralizes the impact of an overly mechanized society or lifestyle. Also makes it easier to make the transition from city to country living.

**Coronadite:** (Black in color). Same in effect as Wulfenite.

**Corvusite:** (Blue-black in color). A protective device useful when one is going into highly dangerous situations. Enables one to notice which objects in one's environment could be used as a weapon, or as a means to protect one in some manner.

**Covellite:** (Metallic blue-black in a silvery matrix. Occasionally some green matrix is included as well). a) A concentration stone. Promotes focus and clarity. Makes it easier to engage in tasks that require a high degree of concentration. b) In the Michael system, enables one to use one's male-energied side more easily, even if one is high-female energied.

**Crazy-Lace Agate:** See Agate, Crazy Lace.

**Creedite:** (Pale to medium lilac crystals). a) Enables one to feel directly connected with the Tao and thus with one's spirituality. One feels directly connected to God. b) In the Michael system, balances the Higher-Moving Center and connects one with the energy of the Tao.

**Cristobalite:** Same stone as Quartz Crystal.

**Crocidolite:** Same stone as Long Hair Asbestos.

**Crocoite:** (Red-orange crystals). Heals back pain and headaches. Quickest effect is achieved by holding the rock on the sore spot.

**Crossite:** (Fibrous and gray in color). Enables one to come up with creative solutions to problems that are accessed from the deepest, most primal subconscious. When a person feels most miserable or desperate about something that is going on, this stone draws up solutions from the survival instincts. These solutions can be very extreme: tailored to fit an extreme situation, such as letting the lion eat your arm off in order to escape from the quicksand. Problems can arise if an individual feels, on the instinctive level, that the problem he/she is facing is of these proportions. The solution this stone might then generate, could be more extreme than would be appropriate in our modern day and age, where life and death rarely hang in the balance. This is where a potential, to misuse the energy of this rock, can arise.

**Cryolite**: Same in effect as Ralstonite.

**Crystal, Aqua Aura**: (Blue-tinted Crystal. Created by giving clear Quartz Crystal a very thin wash with Gold). The blue sheen gives the Crystal an intense sharp focus that produces a laser-beam effect. If the clear Crystal is not programmed, then its natural metaphysical properties are enhanced. If programmed, it augments the ability of the Crystal to manifest whatever it is programmed to do, with more power. For example, one group in the metaphysical community has used it successfully to communicate with non-human sentient beings.

**Crystal, Clear**: a) Increases one's powers of observation and promotes clarity of thought. The clearer the stone, the more effective it is in enabling one's perceptions to be accurate and clear. See discussion on Clear Quartz Crystals in the section "Gemstones: Nature's Gift" for more information. b) In the Michael system, reflects the positive pole of Observation Mode.

**Crystal, Grayish-Brown**. Same stone as Smoky Quartz.

**Crystal, leaded or glass**. Leaded or glass Crystal is man-made Crystal. It has the same qualities of naturally occurring Quartz Crystal when of the same color, although milder in effect. There is also a wider range of colors available in leaded or glass Crystals since they are man made. The effect then varies with the color and, again, is very mild.

> **Blue-Green**: Open-hearted acceptance:
> **Brown**: Puts one in the space of thinking: i.e., processing intellectually.
> **Green**: Puts one in the mood for talking.
> **Lavender**: Balancing physically.
> **Light Green**: Calming.
> **Light Blue**: Projects an aura of strength and authority.
> **Orange, Champagne, Tan**: Makes one feel happier.
> **Pink**: Encourages simplicity in one's point of view.
> **Raspberry Pink**: Makes one feel exuberant and festive.
> **Red**: Makes one more dynamic and lively.

**Royal Blue:** Softens impatience or a tendency toward martyrdom.

**Yellow:** Makes one feel more energetic.

**Crystal, Purple:** Same stone as Amethyst.

**Crystal, Yellow to Gold:** Same stone as Citrine.

**Cubic Zirconia:** (All colors: A man-made Garnet). **a)** Aids in maintaining a high productivity level. **b)** Increases one's prosperity and the ability to have what one wants in one's life. Produces a higher "havingness". **c)** When Cubic Zirconia is colored, each color adds a slightly different twist to the basic energetic effect: that of productivity and prosperity.

**Blue:** Adds an element of calm.

**Brown:** Prompts the body to relax and let go of physical tension.

**Green:** Puts a stronger emphasis on prosperity: focuses one on making life just like one wants it to be.

**Pink, Lilac or Purple:** Creates a mood of relaxation and a desire for spiritual pursuits. Would not not promote productivity in the arena of "getting things done."

**Red:** Adds a little extra punch and a dynamic quality.

**Yellow to Orange:** Adds an element of contentment or happiness: promotes a mildly pleasurable state.

**Cumengite:** (Indigo blue. Found as a growth on Boleite). Encourages a passionate fervor for taking advantage of the opportunities that come one's way, particularly those arising out of the good-luck energy stimulated by Boleite.

**Cuprite:** (Red in color). **a)** Aids in avoiding conception. Do not use this stone as the only form of birth control. This stone works only as long as intention is with it. If one, even subconsciously, wants to get pregnant, this stone will not stop that from happening. **b)** If one has already conceived, this stone can help prevent pregnancy by making it difficult for the fetus to attach itself to the uterine wall. A good stone to avoid if one desires the pregnancy. (Poisonous. Don't eat it!)

**Cuprolite:** (Mottled blue, brown, black and green. Sometimes yellow dots or red streaks). **a)** For service, practicality and attention to detail. Enables one to be practical and grounded while working in a capacity of servce to others. Makes it easier to pay attention to the details of what needs to be done to create excellence in service. **b)** In the Michael system, balances Servers and helps them stay on track.

**Cuprosklodowskite:** (Bright green metallic flakes). Increases one's sense of fun. Encourages greater friendliness and affability. A great stone to take to parties, particularly if one is shy.

**Cuprosmithsonite:** Same stone as Herrerite.

**Cyanotrichite:** (Blue in color). **a)** Balances hormones and stimulates new hair growth. **b)** Promotes psychological transformation. Transforming due to its ability to pull one into emotional intensity and depth. It works by stimulating the hormones which in turn stimulates emotional intensity.

**Cymrite:** (Blue green in color). When wearing this stone, one's most loveable qualities become apparent to those around one. Even one's enemies are drawn to one, are able to see one's positive qualities, and are more willing to give one the benefit of the doubt. Further, even the most obnoxious person can wear this stone, and people around them can find them appealing for the few good qualities they have. A very powerful rock, so a very tiny piece is effective. Acts on the perceiver's abililty to see one's good qualities Does not change the perceptions of the "wearer".

**Cyprine:** Same stone as blue Idocrase.

**Danburite:** (Colorless, wine-yellow, pink, sometimes streaked with white) **a)** Enables one to be more patient. Particularly good for the very heavily impatient who can be extremely intolerant: the type of person who will hyperventilate if caught in a traffic jam, because they can't stand the slow pace. **b)** In the Michael system, softens the Chief Negative Feature of Impatience.

**Datolite:** (Pale, yellowish-green in color). **a)** Produces clearer thinking. Heals exhaustion around communication. **b)** Balances the fifth chakra. **c)** In the Michael system, balances the Intellectual Center.

**Demantoid Andradite:** (Emerald green in color). Heals veins.

**Dendritic Agate:** See Agate, Dendritic.

**Desautekite:** (Grey-blue rock). Enables one to predict future trends and assess more accurately the probabilities of various events occurring in the future.

**Desautelsite:** (Orange in color). **a)** Puts one in touch with one's deepest emotions. Encourages emotional rather than intellectual processing of one's problems. **b)** In the Michael system, opens and balances the Emotional Center.

**Descloizite:** (Dark brown in color). **a)** Removes external aberrant growths such as warts, moles, skin growths, blisters, and hives. **b)** Promotes a tendency to reject anything foreign, including man-made objects, from one's environment.

**Desert Rose:** (Brown-beige platey crystals of Barite arranged in a rosette). Helps the body keep calcium in the bones. Especially good for women.

**Desmine:** Same stone as Stilbite.

**Deutschner:** Same stone as Rim Jasper.

**Devilline:** (Pale to very dark blue to green). Enables one to see when one is being loved and cared for. Enables one to see what one does, that is appreciated by others.

**Devillite:** Same stone as Devilline.

**Diabase:** (Dark gray, greenish-black). For fertility and potency. Makes it easier to "get" pregnant or "make" someone pregnant. Steps up sperm production. Has a beneficial influence on the health of the sexual organs. Helps maintain erections.

**Diadochite:** (Yellow to brown in color). Puts one in touch with the larger picture of one's life plan. Enables one to step back and get perspective. Not good for planning, as details tend to fall away. Particularly good for those who get stuck in the details of everyday life and have no perspective on where they are going.

**Diamond:** a) Promotes the pursuit of excellence, the development of competence, and the mastery of oneself or one's environment. Enables one to take on projects that are vast in scope and succeed with them. b) Promotes a feeling of richness and abundance. c) Promotes mastery of the activities associated with the chakra it is worn closest to. For example, Diamonds worn near the second chakra, promote excellence as a lover and high quality in one's creative projects. d) In the Michael system, a power stone for Kings. e) Diamonds also come in a variety of colors, and each color tends to resonate best to a particular chakra or Role.

| | | |
|---|---|---|
| **Black:** | First Chakra. | Kings. |
| **Pink-Red:** | Second Chakra. | Artisans. |
| **Clear:** | Third Chakra. | Warriors. |
| **Yellow:** | Fourth Chakra. | Servers. |
| **Green:** | Fifth Chakra. | Sages. |
| **Brown:** | Sixth Chakra. | Scholars. |
| **Blue:** | Seventh Chakra. | Priests. |

**Diamond, Herkimer:** See Herkimer Diamond.

**Diaspore:** (Colorless, white, greenish, brown, pale violet, or pink in color). a) For clear observation of one's personal life. Makes one look within and see what one has been ignoring. Doesn't dig up primal, survival issues. Also enables one to evaluate the effectiveness of one's actions. b) In the Michael system, reflects the positive pole of Observation Mode.

**Dichroite:** Same stone as blue Iolite.

**Diopside:** (Pale green fading to black; sometimes dark brown in color). Reduces fever and aches by balancing body temperature.

**Dioptase:** (Emerald green, blue-green). Healing for the brain. Includes anything that physically stresses the brain: e.g., edema, a mild concussion, or stress chemicals released into the brain from overstudying, or overworking.

**Dog's Tooth Calcite:** See Calcite, Dog's Tooth.

**Dolomite:** (Pale brown, or greyish, or greenish, or pink in color). Good for digestion. Promotes general internal bodily health. Kills off aberrant cells and promotes correct bone growth. Very mild in its action.

**Donathite:** (Brown). a) Makes one notice when one is being arrogant or bossy. Encourages one to soften one's approach. b) In the Michael system, softens the Chief Negative Feature of Arrogance.

**Dravite:** Same stone as yellow Tourmaline.

**Drusy Quartz:** See Quartz, Drusy.

**Duftite:** (Green in color). a) Makes it easier to learn any mechanical skill. This includes, for example, basketweaving, car repair, woodcarving, or football. b) In the Michael system, promotes skillful use of the Moving Center.

**Dumortierite:** (Blue, violet in color). Encourages a business-like attitude and helps one prioritize. Creates more organization, but does not necessarily affect productivity levels.

**Dundasite:** (White in color). a) Makes one calm, serene and reflective. b) In the Michael system, pulls one into the positive pole of the Attitude of Stoic.

**Dypingite:** (Forms in white balls). a) Enables one to stop all physical, emotional and mental activity. One can then sit back and, with this clean slate, envision new directions or see old events in a new light. b) Balances and heals the third, fourth and fifth chakras. Particularly good for healing and closing down these chakras when abused.  **c)** In the Michael system, especially good for Warriors, Kings and Scholars, or for stubborn types who have difficulty being flexible.  **d)** In the Michael system, balances and heals the Moving, Emotional and Intellectual Centers.

**Dyscrasite:** (Silvery). Encourages anyone in a male body to fully appreciate, and operate from, their innate maleness.

**Eckermannite:** (Green and fibrous). A memory stone. To stimulate one's memory of the key elements of any event. Useful for recalling key aspects of minor, as well as more major, events that have occurred in one's life.  For example, enables one to focus on where one last left one's keys or wallet, or the most important elements of the motorcycle accident one saw last week, or what was most significant about the heart attack one's father had when one was 12. Does not aid past life recall.

**Edingtonite:** (Yellow in color). If one is experiencing heavy grief, this stone softens it and allows one to get through recovery without collapse.

**Eilat:** (Blend of Chrysocolla, Turquoise, and Malachite).  **a)** The Malachite keeps one balanced and better able to use the energies of the Chrysocolla and Turquoise.  Infuses one with feelings of love.  **b)** Balances and opens the seventh chakra.  **c)** In the Michael system, balances the Higher-Emotional Center and connects one with the energy of the Messianic Plane.

**Elbaite:** Same stone as pink or red Tourmaline.

**Elestial Quartz:** See Quartz, Elestial.

**Emerada:** (Light green) For fearlessness. Wear in situations where one would normally feel afraid or anxious, and one will feel much calmer.

**Emerald:** (Emerald green in color).  **a)** Puts one in the mood for communication. Extremely balancing for anyone who has to deal with communication difficulties or with trying to discover the truth when there is a lot of information to sort through.  **b)** Useful when feeling a great deal of confusion about "what I should do with my life", especialy when one is trying to answer this question from several different levels at once. **c)** Softens an arrogant attitude. Brings up the question, "Am I thinking I am better than anyone else? I know I am privileged, rich, and good-looking, but am I using this to make me think I'm better than somebody else?" **d)** Balancing for "buzzy", fast-moving people and is energizing for those who take life at a slower pace. **e)** Enables one to use one's focused, organizational abilities, and one's creative, innovative abilities, in a balanced fashion. **f)** In the Michael system, balances Sages and softens the Chief Negative Features of Arrogance and Self-Deprecation. Balances high-frequency types of people, or those whose proportion of male to female energy is more or less equal.

**Empressite:** (Pale bronze). Encourages anyone in a female body to fully appreciate, use, and feel fulfilled in their femaleness.

**Enargite:** (Grey black to sooty-black in color). **a)** Puts one in alignment with one's spiritual self. **b)** Promotes vivid dreaming. Can be used by those who wish to remember more of their dreams. **c)** A shaman stone. Discovered centuries ago and used by shamans for vision quests and in combination with drugs for heavy hallucinatory experiences.

**Endlichite:** (Brown, white or yellow in color). (A form of Vanadinite). **a)** A service-oriented stone. Inspires one to feel good about taking care of other people, on an individual basis, and to feel calm and serene about day-to-day tasks that other people might consider drudgery. **b)** In the Michael system, balances Servers.

**Enhydritic Agate:** See Agate, Enhydritic.

**Enigmatite:** Same stone as Aenigmatite.

**Enstatite:** (Brown, grey-green, cat eyed). Same stone as Bronzite.

**Eosphorite:** (Pink or orange in color). Helps children (anyone prior to puberty and before the hormones start to change) to feel more secure, independent, and able to handle temporary absences of parents or primary caretakers. For an infant, this might mean several hours. Whereas, for a ten-year old, it might mean several weeks. We intend to convey that this stone is best used to reduce homesickness, to increase comfort with a new babysitter, etc., but not as a substitute for childcare.

**Epidote:** (Green to pistachio, to dark brown). **a)** Promotes the mastery of one's own power and enables one to remain powerful in a situation where another would like to victimize one, harm one, or undermine one's power. **b)** Promotes regular and steady evolution of the self. **c)** Protects the third chakra. **d)** In the Michael system, pulls one into the positive pole of the Goal of Growth and erases the Chief Negative Feature of Martyrdom, and facilitates the mastery of the Moving Center.

**Epidote, Piemontite:** See Piemontite Epidote.

**Erythrite:** (Purplish-red or pale pink in color). **a)** Discourages martyred behaviors or attitudes. Moves one away from regarding one's self as a victim and encourages one to be more selfless in one's actions. Good for those who have a tendency to be self centered and think too often of only themselves. **b)** In the Michael system, pulls one into selflessness, the positive pole of the Chief Negative Feature of Martyrdom.

**Esperite:** (Rich yellow in color). **a)** Enables one to see clearly one's purpose, or path in life, in the spiritual rather than career sense. "Spiritual" refers here to that which advances one's essence. This is accomplished by putting one in touch with that part of one that sees the overlying patterns of one's existence. Enables one to see the overview of one's life more clearly. This stone can not only be used to identify the general area of one's life purpose, such as being a healer or promoting world peace, but also to identify the specific tasks needed to accomplish this purpose. **b)** In the Michael system, balances the Higher-Intellectual Center.

**Ettringite:** Tends to attract money or energy in the form of goods (things that are worth money) into your life.

**Euclase:** (Sea-green, or light blue in color). a) Motivates one to strive for excellence and to achieve perfection. Makes one want to be exactly correct on all levels. Good to wear when one wants to make an incredibly good impression. In a difficult situation, this stone will help one remain diplomatic and tactful. b) In the Michael system, promotes appropriate use of Repression Mode.

**Eucryptite:** (White, usually with red fluorescence). a) Encourages anything hidden or secretive in its vicinity to reveal itself. While carrying it, one will find oneself blurting out secrets or saying exactly what one believes. Others would find it difficult to tell lies in one's presence. b) Also makes it easier to find hidden and lost things, like keys or buried treasure.

**Eudialyte:** (Mottled black, gray and pink). Aids vitamin absorption, particularly those that are fatty based or occur in complex foods or "yang" foods; e.g., nuts, fish, meats.

**Euxenite:** (Brownish black in color). Healing to the eyes. Helps heal injuries, eye strain and, over a long period of time, can improve nearsightedness or farsightedness.

**Falcon's Eye:** Another name for Spectrolite.

**Fancy Jasper:** See Jasper, Fancy.

**Fayalite:** (Orange in color). Increases female sexuality and fertility. Similar in effect to Ryalite, but Fayalite is more oriented toward increasing fertility, whereas Ryalite is more oriented toward balancing men and women sexually.

**Feitknechtite:** Same in effect as Manganite.

**Feldspar, Albite:** (Blue, clear and white). a) Balancing to those involved in furthering the spiritual development of others. Keeps one from becoming martyred, self-deprecating, overly emotional or overly involved. b) In the Michael system, balances Mature and Old Priests.

**Feldspar, Andesine:** (Metallic blue-green). a) Balances and grounds those involved in artistic or creative projects. b) In the Michael system, balances Mature and Old Artisans.

**Feldspar, Anorthite:** (Red or pale yellow in color). a) Promotes the pursuit of knowledge and keeps one from becoming close minded or overly theoretical. b) In the Michael system, balances Mature and Old Scholars.

**Feldspar, Bytownite:** (Red or pale yellow in color). a) Balancing to those in a position of power. b) In the Michael system, balances Mature and Old Kings.

**Feldspar, Labradorite:** (Lustrous. Grayish or pale straw yellow). a) Enables one to work for long periods of time without tiring. Balances and re-energizes those who have been overworking. b) In the Michael system, balances Mature and Old Warriors.

**Feldspar, Oligoclase:** (Orange or red-brown in color) a) Ensures that important information will be imparted clearly and in a balanced fashion. b) In the Michael system, balances Mature and Old Sages.

**Feldspar, Red to Brown:** a) Enables those in a position of service to stay balanced and not fall into negative patterns, such as being overly emotional, overly involved, martyred or self deprecating. b) In the Michael system, balances Mature and Old Servers.

**Ferberite:** (Black in color). Encourages one to be more willing to let go of familiar structures; allows one to be more accepting of new things, people and places; and to be more flexible and fluid about changes in one's life.

**Fern Agate:** See Agate, Fern.

**Fernandinite:** (Dark green in color). Stimulates feelings of pleasure. One feels generally happy and optimistic. Mild in effect.

**Ferroaxinite:** (Shades of brown, brownish gray and reddish brown). a) Promotes a sense of caution about one's actions, thoughts, feelings, or one's communications. Encourages one to proceed carefully, deliberately, and exactly, making sure all bases are covered.   b) In the Michael system, promotes positive use of Caution Mode.

**Ferrocolumbite:** Same stone as Columbite.

**Fire Agate:** Same in effect as Fire Opal.

**Fire Opal:** See Opal, Fire.

**Fish-Eye Stone:** Another name for Apophyllite.

**Flint:** (Many colors). a) Heals one of survival fears. Makes one feel like one can survive no matter what.  A good healer when one has gone through experiences that threaten one's survival.  b) In the Michael system, balances and heals the Instinctive Center.

**Fluorite:** (Clear, green, blue, blue-green, purple or yellow). a) Excellent aura cleanser. Fluffs the aura and rids it of any unwanted energies. Keeps others from making energetic attachments (cording) that are not desired.   Hold to forehead for 15 seconds for effect.  b) Balances and clears all chakras.  c) Useful as a channeling aid: allows the channel to remain uncorded while channeling.  c) All colors are equally effective. Use the color that seems most attractive for greatest compatibility and comfort.

**Fluorspar:** Another name for Fluorite.

**Francevillite:** (Canary yellow in color). Makes one feel secure on one's own land or home turf. Healing when one has been robbed.

**Franklinite:** a) Allows one to communicate about intense issues in a calmer fashion.  b) Softens emotional intensity and aids the release of emotion-based tensions. Keeps the emotions flowing in a steady fashion so they don't become blocked.  c) In the Michael system, balances the Emotional Center.

**Freibergite:** (Gray, metallic). a) Makes one more pragmatic. Puts one into a practical and reasonable frame of mind. Enables one to coolly and calmly perform tasks in the most logical manner.   b) In the Michael system, promotes the positive use of the Attitude of Pragmatist.

**Friedalite:** (Marbled orangey-pink and white in color). Enables one to feel more at home on the East Coast of the United States.  This is also where it is found.  Good for immigrants to the U.S. or citizens from other parts of the U.S. who are transplanted to the East Coast.

**Fuchsite:** (Green in color).  Increases one's appreciation of the artistic endeavors of others.  Also enhances one's talent around anything that requires artistic ability, flair, or an eye for design.

**Galena:** (Blue-grey in color).  **a)** A philosopher's stone. Promotes telling the truth and encourages one to look for what's true.  **b)** In the Michael system, pulls one into the balanced use of the Intellectual and Higher-Intellectual Centers.

**Galenite:** Another name for Galena.

**Garnet:** (Orange through red, purple and brown).  **a)** Best all-round stone for productivity.  Also promotes prosperity and having life exactly as one would like it to be.  The types of Garnet listed below, vary from one another by having a slightly different chemical composition and color.   **b)** In the Michael system, balances Warriors.

**Garnet, Almandine:** (Red with a violet tint).  **a)** Increases one's productivity.  Enables one to stay focused and to get things done in a competent, purposeful fashion.    **b)** Promotes prosperity.

**Garnet, Man-made:** Another name for Cubic Zirconia.

**Garnet, Pyrope:** (Red with brown tint, orange-red, purple-red, purple)  For productivity with the qualities of happiness and abundance.  Keeps one not only producing, but producing abundantly with a sense of happiness at the same time.

**Garnet, Rhodolite:** (Rose-red or pale violet type of pyrope). Promotes productivity and prosperity in the arena of one's career. Makes one feel productive while on the job.

**Garnet, Spessartite:** (Orange-brown, orange, yellow-orange in color). **a)** A productivity stone for the homemaker. Enables one to focus on the home and get a lot accomplished. **b)** Makes one feel grounded and rooted in the home. Brings forth a strong feeling of belonging with the family. Makes one feel happy and contented with one's home life. **c)** Boosts self confidence and decreases self-deprecation and arrogance. Brings up such feelings as "I'm a good person". "I have my niche and I know where I belong. So, it's unecessary for me to compare myself with others in any way." **d)** In the Michael system, softens the Chief Negative Features of Arrogance and Self-Deprecation. Balances Warriors

**Garnet, Star:** (Star is formed by Rutile). **a)** For high-powered productivity. The productivity of the Garnet is powered by the Rutile that "stars" it and keeps one moving "full steam ahead" for long periods of time. It is usually the Almandine Garnet that is found with the Rutile. **b)** In the Michael system, a stone preferred by Warriors.

**Gaudefroyite:** (Black, metallic). **a)** Enables one to transcend ego and one's sense of individual identity. Enables one to go beyond one's self and feel a part of the greater whole. **b)** In the Michael system, balances the Higher-Moving Center and connects one with the Tao.

**Gehlenite:** (Green/black in color). Encourages one to strengthen family ties and to recognize the family as important. Also makes one willing to go out of the way to insure the biological success of one's genes and, thus, protect the family lineage.

**Gem Silica:** (Gem quality of Chrysocolla). Same in effect as Chrysocolla, but stronger.

**Geodes:** (Hollow nodules with Crystal or Agate centers). **a)** Geodes are unique and individual. Each Geode represents a different observation about something that's true. One will be attracted to the Geode that reminds one of a particular observation that one has made and wishes to remember. For example, one Geode might encapsulate the observation that one needs to exercise. Another one might remind one of the observation that meditation has beneficial effects. For this reason, Geodes are best selected on a personal and individualized basis. **b)** In the Michael system, reflects the positive pole of Observation Mode.

**Getchellite:** (Metallic dark red in color). Encourages one to take risks to protect one's loved ones. Whatever risk is necessary will be undertaken, including the possible loss of one's life.

**Girasol:** Same stone as Fire Opal.

**Glaserite:** Same stone as Aphthitalite.

**Glauberite:** (Beige, sandstone-like platelets). Enables one to feel more comfortable around modern technological inventions. Helps ease the discomfort one feels with new advances in science and technology.

**Glaucocerinite:** (Bluish green in color). For emotional mastery. Allows one to feel in control of one's emotions and gives a comforting sense that one will make it through emotionally trying times.

**Gmelinite:** (Beige Crystals). **a)** Increases the delicacy of one's movements and enables one to project a general aura of refinement. **b)** In the Michael system, supports the positive use of Repression Mode.

**Goethite:** (Black, brownish-black, brownish-yellow in color. Found in Fluorite or Quartz Crystals). **a)** Enables a highly creative, sensitive man to be more comfortable in a male body. Good for men having a hard time with masculinity issues such as feeling they're not masculine enough or not in touch with their maleness. **b)** Enables women who are highly focused energetically to feel more comfortable within a female body. Because this stone reduces the amount of conflict going on between body type and energy, one feels much more relaxed. **c)** In the Michael system, attractive to those with male bodies or high-male energied females paired with a disparate energy or body type   d) A counterpart to green Chlorite.

**Gold:** Lowers frequency the most of any metal. Slows down the internal clock, and makes one feel more mellow.

**Goldstone:** (Glass with Copper flecks). Copper raises one's frequency or "buzziness", but is somewhat softened by the glass which surrounds it.

**Goldstone, Blue:** (Glass with copper flecks. The blue color is a dye). Copper raises one's frequency or "buzziness," but is somewhat softened by the glass which surrounds it. The dark blue color is very calming, particularly if one is intellectually stressed. The total effect is one of making one feel one can enjoy one's time off or feel a little peppier if tired.

**Goosecreekite:** (White in color). Helps one break through one's emotional and intellectual blocks to increasing one's prosperity.

**Gorceixite:** a) Increases one's self confidence. Makes it easier to believe in one's self.   b) In the Michael system, softens the Chief Negative Feature of Self-Deprecation.     c) Different colors work best for different types of roles. Choose the color one resonates to the most, if one's role is unknown.   When found as a mixture of colors such as yellow-green or orange-red, it works equally well for all Roles.

> **Red:**      Priests and Servers.
> **Orange:**   Sages and Artisans.
> **Yellow:**   Kings and Warriors.
> **Green:**    Scholars.

**Gordonite:** Healing to the myelin sheath; the outer covering of muscle cells.

**Goshenite:** (Colorless) a) Balances those who process life intellectually and have little or no emotional empathy.   b) An anti-pigheadedness stone.   Centers one in the appropriate use of the intellect and encourages one to depend on knowledge rather than theory. Good for those who get into rigid, opinionated theorizing; who resist any information that might challenge their pet theories or those who pontificate from an unbalanced emotional state. **c)** In the Michael system, balances Infant, Baby and Young Scholars. Also corrects an inappropriate use of the Intellectual Center.

**Goudeyite:** (Greenish-yellow). **a)** Decreases arrogance and keeps one from having "shy episodes": that agonizing flipping back and forth between self-deprecation and arrogance. This stone short circuits the process. Good for children since they usually go through episodes of this. **b)** In the Michael system, softens the Chief Negative Features of Self-Deprecation and Arrogance.

**Granite:** (Many colors). **a)** Allows one to feel directly connected to God: the Supreme Reality. **b)** Balances all chakras and makes one feel grounded and connected to the earth. **c)** Grounds one while channeling. **d)** In the Michael system, balances all Centers and connects one with the Tao.

**Graphite:** (Lead colored). Encourages a sense of orderliness and a desire for things to be in place. Makes it easier to get things done in an organized fashion.

**Gratonite:** (Gray metallic nodules). **a)** A survival stone. Helps one to believe that even under the most difficult of living situations such as poverty, starvation and extreme illness, that one can not only survive, one can thrive against all odds. The promotion of this attitude enables one to keep going when others would lose heart and aids one to succeed against all odds. **b)** In the Michael system, balances the Instinctive Center.

**Green Aventurine:** See Aventurine, Green.

**Grossular, Gray to Black:** **a)** Enables one to face survival threatening events, such as the loss of a job, with equanimity. One then feels calmer and less afraid. Functions similarly to Bone. **b)** In the Michael system, balances and heals the Instinctive Center.

**Grossular, Green:** Makes one more comfortable with communicating: i.e., one feels more comfortable with what one wants to say and with one's ability to communicate it.

**Grossular, Orange-Brown:** Same stone as Hessonite.

**Grossular, White:** Healing to the immune system.

**Grossular, Pale Yellow: a)** Reduces impatience about communication. Creates the feeling that one will be able to say it all, get all the information out, and that one can stay relaxed behind the push to communicate. Very good for those in the acting professions or media. **b)** In the Michael system, balances Sages, especially those who talk a lot. Particularly effective for Infant, Baby, and Young Sages.

**Groutite:** Same in effect as Manganite.

**Grunerite:** (Green/black in color). Same in effect as Bismuth.

**Gypsum: a)** Promotes intellectual clarity and competency. **b)** In the Michael system, balances the Intellectual Center. **c)** Colors relate to certain Roles. Where one is not sure of their Role, choose the color to which one resonates most.

| | |
|---|---|
| **Champagne & Pink:** | King. |
| **Clear:** | Scholar. |
| **Green:** | Sage. |
| **Lt. Brown:** | Warrior. |
| **White:** | Artisans. |
| **Yellow:** | Server. |
| **Yellow-Green:** | Priest. |

**Gyrolite: a)** Promotes one's ability to see the "larger picture" and be creatively expansive. Encourages one to become less focused, more fluid, and more versatile. **b)** In the Michael system, puts one more in touch with one's female-energied side and one's ability to use it. Accentuates female-energied qualities.

**Hackmannite:** (Purple-pink variety of Sodalite). Same in effect as Sodalite.

**Halite, Blue:** **a)** Helps one to attract one's soul mate into one's life. If one is already acquainted with this person, this stone helps one to get along with him or her. **b)** In the Michael system, helps one to attract one's essence twin into one's life.

**Halite, Pink:** **a)** Creates a sense of spirituality in which one feels visionary, inspired and larger than life. **b)** In the Michael system, pulls one into the positive pole of the Attitude of Spiritualist.

**Halotrichite:** **a)** Calms one's fear of heights. Most effective with fears about heights stemming from traumatic incidents in past lives that still affect one now. **b)** Creates a sense of ascending into spiritual heights as well as creating a sense of calm about physical heights. Puts one in touch with one's spiritual nature.

**Hambergite:** (Colorless to white). **a)** Promotes a spiritualistic, utopian viewpoint in which one becomes inspired by utopian concepts and the wonderful possibilities that exist in the universe. Excellent for fomenting ideas that are visionary in scope. **b)** In the Michael system, a stone for those with the Attitude of Spiritualist.

**Hanksite:** (Cream color). Enables one to understand action-oriented and production-oriented people, especially if one is not so inclined. Makes it easier to deal with these people, particularly if the case is extreme, such as one's mate being a workaholic.

**Hauynite:** (Lazuli-blue in color). **a)** Puts one in alignment with one's spiritual self. One can feel connected to all that is and be able to access unconscious symbols to reach higher spiritual states of awareness. **b)** Amplifies shamanic abilities. Operates by pulling one into the emotions and reconnecting one with the memories of those early lifetimes when one was still in touch with the Tao. **c)** In the Michael system, balances the Higher-Moving Center and connects one with the energy of the Buddhaic Plane and the Tao.

**Hawk's Eye:** Another name for Spectrolite.

**Hedenbergite:** (Green crystals). **a)** Healing to the physical body. **b)** Promotes serenity, calms impatience, and creates an ability to move at a slower pace. **c)** Calms highly-energized, over-stimulated persons. **d)** In the Michael system, balances high-frequency types of people.

**Heliodor:** (Lemon-yellow to gold in color). **a)** Makes one very comfortable with being in a position of nurturing others. Can feel very relaxed about giving to others, as one feels confident one will not be victimized or allow one's self to be trapped in any way. One of the most comforting types of stones to wear. **b)** In the Michael system, balances Old and Mature Servers and those in positions of service to others.

**Heliotrope:** Same stone as Bloodstone.

**Hematite:** (Black, black-grey, or brown-red in color). **a)** An aid to re-evaluation. Promotes awareness of personal issues and patterns. Enables one to pull up anything that needs to be looked over to make it really clear what the issue is. **b)** Also useful for focusing on past lives. **c)** In the Michael system, enables one to positively use the Goal of Re-Evaluation. Particularly good for Priests who tend to forge ahead and re-evaluate life infrequently and those in Passion Mode who tend to enthusiastically skip past things they need to learn.

**Hemimorphite:** (Blue, blue-green, or colorless). **a)** Enables one to be assertive, enthusiastic, and dynamic in one's undertakings. **b)** In the Michael system, pulls one into the positive pole of Aggression Mode.

**Hendricksite:** (Brown to copper-brown in color). Increases one's ability to work with one's female energy; to get in touch with it, play with it, express it, and operate through it. One totally relaxes one's concentration to be creative, expansive and playful.

**Herderite:** (Purple crystals). **a)** Encourages one to be very powerful in service to others or in service to causes that benefit others. Particularly fosters the ability to know what would enhance the emotional well being or spiritual growth of another person.   b) In the Michael system, a power stone for Priests and Servers.  Helps Priests and Servers be powerful in all areas of their life.  Other Roles find this stone empowering when in positions of service to others.

**Herkimer Diamond:**  (A type of Quartz Crystal).  a) Same in effect as clear Crystal, but more powerful.  Combines the clarity of clear Crystal with masterful energy because of the double-edged shape.  b) Good for vivid dreaming.  With Rhodocrosite, helps one remember one's dreams.  c) In the Michael system, pulls one into the positive pole of Observation Mode.

**Herrerite:**  (Pale, blue-green crystals).  a) Enables one to open up one's psychic abilities particularly where blocked.  b) Heals and balances the sixth chakra:  frees the energies of the sixth chakra for higher work.  c) In the Michael system, makes the Higher Intellectual Center available for use.

**Hessonite:**  (Orange-brown).  a) Keeps one from falling into non-productive communication habits such as being verbose or gossipy.  Also helps one avoid a tendency to talk at people rather than with them: to avoid falling into oratory or non-stop talking.  b) Puts one in touch with basic truths and the ability to communicate them.  c) In the Michael system, mellows and balances Mature and Old Sages.

**Heterosite:**  (Rose to purple in color).  a) Enables one to feel more comfortable with emotional openness.  Very useful for those who are emotionally blocked.  b) Balances the fourth chakra.  c) In the Michael system, balances the Emotional Center.

**Heulandite:**  (Clear, white to pale pink or peach, opaque crystals).  a) For spiritual awareness.  Enables one to experience the connectedness of the whole; oneness with all that is; awareness of and oneness with the Supreme Reality.  b) Connects one with those spirits one is closest to who are no longer incarnating on the physical plane.  Easily used by those who are skeptical and cautious about accepting the unusual without a lot of proof.  c) In the

Michael system, balances the Higher-Moving Center and connects one with the Buddhaic Plane and the Tao. Also connects one to the Astral Plane and the cycled-off members of one's entity.

**Hewettite:** (Deep red to rust in color). Decreases allergies to anything organic (plant or animal matter).

**Hexagonite:** (Lavender in color). **a)** Same in effect as Actinolite. Keeps those involved in creative projects paying attention to detail and being less impatient. **b)** In the Michael system, balances Artisans.

**Hidalgoite:** (Rich green in color). Increases one's tolerance for extreme temperatures: hot or cold. The amount of increase depends on the individual and what that person's tolerance was in the first place.

**Hiddenite:** (Green or yellow) **a)** For spiritual awareness. Enables one to experience a feeling of love and connectedness with the entire universe. One feels harmoniously connected to the whole, and that everything is perfect just as it is. **b)** In the Michael system, balances the Higher-Moving and Higher-Emotional Centers, and connects one with the energy of the Messianic and Buddhaic Planes.

**Hollandite:** (Metallic black). **a)** Empowers one to be productive, purposeful, and focused in getting things accomplished. **b)** In the Michael system, a power stone for Warriors. Particularly, empowers them to feel masterful in manifesting the positive pole of their Role.

**Holmquistite:** (Gray-blue to green in color). Increases one's ability to understand, and work with mathematical concepts, and solve puzzles.

**Hopeite:** (Blue in color). For healing bone marrow.

**Horn:** **a)** Makes one feel connected to other live, warm things. Makes one feel loved. **b)** Balances the fourth chakra. Produces a warm-hearted feeling state. **c)** In the Michael system, balances the Emotional Center.

**Hornblende:** (Dark greenish black). Same in effect as Actinolite.

**Hornstone:** (Gray in color). A name given to several different minerals that are not related to one another except they are all more or less gray. We have found three. See Gray Jasper, Nunkirchner Jasper, and Neptunite.

**Howlite:** (Snow white with black, brown or gray veins. Often dyed a turquoise blue or lapis color). a) Brings new ideas into clear focus. Pulls one into artistic creation and inspiration. Helps one bring new things into one's life in a creative way. b) Balances and heals the sixth chakra. Especially good for one that has been overworked. c) In the Michael system, balances the Higher-Intellectual Center. Artisans particularly enjoy using this stone.

**Hubnerite:** (Reddish-brown in color). Brings new karmas into one's life. Good when one feels ready for a new cycle. While some may recoil at the thought of karma, it is important to remember that karma can be positive as well as negative.

**Huntite:** (Warm brown mottled with white). a) Allows one to prioritize so one can productively accomplish everything. Clears any excess out of the space and allows one to concentrate on just what needs to be done. b) In the Michael system, a stone that Warriors particularly enyoy.

**Hyalophane:** (Clear crystals). a) Increases mental activity. Enables one to think more quickly and of more things. Focuses the mind when one has been feeling foggy. This stone steps up the intellectual pace to such an extent that emotion and action can get set aside temporarily. b) In the Michael system, balances the Intellectual Center.

**Hydrogrossular:** Same stone as green Grossular.

**Hydrotalcite:** a) For feeling connected with anyone that has parallel experiences to one's own. Examples are: being involved in the same project or going off to the same college. One feels in communion with, and empathetic with, that other person. b) In the Michael system, allows one to feel in alignment with, and attuned to, parallel selves (those in parallel universes) that are taking different paths from the path one is taking in this universe.

**Hydroxyl-Herderite:** Same stone as Herderite.

**Hypersthene:** (Clear, black-green, or black-brown in color). Helps reduce fear of being in public view. Useful in public speaking, board meetings, or even crowded grocery stores.

**Iceland Spar:** Same stone as clear or white Calcite.

**Idocrase:** Releases tension. Drains out excess energy. The different varieties affect different types of tension.

**Idocrase, Blue:** a) Releases emotional tension. b) Balances the fourth chakra and drains out excess energy. c) In the Michael system, balances the Emotional Center.

**Idocrase, Green:** a) Releases physical tension. b) Balances the second and third chakras and drains out excess energy. c) In the Michael system, balances the Moving and Higher-Moving Centers.

**Idocrase, Yellow:** a) Releases intellectual tension. b) Balances the fifth and sixth chakras and drains out excess energy. c) In the Michael system, balances the Intellectual and Higher-Intellectual Centers.

**Idocrase, Yellow-Green or Brown:** a) Releases survival fears. b) Balances the first chakra and drains out excess energy. c) In the Michael system, balances the Instinctive Center.

**Ilmenite:** (Grey or purple/black metallic crystals). Increases one's understanding of the way mammals, other than human, think. Good for animal trainers, pet-owners, farmers, etc.

**Ilvaite:** (Black color). Increases the appetite of animals that are off their feed. Is related more strongly to animals than to humans.

**Imperial Jasper:** See Jasper, Imperial.

**Inderite:** Same stone as Kurnakovite.

**Indialite:** Same stone as Iolite and Cordierite.

**Indicolite:** Same stone as blue or blue-green Tourmaline.

**Indigolite:** Same stone as blue or blue-green Tourmaline.

**Inesite:** (Pinkish gray). Balances water gain and loss in the body.

**Iolite: a)** Makes one feel comfortable taking a leadership role and creating win-win situations for everyone. Promotes a sense of self-confidence that makes it easy for others to accept one's leadership. This stone is particularly good for the overly mushy, overly ingratiating, or overly submissive person. **b)** Good as an anti-martyrdom stone since it makes people feel so confident about their ability to take charge of their lives, that it becomes very difficult to continue to feel that one is a victim of circumstances. **c)** In the Michael system, pulls one into the positive use of the Goal of Dominance and softens the Chief Negative Feature of Martyrdom. **d)** Different colors affect different areas of one's life.

> **Blue:** Enables one to take a leadership role in one's friendships and make things work out in a way that is satisfactory to all.
> **Gray:** Makes one feel comfortable taking a leadership role in one's job or profession.
> **Purple:** Enables one to take a leadership position in one's sexual or familial relationships. Good for wishy-washy parents.

**Iron Pyrite:** (Brass yellow or grey-yellow in color). **a)** Helps one harmonize one's energy with another and makes it easier to move at the same pace, especially if that pace differs from one's own. **b)** In the Michael system, helps one match one's frequency with someone of a higher or lower frequency than oneself.

**Iron Pyrite, Dodecahedron:** (Iron Pyrite that has a twelve-sided shape). Assists one in feeling comfortable with the members of one's support circle and makes it easier to bring them into one's life. Enables one to match frequencies with members of one's support circle and feel automatically more at ease relating to them. Most effective with the friends one works with each lifetime.

**Ivory:** a) Calms basic fears about survival and helps one feel assured that survival is not an issue. b) Balances and heals all chakras, but has strongest impact on the first chakra.. c) Has a capacity to calm survival fears associated with the chakra it is worn closest to. When worn near the second chakra, calms survival-related fears about one's sexuality or creativity. When worn near the third chakra, calms survival issues about money, or the use of power. When worn near the fourth chakra, one's emotions will not be survival based. When worn near the fifth chakra, calms survival-based thought patterns. When worn at the sixth chakra, produces inspiration about ways to solve survival issues. d) Stabilizes one's energy level and keeps one moving through life at a comfortable pace: one that is neither too hurried nor too plodding. e) In the Michael system, balances and heals all Centers in general, and the Instinctive Center in particular. A good energetic balancer that enables one to keep one's frequency rate stable.

**Jade, African:** Same stone as green Grossular.

**Jade, Apple:** Same stone as green Grossular.

**Jade, Black:** a) Enables one to deal with issues which involve survival, sex, and power, in a balanced fashion. Good to wear when one wants to open up, but feels attacked or that survival is an issue. b) Balances, opens and integrates the first three chakras, so one can be appropriate with all three. c) In the Michael system, balances and integrates the Instinctive, Moving, and Higher-Moving Centers.

**Jade, Blue:** Neutralizes the impact of karmic influences. Allows one to see what's going on and remain neutral about it emotionally.

**Jade, Brown or Gray:** a) Helps one to relax by draining excess energy out of the body. When worn during the day, keeps excess energy from building up and helps one to operate from a relaxed state. b) Temporarily suspends the impact of karmic influences and allows one to view things from a detached perspective. **c)** Drains excess energy from all chakras which allows the chakras to realign themselves. **d)** In the Michael system, drains excess energy from all chakras through the Instinctive Center.

**Jade, Butterfat:** Same stone as brown or gray Jade.

**Jade, China:** Same stone as Bowenite.

**Jade, Gray:** See Jade, Brown or Gray.

**Jade, Green:** (Darkish green, mossy color. Also known as Nephrite). **a)** Creates a mood of tranquility in which one emanates an aura of calm, peacefulness and harmony. Allows one to find inner peace more easily. **b)** Enables one to be resigned to, and more tranquilly accepting of, difficult or unpleasant aspects of one's life that cannot be avoided, and must be handled. Makes one feel more grounded and capable of dealing with any situation. Good to counteract depression. **b)** In the Michael system, balances those with the Attitude of Stoic.

**Jade, Lavender:** **a)** For a more idealistic approach to life. Useful when one feels too cynical or unimaginative. Not for someone who lacks the ability to concentrate, because it can promote daydreaming. **b)** In the Michael system, balances those with the Attitude of Idealist. Those with the Attitude of Skeptic like it because it puts them into an optimistic mood.

**Jade, Nevada:** See Nevada Jade.

**Jade, New:** Same stone as Bowenite.

**Jade, Orange:** **a)** Allows one to be appropriately skeptical. Encourages one to investigate a situation rather than automatically reject it. **b)** Useful when one is unsure of one's sophistication about life. Reduces any tendencies to be gullible and naive about what's actually so. **c)** In the Michael system, pulls one into the positive pole of Skeptic. Good with Golden Sapphire (a Scholar stone) for people who tend to be naive.

**Jade, Pakistan:** a) Puts one in touch with spiritual, visionary energy and enables one to come up with some great, wild ideas. Similar in effect to Hambergite.   b) In the Michael system, good manifesting stone for those with the Attitude of Spiritualist.

**Jade, Pink:** Same in effect as orange Jade.

**Jade, Soo-chow:** Same stone as Bowenite.

**Jade, Southern:**  (Nephrite that has been heat treated to become dark rust-red in color). a) Puts one in touch with spiritual, visionary energy.   b) Moves one from a position of being resigned to one's fate to a position of being able to see the variety of possibilities inherent in a situation. Encourages one to come up with new possibilities instead of just accepting things as they are.   c) In the Michael system, pulls one gently out of Stoicism into the positive pole of Spiritualism.

**Jade, Transvaal:** Same stone as green Grossular.

**Jade, White:** a) Makes it easy to perceive objective reality.   b) Can have an extremely calming effect for those who usually can't tell what's going on.  For those who tend daydream or to "float out of their bodies", White Jade makes them feel grounded and that they know what's really going on.   c) In the Michael system, balances those with the Attitude of Realist.

**Jade, Yellow:** (Varies from a soft, creamy color that turns translucent with use to a deep yellow gold).  Takes the mystery out of the opposite sex and gives one a sense that one really can understand what goes on with them.

**Jamesite:** (Reddish brown in color).  Gives a one a feeling of security.   One feels confident that any endeavor undertaken will come out well.  Enables one to believe that support will be there when needed, which gives the confidence to take on projects that might otherwise seem too difficult or overwhelming.

**Jamesonite:** (Steel gray to dark lead gray).  a) For stability, security, and steadfastness.  A good "stick-to-itiveness" stone. Makes one feel grounded and secure that one can perservere over very long periods of time regardless of what comes up. A very hard-working rock. **b)** In the Michael system, Pulls one into the positive pole of Perserverance Mode.

**Jarosite:** (Brown in color). **a)** Helps one bring diverse and confusing ideas into focus or gather scattered thoughts together. Gets the mental process into gear and functioning smoothly. **b)** In the Michael system, balancing to the Intellectual Center.

**Jasper:** All Jaspers and Agates are very healing. They share the same basic chemical compound.

**Jasper, Black: a)** This stone has a repulsing quality. If one wears it or keeps it on one's person, others will assume that privacy is desired and will not approach without a very good reason. **b)** Can be used in one's environment to keep the energy protected. Particularly good for sacred or personal sites. One should create the energy desired, then put the stone in place and it will repulse all unwanted energies.

**Jasper, Biggs:** Same stone as Picture Jasper.

**Jasper, Brecchiated: a)** Heals mental stress. Centers one intellectually and makes it easier to be logical, clear-headed, and clear-thinking. Wakes one up and increases one's intellectual capacity. **b)** In the Michael system, heals and balances the Intellectual Center.

**Jasper, Brick-red: a)** Helps one get along with the same sex, and maintain compatible same-sex relationships. **b)** If homosexual, makes one very comfortable with one's sexuality. **c)** Balances all chakras. **d)** Stabilizes one's energy level and keeps one moving through life at a comfortable pace: one that is neither too hurried nor too plodding. **e)** In the Michael system, an all-purpose energetic balancer although mild in effect.

**Jasper, Brown:** Keeps others from making energetic attachments (cording) that are not desired.

**Jasper, Bruneau:** (Red and tan-gray opaque blend). **a)** Encourages one to handle crises or difficulties in a balanced fashion: i.e., without getting too stubborn, too impatient, too martyred, too self deprecatory or arrogant or too self destructive or heedless. **b)** In the Michael system, reduces all Chief Negative Features, and pulls one into the positive pole of one's Attitude.

**Jasper, Fancy:** (Multi-colored green, golden-brown and lavender). A "let's party" stone. Particularly good for helping serious, highly-focused types to lighten up and have a little fun.

**Jasper, Gray: a)** Makes it easier to utilize one's own personal power and have confidence that one's power cannot be taken away. **b)** Balances, heals and protects the third chakra. **c)** In the Michael system, protects and heals the Moving Center. Pulls one out of the negative pole of Martyrdom.

**Jasper, Green: a)** Removes energy blocks in the body. Balances and clears all chakras. **b)** Healing to highly focused people, especially those who have worn themselves out with concentrating. **c)** Makes those who like to take life at a slower pace feel peppier. **d)** In the Michael system, balances low-frequency types of people, and/or those who are high-male energied.

**Jasper, Bright Green:** Draws one into a cool, calculating intellectual energy.

**Jasper, Pale Green to Yellow:** Calms aggressive energy.

**Jasper, Imperial:** (Purplish-red in color). **a)** Useful for a highly female-energied, creative person who wants to be more grounded. For someone who's very unfocused and wants to more focused. **b)** Also useful for someone who likes to move through life at a slower pace to feel healed. Slower moving people often have difficulty feeling adequate, because they're always striving to move faster. **c)** In the Michael system, balances low-frequency types and/or those who are high female-energied.

**Jasper, Morrison Ranch:** (Brown, olive green, and/or tan, sometimes with streaks). **a)** Related to shamanistic rituals. Makes it easier to get in touch with inner parts of the self, using rituals and ritualistic symbolism. Puts one in touch with the Tao, or Universal Consciousness, in a shamanistic way. **b)** Useful in certain types of therapy such as past-life regressions or dealing with one's deeper, unconscious issues. Helps bring instinctive issues to the surface, and makes one feel more comfortable handling them. **c)** Good for accepting certain types of change in one's life. Examples are moving away from home for the first time, graduating from college, getting married, having a baby, turning 40, etc. Makes one feel capable of handling these changes and seeing clearly what challenges they bring. **d)** Opens, balances, and connects all the chakras. **e)** The more avocado green the color, the more effective the stone is. **f)** In the Michael system, balances the Instinctive Center, and is useful for doing Instinctive Center work such as past-life regressions. Also puts one in touch with the Tao.

**Jasper, Mustard:** Same stone as yellow Jasper.

**Jasper, Nunkirchner:** Same in effect as Bloodstone.

**Jasper, Owyhee:** (A combination of Mustard Agate, and pale green Jasper with a touch of red Jasper). **a)** Useful to have around if there is something one needs to deal with dynamically, but not too aggressively, over a long period of time. Enables one to come up with unusual solutions for problems that are not easily solvable. Good to combine with Green Jade for tranquility and harmony. **b)** In the Michael system, pulls one into the positive pole of Perserverance Mode.

**Jasper, Parrot Wing:** (Combination of Chrysocolla, Turquoise & Malachite). Same in effect as Eilat.

**Jasper, Picture:** **a)** Aids in the evaluation of one's issues by prompting the recall of past experiences that are associated with the issue. One remembers the story that goes along with the memory, as well as what went wrong, or where one went off a correct path. Makes it clearer what needs to be done to resolve the issue, or what needs to be understood about it.   b) In the Michael system, allows one to use the positive pole of the Goal of Re-Evaluation.

**Jasper, Pink:** Hormone balancing.

**Jasper, Poppy:** a) For animal-related allergies.  Keeps one from being allergic to animals or to their products: e.g., feathers in pillows, househair, or any part one might eat such as meat.   b) Also helps one to understand animals and be more in tune with them.   Creates more compatibility with one's pets.

**Jasper, Rain Forest:** (Combination of blue-green Agate, Green Jasper and Quartz).  Makes one feel expansive and happy.

**Jasper, Red:** (True red in color).  a) Produces a dynamic and lively energy.  Puts one in touch with feeling powerful and reduces feelings of victimization.   b) Balances the third chakra.   c) In the Michael system, balances the Moving Center.   Pulls one into the positive pole of Aggression Mode.

**Jasper, Rim:** (Brown in color).  a) Creates a positive attitude, and reduces one's inclination to be arrogant self-deprecating, greedy, self-destructive, victimized, impatient or stubborn.   b) In the Michael system, softens all Chief Negative Features and pulls one into the positive pole of one's Attitude.

**Jasper, Serape:** Enhances female sexuality.  Stimulates sexual interest and arousal in women.   Facilitates getting pregnant.

**Jasper, Spider Web:** Soothes frayed nerves.  Valium-like in its effect.

**Jasper, Stromatolitic:** (Black, brown, and gold blend).  Similar in effect to Andalusite with more emphasis on the element of risk taking.

**Jasper, Variegated:** One of the strongest healing stones for the physical body.  Especially good for those who have been extremely ill and are recuperating.  Anything shattering or extremely debilitating to the body, can be soothed by this stone.

**Jasper, Willow Creek:** Same in effect as Serape Jasper.

**Jasper, Wood:** Same in effect as Rim Jasper.

**Jasper, Xmas-Tree:** (Tri-colored: mustard yellow, red-red, and bright green). **a)** A combination of aggressive dynamic energy (red), cool, calculating intellectual energy (green), and uranian energy for a long-lasting impact (mustard yellow) that powerfully promotes success. Empowers one to achieve whatever one has set out to do. Keeps one anchored in mastery and excellence; completely focused and looking ahead to what is going to be accomplished next without being distracted. **b)** One can produce a similar effect by combining Garnet, blue Topaz, and Rutillated Quartz. Michael suggests throwing in a little Blue Sapphire for compassion. Most similar in effect to Andalusite, the "empire builder."

**Jasper, Yellow:** Hormone balancing.

**Jeanbandyite:** (Orange-brown in color). Enables one to remain firm in one's convictions. Helps one not to be wishy-washy, easily swayed or convinced of anything other than what one truly believes. Not necessary for people who are stubborn, or have difficulty seeing other points of view once they are on a determined path.

**Jerrygibbsite:** (Violet-pink in color). **a)** Promotes a sense of calm and an ability to remain stoically tranquil in the face of any mishap or difficulty. **b)** In the Michael system, pulls one into the positive pole of the Attitude of Stoic.

**Jet:** **a)** Enables one to see all the possible pitfalls in a situation and come up with constructive solutions. Wear when it is necessary to go into a situation with all eyes open. For example, being in a war where it's useful to keep oneself in survival mode, or in a business where much back-biting occurs, or when being undermined by an enemy. Keeps one alert for what might go wrong so one can correct the situation with some kind of positive action. **b)** In the

Michael system, pulls one into the positive pole of the Attitude of Cynic.

**Jinshajiangite:** (Blackish-red to golden-red in color). **a)** A meditation stone. Leads one directly and with surety to one's personal truths and inner principles. Eliminates self-deception and clarifies one's beliefs. Useful during meditation. **b)** In the Michael system, balances the Higher-Intellectual Center.

**Joaquinite: a)** Heals fears or traumas in the area of one's sexuality. Healing for anyone who has ever been sexually abused or molested. **b)** Healing to the second chakra. Opens it if too closed and closes it down, and repairs it, if ragged and bruised. Heals and balances the Higher-Moving Center.

**Johannsenite:** (Brown-black to black crystals). Same in effect as Hedenbergite.

**Jokokuite:** (Pink in color). **a)** Opens one to spiritually-based, emotional experiences. Enables one to feel a sense of lovingness toward all beings. **b)** A stone that is particularly appealing to children. The younger the child is, the stronger the attraction. The effect of this stone on a person, however, is the same regardless of age: it is only affinity to the stone that shifts. **c)** Opens and balances the seventh chakra. Similar in effect to Chalcanthite. **d)** In the Michael system, balances the Higher-Emotional Center, and connects one with the energy of the Messianic Plane.

**Julienite:** (Blue in color). Helps one get in touch with, and maintain, mental contact with other sentient beings and species, on this planet and others. Must be discriminating about who one has contacted, as this stone helps one make contact with any life form that has thoughts no matter how rudimentary.

**Kammererite:** (Lavender in color). **a)** Promotes spiritual awareness. Gives one a sense of being at peace: a sense of harmony and connectedness with the whole. **b)** In the Michael system, connects one to the Buddhaic Plane and Higher-Moving Centered experiences.

**Kettnerite:** A friendship stone. Helps one attract and maintain appropriate relationships with friends. It has no effect on relationships with family members or mates. The different colors have different effects.

> **Yellow:** Attracts new friends.

> **Green:** Helps one maintain friendly relations and stay in good communication with those one already knows.

> **Blue:** Encourages one to do everything possible to save a failing friendship and gives one the courage to end the relationship if not successful.

**Kidwellite:** (Soft yellow-green in color). Enables one to understand the hidden meanings in the communications of another person. Makes it easier to grasp the meta-message: i.e., that which is not said, but is a message contained in what is said. Makes it easier for people to truly understand one another, and reduces the tendency to misinterpret the communications one receives.

**Kinoite:** (Azure blue in color). Promotes a feeling of peace and harmony. Aids in the easing of grief.

**Koettigite:** (Grey-green, fan-shaped crystals). a) Enables one to feel less stressed when in the process of creation. As a result, one's projects run more smoothly. b) In the Michael system, balances Artisans, and is particularly helpful to Artisans for releasing stress.

**Kolwezite:** (Fuzzy moss green to dark green in color). Balances the physical body. Brings various parts of the physical system or body into harmony with one another to reduce allergies, build the immune system, and increase physical stamina.

**Kornerupine:** (Grass green, pine green, or green-brown in color). Enables one to communicate better and more clearly. The greener the color, the stronger the effect.

**Kunzite:** (Lilac or pink in color). a) For surrender. Makes one feel that one can accept something that's out of one's control and surrender to it. Very useful because people spend so much time resisting things that are truly out of their control. Michael regards this as one of the most useful of stones and recommends it highly. b) In the Michael system, balances those with a Goal of Submission.

**Kupletskite:** (Amber colored). Encourages the body to flush out any toxic materials by making it crave clean water. One will not experience this craving unless there is some toxic substance in the body. If there are toxic materials present, one will continue to crave and drink water until the body has been flushed. Not useful for toxic processes in the body which cannot be effectively flushed such as a fungus infection, an ear infection or appendicitis. If one carries this stone and continues to crave water past a reasonable period of time required to flush the body of toxins, (like one week), one should seek medical attention to verify the source of the problem.

**Kurnakovite:** (Transparent and colorless or pink in color). Reduces dizziness and motion sickness.

**Kyanite:** (Blue-gray, pale to deep blue with overtones of violet in color: metallic and mica-like). a) Connects one with teachers on higher planes of existence. b) In the Michael system, connects one with the Causal Plane. This connection not of interest usually unless one has a teacher on that plane. Michael is a causal plane teacher and those who wish to connect with him or another such teacher will find this stone useful.

**Kyanite, Black:** (Black to midnight blue in color: metallic and mica-like). Enables one to contact, or channel beings, from the lower Astral Plane. This refers to people between lives, or devas who have not yet had a lifetime. Useful for mediums or channels who want to contact a loved one for a client. Also useful for communicating with devas. Must use caution when using this stone, as it will open one up to anyone without a body, even not very developed beings.

**Kyanite, Green:** a) Creates delighted shivers and rushes of well being. Opens one to inspirational bursts of truth, love, or healing from higher planes of existence. b) Enables one to contact, or be a channel for, beings of higher consciousnes. c) In the Michael system, balances the

Higher Intellectual Center and connects one with the energy of the Mental Plane.

**Labradorite:** Same stone as Labradorite Feldspar. See Feldspar, Labradorite.

**Lanarkite:** (White-lavendar crystals). Helps one lose weight. Boosts the metabolic rate.

**Lapis Lazuli:** (Deep blue). **a)** Allows one to perceive emotional issues more clearly. Not useful for calming down when one feels over-emotional: this stone does not affect the type of emotion felt or its intensity. Enhances neutral perceptivity. **b)** In the Michael system, balances the Emotional Center.

**Lapis, Nevada:** Same stone as Nevada Jade.

**Laramar:** (Sky blue in color). **a)** For eternal love. Allows one to keep on loving where one has started loving. Also makes the wearer feel emotionally supported. Very useful when a relationship is undergoing stress and love may be jeopardized. Laramar ensures that the love that's underneath the obstacles and challenges will still be there. Also good in a divorce or a split relationship where both would like to remain friends. **b)** In the Michael system, balances the Higher-Emotional Center.

**Lattice Agate:** See Agate, Lattice.

**Laubmannite:** (Green-brown in color). Relaxes muscle tension in the feet, and encourages the muscles to stay in alignment. This is important, because how one walks governs whether the body is chiropractically sound.

**Laumontite:** (White in color). **a)** Reduces obsessive or compulsive tendencies. Obsessions refer to repetitive thoughts and compulsions are repetitive behaviors one feels compelled to perform. **b)** Good for those who are trying to give up addictions, as one will notice that one is thinking about "reaching for that cigarette" and in noticing, one will feel uncomfortable and it will be easier to stop. **c)** If the obsession or compulsion is not related to an addiction, and is not apparently related to anything else, one should use this stone in conjunction with therapy. Therapists should note this stone brings to the surface the anxiety, an obssessive or compulsive behavior might be masking.

**Lavender Quartz:** See Quartz, Lavender.

**Lavrentievite:** Same stone as Corderoite.

**Lavulite, Royal:** Same stone as Sugilite.

**Lawsonite:** Same in effect as Leopard Skin Agate.

**Lazulite:** (Blue, green-blue). Same in effect as Lapis Lazuli.

**Lazurite:** Gem quality Lapis Lazuli.

**Legrandite:** (Red to black metallic). For karmic intensification. It brings in karmic lessons through imbalance; it makes one feel unbalanced which propels one into either self karma or karma with another to feel balanced again.

**Leopard-Skin Agate:** See Agate, Leopard-Skin.

**Lepidolite:** (Lavender in color). a) Promotes spiritual awareness. Gives one a sense of being at peace: a sense of harmony and connectedness with the whole. b) In the Michael system, connects one to the Buddhaic Plane and promotes Higher-Moving centered experiences.

**Leucite:** (Clear or white). Helps clear mucus membranes. Good for colds.

**Levyne:** (White in color). Same in effect as Apophyllite.

**Levynite:** Another name for Levyne.

**Libethenite:** (Dark green in color). Kills off aberrant cells, especially sex cells. This stone is good to keep around when one is trying to get pregnant. Enhances the probability of a normal baby, and it lowers the risk of having a baby that's mentally retarded or deformed.

**Liebigite:** (Apple green). a) Brings intense, growthful experiences into one's life. Good to wear when getting bored or stuck in a rut.   **b)** Attract's one's karmas or spiritual debts, and brings them into one's life when worn. These will be the karmas one had planned on having in one's life before birth.   Remember these could be positive karmas and highly desirable, such as bringing in a lifetime mate, changing one's monetary status for the better, or discovering a new, exciting career.   **c)** In the Michael system, pulls one into the positive pole of the Goal of Growth.

**Limestone:** (Usually gray.  Often found dyed in various colors).  **a)** Extremely healing to the immune system. Totally cleanses and purifies the system.  **b)** Creates a sense of balance for those who like to take life at a more leisurely pace and makes them feel peppier.  **c)** Calming to highly-energetic people, who when they become over stimulated, are often unable to slow down.  Helps them relax and set a more comfortable pace.  **d)** Balances those people who are either highly focused and driven in their approach to life; or those who are highly creative, but chaotic in their way of dealing with things.  Brings both out of the extremes, into a more balanced state near the middle.  **e)** In the Michael system, balancing and grounding for those who are either very high-male energied or who are very high-female energied.  Balances people of either very high or very low frequency.

**Limonite:** Similar in effect to Iron Pyrite.

**Linarite:** (Azure-blue in color).  Makes one feel very good humored and optimistic about life.

**Litharge:** (Orange and red in color).  Encourages one's body to purge itself of ingested poisons or toxins through vomiting and diarrhea.  An emetic that functions in a fashion similar to Ipecac.  Wrap this one in plastic and take out for a specific use.

**Lithium Mica:** Same stone as Polylithionite.

**Lizardite:** (A green, yellow, or brown form of Serpentine).  **a)** Calms anxiety and survival-based fears.  **b)** Enables one to access primitive, unconscious fears.  Brings one's fears up to conscious awareness so they can be processed.  Useful in therapy. **c)** In the Michael system, calms the Instinctive Center.

**Llanoite:** (Pink or lavender in color). For creativity of the "genius" sort. Promotes unusual thought patterns for the creation of highly unusual solutions to problems. Makes it easy to generate fresh perspectives. An example might be that one knew there were three planes, and suddenly realized there was a fourth dimension. A different way to process intellectually, which can make one look eccentric when viewed from the outside.

**Lodestone:** (Iron-black or grey-black in color). Helps one communicate with dolphins and whales.

**Long-Hair Asbestos:** See Asbestos, Long Hair.

**Ludlamite:** (Olive-green crystals). **a)** Very calming, particularly when one has gone through difficult or anxious times. Keeps one from acting out one's stress with inappropriate behavior. **b)** In the Michael system, very calming to the Instinctive Center, particularly when it has been severely taxed.

**Ludwigite:** (Black metallic). Reduces fear of carnivores. Keeps one from fear that one is going to be eaten. If not paralyzed by fear, one can use one's resources more effectively to avoid being eaten. This includes running away if that's what's most logical. Take when camping in the wild or when having dinner at the house of a friend who owns a pet python.

**Luzonite:** Same in effect as Enargite.

**Magnesiohornblende:** (Red in color). Intensifies the effect of Hornblende.

**Magnetite:** (Iron black or Gray black). **a)** Pulls one into objective reality. Promotes a straight forward, reality oriented, truth-telling approach. **b)** In the Michael system, pulls one into the positive pole of the Attitude of Realist.

**Mahogany Obsidian:** See Obsidian, Mahogany.

**Malachite:** (Bright green in color). **a)** Enables one to stay in a mood of loving tolerance toward others, balanced internally and able to respond flexibly to events, regardless of what is happening and no matter how bizarre and unsettling the events. One is able to be truly appropriate in one's reactions. **b)** Makes one feel very willing to communicate who one is and where one is coming from. Promotes a willingness to relate to others and let them know who one truly is. **c)** Stabilizes one's energy level, and allows one to move at a steady, comfortable pace through the day. **d)** Balances and heals all chakras. One of the most powerful balancing stones. It is almost impossible to be around Malachite for long, and remain unbalanced. **e)** In the Michael system, an energetic balancer that keeps one's frequency rate stable. Balances all Centers.

**Manganaxinite:** (Pink to purplish gray). A stone for locating objects. Enables one to find things one has lost in, or under the ground, by following one's inner promptings, which will push one to move in the right direction. Also helps one to find new things located underground that one would enjoy, like crystals, gold or oil.

**Manganite:** (Silver and black). Makes one more attractive or charismatic to others. Brings one's friendlier aspects to the fore and makes one appear more outgoing and approachable.

**Manganocalcite:** (Pink in color. Grows in round nodules). The "adorable" stone. A stone whose effects are noticed by others, but not noticed by the person wearing it. Greatly increases one's "adorable quotient". Intensifies positive pheromonic potential. Thus, any positive reaction tends to be heightened, and any negative reaction a person might have towards one will be toned down.

**Manjiroite:** (Black crystals). **a)** Softens cruelty toward self or others. Operates by reducing the internal stress state that causes one to engage in compulsively destructive acts. Examples of such behaviors might be: pulling the wings off butterflies, burning one's self or a child with cigarettes, or slashing one's arm repeatedly with razor blades. The intention behind these behaviors is to reduce the pain one feels inside. Manjiroite opens one up to other ways of reducing the pain, and makes one see how inappropriate such behaviors are. **b)** In the Michael system, reduces the Chief Negative Feature of Self-Destruction.

**Marble:** (Comes in a variety of colors). **a)** Enables one to be very focused and clear, without undue stress. Makes it easier to accomplish projects that require a high degree of concentration. **b)** In the Michael system, balances one's male-energied side regardless of the amount of male energy a particular person has. Darker colors are often preferred by the more solid roles, such as Warriors, Kings, and Scholars or high male-energied types. Lighter colors of Marble are generally preferred by the high-female energied types, by the lighter roles, Artisans, Servers and Priests, or by those who feel very unhealed and sensitive. **c)** Marble comes in many colors and each color gives a slightly different flavor to the main definition.

**Black:** Focuses one's energy in a very refined manner.

**Brown:** Focuses one's attention a little more on issues relating to the home.

**Gray:** No added qualities.

**Green:** Focuses one's attention a little more on prosperity issues.

**Pink:** Calms and heals.

**Salmon:** Makes one more aware of what one might be angry about.

**Tan:** Enables one to remain physically balanced.

**White:** No added qualities.

**Marcasite:** (Metallic silver-gray). **a)** Helps one evaluate one's life issues. Same in effect as Hematite, although a little more gentle: one can kick back with one's slippers and pipe, and reflect for awhile. **b)** In the Michael system, pulls one into the positive pole of the Goal of Re-Evaluation.

**Margaritasite:** (Pale yellow). Gives one a green thumb. Expands one's abililty to instinctively know how to take care of one's plants and help them grow.

**Margerite:** (Looks like salmon-pink Rhodocrosite crystals). **a)** Helps one get rid of preconceived notions, by taking one back to a state of innocence and simplicity. Allows one to take a look at one's life without a sense of struggle. Good for cynics, skeptics, and over-achievers. **b)** In the Michael system, creates the positive use of the Goal of Re-Evaluation.

**Marialite:** (White in color). **a)** Reduces trauma to the body, thus encouraging wounds of a physical nature to heal more quickly. **b)** Also strengthens the immune system.

**Mariposite:** (Deep green, light green and white swirls). **a)** Enhances one's self expressiveness and one's ability to communicate with others. Stimulates one's self expressiveness in the area of one's creative projects. **b)** Helps one to build an empire that is based communication or media skills. **c)** In the Michael system, a power stone for Artisans and Sages.

**Marmatite:** (Found with Siderite). **a)** Neutralizes the impact of astrological influences. A type of Sphalerite that allows one to be less impacted by the moon and other planetary energies outside one's own body. For example, great to wear when Mercury is retrograde or Saturn is transiting one's Venus. **b)** Also makes it easier to avoid karmas and other predestined happenings dictated by one's astrology.

**Massicot:** (Yellow in color). Same in effect as Litharge.

**Matildite:** (Blue in color). Encourages inter-racial and inter-cultural communication. Makes one curious about, interested in, and open to hearing about other perspectives.

**Melanite:** See Andradite, Melanite.

**Melanotekite:** (Black, metallic crystals). Same in effect as Tektite.

**Meneghinite:** (Rich black metallic crystals). Same in effect as Sulfur.

**Merlinoite:** (White in color). Strengthens the digestive system by promoting proper functioning of all aspects of digestion.

**Merwinite:** (Bluish-gray in color). Same in effect as Bloodstone.

**Mesolite:** (White). **a)** A "go with the flow" rock. Allows one to be more free-flowing. Stops one from putting boulders in the middle of one's own stream. Particularly good for those who are over-stressed or who work too hard, as it would enable them to relax somewhat. One can move immediately into a restful state instead of taking several days to wind down. A "let's-go-on-vacation" rock; totally relaxes and detoxifies. **b)** In the Michael system, pulls one into the positive pole of the Goal of Stagnation.

**Metahewettite:** (Red in color). **a)** Promotes one's ability to tackle one's problems forcefully and move into action dynamically and appropriately. **b)** In the Michael system, pulls into the positive pole of Aggression Mode.

**Metals:** Metals either raise or lower one's frequency. When one's frequency is raised, one feels "zippier" and when one's frequency is lowered, one feels more mellow. See further discussion in section on Frequency.

> **Bronze and Brass:** Lowers frequency, but not as much as Gold.
>
> **Copper:** Raises one's frequency the most and is quite energizing. Copper also has healing properties. See Copper for further discussion.
>
> **Gold:** Lowers one's frequency the most.
>
> **Silver:** Raises frequency a moderate amount.

**Metatorbernite:** (Dark green metallic platelet crystals). **a)** Affects one simultaneously on the physical and emotional levels. On the physical level, increases metabolism, raises adrenalin levels, and raises body heat. **b)** On the emotional level, stimulates enthusiasm about taking care of others and being of service to them. **c)** In the Michael system, inspiring to Servers.

**Mexican Opal:** Same stone as Fire Opal.

**Mexican Red-Lace Agate:** See Agate, Mexican Red Lace.

**Miargyrite:** (Silver metallic). **a)** Encourages athletic activity and stimulates one to hone one's athletic abilities. **b)** In the Michael system, stimulates the Moving Center.

**Microcline:** (Pale white or pink). **a)** Makes one's bad habits show up more clearly, particularly their self-destructive aspects. For example, one can see just how self-destructive one is being when one is taking that next drink or saying something hurtful to another person. One really feels how unnecessary it is. **b)** Similar in effect to Amazonite, but stronger in it's ability to foster awareness of self-destructiveness. Amazonite is, technically, the blue-green variety of Microline. **c)** In the Michael system, softens the Chief Negative Feature of Self-Destruction.

**Microlite:** (White in color). Same in effect as Actinolite.

**Milarite:** (Rust-colored platelets). **a)** Enhances and sharpens one's observations. Helps one to see things with greater clarity. **b)** In the Michael system, pulls one into the positive pole of Observation Mode.

**Millerite:** (Brass-yellow, bronze-yellow to grey-green in color). Helps one to get in touch with, and eliminate, beliefs obtained from significant others during childhood, as a part of one's imprinting, that have no actual basis in fact.

**Mimetite:** (Yellow to brown in color). Keeps reptiles balanced.

**Minium:** (Bright pink to bright red in color. Powdery). Same in effect as Cerussite.

**Mirabilite:** (Clear crystals like chunks of ice). **a)** Increases one's emotional perceptivity and empathic understanding of others. Makes hunches and intuitions, of any sort, stronger. **b)** In the Michael system, pulls one into the positive pole of the Emotional Center.

**Miserite:** (Rose to lilac to violet in color. Fibrous). Releases tension. Promotes a "holiday-like" atmosphere. Encourages one to let go and get into the festivities.

**Mixite:** (Light green). Same in effect as Conichalcite.

**Mizzonite:** Same in effect as Marialite.

**Moldavite:** (Dark olive green in color). Enables one to communicate telepathically with sentient beings, both human and non-human. The other sentient beings on this planet are whales and dolphins. This stone also aids one to connect telepathically with sentient beings on other planets.

**Molybdenite:** (Blue-grey in color). Helps one to feel more comfortable in the dark. Works equally for adults and children.

**Monticellite:** (Clear, green or black crystals). Strengthens the immune system.

**Montroseite:** (Jet black in color). Same in effect as Sard.

**Moolooite:** (Turquoise green in color). Increases the retention of water in the digestive tract. Functions as a very mild, natural laxative.

**Moonstone:** (Translucent milky white or peach. Has a silvery to bluish luminescence). a) A visionary stone. Reduces tendencies toward tunnel vision and enables one to see the variety of possibilities inherent in a situation. Helps one achieve one's heart's desire by clearly seeing the possibilities that exist. b) In the Michael system, stimulates use of the positive pole of the Attitude of Spiritualist.

**Morganite:** Same stone as pink to pale violet Beryl.

**Morion:** Dark form of Smoky Quartz.

**Morrison Ranch Jasper:** See Jasper, Morrison Ranch.

**Morrisonite:** (Brown, olive green, and/or tan, sometimes with streaks). Same in effect as Morrison Ranch Jasper.

**Moss Agate:** See Agate, Moss.

**Mother of Pearl:** (Rose and creamy-white in color). **a)** Same in effect as Abalone. **b)** In the Michael system, especially healing for those with ordinal Modes, Goals, and Attitudes. One of the strongest Instinctive Center healers.

**Mottramite:** (Olive-green opaque). Increases one's ease with man-made objects. One can be surrounded by synthetics such as plastic, nylon, computers and the plethora of man-made items in our modern world, and feel comfortable.

**Moukaite:** (A composite rock. Striped burgundy, tan, black, and white). For adjusting to and enjoying one's body. Same in effect as Zebra Agate.

**Mountain Opal:** See Opal, Mountain.

**Mullite:** (Light pink in color). Encourages thriftiness. Encourages one to make a budget and then stick with it. Helps one acknowledge that one has personal, monetary limitations.

**Murataite:** (Black in color). Same in effect as Wulfenite.

**Murdochite:** (Black in color). Helps the body adjust to, and feel more comfortable with, high temperatures. Useful for those who live in hot climates or must work in overly warm places.

**Muscovite:** (Brown, red-brown, yellow, green, yellow-green in color). **a)** Connects one with spiritual teachers or guides. Enables one to get in touch with those higher beings who care about, and want to communicate with one. **b)** In the Michael system, connects one with one's spirit guides, and with the Astral Plane. Assists solid roles, Kings, Warriors and Scholars, to leave their bodies when desired.

**Mustard Jasper:** See Jasper, Mustard.

**Myrichite:** (Bright red, orange, yellow and black in thin well-defined stripes). For accuracy and speed of communication. Communication is more intense in quality and one feels a strong push to get one's communications out there quickly, while using this stone. Good for those in the media and for others who just need to have an "important" talk with someone. The darker colors are for more intense communication.

**Natrojarosite:** **a)** Reduces sexual repression and stimulates sexual passion. **b)** Balances and heals the second chakra. **c)** In the Michael system, balances the Higher-Moving Center.

**Natrolite:** (Clear white in color). Heals foot problems by resolving the emotional issues connected to them. People put energy blockages in their feet relating to love issues (right foot ) or support issues (left foot). Calms issues relating to love or support depending on color.

**Clear or Yellow:**     Left foot.
**Red or White:**     Right foot.

**Natrolunite:** (White and tan in color). Prevents cavities in teeth and calcium loss in bones.

**Navajo Turquoise:** (Combination of Sard and Turquoise. Green Turquoise in a yellow-brown matrix). **a)** Centers one's being on love and connectedness with others. Also makes one feel secure and "at home" no matter where one is. **b)** In the Michael system, balances the Higher-Emotional Center and connects one with the energy of the Messianic Plane.

**Neoticite:** (Purple/red brown in color). Increases the wearer's ability to seem friendly and outgoing even though inside they may be feeling a little inhibited and closed down.

**Nephrite:** (Mossy, darkish green Jade: may tend toward a brownish color). Same stone as Green Jade.

**Neptunite:** Same in effect as Grey Jasper.

**Nevada Jade:** (Pale green and pink in color). Helps one to become a master healer; really in charge of and in control of one's healing powers. Aids one in healing others rather than oneself.

**Nevada Lapis:** Same stone as Nevada Jade.

**New Jade:** Another name for Bowenite.

**Nontronite:** (Green to black in color). Helps the body fight off bacterial infections.

**Norbergite:** (Yellow in color). **a)** Stimulates one to act on one's thoughts or plans. If one is thinking about something, the impulse will occur to take some action that handles whatever one was considering. For example, if one were thinking about writing a letter to Aunt Minnie, one would find one's self engaged in writing the letter very quickly, after picking up one's Norbergite. **b)** In the Michael system, balances and activates the Moving Center.

**Northupite:** Increases muscle strength.

**Nullaginite:** (Bright green in color). **a)** Makes one feel more in touch with the earth and physically balanced. One feels integrated with the earth and, in fact, all other physical objects. **b)** Enhances the ability to keep one's balance in a physical sense. Great for tight rope walkers, horseback riders, sailors, dancers, hang gliders and in any endeavor where keeping one's balance is essential.

**Nunkirchner Jasper:** See Jasper, Nunkirchner.

**Obsidian, Black and Brown:** Helps eliminate bad habits by reducing craving. Good for dieting, giving up smoking and other bad habits.

**Obsidian, Black:** Same in effect as Leopard-Skin Agate.

**Obsidian, Golden:** Same stone as black and brown Obsidian.

**Obsidian, Mahogany:** (Rust-red brown in color). Increases ones sexuality and sensuality. One feels sexier and more "in touch with touch".

**Obsidian, Rainbow:** **a)** Good all-purpose, energetic balancer. Stabilizes one's energy level, and allows one to set a pace, as one moves through the day, that is comfortable: neither too hurried nor too plodding. **b)** Helps one harmonize one's energy with that of another and makes it easier to move at the same pace, especially if the other person's pace differs from one's own. **c)** Enables one to use one's focused, organizational abilities and one's creative, innovative abilities in a balanced fashion.  d) Calms, relaxes, and heals one of survival fears.  Makes one feel safe.  e) Balances those who are mentally unstable due to extreme chemical imbalances, such as that found in Schizophrenia or Manic Depressive illnesses.  f) In the Michael system, an all-purpose energetic balancer that enables one to keep one's frequency rate stable.  Balances those who are either very high-male energied or who are very high-female energied.  Enables one to match frequencies with another person.  Balances and heals the Instinctive Center.

**Obsidian, Silver or Gold Sheen:**  a) Energizes by getting one in touch with the movement of one's body.  Stimulates one to engage in activities that promote bodily health.  b) In the Michael system, stimulates the Moving Center.

**Obsidian, Snow-Flake:**  (Black and gray).  Balances and calms "high frequency", "buzzy" types of persons who move through life at a very fast pace.  Makes it easier for them to slow down and mellow out.

**Okenite:**  (White and fuzzy).  a) Balances those people who approach life in a highly creative, expansive and fluid manner.  Enables them to put a focus on their creative energies and keep from getting too scattered or sidetracked.  b) In the Michael system, enables high-female energied people to feel more focused.

**Oligoclase Feldspar:**  See Feldspar, Oligoclase.

**Olivenite:**  (Grey/green black crystals).  Promotes one's business endeavors by making it easy to focus on work or career issues.  Encourages a "hard-working atmosphere".

**Omphacite:**  (Green, often with red Garnet and blue Azurite matrix).  a) Fills one with a sense of adventure.  Increases boldness and prepares one to tackle the next task with fervor.  When found with red Garnet, adds a strong element of productivity.  When blue Azurite is also present, one communicates appropriately about the task or adventure.  b) In the Michael system, promotes the positive use of Aggression Mode.

**Onyx:** (Layered stone; useful for cameos and intaglios).  **a)** Useful when one wants to pursue creative projects and see things from a more expansive, "larger picture" perspective. **b)** In the Michael system, balances one's female-energied side.  **c)** Onyx comes various colors.  Each color adds a slightly different flavor to the basic definition.

> **Black:**  Calms primal or basic fears and enables one to feel stable and secure.
>
> **Milky White or Cream:**  No added qualities.
>
> **Orange to Brown:**  Enhances and intensifies the basic effects.
>
> **Pale Green or Olive Green:**  Soothes and calms the emotions.
>
> **Red:**  Adds a dynamic element.

**Opal, Black: a)** Makes one feel energetically connected to the whole and one with all that is.  **b)** Enhances one's sexuality and sexual attractiveness.  Enables one to have a highly spiritual and divinely intense sexual experience, in which one loses the boundaries of one's ego, and merges with the cosmos.  **c)** Creates an energetic field of resonance between oneself and others.  Enables one to have the experience of being on the "same wavelength" as one's friends and intimates.  **d)** Because of this resonance however, others are drawn to connect with one energetically, and one can be easily corded when wearing this stone.  Can use with Fluorite, or any other aura cleanser, to prevent unwanted cording.  See section on Chakras.  **e)** A very energizing stone.  Makes one feel physically energetic and alert.  **f)** In the Michael system, stimulates the Higher-Moving Center and connects one with the energy of the Buddhaic Plane.

**Opal, Boulder:** (Opal still growing in the matrix.  Blue with flashes of light).  **a)** Inspires creative, imaginative ideas of an unusual and, sometimes, bizarre sort.  Stimulates one to come up with wild and crazy ideas, to make leaps to higher levels of knowledge, or to think of something that pulls a lot of ideas together in a way that suddenly works when it didn't before. A truly elegant, unusual stone that people who have a sense of difference would appreciate. **b)** In the Michael system, an enjoyable stone particularly for Artisans or anyone at the 5th (or ecccentric) level of any soul age. Useful, when working in five person groups, to aid the "eccentric" to come up with innovative and unusual ideas.

**Opal, Cacholong:** (Translucent white to yellowish in color). **a)** Clears up energy blockages in the body, so one can open up to new experiences including those of a spiritual nature. **b)** Balances all chakras. **c)** An aid to channeling.

**Opal, California:** Another name for Sonoma Opal.

**Opal, Fire: a)** Allows one to project with incredible charisma The effect is less intense with a timid person. **b)** Increases one's personal power and one's ability to operate effectively in the world. Especially enables one to operate powerfully in circumstances that require action. **c)** Enables one to take command assertively and with a good eye for strategy. **d)** In the Michael system, pulls one into the positive pole of Power Mode.

**Opal, Jelly:** Same in effect as Black Opal, although not as powerful in its effect.

**Opal, Mexican:** Same stone as Fire Opal.

**Opal, Mountain:** Another name for Sonoma Opal.

**Opal, Sonoma: a)** Stabilizes the emotions. Evens out mood swings and keeps one from getting easily upset. Good for anyone who is pursuing a hobby, career, or artistic endeavor that requires they be creative and emotionally stable at the same time. Also stabilizes the emotions of one who is involved in a sexual relationship. **b)** Creates a link between the second and fourth chakras, keeping them aligned and operating in a blended fashion. **c)** In the Michael system, balances and stabilizes Mature Artisans. Balances the Emotional and Higher-Moving Centers.

**Opal, Sun:** Same stone as Fire Opal.

**Opal, Sunflower:** Same stone as Fire Opal.

**Opal, White:** a) Makes one more productive. Energizes the body and encourages one to get a lot done. b) In the Michael system, balances the Moving Center.

**Opalite:** (A composite rock. Pale brown, pale yellow or gray sometimes with pink areas or a dark blue thread running through). a) A stone that relaxes one by pulling excess energy up and out of the body. Also keeps excess energy from building up and can help release that "headachy" feeling one gets from overusing the mind. b) Reduces fevers. c) Balances and heals the sixth chakra. d) In the Michael system, particularly useful for those who tend to overuse the Intellectual Center.

**Orpiment:** (Yellow in color). For feeling nurtured and emotionally connected with others. Makes one feel that one is getting what one wants, and needs, from loved ones.

**Orthoclase:** (Champagne in color). Aids in the healing of any cancer.

**Orthochrysotile:** A variety of Clinochrysotile.

**Orthoferrosilite:** (Brown, gray-green, or cat eyed. Sometimes called Enstatite incorrectly). Enhances short-term memory.

**Osarizawaite:** (Greenish-yellow, yellowish-green, green, blue-green and green-blue in color). Promotes a fine, pin-point accuracy in whatever one attempts to manifest or bring into one's life. Whatever one is trying to produce, emerges in its purest, finest and most exact form.

**Osumilite:** (Blue-black crystals. Often occurs in a Ryalite matrix). For male sexuality. A powerful fertility stone. Steps up the production of strong, healthy sperm. Keeps sexual organs healthy and heals genital damage.

**Padparadschah:** Same stone as Orange Sapphire.

**Pakistan Jade:** See Jade, Pakistan.

**Palygorskite:** (Grey/white opaque). Makes children, or the inexperienced person, feel more experienced, more capable and more adult.

**Parachrysotile:** A variety of Clinochrysotile.

**Parajamesonite:** Same stone as Jamesonite.

**Parrot-Wing Jasper:** See Jasper, Parrot-Wing.

**Partheite:** Same stone as Lawsonite.

**Pascoite:** (Orange, yellow or yellow-orange in color). **a)** Releases tension and drains excess energy from the body, so one can relax. **b)** Balances all chakras. **c)** Draws impurities to the surface of the skin to be dissipated into the air or cleansed from the body with a bath. This includes physical matter such as chemicals and minerals, as well as non-physical matter, in the form of energy, that needs to be released in order to balance the system.

**Paua Shell:** (Dark blue and pearly lining of an Abalone Shell). Heals stress by keeping the body clear of stressful body chemicals and hormones. Helpful in times of difficult challenges, heavy karmas, or soul-level transitions.

**Peacock Copper:** Another name for Chalcopyrite.

**Pearls: a)** For wisdom. Each Pearl absorbs and holds different inspirational thought. Each Pearl is unique, and the energy of one doesn't blend with the energy of another. The more misshapen the Pearl, the more eccentric the thought. **b)** Balances and heals all chakras. Pearls can be placed near a chakra, when one desires the highest truth and wisdom about an issue that pertains to that chakra. **c)** In the Michael system, balances the Higher-Intellectual Center and connects one with the energy of the Mental Plane.

**Pearls, Biwa:** (Oddly shaped Pearls found in fresh water). Same in effect as Pearls, but for thoughts that are more eccentric in nature.

**Pectolite, Pink:** Enables one to increase the amount of oxygen one draws out of the air, as well as to increase the amount one utilizes as one breathes. Good for cigarette smokers, those with emphysema, or anemia (low red blood cell count). Do not eat.

**Pectolite, White or Clear:** Augments the body's ability to use nutrients to strengthen bones, teeth, hair and nails. Do not eat.

**Periclase:** (Clear and yellowish in color). Aids in healing sun damaged skin.

**Peridot: a)** Stimulates one's growth on the essence level: opens up the adventure box of life and new challenges abound. The effect can be too intense for some. The yellower color produces the most intense effect; greener a milder effect. Wear with Amethyst and Citrine to slow the growth aspect down, and keep one balanced. **b)** In the Michael, pulls one into the positive pole of the Goal of Growth.

**Perovskite:** (Black in color). **a)** Enables a person, who tends toward gullibility, to see what might be wrong with something that is being offered. Encourages one to develop some healthy cynicism. **b)** In the Michael system, enables one to use the positive pole of the Attitude of Cynic.

**Petalite:** (Clear or pink in color). Aids in fertility. Promotes sperm production. Acts on the sexual organs to stimulate healthy functioning.

**Petersite:** (Silver-blue metallic swirls). Aids one to become a better teacher. Increases one's clarity of presentation and improves one's public-speaking skills. Enables one to each for longer periods of time without tiring and heals teacher "burn-out".

**Petrified Wood:** (Brown, grey, or red in color). **a)** Calms survival-based fears. Makes one feel safe and secure that everything will turn out all right. Gives one a sense of agelessness, and a feeling that one will last forever. **b)** Stabilizes one's energy level, and allows one to set a pace, as one moves through the day, that is comfortable: neither too hurried nor too plodding. **c)** In the Michael system, balances and heals the Instinctive Center and is an all-purpose energetic balancer that allows one to keep one's frequency rate stable.

**Pharmacolite:** (Pale cloudy white, yellowish or tan). Heals by drawing impurities from the body to the surface of the skin which can then be washed away. Works locally or systemically depending on the type of impurity or problem. Place on the body near the toxic area. Do <u>not</u> ingest.

**Phenakite:** In general, keeps one from forming bad habits.

**Phenakite, Blue:** (Pale in color). Keeps one from forming bad emotional habits. This includes throwing a tantrum when one doesn't get one's way, or any way of acting out of one's emotions inappropriately.

**Phenakite, Colorless to White:** Keeps one from forming bad mental habits. For example, assuming that one is right, when one hasn't collected enough evidence, or had enough experience, to know.

**Phenakite, Yellow or Pink:** (Pale in color). Keeps one from forming bad physical habits. Examples include not eating right, not exercising enough, or letting one's addictions get out of control.

**Philipsburgite:** (Bright green to deep green in color). Makes anything seem funny or amusing.

**Phillipsite:** (Orangeish in color). Enables one to look at things from a broad perspective. One can step back and separate the "forest from the trees".

**Phosgenite:** (Clear, colorless crystals). Makes birds, etc., lay stronger eggs.

**Pickeringite:** (Light, white and feathery. Sometimes referred to as "Angelic Feathers"). **a)** Allows one to create an island of calm in an otherwise frantic period. **b)** Allows one to suspend karma temporarily.

**Picture Jasper:** See Jasper, Picture.

**Piemontite Epidote:** (Cherry red in color). **a)** A very powerful stone. Good for getting people motivated, feeling empowered, and ready to go. Makes one feel infused with power and pulsing with "get-up-and-go" energy. A good cure for laziness. b) In the Michael system, pulls one into the positive pole of Power Mode.

**Pink Halite:** See Halite, Pink.

**Pioche:** (Creamy yellow-brown in color). Heals the digestive tract. Do not eat.

**Pistacite:** Another name for Epidote.

**Plancheite:** (Fuzzy pale blue). a) Very strong healer when one is going through an intense tragedy or grieving period. Temporarily numbs the emotions until healing can begin, then it eases a person through the various stages of the grief process. b) Has a different effect at each stage: 1) Causes a feeling of numbness emotionally. 2) As the numbness wears off, which usually happens (if carried constantly) after 3 days to 2 weeks depending on the person, one gets back in touch with whatever the original grief was about, but only for a few hours of crying and release and then back to numbness. This process continues for a month to six weeks. 3) The numbness is gone and the person begins to feel some capability to handle things, but will continue to vary between feeling capable and breaking down and crying for a few hours. Emotions will stay in this phase as long as rock is on the person, or until one has completed the grief process. c) Aids children in going through the grieving process when they have lost someone they love. d) In the Michael system, heals the Emotional Center.

**Planerite:** (Light green in color). a) Makes one feel personally competent and powerful. Encourages a winning attitude. Enhances one's personal power when communicating, as well as one's ability to debate effectively. Good for winning arguments. b) In the Michael system, pulls one into the positive pole of Dominance.

**Plattnerite:** (Black crystals). a) Reduces clumsiness and increases one's ability to move with grace and ease. b)

Encourages greater craftsmanship and skill in using one's hands.

**Pleonaste:** Same stone as dark green Spinel.

**Plume Agate:** See Agate, Plume.

**Pokrovskite:** (White, silky sprays). Enables one's body to tolerate low temperatures more easily, particularly when living in snowy areas for long periods of time.

**Polyhalite:** Another name for Pink Halite.

**Polyhedroids:** (A pseudo Agate with a triangular shape). Enables one to relate to alien thoughts and cultures.

**Polylithionite:** (Light violet-gray in color. Mica like). Helps correct chemical imbalances of the brain, such as is found in certain types of mental illness.

**Poppy Jasper:** See Jasper, Poppy.

**Powellite:** (Clear octahedral chunks). a) Encourages self confidence and imbues one with a sense of dignity. Particularly good for those who were brought up not to believe in themselves. b) In the Michael system, softens the Chief Negative Feature of Self-Deprecation.

**Prase or Prasolite:** (Leek green in color). Same in effect as Actinolite.

**Prehnite:** (Green in color). Promotes calm.

**Proustite:** (Scarlet red. Often occurs in a shiny silvery matrix). Heals the colon.

**Pseudoboleite:** (Dark blue crystals). a) Encourages one to pay attention to appropriate and proper social behavior. Enables one to behave in a refined manner. b) Contains impulsiveness. Provides an internal monitor that keeps one from going over the edge emotionally into rash behavior. c) When found on Boleite, helps one to contain the energetic rush of opportunites, and the good luck energy that Boleite brings, appropriately. d) In the Michael system, pulls one into the positive pole of Repression Mode.

**Purpurite:** (Clear, purple, deep pink, dark brown in color). **a)** Increases physical strength and stamina. **b)** Makes one more capable of doing anything that requires agility and good motor coordination. Improves one's fine motor coordination as well. **c)** Balances the third chakra, and keeps one moving steadily into appropriate action. **d)** In the Michael system, keeps the Moving Center balanced.

**Pyrite, Iron:** See Iron Pyrite.

**Pyrolusite:** (Black in color). **a)** A stone that enhances qualities of determination, willfulness, and ambition. Makes it easier to keep going, when the going gets tough. Good for stiffening the spine of a passive, indecisive type of person. When combined with White Calcite, there is an added element of love and acceptance toward others, that tempers the willfulness of this stone. **b)** In the Michael system, this stone is attractive to a Warrior who is Young in soul age. Young Warriors (and overly-ambitious types) definitely need to use this stone with White Calcite, as they can go overboard and get into clawing their way to the top.

**Pyromorphite:** (Brown, green, yellow, or orange in color). Attracts money, or energy in the form of goods.

**Pyrope:** See Garnet, Pyrope.

**Pyrophyllite:** (White, pink, or brown in color). Heals and detoxifies the blood.

**Pyrrotite:** Same in effect as Iron Pyrite.

**Qingheiite:** (Jade green in color). Same in effect as Rosasite.

**Quartz Crystal:** See Crystal, Clear.

**Quartz Lignite:** Same in effect as Tiger Iron.

**Quartz, Amethyst:** See Amethyst Quartz.

**Quartz, Analcime:** Same stone as Analcime.

**Quartz, Analcite:** Same stone as Analcime.

**Quartz, Drusy:** Same in effect as Quartz Crystal, but has a dreamier quality than regular Quartz.

**Quartz, Elestial:** (Gray). **a)** Opens the emotions, releases emotional blocks and heals. Allows one to see one's emotional truths clearly. Particularly good for those who have had a past history of abuse, or a very dysfunctional family, to heal up from. **b)** In the Michael system, balances and heals the Emotional Center.

**Quartz, Green::** Metaphysical meaning can be found by determining the type of mineral that is responsible for the green color. Most common inclusions are Hedenbergite, Actinolite, or Pargasite (type of Hornblende).

**Quartz, Lavender:** (Pale, opaque lavender color. Often sold as Amethyst or Cape Amethyst). **a)** Promotes calm. Relieves stress. **b)** Aids in "self-remembering", and produces an intense, super self awareness. Self-remembering is being aware of what one is actually doing and saying on all levels. For this reason, Lavender Quartz is a good stone for meditation and is an aid in self realization and transformation.

**Quartz, Rose:** See Rose Quartz.

**Quartz, Rutillated:** (Quartz with Rutile inclusions). **a)** Enables one to project an aura of authority. Pulls one into powerfulness and produces clarity with regard to what one is being powerful about. One not only looks very clear and capable of handling everything, but one feels that way as well. **b)** In the Michael system, pulls one into the positive pole of Power Mode.

**Quartz, Skeletal:** Same stone as Elestial Quartz.

**Quartz, Smoky:** See Smoky Quartz.

**Quartz, Snow:** **a)** An observation stone. When Quartz is snowy in color rather than clear, one moves into "childlikeness" and can observe from a place of innocence. One's insights are fresh and clear, free of preconceptions and free of "adult" cynical viewpoints.  b) Good balancing stone for children.  Helps them be clear about the world they're in and be comfortable in a child's body   c) In the Michael system, pulls one into the positive pole of Observation Mode.  Sages are attracted to Snow Quartz, because they grow up at a slow rate, and Sages often feel like their bodies are maturing at a faster rate than they are.

**Quartz, Strawberry:** a) Has an intense, dreamy quality.  b) Keep's one attached to one's body, especially while sleeping.  c) Helps one to remember dreams.  d) In the Michael system, balances Artisans.

**Quartz, Tourmalinated:**  (Quartz with Tourmaline inclusions).  Same in effect as Rutillated Quartz.

**Quenstedtite:** (Violet in color).  Attracts people to one another who have strong agreements to be together in the present lifetime.  This includes all types of agreements such as mates, friends, and work partners.

**Quetzacoatlite:** (Blue in color).  Encourages one to zero in quickly, on whether someone else is appropriate mate material or not.  A mate screening rock.

**Quietite:**  (Pale yellow in color).  Very calming to domesticated animals.  Makes wild animals nervous.  No effect on humans.

**Rain Forest Jasper:** See Jasper, Rain Forest.

**Rainbow Obsidian:** See Obsidian, Rainbow.

**Ralstonite:** Encourages one to see things with a sense of humor.

**Ramsdellite:** (Gray to black in color).  Increases courage and bravery.  Gives one the courage to continue on in very difficult, or potentially dangerous situations.  Helps one operate from "fight" rather than "flight".

**Raspite:** (Brownish-yellow).  Helps eliminate, or tone down, muscular tics and twitches.

**Rauvite:** (Red-brown, purple or black in color). Enables a group of people to work together on an action-oriented project, with a great deal of synchronicity and a telepathic awareness of the members of the group and of the group dynamics.

**Realgar:** (Transparent. Dark red to orange red in color). For balanced harmony. One feels a sense of harmony and balance about one's life, one's relationships and one's possessions. Often found mixed with Orpiment.

**Red Amber:** See Amber, Red.

**Red Aventurine:** See Aventurine, Red.

**Red Serpentine:** See Serpentine, Red.

**Red Tiger Eye:** See Tiger Eye, Red.

**Reevsite:** (Yellow to greenish-yellow). Helps one empathize with, and have a clear intellectual understanding of, the point of view of someone who has a very different point of view from one's self. A harmonizer for those who are in great conflict. Does not change one's point of view, but it will enable one to really understand what's going on with the other person.

**Rhodochrosite:** (Pink to salmon pink in color). Increases long term memory. One is better able to access memories from the present life, as well as from past lives. Enables one to remember what one is supposed to be doing in the present moment: to stay aware, be present and be relevant.

**Rhodolite:** See Garnet, Rhodolite.

**Rhodonite, Pink with Brown, Yellow or Grey markings:** Enables one to be cool and dignified even while facing stressful circumstances.

**Rhodonite, Pink or Pink with Black markings:** For feeling, as well as projecting, an aura of elegance.

**Richterite:** (Blackish green in color). **a)** Gives oes mental stamina. Enables one to keep paying attention, for long periods of time, to even somewhat boring material. One can study tedious materials longer.   **b)** In the Michael system, promotes efficient use of the Intellectual Center.

**Riebeckite:** (Long, dark-blue crystals).  Helps one recognize what's missing.  One might identify what thieves stole in a robbery, or look at larger issues such as what is missing in one's life.

**Rim Jasper:** See Jasper, Rim.

**Rockbridgeite:** (Brownish-green, spherical shaped crystals). Enhances one's coordination and physical balance. Decreases clumsiness.

**Romanechite:** (Opaque white and gray in color).  Heals the abnormal fear of open spaces.  The effect is temporary, and only lasts as long as one is wearing it.  The basic issue underlying the fear will not be healed.  A useful aid, in psychotherapy, to heal Agoraphobia.

**Romerite:** (Chocolate brown in color).  Same in effect as Danburite.

**Rosasite:** (Looks like Turquoise).  **a)** Helps one shift out of a negative emotional state into a more positive one.  This stone works by enabling one to produce an appropriate action or thought, that then shifts the emotional state.   **b)** In the Michael system, stimulates the Moving or Intellectual Centers to produce an action or thought, that balances the Emotional Center.

**Rose Quartz: a)** Puts one in touch with one's self on the essence level.  Enhances awareness of one's true self.  **b)** Assists one in communicating with one's spirit guides. Since Rose Quartz keeps one in one's body, the communication would take place internally.

**Rubellite:** Same stone as pink or red Tourmaline.

**Rubicelle:** Same stone as yellow Spinel.

**Ruby: a)** Makes one feel giving toward others and happy about being able to be of service to them.  Reduces resentment about it.  One can approach caretaking of others in a relaxed fashion; knowing that one will not be victimized or trapped in any way. Enhances one's ability to be warm, caring and tuned into the needs of others. Inspiring in its devotional quality. b) In the Michael system, balances Servers.

**Ruby Silver:** Another name for Proustite.

**Ruizite:** (Salmon pink fibrous tufts). Enables one to feel a heart connection with someone, even though separated by great distances, continents, and oceans: even beyond death. Usually found with Apophyllite.

**Rumanite:** Same stone as Burnite.

**Rutile:** (Black, gold or red). a) Adds power to whatever rock it flows through. The stone then becomes a magnifier of the power of one's own personal aura. One stands out as a more powerful or noticeable person in one's way of being. It is important to note that it is the power of one's presence that is augmented, rather than one's actions becoming more powerful or having more power over another person. b) In the Michael system, pulls one into the positive pole of Power Mode.

**Rutillated Quartz:** See Quartz, Rutillated.

**Ryalite:** (Pink/orange, brown, grey, or purple in color). The generic name for Serape Jasper or Wonder Agate. The more pink/orange the tones are, the more the stone relates to female sexuality. The more brown/gray//purple the tones are, the more the stone relates to male sexuality.

**Sagenite Agate:** See Agate, Sagenite.

**Sanbornite:** (White, or pale blue-green in color). a) Increases one's ability to achieve inner peace. Promotes a feeling of security and great stability. b) Promotes one's ability to perservere; to continue at a steady pace regardless of the circumstances. c) In the Michael system, pulls one into the positive pole of Perserverence Mode.

**Sanidine:** Anti-cancer agent.

**Saponite:** (Green to brown spheres). Same in effect as Pyromorphite.

**Sapphire, Dark Blue: a)** Enhances creativity and enables one to tap into one's full creative potential. This stone feels nurturing because it allows anyone to creatively express who they are. It is grounding during the creative process: keeps one from becoming too scattered and assists follow through to completion. Also helps one find creative solutions to problems when needed. **b)** Good for imtinate sexual relationships, as it inspires a sense of loyalty and bondedness. **c)** Opens the second chakra and frees it for creative use. **d)** In the Michael system, balances Artisans.

**Sapphire, Light Blue: a)** Inspirational in quality. Promotes inspired conceptual thoughts and inspiration in one's intellectual projects. Makes one feel excited about life; that it will really work. Good for therapists as it will inspire them to see through people's blocks and find ways to work them out. **b)** With regard to the color range, the darker the blue of the Sapphire, the more creative it is. The lighter the blue of the Sapphire, the more intellectually centered and philosophical it is. **c)** In the Michael system, balances Priests.

**Sapphire, Green:** Good luck stone. Creates the atmosphere for serendipitous events to occur in one's life.

**Sapphire, Lilac:** (rare) **a)** This stone allows one's creativity to flow freely and intensely. Can be used by anyone who has already developed their creative talent, or is involved in a creative project, but at the moment, feels blocked. **b)** In the Michael system, balances Mature and Old Artisans who have already learned to use their creativity, but are feeling lazy or blocked because they're stuck in the negative pole of their Chief Feature.

**Sapphire, Orange: a)** Promotes a clear perspective that enables one to acquire knowledge in its most basic and pure form, without distorting it to conform to one's own biases. **b)** Empowers one to build an empire based on scholarly pursuits. This could include the writing of books, doing research on a large scale, or being in charge of ten libraries at once.  c) In the Michael system, a power stone for Scholars.

**Sapphire, Pink:** a) Brings out one's ability to surrender to, or devote oneself to, a cause or another person for the greater good.  A delegation and surrender stone that allows one to surrender power or control to people who can handle things better.  Makes it easier to accept when one is not "in control".  Allows one to be really devotional and appreciative of those one has surrendered to.  A very people-oriented stone.  b) In the Michael system, pulls one into the positive pole of the Goal of Submission.  Good for those in Aggression Mode or with a Goal of Dominance: tones them down and enables them to let life flow a little more.

**Sapphire, Star:** See Star Sapphire.

**Sapphire, White:** a) Encourages one to be good to oneself and self-nurturing.  Keeps one serving oneself appropriately by making sure one does nice things for oneself.  Enables one to be gentle with oneself, and helps prevent needless suffering.  b) In the Michael system, balances Servers who most often forget to maintain the balance by serving themselves as well.

**Sapphire, Yellow:** a) Puts one directly in touch with what one knows.  Also helps one realize what one doesn't know Enables one to use one's intellect and knowledge very appropriately.  Enhances one's ability to learn and retain information.   b) When wearing this stone, new opportunities start to arise and new options open up for one to take advantage of.  c) In the Michael system, pulls one into the positive pole of the Intellectual Center. Balances Scholars.

**Sarabauite:** (Bright carmine red).  Stimulates courage. Increases one's willingness to take risks of an emotional nature as well as those of a physical nature.  Promotes courageous action.

**Sarcopside:** (Brown-green in color).  Encourages one to focus in on why one is lonely and/or not allowing in any support from others. Stimulates a desire to shift by sharpening the poignancy of the aloneness.

**Sard:** a) "Homestone." Brings up memories of home and keeps a person mindful of their emotional attachments and family commitments. Those who are without family or home feel more rooted and comforted. b) Also enables the body to assimilate food more easily. Light brown Sard aids in the digestion of vegetable proteins. red-brown Sard aids in the digestion of animal proteins.

**Sardonyx:** Same stone as Orange Agate with White Stripes.

**Sauconite:** (Pink and clay-like). Same in effect as pink Rhodonite with black markings.

**Scheelite:** (Colorless, white, yellow-white, yellow, reddish-yellow, brownish in color). a) Opens up awareness of one's personal survival issues or deeply buried conflicts. Enables one to stay balanced while dealing with them. b) Balances and opens the first chakra. Good because the first chakra is often closed down. c) In the Michael system, balances the Instinctive Center.

**Schorl:** Same stone as black Tourmaline.

**Schrockingerite:** (Greenish-yellow to bright yellow in color). Promotes a deep sense of well being, happiness and a sense of humor.

**Scolecite:** (Snow white in color). a) Balancing for those who are involved in artistic or creative endeavors. b) In the Michael system, particularly balancing for Infant, Baby and Young Artisans. Enables them to stay out of self-deception, moodiness and wishy-washiness.

**Scorodite:** (Gray-green crystals). Encourages one to leave hopelessly dysfunctional emotional relationships. Especially useful where one clings addictively to a relationship that will never work. Makes it easier to let go and move on.

**Scorzalite:** (Deep blue in color). Deepens and underscores the effect of any other mineral it is bonded to or in matrix with.

Doesn't work if another rock is merely set near it: must be a bonding or melding of materials. Oten found with Andalusite, Citrine, Scorodite, Kyanite, Quartz, Pyrophyllite and Garnet.

**Sea Amber:** Same stone as Burnite.

**Selenite:** (The clear variety of Gypsum) **a)** Promotes intellectual clarity and competency. **b)** Assists in the digestion and absorption of minerals. **c)** After being used for a while, a gemstone or mineral can be drained of its energy or soak up undesirable energies occurring in its proximity. Selenite can be used to clean and recharge other gemstones and minerals. For further information, refer to the discussion on cleaning and recharging gemstones and minerals in the section, "Gemstones: Nature's Gifts". **d)** In the Michael system, balances Scholars. See Gypsum.

**Septarian Nodule:** (Combination of Aragonite, Brown Calcite, and naturally occurring concretions or concrete). **a)** This combination is energizing and enhances the ability to perceive higher truth and love. The Aragonite keeps one emotionally and intellectually centered in the truth. The Brown Calcite allows one to connect with higher planes of existence that are a source of spiritual knowledge and wisdom. The concretions hold energy that can be drawn on as needed. **b)** The Aragonite keeps chakras four, five, and six open, in balance and aligned. **c)** The concretions can also be used by spirit guides as a base from which to contact their student on the physical plane. **d)** Useful for a channel as a source of energy and to insure the clarity of information. **e)** In the Michael system, balances the Emotional, Intellectual, and Higher-Intellectual Centers and allows them to operate in a blended fashion. Connects one with the energy of the Astral Plane and the Mental Plane.

**Serandite:** (Pink or peach in color). **a)** Encourages one to believe in one's own attractiveness and appeal to others. Makes it easy to believe that others would like to spend time with one, work with one, or love one. **b)** In the

Michael system, pulls one out of the negative pole of the Chief Negative Feature of Self-Deprecation.

**Serape Jasper:** See Jasper, Serape.

**Serpentine:** In general, Serpentine is the same in its effect as Jade. Both Jade and Serpentine occur in a variety of colors (white, green, orange, pink, black, gray, and lavender). The colors correspond in effect. So, green Jade has the same effect as green Serpentine, gray Jade has the same effect as gray Serpentine, etc. Colors that are unique to the Serpentines are listed below as they have no correspondents in the Jade group.

**Serpentine, Chartreuse:** (Pale yellow or chartreuse green in color). Reduces allergic reactions to animals, birds, fish, reptiles, pets, and meats that one eats.

**Serpentine, Chrysotile:** Same stone as Long Hair Asbestos.

**Serpentine, Pale Green to Yellow-Green:** (Translucent). Same stone as Bowenite.

**Serpentine, Red:** (Looks somewhat like Red Aventurine except it's lighter in color and has some brown in it.). **a)** Enhances one's sexuality with one's soul mates. **b)** In the Michael system, helps one to have good sex with one's essence twin.

**Shattuckite:** (Blue in color). **a)** Puts one in touch with the different facets of one's higher self. These facets include the ability to be in accord with nature and animals, to appreciate the finer aspects of power, prosperity, and relationships with one's fellow man, as well as the experience of higher truth, transcendent love and wisdom. **b)** In the Michael system, puts one in touch with different degrees of essence: from the least, to the most developed aspects of one's essence.

**Shell:** Similar in effect to Bone and Ivory. See types by name such as Mother of Pearl, Cameo Shell, or Clam Shell.

**Siderite:** (Yellow, tan or brown). Same in effect as Blue Aventurine.

**Siegenite:** (Metallic black). Increases eye-hand coordination.

**Sillimanite, Pale Blue:** Same in effect as blue Kyanite.

**Sillimanite, Dark Brown:** Same in effect as Andalusite.

**Silver:** Has a mildly energizing effect.

**Simetite:** Same stone as Burnite.

**Sinhalite:** (Yellow-brown or green-brown in color). **a)** Steps up the pace of one's growth on an essence level. Allows challenges to come into ones life at a more rapid pace. Good if bored and one wants a little more excitement. Similar in effect to Peridot. **b)** In the Michael system, pulls one into the positive pole of the Goal of Growth.

**Skeletal, Quartz:** Same stone as Elestial Quartz.

**Skutterudite:** (Opaque, tin-white in color). Aids in the recall of past life material.

**Smaragdite:** Same stone as Actinolite.

**Smithsonite:** Clears the chakras of any blockages and enables one to use them more effectively. Smithsonite comes in a variety of colors. Each color works on a different chakra: it clears the chakra and makes it easier to use the energy of that particular chakra.

**Smithsonite, Brown:** **a)** Stimulates the use of the intellect and produces clearer thinking. **b)** Balances the fifth chakra. **c)** In the Michael system, balances and stimulates the Intellectual Center.

**Smithsonite, Green or Blue:** **a)** Makes it easier to experience emotions. Especially good if one has been emotionally blocked. **b)** Balances and clears the fourth chakra. **c)** In the Michael system, balances the Emotional Center.

**Smithsonite, Pink:** **a)** Helps make children more psychic. Can also be used by adults, but is more effective for children. **b)** Balances the sixth chakra. **c)** In the Michael system, balances the Higher-Intellectual Center.

**Smithsonite, Purple:** a) Makes one more psychic and able to use one's psychic abilities. b) Balances the sixth chakra. c) In the Michael system, balances the Higher-Intellectual Center.

**Smithsonite, Yellow:** a) Makes one more movement oriented and ready for action. b) Balances the third chakra. c) In the Michael system, balances and stimulates the Moving Center.

**Smoky Anydrite:** Same stone as Elestial Quartz.

**Smoky Quartz:** (Dark grayish-brown in color). a) A discrimination stone. Helps one to be more appropriately selective when responding to people or situations. Enables one to distinguish that which one wants, and that which one doesn't want, in one's life, and to be clear about which is which. Assists one in cutting the "dead wood" away. Use Smoky Quartz with Hematite to evaluate personal matters. b) In the Michael system, facilitates the positive use of the Goal of Discrimination.

**Snake Skin Agate:** See Agate, Snake Skin.

**Snow Flake Obsidian:** See Obsidian, Snow Flake.

**Snow Quartz:** See Quartz, Snow.

**Soapstone:** Same in effect as Jade. Comes in a variety of colors. Effect varies with color. Each color of Soapstone has the same effect as its corresponding color in Jade.

**Soapstone, Pale Green:** (Translucent). Same in effect as Bowenite. A form of Serpentine.

**Sodalite:** (Pale to deep blue, white, grey, or pink in color). a) Stimulates one to use one's creativity. b) Increases sensuality, sexual attractiveness, and sexual interest. c) Balances and stimulates the second chakra. Very healing to a second chakra that has been overused or too shut down. d) In the Michael system, balances the Higher-Moving Center.

**Sogdianite:** (Light pink to violet). Enables one to push beyond one's ordinary limitations to survive.

**Sonolite:** (Reddish-orange in color). **a)** Puts one into a spiritualistic, visionary frame of mind, able to envision all possibilities and open new horizons. **b)** In the Michael system, pulls one into the positive pole of the Attitude of Spiritualist.

**Sonoma Opal:** See Opal, Sonoma.

**Southern Jade:** See Jade, Southern.

**Spangolite:** (Dark green to blue in color). Same in effect as Chalcanthite.

**Spectrolite:** (Dark, opalescent blue). **a)** Keeps one active. Stimulates one to exercise, dance, hop and skip about. Similar in effect to Bronzite. **b)** Opens and stimulates the third chakra. **c)** In the Michael system, stimulates the Moving Center.

**Specularite:** Same stone as Hematite.

**Spessartite:** See Garnet, Spessartite.

**Sphalerite:** **a)** For spiritual awareness and transcending the ego. The stone is empathic with one. It senses where one is and empathizes with one. It takes one beyond petty problems, into a higher space of calm and true self-knowledge. This is why it transcends ego. **b)** In the Michael system, balances the Higher-Intellectual Center. **c)** The different Roles resonate best to different colors. If Role is unknown, choose the color one finds most attractive.

| | |
|---|---|
| **Black:** | Warrior. |
| **Brown:** | King. |
| **Clear:** | Scholar. |
| **Reddish-Brown:** | Sage. |
| **Red:** | Priest. |
| **Green:** | Artisan. |
| **Yellow:** | Server. |

**Sphene: a)** Encourages compassion of an extremely durable type. Helpful in situations that really put a strain on one's compassion, such as working in a hospital or with very disturbed people for extended periods of time. **b)** In the Michael system, balances Priests. **c)** Each color is for a different perspective that is related to how long the soul has been on the planet. If soul age is unknown, select the color one finds most attractive.

| | |
|---|---|
| **Black or Brown:** | Infant souls. |
| **Clear to Gray:** | Baby souls. |
| **Green:** | Young souls. |
| **Yellow:** | Mature souls. |
| **Orange-Brown:** | Old souls. |
| **Red-Brown:** | Old souls |

**Spider-Web Jasper:** See Jasper, Spider Web.

**Spinel:** Effect varies with color. Synthetic Spinels have the same effect as naturally occurring Spinels.

**Spinel, Black:** Promotes a sense of beneficence. Makes one feel so in charge of situations and oneself, that one can afford to be really giving to, and understanding of, others no matter what they're doing.

**Spinel, Blue or Gray: a)** Strongest discrimination stone. Enables one to be very discriminating about what one allows to exist in one's space. This stone works on the conscious as well as the unconscious level. Thus, one is able to reject anything out of one's space, from people out of one's life to germs out of one's body. Wonderful for illness, super dumping jobs and cleaning the garage. **b)** Enables those who are more evolved to relate appropriately and comfortably to those who are relatively new to the physical plane and, thus, not quite as evolved. Have to exercise some caution with this stone, as one can be rejecting if not careful. **c)** In the Michael system, pulls one into the positive pole of the Goal of Discrimination. Helps Young, Mature, or Old souls who have constant dealings with Infant or Baby souls, to relate to them better. One is able to discriminate very clearly about how to behave appropriately around an Infant or Baby soul.

**Spinel, Dark Green:** a) Emphasizes wisdom and increases the ability to communicate what one knows to be true in an effective manner. b) Increases one's vocabulary by enabling one to remember more of the words one comes in contact with. c) In the Michael system, balances Sages.

**Spinel, Light Green:** Same stone as Emerada.

**Spinel, Peach:** a) Aids in building self esteem. Softens the tendency to be critical of oneself or of others. Hits one very hard with the realization that one just did or said something indicative of low self esteem and prompts one to self correction. b) In the Michael system, softens the Chief Negative Features of Self-Deprecation and Arrogance.

**Spinel, Pink or Red:** a) An other-oriented stone that fosters devotion to those one loves. Enables one to surrender, and be devoted to another person. Can set one's ego aside when with a significant other, and be loving even when it's tough. A good wedding ring stone. b) In the Michael system, facilitates the positive use of the Goal of Submission.

**Spinel, Violet:** a) Enables one to be appropriate about the ways one takes care of others or nurtures them. Most useful when one is in a position of service to others and is being victimized by them or, at least, feels that one is. This stone enables one to pull out of the victim role and gain control. b) Also, a "generation gap" stone. Makes it easier to communicate with those who are 20 years older or more, than oneself, or more than 20 years younger than oneself. c) In the Michael system, balances Servers who tend to get trapped most often by the needs of others.

**Spinel, Yellow:** a) Encourages feelings of pride and confidence in one's accomplishments. Especially good for people with very low self esteem, as it enables them to start believing in themselves. b) In the Michael system, softens the Chief Negative Features of Self-Deprecation and Arrogance.

**Spodumene, Green:** Same stone as Hiddenite.

**Spodumene, Lilac or Pink:** Same stone as Kunzite.

**Spodumene, Yellow:** Same stone as Hiddenite.

**Sponge Coral:** See Coral, Sponge.

**Stanite:** (Rich blue-black in color). Enables one to feel as stable as the Rock of Gibralter; very grounded, and capable of standing up to any pressure.

**Star Garnet:** See Garnet, Star.

**Star Sapphire: a)** An isolation stone. Projects a message to others that says: "Don't interfere with me. I want some privacy right now". **b)** Comes in a variety of colors. In the Michael system, color selected depends on frequency at which one vibrates. See discussion of frequency elsewhere in this book, for further information. If frequency rate is unknown, select the color that seems most attractive.

    **Black:** For a person who moves through life at a very slow pace. Lower 1-30% of frequency range.

    **Blue:** For a person who's pace is average. Middle 30-70% of frequency range.

    **White:** Same as in effect as blue.

    **Red:** For a person who's fast paced and "buzzy". Upper 70-100% of frequency range.

**Staurolite:** (Brown with a tinge of red or orange in color). **a)** Aids one in remembering past lives, particularly those when one was first on the planet. **b)** In the Michael system, helps one to remember lessons from the Infant Cycle.

**Stellarite:** (Metallic green, blue and black). Puts one in touch with with the highest degree of one's essence, or one's highest self.

**Stibiconite:** (Yellow to greyish-yellow in color). Balances fish and crustaceans.

**Stibnite:** (Pale to dark lead-grey to blue, sometimes white in color). Encourages bravery and helps in conquering one's fears.

**Stichtite:** (Purple and pink variety). Aids in completing old cycles and clearing up one's incompletions. Cycles have a beginning , middle, and an end. Stichtite encourages one to continue through to completion.

**Stilbite:** (Aqua-blue, pink, peach, white, grey or clear in color). Makes one seem more adorable to others. Need to have it very near one's body for the other person to regard one as adorable. Very similar in effect to Manganocalcite. All colors work equally well. Color choice based on preference only.

**Stilpnomelane:** (Golden-brown and shiny). Makes one more comfortable with all activities related to water, from swimming to making one's living. Reduces fear of drowning.

**Stishovite:** Same stone as Quartz Crystal.

**Strashimirite:** (Light green to green). Gives one a green thumb. Enhances one's natural empathy with plants and one's ability to grow them well.

**Strawberry Quartz:** See Quartz, Strawberry.

**Strengite:** (Dark purple crystals. Often found near Variscite). a) For bravery, courage, and perserverance in the face of adversity. b) In the Michael system, promotes positive use of Perserverance Mode.

**Stringhamite:** (Azure blue to bluish purple in color). a) Allows one to take the leadership position and guide a situation to an outcome that benefits all. Makes it easy to convince others to follow one's lead. Can be effective regardless of the difficulties encountered. b) In the Michael system, facilitates the positive use of the Goal of Dominance.

**Strontianite** (Silvery, greenish or yellowish metallic stone). a) Increases physical strength by stimulating the body's ability to build muscle.    b) In the Michael system, stimulates the Moving Center.

**Strunzite** (White to yellow in color). Increases one's ability to learn other languages.

**Sturmanite:** (Yellow in color). Attracts money, and energy in the form of goods.

**Sugar Quartz:** Another name for Drusy Quartz.

**Sugilite:** (Also called Royal Lavulite).  a) Creates a state of receptiveness to spiritual influences from higher planes of existence.  b) Balances, heals, and opens all chakras, particularly the seventh.  c) A valuable aid to channeling.

**Sulfur:** (Yellow in color). Heals plant allergies.

**Sun Opal:** Same stone as Fire Opal.

**Sunflower Opal:** Same stone as Fire Opal.

**Sunstone:** Aids one in finding, maintaining, or completing sexual relationships. Effect varies with color.

**Sunstone, Blue or Green:** Enables one to end inappropriate or dysfunctional sexual relationships.

**Sunstone, Clear or Yellow:**  For maintaining sexual relationships and keeping them balanced. All couples could use this. Helps avoid the tendency to blame the partner for difficulties.

**Sunstone, Orange or Pink:** Useful for finding sexual relationships. Gives the wearer an aura of sexual attractiveness.

**Sylvite:** (Pink). a) Enables those in a position of service to stay appropriately nurturing, care-taking, and tuned into the needs of others.  b) In the Michael system, a power stone for Servers.

**Szaibelyite:** (Rich silky white in color). Increases one's sensuality, sexual attractiveness and sexual interest.

**Tacharanite:** (Red in color). Aids the body in cleansing, flushing, and elimination of excesses, e.g., excess bacteria and viruses, excess toxins, excess water, or excess fat. Good for losing weight. Do not ingest.

**Taikanite:** (Emerald green). Promotes loving alignment, understanding, and great depth of empathy between parents and children of the same sex.

**Takovite:** (Blue-green). Promotes understanding of other people's tribal, racial, nationalistic, patriotic, philosophical, or religious orientation. Puts one in touch with why that person likes being identified with that particular group or philosophy.

**Tantalite:** (Black with deep red on edges). **a)** Encourages one to seek interesting and self-actualizing experiences. Helps those who tend to be repressed or restrained in manner, to let go and move into open-hearted enthusiasm. **b)** In the Michael system, helps those in Repression Mode move to the positive pole of Passion Mode.

**Tanzanite:** (Lavender). **a)** Calming to "high frequency", "buzzy" types of people who tend to live in a very intense state. Slows them down and mellows them out. **b)** Balancing for people who are either highly focused and driven in their approach to life, or people who are highly creative but chaotic in their way of dealing with life. Brings both out of the extremes into a more balanced state near the middle. **c)** In the Michael system, balancing for high-frequency types and balances those who are either high-male or high-female energied.

**Tektite:** (From meteors). Assists one in contacting and communicating with sentient races from other planets.

**Tennantite:** (Bright grey to dark grey to dead black in color). Helps one gain weight. Slows down the metabolic rate.

**Tenorite:** Same in effect as Iron Pyrite.

**Tephroite:** (Grey-brown, reddish brown and flesh-red in color). Gives one an air of dignity.

**Thenardite:** (Yellow). **a)** Improves one's memory. Promotes more efficient accessing of existing memory banks. **b)** Aids in the storage of new information in a more efficient manner and in the creation of new memory banks.

**Thinolite:** (White to gray to pinkish-beige in color). Makes one more effective in the training of animals and enhances one's ability to communicate with them.

**Thomsonite:** (White Agate with small green sprays that look like the irises of eyes). Same stone as Eye Agate.

**Thulite:** Same stone as pink Zoisite.

**Thunder Eggs:** Another name for Geodes.

**Tiger Eye, Blue:** Same stone as Spectrolite.

**Tiger Eye, Gold:** (Golden or yellow-brown in color). **a)** Softens stubbornness and makes it possible to be more flexible in one's behavior and determined rather than obstinate in one's approach. **b)** Balancing for more solid types who like to move slowly and take their time about things. Can help those who are a little too "buzzy", to mellow out. **c)** In the Michael system, softens the Chief Negative Feature of Stubbornness. Balancing for low-frequency types.

**Tiger Eye, Red:** **a)** Enables one to slow down, and take a break from action and the need to get things done. Particularly good for those who get too hyper and can't stop moving. **b)** Slows the third chakra down and flushes excess energy out. **c)** In the Michael system, gives the Moving Center a rest.

**Tiger Iron:** **a)** Enables one to be powerful and influential in one's relationships, one's political ventures, or one's career. Promotes the mastery of skills necessary to deal effectively with situations external to one's self. Stimulates the pursuit and achievement of excellence. **b)** In the Michael system, a power stone for Kings.

**Tiger-Eye Matrix:** Same in effect as Tiger Iron.

**Tigillite:** (Fossilized worm tunnels). **a)** Heals and calms one's strongest fears about survival. **b)** In the Michael system, heals and balances the Instinctive Center.

**Tilasite:** (Pink in color). Encourages hereditary blondness and blue-eyed recessive genes of all sorts to manifest themselves in the children of those who wear, or live near, this rock. Most specimens found in Scandinavian countries.

**Tinzenite:** (Yellow to red in color). Encourages one to lose the things one no longer has use for, but has been hanging onto. This includes not only inanimate objects like an old sweater, but also includes outmoded relationships.

**Titanite:** Same stone as Sphene.

**Todorokite:** (Black in color). **a)** Calms and soothes highly excitable or creative types of people when they are under stress. **b)** In the Michael system, balances and calms a high-female-energied person. Balances Artisans.

**Topaz, Blue: a)** Enhances one's leadership abilities. Gives one an aura of competence that encourages others to accept one in a position of leadership. Makes one feel more in control of oneself, or of the situations one encounters, and more able to handle things competently. Good stone to wear for a meeting with the IRS. **b)** In the Michael system, facilitates the positive use of the Goal of Dominance.

**Topaz, Clear·** For better relationships with non-human species on this planet: the plant and animal kingdom.

**Topaz, Golden:** (Yellow to rich yellow). **a)** Enables one to be very pragmatic in one's outlook, and practical in one's methods. Useful for knowing what procedures will work best in a particular situation. Enables one to delineate steps a, b, and c, without wasting time. Good with Garnets, as this combination will produce practical ways of being productive. **b)** In the Michael system, pulls one into the positive pole of the Attitude of Pragmatist.

**Topaz, Green:** For benevolence with regard to the mistakes of others. Useful in situations where another person does something really stupid, and one would rather be benevolent and understanding, than rub their nose in it and further the karma. Keeps one from doing something ineffective when someone else already has.

**Topaz, Imperial:** (Sherry colored). a) Enables one to exercise all one's scholarly abilities and talents. Makes anyone feel they are intelligent enough, they have enough information and, in general, that they have enough scholarly ability to handle any situation. b) In the Michael system, a power stone for Scholars.

**Topaz, Pink:** Encourages one to behave with integrity and honesty.

**Topaz, Smoky:** See Smoky Quartz.

**Topaz, White:** a) Stimulates one to use the mind, and helps one to maintain a clear, intellectual focus. Same in effect as Amber, although not quite as strong. b) Balances and opens the fifth chakra. c) In the Michael system, balances the Intellectual Center.

**Topazolite:** See Andradite.

**Torbernite:** (Greenish blue in color). a) Encourages compassionate and nurturing behavior toward others. Enables one to be effectively powerful in the ability to heal or aid others, and in the ability guide others, toward the fruition and completion of projects that are beneficial to all. b) In the Michael system, a power stone for Priests and Servers.

**Tourmalinated Quartz:** See Quartz, Tourmalinated.

**Tourmaline, Black:** Healing for house plants. Has no effect on humans other than producing a mild empathy for the plant kingdom

**Tourmaline, Blue:** (Color can range from very light to very dark blue). a) Enables one to be very clear, calm, and centered about what one doesn't want in one's life. Be careful in its use because the calm can verge on being cold and calculating. b) Can use in conjunction with light blue

Sapphire (compassion) or blue-green Tourmaline (acceptance) to soften this aspect. Similar in effect to Blue Spinel, but much more gentle.   c) In the Michael system, pulls one into the positive use of the Goal of Discrimination.

**Tourmaline, Blue-Green: a)** Wear to be more open-hearted, giving, and accepting of what's going on one's life, or of other people.   Enables one to move closer to the experiences of "agape" or unconditional love, and one is generally more tolerant of others.  Invites people in, rather than closing them out.   **b)** In the Michael system, pulls one into the positive pole of the Goal of Acceptance. Useful for those with a Chief Negative Feature of Impatience as it pulls them out of intolerance, into tolerance.

**Tourmaline, Green to Dark Green: a)** Produces a greater ability to communicate in everyone.   One can be quite eloquently charismatic.    Emphasizes the clear communication of information, wisdom, and truth.   **b)** In the Michael system, balances Sages.

**Tourmaline, Pink to Red: a)** Releases free-flowing energy. Enables one to go with the normal flow of one's life, rather than be in resistance to it.  Makes it very easy to relax and unwind.  Good to wear when one wants to take a week off. Best not to use it, when one wants to be dynamic and out there in the world accomplishing things.   **b)** In the Michael system, pulls one to the positive pole of the Goal of Stagnation.

**Tourmaline, Watermelon:** (Bi-color pink and green).  **a)** Increases one's quotient of "stick-to-itiveness" and strengthens the ability to perservere.   **b)** Helps people create the impression they are stable and reliable whether they are or not.  It also enables one to draw on those qualities to the extent one possesses them.  Especially good for those fluid, expansive types of people who can appear "fluff-headed".   Enables them to be more focused and solidly grounded.   **c)** In the Michael system, pulls one into the positive pole of Perservence Mode, and balances high-female energied persons. Helps them tap into, and use, their male-energied side more effectively.

**Tourmaline, Yellow, Brown or Clear:** a) Assists one in endeavors that require intellectual processing. b) Balances the fifth chakra. c) In the Michael system, balances the Intellectual Center.

**Tourmaline, Yellow-Green:** a) Helps those souls with a lot of lifetimes of experience "under their belts" to relate to each other well. b) In the Michael system, helps Old, Mature and Young souls relate to one another other well.

**Trainite:** Same stone as Variscite.

**Tree Agate:** See Agate, Tree.

**Tremolite:** (White, pink, brown or gray in color). Same in effect as Actinolite.

**Trevorite:** (Tan, or grey in color). Increases honesty. Cures the tendency to be sly or manipulative. Increases one's awareness of a tendency to be sneaky, and the resulting embarrassment, encourages a more honest approach.

**Tridymite:** Same stone as Quartz Crystal.

**Triphylite:** (Blue gray or pale lavender in color). Reduces fear of accidents and actually contributes to one having fewer accidents, by keeping one's consciousness on what one is doing, rather than on one's fear of something going wrong.

**Triplite:** (Brown in color). Same in effect as Amber.

**Trippkeite:** (White, blue/green, gray opaque). a) Opens up one's ability to experience all emotions. Aids in experiencing one's joy and love to the fullest. b) Since this stone removes defenses around feelings, those who regularly block their emotions, might open up painful feelings to deal with. Persons in this category should use this stone purposefully, and in combination with other stones that would aid them in processing difficult emotions, such as Pink Calcite, Kinoite, etc. c) Balances and heals the fourth chakra, particularly when blocked. d)

In the Michael system, balances and heals the Emotional Center.

**Tsavorite:** (Green in color). **a)** Promotes the ability to master one's personal issues and take control of one's own destiny. Gives one a feeling of happiness and confidence that one's life is in good shape, whether it pleases someone else or not. **b)** In the Michael system, balances Kings.

**Tufa:** Same stone as Aragonite.

**Tugtupite:** Increases the ability to remember.

**Turitella Agate:** See Agate, Turitella.

**Turquoise:** (Blue to green in color). **a)** Centers one's being on love and connectedness with others. Pulls one into the experience of unconditional love for all beings. **b)** In the Michael system, balances the Higher-Emotional Center and connects one with the energy of the Messianic Plane.

**Turquoise, Navajo:** See Navajo Turquoise.

**Tyrolite:** (Green in color). Encourages one to feel happy and cheerful.

**Ulexite:** (White, sometimes greenish or greyish in color). Encourages a philosophical and positive outlook on one's life and a willingness to be adventuresome. One feels free to do whatever one wants to do: not restricted or stuck. It seems possible to really make changes and transform oneself in a positive, adventurous way.

**Unikite:** (A moss-green and salmon pink composite rock). **a)** Enhances one's personal power and the ability to completely take charge of one's own life. Helps ensure that one will be the guardian of one's own fate and not be taken over by anyone else. **b)** In the Michael system, balances Kings and pulls one out of the negative pole of the Chief Feature of Martyrdom.

**Uranophane:** (Yellow sprays). Encourages a feeling of accomplishment. Allows one to savor completions.

**Utahlite:** Same stone as Variscite.

**Uvarovite:** (Vivid green). A "Storyteller" stone. Stimulates one's imagination and enhances one's ability to tell stories that fascinate. Increases charisma and improves one's verbal skills.

**Uvite:** Same stone as pink or red Tourmaline.

**Valentinite:** (Long, clear needles of mineral). Encourages one to sing and enjoy music.

**Vanadinite:** (Orange to red in color). **a)** For inspiration of a spiritual nature. Promotes the experience of an exalted, inspirational space wherein one is in touch with God, the Universal Consciousness. **b)** In the Michael system, balances Priests. Puts one in touch with the Tao.

**Variegated Jasper:** See Jasper, Variegated.

**Variscite:** (Pale green to medium green). **a)** Empowers one to come up with solutions or actions that will produce win-win results for everyone. Allows one to simultaneously see what it is that pulls everything together, and to feel that one has the power to make it happen. Boosts self-confidence. **b)** In the Michael system, pulls one into the positive pole of the Goal of Dominance.

**Vauxite:** (Tiny, dark blue crystals). Makes one very sleepy. Good for insomnia.

**Veatchite:** (Black with gray, white and beige inclusions). Reduces fear of animals.

**Verdelite:** Same stone as green or dark green Tourmaline.

**Vesuvianite:** (Dark brown-green. A type of Idocrase). **a)** Enables one to compete, and at the same time, to be appropriate with one's competitiveness. Encourages a "win-win" attitude, rather than one of tromping on the competition. **b)** In the Michael system, facilitates positive use of the Goal of Dominance.

**Veszelyite:** (Dark greenish-blue crystals). **a)** Makes one more accepting of people one is having difficulties with. Makes it easier to get along with others. Allows one to be more compassionate. **b)** Enables one to build an "empire" that is spiritually based, usually in the ministry. c) In the Michael system, a power stone for Priests.

**Villiaumite:** (Red, yellow or purple in color). Enables one to appreciate the unusual, the eccentric, and the bizarre.

**Violane:** (Violet in color). Balances body temperature and reduces fever.

**Viridine:** Same in effect as Andalusite.

**Vivianite:** (Blue in color). a) Helps one relate well to person's whose level of spiritual awareness is markedly different from one's own. b) In the Michael system, helps one get along with Infant and Baby souls.

**Volborthite:** (Rich yellow-green to dark green in color). Decreases one's tendency to worry, particularly when the worry is needless.

**Volcanic Ash:** a) For acceptance and surrender to the inevitable. Doesn't help one with the emotional aspects of accepting a difficult situation. Helps one recognize, and then acknowledge, when nothing can be done and surrender is appropriate. Same effect regardless of color. b) In the Michael system, pulls one into the positive use of the Goal of Acceptance.

**Volkonskoite:** (Green) Improves one's ability to keep one's balance. One feels more in touch with the earth and physical objects.

**Water Sapphire:** Same stone as blue Iolite.

**Watermelon Tourmaline:** See Tourmaline, Watermelon.

**Wavellite:** (White, greenish-white, pale grey, brown, yellowish-brown, yellow and green in color). Healing for bones. Effect varies with color:

| | |
|---|---|
| Blue: | Small bones. |
| Brown: | Teeth. |
| Colorless: | Large bones. |
| Green: | Medium-size bones. |
| White: | Bone marrow. |

**Yellow:** Bone marrow.

**Weeksite:** (Yellow in color). When worn on the body or placed near it, attracts in members of one's basic support group. That is, people who have support relationships of various types with one, even though one has not yet met them this lifetime.

**Wermlandite:** (White and brown opaque rock). a) Increases curiosity, stimulates the intellect, and allows one to think for long periods of time without mental fatigue. b) Balances the fifth chakra. c) In the Michael system, stimulates and strengthens the Intellectual Center.

**Whiteite:** (Opaque, mottled brown in color). Decreases stiffness of the joints, by encouraging excess minerals to be processed out of the body.

**Willemite:** (Light green to bright green. Often found in Calcite matrix). Similar in effect to Laramar.

**Willemseite:** (Bright translucent green with black inclusions). a) Encourages one to be appropriately choosy and discriminating. This stone is particularly effective for those who have a hard time making decisions or knowing what their true opinions are. b) In the Michael system, encourages the appropriate use of Discrimination for those who do not have a Goal of Discrimination.

**Willow Creek Jasper:** See Jasper, Willow Creek.

**Wiluite:** Same stone as yellow-green or brown Idocrase.

**Window Pane Calcite:** See Calcite, Window Pane.

**Winstanleyite:** (Yellow). a) Stimulates one's curiosity, promotes use of the intellect, and allows one to think for long periods of time without mental fatigue. b) Balances the fifth chakra and strengthens it. c) In the Michael system, balances the Intellectual Center.

**Witherite:** (White to gray white). a) Helps control compulsive behavior. In a compulsive sequence, one acts without thinking, then feels negatively about one's action. This is followed by the same action and negative emotion, again and again. This stone breaks the cycle, by allowing one to take a more intellectual approach in which one can think about what one is doing, and then initiate a different, more appropriate, action. This, in turn, produces a more positive emotional state. **b)** In the Michael system, balances the use of the Moving Center.

**Wogdinite:** (Lustrous black crystals). For love and affection. This stone reminds everyone of the love they feel for the person wearing the stone. Reinforces the love and affection one's friends and intimates have for one.

**Wolframite:** (Black tablets often found in Quartz). Same in effect as Hubnerite.

**Wolsendorfite:** (Orange-red in color). Starts people laughing and giggling. No internal experience of humor need occur, but one will find oneself laughing. Healing in its power to promote laughter.

**Wonder Agate:** See Agate, Wonder.

**Wood Jasper:** See Jasper, Wood.

**Woodhousite:** (Yellow-brown in color). **a)** Makes it easier to surrender when necessary, and not be so controlling. Enables one to let go of any false pride, arrogance, stubbornness, or self deprecation that would stand in the way of surrendering, or compromising appropriately. Makes one feel one can submit to the greater good. **b)** In the Michael system, facilitates the positive use of the Goal of Submission.

**Wood-Tin Cassiterite:** (Yellow-brown to red-brown lumps). For lowering one's internal energy and drive, so that one can slow down, come to a standstill and set the stage for re-evaluation. Doesn't help one re-evaluate, it just helps one "get off the merry-go-round".

**Wulfenite:** (Yellow to orange to red-orange in color. Rarely black). Enables one to commune with the spirits of nature. Connects one to the "devas". One feels in touch with their energies and intentions.

**Wyartite:** (Violet to black). **a)** Enables very focused, straight-forward people to understand, and get along with, people who are very unfocused and scattered in purpose and vice-versa. **b)** In the Michael system, enables high male-energied people to understand high-female energied, people, and vice-versa.

**Xanthiosite:** (Golden yellow). Heals the sexual organs of illness, imbalance or disease. Works for all mammals of both sexes.

**Xanthite:** Same stone as yellow Idocrase.

**Xiangjiangite:** (Yellow in color). Enables one to use at least five more percentage points of one's mental capacity.

**Xitieshanite:** (Bright green in color). Increases one's overall physical agility and motor coordination. Particularly enhances one's eye-hand motor coordination as required for finer applications, such as fencing, microcircuitry, surgery and art.

**Xocomecatlite:** (Emerald green in color). **a)** Reduces one's resistance to following another's lead. Enables one who has natural leadership abilities, or a natural tendency to be pushy and domineering, to follow someone else's lead when necessary. **b)** In the Michael system, pulls one into the positive pole of the Goal of Dominance.

**Yafsoanite:** (Brown in color). Brings up thoughts of home and keeps a person mindful of their emotional attachments and family commitments. Those who are without family or home, feel more rooted and comforted.

**Yecoraite:** (Orange to yellow crystals). Same stone as Benjaninite.

**Yedlinite:** (Red-violet in color). Encourages strong feelings of loyalty and faithfulness toward one's mate. Or, if one has no mate, towards one's intimate family members primarily focusing on one's parents. Increases the bondedness of the immediate family.

**Yoshimuraite:** (Orange-brown). Promotes loving alignment, understanding, and great depth of empathy between parents and children of the opposite sex.

**Youngite:** (A composite rock with a pinkish-gray or salmon-gray center overlayed with a grayish translucent material. Looks like fuzzy brains). **a)** Inspires solutions to problems requiring action on the physical plane. Energizes one to solve difficult problems. Productivity oriented. **b)** In the Michael system, a power stone for Kings and Warriors.

**Yttrocerite:** (Many colors). Same in effect as Flourite.

**Yugawaralite:** (Clear to white). Same in effect as Manganocalcite.

**Yuksporite:** (Pink in color). Enables one to become inventive with language. Helps people invent new types of poetry, come up with jingles, understand puns, solve crossword puzzles, invent new words, and have fun while one is doing it. Helps one to write in a spirit of creative adventure.

**Zapatalite:** (Pale blue in color). Increases the younger person's understanding of the points of view of those older than themselves. Does not work in the other direction.

**Zebra Agate:** See Agate, Zebra.

**Zebra Gneiss:** (A white and black striped composite rock). Anti-prejudice or anti-xenophobic rock. Encourages one to feel one can understand other races and other sentient beings. Makes it easier to understand how they're thinking and what they're doing.

**Zektzerite:** (Colorless to pink in color). Provides protection for any child under the age of five, against threats to their survival. Often found with Sogdianite or Granite.

**Zeunerite:** (Forest green platelet crystals). **a)** Inspires one to operate powerfully in the area of service to others. Creates a sense of enthusiasm and inspired excitement about ways to be of service or to spiritually aid others. **b)** In the Michael system, a power stone for Servers and Priests.

**Zinkeinite:** (Silver metallic). Same in effect as Bismuth.

**Zinnwaldite:** (Brown in color). Encourages the manifestation of the dominant genes in one's children. Useful for those who have a recessive, gene-linked hereditary disease in the family they would wish to avoid, such as hemophilia.

**Zippeite:** (Yellow in color). Same in effect as Carnelian.

**Zircon, Light Blue: a)** Makes one feel balanced and gently stabilized. Has an uplifting quality. **b)** Opens and balances all Chakras. **c)** In the Michael system, balances and stabilizes Priests, or those who have Priest essence twins.

**Zircon, Brown or Brownish-Red:** Heals headaches. Drains excess energy from head, and keeps the energy properly balanced in that area.

**Zircon, Green:** Increases gregariousness. Similar in effect to Ardennite.

**Zircon, Colorless:** Clears the aura. Fluffs up the aura and rids it of any unwanted energies (cording) or impurities from the environment.

**Zircon, Pink:** Pushes one out of the body at night, while sleeping, to take on lessons of an emotional nature on the Astral Plane. This can result in a rather restless night.

**Zircon, Red:** Helps ear infections heal more quickly.

**Zircon, Violet:** "Penny" stone for monetary resourcefulness. Makes one feel like there will always be enough money, especially if it is really needed.

**Zircon, Yellow:** Clears the aura in the same way as colorless Zircon. Motivates one to clear one's space of clutter. Also impels one to clear one's environment energetically.

**Zoisite, Brown: a)** Balances those engaged in intellectual pursuits. Prevents one from falling into an opinionated, "know-it-all" attitude. **b)** In the Michael system, balances Young Scholars.

**Zoisite, Gray: a)** Keeps one organized, productive and able to get a lot accomplished without being insensitive to others, bossy or too demanding.   **b)** In the Michael system, balances Infant, Baby and Young Warriors.

**Zoisite, Green:** (With Ruby Crystals, called Anyolite). **a)** Balances those in a position of power in the area of service to others. This could be the administrator of a hospital, the director of a research project to find a cure for cancer, or the relationship between doctor and patient, therapist and client, healer and healed. Enables one to use one's power to act effectively in the best interests of the agency, the project or the individual.   **b)** In the Michael system, a power stone for Servers.

**Zoisite, Lavender:** Same stone as Tanzanite.

**Zoisite, Pink: a)** Balancing to those in a position of service to others, and keeps them from over-extending themselves, or falling into any negative habit patterns, such as being overly bossy, too self-effacing or martyred.   **b)** In the Michael system, balances Infant, Baby and Young Servers.

**Zoisite, White: a)** Balancing to those in a position of power. Keeps one aware of the power of one's position. Enhances one's ability to use one's power appropriately.   **b)** In the Michael system, balances Infant, Baby and Young Kings.

**Zorite:** (Rose colored). **a)** Increases one's ability to judge appropriate choices more accurately. Good for delicately balanced decision making, such as that in which arbitrators and judges engage.   **b)** In the Michael system, pulls one into the positive pole of the Goal of Discrimination.

**Zunyite:** (Light brown in color). Encourages a deep sense of patriotism toward one's tribe, nationality, race, religion-- anything that distinguishes one as a group member.

# INDEX
## Of Gemstones and Minerals
## Categorized by Subject

Binghamite, 141
Biotite, 112
Bisbeeite, 47, 162, 209
Bismuth, 35, 151
Bismuthinite, 35, 151
Bismutite, 35, 151
Bixbyite, 92, 95, 224
Bjarebyite, 84
Blixite, 61
Bloedite, 104, 109
Bloodstone, 43, 92, 97, 138,
   141, 146, 228
Boevnite, 109
Bogdanovite, 65, 104
Boggildite, 166
Boleite, 43
Bolivarite, 114
Boltonite, 52, 188
Boltwoodite, 40, 115
Bonaccordite, 31
Bone, 58, 126, 131, 136, 218
Boothite, 84
Boracite, 116, 164
Borcarite, 95
Bornite, 152
Bostwickite, 90
Botryogen, 168
Boulangerite, 80, 103, 198
Bournonite, 40, 118
Bowenite, 33, 71, 112, 118,
   119, 120, 229
Bracewellite, 80
Brass, 139
Braunite, 32, 120
Bravoite, 139
Brazilianite, 60, 184
Breithauptite, 116, 164
Brochantite, 111, 112
Bronze, 139
Bronzite, 116, 127, 215

Brookite, 78
Brucite, 56, 185
Brushite, 61
Buergerite, 38
Bukovskyite, 52, 188
Burckhardtite, 168
Burnite, 64, 83, 129, 203, 212
Buttgenbachite, 85, 195

# C

Cacoxenite, 74, 157
Cahnite, 66, 116, 122
Calcite, Black, 71, 203
Calcite, Blue, 55, 56, 128,
   131, 208, 221, 239
Calcite, Brown or Gold, 49,
   130, 214, 243
Calcite, Gray, 39, 57
Calcite, Green, 110, 114
Calcite, Orange, 55, 100, 202,
   208
Calcite, Red, 56, 57, 128, 208
Calcite, Violet, 49, 99, 216,
   243
Calcite, White, 47, 130, 209,
   243
Caledonite, 160
Callaghanite, 72
Calomel, 66
Cameo Shell, 87, 95, 218
Campbellite, 117
Campiglaite, 44
Cancrinite, 162
Cape Chrysolite, 99
Carminite, 61, 65, 199
Carnallite, 122
Carnelian, 93, 137, 141, 145,
   224

Tourmaline, Black, 38
Tourmaline, Blue, 83, 191
Tourmaline, Blue-Green,
164, 190
Tourmaline, Green to Dark
Green, 150, 156, 149, 181
Tourmaline, Pink to Red,
105, 194, 247
Tourmaline, Watermelon,
80, 104, 144, 198
Tourmaline, Yellow,
Brown or Clear, 63, 129,
213
Tourmaline, Yellow-
Green, 159, 246
Tremolite, 37, 76, 180
Trevorite, 79, 96
Triphylite, 94
Triplite, 63, 129, 135, 213
Trippkeite, 56, 88, 129, 209
Tsavorite, 79, 183
Tugtupite, 62
Turquoise, 48, 211
Turquoise, Navajo, 48, 170,
211
Tyrolite, 100

**U**

Ulexite, 85
Unikite, 79, 183, 229
Uranophane, 94
Uvarovite, 37, 151

**V**

Valentinite, 32
Vanadinite, 50, 178, 244
Variscite, 42, 77, 193

Vauxite, 119
Veatchite, 31
Vesuvianite, 77, 193
Veszelyite, 76, 154, 157, 164,
178
Villiaumite, 37
Violane, 111
Viridine, 76
Vivianite, 159, 246
Volborthite, 59
Volcanic Ash, 81, 190
Volkonskoite, 38, 115

**W**

Wavellite, 114
Weeksite, 162
Wermlandite, 61, 63, 213
Whiteite, 114
Willemite, 164
Willemseite, 83, 191
Winstanleyite, 61, 63, 129,
213
Witherite, 96, 216
Wogdinite, 84, 164
Wolframite, 40
Wolsendorfite, 102
Woodhousite, 81, 194
Wulfenite, 50, 245
Wyartite, 145, 164

**X**

Xanthiosite, 120
Xiangjiangite, 63
Xitieshanite, 116
Xocomocatlite, 158, 193

# REFERENCES

1. Fleischer, Michael. <u>Glossary of Mineral Species</u>. The Minerological Record Inc: Tuscon, AZ, 1983.

2. Schumann, Walter. <u>Gemstones of the World</u>. Sterling Publishing Company: New York, NY, 1984.

3. Sinkankas, John. Mineralogy. Van Nostrand Reinhold Company: New York, NY, 1964.

4. Stevens, Jose, & Warwick-Smith, Simon. <u>A Michael Handbook: Essence and Personality</u>. Warwick Press: Orinda, CA, 1986.

5. <u>The Michael Connection</u>. M.C. Clark, Editor. P.O. Box 1873, Orinda, CA, 94563.

6. Van Hulle, JP, Clark, M. C., & Christeaan, Aaron. <u>Michael: The Basic Teachings.</u> Affinity Press: Orinda, CA, 1988.

## ABOUT THE AUTHORS

JP Van Hulle is a well-known Bay Area author, teacher, and consultant. A California native, she graduated from U.C. Berkeley, then ran a Sanctuary Program for Oakland's homeless, and taught courses on communication and sexual dysfunction at the Institute of Human Abilities.

JP presently lives in Orinda, California with her husband, Aaron; her daughters, PJ and Jessica; her parents, Joy and John; and a revolving door of clients, relatives, friends, and cats. She has been channeling Michael exclusively and professionally since 1982, and has personally trained most of Michael's channels. This is her second book using channeled information from Michael and two more are in process.

Dr. Judithann David is a long-standing student of Michael's teachings and a practicing psychologist. As a Scholar, she has done extensive experimentation with many of the stones listed in this book and has proven to her own and other students' satisfaction the validity of properties Michael has ascribed to them. Her dedication to this topic led her to transcribe, compile and explain Michael's teachings in the Gemstone Dictionary.

She lives in Orinda with her husband Desai, her daughter Juliana and several cats. She is a Michael channel and finds it most gratifying to include information from Michael as part of the psychotherapy process. She has begun developing new techniques in psychotherapy based on her association with Michael and the Michael Teaching. A new book on this topic is being planned for the future.

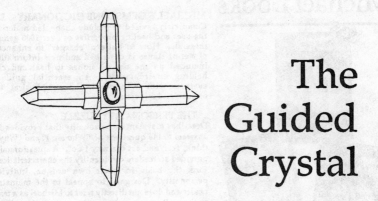

# The Guided Crystal

30% Discount Sale

on

Jewelry, Minerals, Gemstones

Obelisks Spheres Wands Eggs Points Sculptures

**Best Retail Prices**
*Gift certificates available*

Drop by in person -- or order by phone or mail!

Joy Perasso
THE GUIDED CRYSTAL
10 Muth Drive, Orinda, CA 94563
415/254-5736

# Michael Books

**MICHAEL'S GEMSTONE DICTIONARY**   $12.95
Completely revised to include channeled material on the uses and healing properties of over 1000 gems and minerals. How to build a "charger" to enhance the power of stones is described and new information is included on the use of stones to heal and create healing environments. An essential guide for everyone with an interest in the metaphysical value of gems and minerals.

**THE PERSONALITY PUZZLE**   $9.95
Describes a system of personality that provides fresh answers to the questions of, "Who am I" and "Why do I think, feel, and act the way I do". A questionnaire is provided so readers can identify the characteristics that form the basis for their own unique, individual personality. Designed to appeal to the mainstream reader and does not directly refer to Michael as a teacher or channeling as a source.

**EARTH TO TAO**   $11.95
Delves into spiritual growth and its relationship to healing. Such topics as developing unconditional self-acceptance and healing the chakras are explored in a lively manner.

**MICHAEL: THE BASIC TEACHINGS**   $11.95
A reference book that explains the basics of Michael's teachings in a clearly written, logical and intelligent fashion. Complete with charts, diagrams, and effective illustrations, it appeals to readers of metaphysics, philosophy and popular psychology.

**MICHAEL'S CAST OF CHARACTERS**   $8.95
Here's the Michael system explained clearly and simply with tongue-in-cheek humor making the book attractive to the mainstream reader. Includes the personality profiles of 800 celebrities and historical figures as described by Michael.

**THE MICHAEL GAME**   $7.95
Fascinating topics discussed. Including 101 questions to ask a channel, the state of the planet, planes of existance, AIDS, whales and dolphins as sentient beings and more.

**THE MICHAEL HANDBOOK**   $11.95
This book covers the basics in detail; such as soul ages, roles, and overleaves. An excellent reference book to the Michael system.

**TAO TO EARTH**   $11.95
A practical and entertaining guide to such diverse topics as understanding intimate relationships, how the laws of karma work and the nature of prosperity.

**THE WORLD ACCORDING TO MICHAEL** $8.95
A fresh and delightful introduction to the Michael teachings. Michael's unconventional approach to why humans behave as they do. Will be enjoyed by anyone with a curiosity about the universe we live in.

# ORDERING WHOLESALE

## Books Available:

EARTH TO TAO: Michael's Guide to Healing and Spiritual Growth. by Jose Stevens Ph.D. ISBN 0-942663-03-9. $11.95.

MICHAEL'S CAST OF CHARACTERS: A "Not So Serious" Guide to the Michael Teaching. By Emily Baumbach. ISBN 0-942663-07-1. $8.95.

MICHAEL'S GEMSTONE DICTIONARY. By Judithann H. David Ph.D., & JP Van Hulle. ISBN 0-942663-05-5. $12.95.

MICHAEL: THE BASIC TEACHINGS. By Aaron Christeaan, J.P Van Hulle, & M.C. Clark. ISBN 0-942663-01-2. $11.95.

TAO TO EARTH: Michael's Guide to Relationships and Growth. By Jose Stevens Ph.D. ISBN 0-942663-02-0. $11.95.

THE PERSONALITY PUZZLE. By Jose Stevens Ph.D. ISBN 0-942663-06-3. $11.95.

THE WORLD ACCORDING TO MICHAEL. By Joya Pope. ISBN 0-942663-04-7. $8.95.

## Order From:

Affinity Press
P.O. Box 877, Orinda, CA
(415) 253-1889.

Anyone is welcome to order wholesale from Affinity Press. The quantites that must be ordered, to qualify for wholesale prices, are listed below.

## Discount Schedule:

| | |
|---|---|
| 5 of one title, 10 mixed titles: | 40% of Retail. |
| By the box, or 100 mixed titles: | 50% of Retail. |

All orders will be shipped COD, unless you have established an account with us. Residents of California, must have a resale number or pay a tax of 7%.

## DISTRIBUTORS

All books may also be ordered from the following distributors.

| | | |
|---|---|---|
| BAKER & TAYLOR | Reno, NV | (702) 786-6700. |
| BOOKPEOPLE | Berkeley, CA | (800) 227-1516. |
| DEVORSS & CO. | Marina Del Rey, CA | (213) 870-7478. |
| the DISTRIBUTORS | So. Bend, IN | (219) 232-8500. |
| INLAND BOOKS | East Haven, CT | (800) 243-0138. |
| MOVING BOOKS | Seattle, WA | (800) 777-6683. |
| NEW LEAF | Atlanta, GA | (800) 241-3829. |